My Shakespeare

My Shakespeare

A Director's Journey through the First Folio

Greg Doran

methuen | drama
LONDON • NEW YORK • OXFORD • NEW DELHI • SYDNEY

METHUEN DRAMA
Bloomsbury Publishing Plc
50 Bedford Square, London, WC1B 3DP, UK
1385 Broadway, New York, NY 10018, USA
29 Earlsfort Terrace, Dublin 2, Ireland

BLOOMSBURY, METHUEN DRAMA and the Methuen Drama logo are trademarks of
Bloomsbury Publishing Plc

First published in Great Britain 2023
Reprinted in 2023 (five times)

For legal purposes the Acknowledgements on p. xi constitute an extension
of this copyright page.

Cover design: Ben Anslow
Cover image: Parian bust by Copeland after an original by Raffaele Monti,
made for the Crystal Palace Art Union for the Shakespeare tercentenary
celebrations of 1864. (Photo © Andy Williams)

Bloomsbury Publishing Plc does not have any control over, or responsibility for, any
third-party websites referred to or in this book. All internet addresses given
in this book were correct at the time of going to press. The author and publisher regret any
inconvenience caused if addresses have changed or sites have ceased to exist,
but can accept no responsibility for any such changes.

A catalogue record for this book is available from the British Library.

ISBN: HB: 978-1-3503-3019-1
        ePDF: 978-1-3503-3021-4
        eBook: 978-1-3503-3020-7

Typeset by RefineCatch Limited, Bungay, Suffolk
Printed and bound in Great Britain

To find out more about our authors and books visit www.bloomsbury.com
and sign up for our newsletters.

To my beloved siblings:
Mark, Jo and Ruth

To business that we love we rise betime
And go to't with delight.

Antony and Cleopatra (Act 4 Scene 4)

Soul of the age!
The applause, delight, the wonder of our stage!
My Shakespeare, rise!

Ben Jonson

Contents

Illustrations

Acknowledgements

Hearty thanks.
The bounty and the benison of heaven
To boot, and boot!

Gloucester in *King Lear* (Act 4 Scene 6)

If I started to thank all the people who have helped me through my career, and on all the productions mentioned here, the list would be endless, so I will try to restrict myself to the folk who have helped me research this book, write it and edit it.

Firstly to the team at Bloomsbury, in particular Anna Brewer for all the suggestions she made, including the ones I should have listened to; to Ben Anslow for his talent and his patience developing the cover; to Aanchal Vij for her editorial assistance with the images; to Mark Fisher for his eagle-eyed copy-editing; to Merv Honeywood for his diligent typesetting; and to production editor Amy Brownbridge.

At Stratford there are so many people who have helped prepare the book, in particular: Kevin Wright, Michelle Morton, Andy Williams and Jane Tassell.

And many close friends who were good enough to read the drafts and provide vital comments, corrections and encouragement, including Lucy Shepherd, Richard Sharples, Mike Poulton, Sue Powell, John Wyver, Alfred Bradley, Malcolm Taylor and Thelma Holt.

But my greatest debt is to the man with whom I spent thirty-five years of my life, and who in his last months forced me to write. I read him many chapters. He responded with love, laughter and a brilliant incisive instinct, and remained on my shoulder throughout, encouraging me to write only from the heart – Tony Sher.

I would also like to add a special thanks to the generations of young directors who have supported me as assistant and associate directors over many years, including:

Abigail Anderson, Justin Audibert, Phillip Breen, Cressida Brown, Ben Brynmor, Sam Caird, Tom Daley, Jo Davies, Heather Davies, Anna Girvan, Aileen Gonsalves, Owen Horsley, Ellie Jones, Tom King, Titania Krimpas, Steve Marmion, Rebecca McCutcheon, Mitchell Moreno, Jonathan Munby, Gbolahan Obisesan, Aaron Parsons, Ng Choon Ping, Lucy Pitman-Wallace, Kate Raper, Chris Rolls, Jacqui Somerville, Jennifer Tang, Sarah Tipple, Leigh Toney, Richard Twyman, Huan Wang, Zoe Waterman, and Tom Wright.

Introduction

Man cannot live by Bard alone.

Or so the actor Donald Sinden, once said. But I seem to have done pretty much that.

As I step down as the sixth Artistic Director of the Royal Shakespeare Company, and prepare to direct the last play in the First Folio, to celebrate its 400th anniversary, I have the satisfaction of being able to say I have produced every single play in that miraculous book.

While I have directed the work of other writers, too – including Shakespeare's seventeenth-century contemporaries from Ben Jonson to Aphra Behn; classics by Beckett, Wilde, Coward, Miller, O'Neill and Stoppard; new work from Edward Bond, David Edgar, Biyi Bandele and Derek Walcott; and even the odd musical – Shakespeare has been a constant. If J. Alfred Prufrock (in T.S. Eliot's poem) measured out his life with coffee spoons, I have measured mine in Shakespeare plays.

This book is not a manual about how to direct Shakespeare, but rather my own personal experience of working on his plays, and what I have learnt along the way; of the many amazing people I have been lucky enough to work with and what they taught me; of the roads travelled; how life-events sometimes intervened, and how Shakespeare often helped articulate and explain those moments.

My passport came up for renewal in 2016, the quatercentenary of Shakespeare's death. I was delighted to discover that a 3D watermark of Shakespeare's face is embedded on every visa page of the new passport.

Shakespeare runs like a watermark through my career, and through all the work of the RSC, constantly present, identifying a standard of excellence and inspiring us to achieve it.

Shakespeare has been a passport through my life. This book is an account of that journey.

Greg Doran
Artistic Director, Royal Shakespeare Company
Stratford-upon-Avon, April 2022

1

Romeo and Juliet: A Prologue

– 1979: The Poor Players. National Tour summer.

O, I am fortune's fool!

It's the opening night of my production of *Romeo and Juliet*, at the Mayfair Theatre in London, and Romeo has just fainted. It's 1979, and I am twenty years old.

It's the start of Act Three, and in these hot days in the square in Verona, the mad blood is stirring. That king of cats, Tybalt, has just accused Mercutio of sleeping with Romeo, and prompted a fight in which Mercutio is killed. Romeo flies at Tybalt, stabs him to death, and prompted by Benvolio flees, exiting downstage left.

A scene later, in Friar Laurence's cell, I can't understand what is happening. The Friar seems to be holding Romeo up, and Romeo seems to have forgotten his lines, and is muttering the tirade incomprehensibly. When the nurse enters and asks where Romeo is, the friar tells her: 'There on the ground, with his own tears made drunk.'

Drunk? Can it be that Romeo with all the nerves surrounding this performance has actually got pissed? Unfortunately, unbeknownst to me, exiting from the previous scene with the line 'O, I am fortune's fool!' Romeo had crashed straight into the wall in the wings, knocked his head and passed out. Somehow, with the friar's help, he makes it through the scene.

This is only one of a catalogue of disasters that haunts that night. Some misunderstanding that morning meant we had not been able to get into the theatre to prepare for our glittering gala one-off performance. When we did get in, the set did not fit on the stage, and had to be swivelled round by thirty degrees. There had been no time to rehearse, no time to do the lighting, or even run through the fights properly.

We are an ambitious student company, and have invited any number of influential arts folk to attend our debut. But as the two hours traffic of our stage threatens to drag on closer to four, I see all our hopes draining away. My sister Jo is sitting next to me. She slips a reassuring hand into mine. By the time the show finishes, I have nearly wrung it off.

'That's it,' I thought, 'it's the end of my career.'

* * *

Why is it that the first day of any rehearsal is like the first day at school?

I have been in that room, on that first nervous morning, for every single Shakespeare play.

And it is always the same.

Actors shuffle in, clutching their coats, looking for a spare chair on which to deposit their bags, half expecting one of the stage management to inform them they are in the wrong room, or possibly (depending on how acute their particular imposter syndrome is), that there has been some mix up, and though they auditioned, they haven't actually been cast in the play at all.

Everybody seems to know everybody else, and have cups of coffee which they knew where to find. Escape still seems a viable option until someone finally closes the door.

Eventually you realize that the first day of rehearsal is merely a way of getting to the second day of rehearsal.

As an early exercise, I like to use the opening of *Romeo and Juliet*. The 14-line prologue acts as a trailer to the play. No matter what stage of your career you are at, this session breaks down barriers and acts as a leveller.

It's part of something we call the Shakespeare Gym, a regular space in the rehearsal time that is devoted to the exercise of your Shakespeare muscles. It provides a chance to limber up, wrap your mouth around the verse and have a bit of fun, while building up the stamina and dexterity required to deliver that 400-year-old text. It helps to achieve that balance of concentration and relaxation that is at the heart of the craft of acting.

You sometimes hear a suppressed groan as the text of the sonnet is handed round, because the piece is so familiar. But there are some surprises in store for even the most seasoned actor. Those fourteen lines contain within them pretty much all the basics you need to know to speak Shakespeare's verse, or rather how to detect the clues he has given you in order to make the audience listen.

I always preface the session by insisting that no question is too stupid, because what *you* want to ask, someone else on the other side of the circle has been wondering about as well.

Here is the prologue as it is printed in the Quarto edition. For some reason it is left out of the Folio.

Two households, both alike in dignity,
In fair Verona, where we lay our scene,
From ancient grudge break to new mutiny,
Where civil blood makes civil hands unclean.
From forth the fatal loins of these two foes
A pair of star-cross'd lovers take their life;
Whose misadventured piteous overthrows
Doth with their death bury their parents' strife.
The fearful passage of their death-mark'd love,
And the continuance of their parents' rage,
Which, but their children's end, nought could remove,
Is now the two hours' traffic of our stage;
The which if you with patient ears attend,
What here shall miss, our toil shall strive to mend.

So, what do we know? It's a sonnet. It has fourteen lines, essentially three quatrains (four lines each) with an ABAB rhyme scheme and it ends with a rhyming couplet.

And it's in iambic pentameter. That makes the metre sound more complicated than it is. It's very simple. Five di-dums. A light stress followed by a heavy one, repeated five times per line. And those ten beats can encapsulate and convey a simple parcel of information, just enough for the audience to take in, in one go.

I have noticed this recently watching wildlife documentaries on TV. Have you noticed how the narration is often broken up into short readily-understandable phrases? In a documentary about penguins near the South Pole: 'The sun won't rise again, until the spring.' Often these phrases are ten or eleven beats long, a natural human breath. 'Hippos have relatively good night-vision.' You can quickly become obsessed. Some are actually iambic pentameters: 'These chimps have learned to use grass stems as tools.'

In the gym session, we start by reading the prologue in unison, generally the most boring delivery of the text imaginable. Then we pick out the meaning. Each person in turn reads a line out loud and then paraphrases it in their own words. This is pretty straightforward. There may be some questions around words like 'mutiny', 'misadventured' and the precise meaning of 'civil', why it is repeated, and whether it means the same thing both times.

Shakespeare's two invented conjunctions 'star-cross'd' and 'death-mark'd' always prompt interesting discussion about what images they conjure. 'Star-cross'd' suggesting fated or doomed by the malign influence of the heavens, or perhaps even physically stopped in their tracks by the stars barring their way. 'Death-mark'd' summoning up the crosses slashed in red paint on the doors of houses visited by the plague in Elizabethan London, leading to the cruel isolation of the entire household, doomed to die together.

But the revelation comes when the actor paraphrases the second half of the line: 'A pair of star-cross'd lovers <u>take their life</u>'. Nine times out of ten they will say 'the lovers commit suicide'.

If you reverse the order of the lines, it becomes clear that that is not what it means at all:

A pair of star-cross'd lovers take their life
From forth the fatal loins of these two foes.

They take their life from their parents' loins. They are born. Or maybe Shakespeare is allowing a macabre pun.

We beat out the lines to see which are regular iambics, and where the word stress and the verse stress coincide naturally, as they do for example in the second line:

In <u>fair</u> Ve<u>ro</u>na, <u>where</u> we <u>lay</u> our <u>scene</u>,

And in the final couplet:

The <u>which</u> if <u>you</u> with <u>patient</u> <u>ears</u> attend,
What <u>here</u> shall <u>miss</u>, our <u>toil</u> shall <u>strive</u> to <u>mend</u>.

The simplest way of identifying these opportunities, where Shakespeare may be suggesting other things to stress, is to say di-dum fives times, and then say the line precisely in that rhythm. If you exaggerate the rhythm it becomes even more obvious. Where the rhythm breaks down, you are being alerted to something you need to attend to.

The verse stress doesn't coincide with the natural word stress in the very first two words of the chorus. Not surely 'Two <u>house</u>holds', but '<u>Two</u> households'. Shakespeare could have reversed the first two lines just as easily. He doesn't. Why?

Imagine going out in front of an audience of perhaps 1,700 people at the original Rose theatre, or possibly 3,000 when the company takes up residence in the Globe. A sweaty jostle of raucous gallants, noisy oyster wenches, and rowdy apprentices, nattering, squabbling, gobbling, and having their pockets picked. Now try to get their attention. It's two o'clock in the afternoon. There are no lights to dim. No curtain to raise. A trumpet from the roof turret may have announced that the play was about to start to summon latecomers to hurry in. But it's up to you to open their ears. Very hard if your first line is as soft as 'In fair Verona, where ...'

But start with 'Two households ...' and you've got them straight away. And you've made them listen with two words that sum up the whole play. It's all about division.

Shakespeare gives the actor another clue about what to stress in the third line. The verse stress falls on the word 'to'. No actor is going to want to stress such an uninteresting preposition. So what word should they stress? Look either side of 'to'. 'New' is quite interesting, but the word that cracks out, that triggers the new mutiny, is 'break'. Shakespeare breaks the rhythm with the very word 'break'.

The same thing happens with the word 'bury' a few lines further on.

Shakespeare is anxious for you to notice the two occasions when he has invented new words in this sonnet, at any rate, new conjunctions of words: 'star-cross'd' and 'death-mark'd'. These new words are over-familiar to us now, particularly star-crossed, which has become a cliché used by tabloids to describe any teenage tragedy. But it's up to us to fresh-mint them, to remember this is the first time those two words have ever been placed in this partnership. They require two heavy stresses, assigning each word equal weight.

In the third quatrain, the line that always raises a laugh when you try to beat it out, is 'And the continuance of their parents' rage'. It lurches about, and seems to have one beat too many.

And <u>the</u> con<u>tinu</u>ance of <u>their</u> <u>par</u>ents' rage

'Continuance' is the problem. Conventional wisdom would insist that elision is employed here to somehow slide the words back on track, and make them fit. But I would argue that the word 'continuance' itself is giving you the clue. It's the longest word in the entire sonnet, and it's there to convey the terrible amount of time this ancient grudge has consumed. Why squeeze the word to make it sound shorter? Let it last even longer.

Our di-dum exercise lands the verse stress on another uninteresting word in the penultimate line of the third quatrain. 'Which, <u>but</u> their <u>chil</u>dren's <u>end</u>, nought **could** remove'. Why stress 'could'? Scanning around it though, you quickly find the word Shakespeare is pointing out to you, and asking you to consider stressing: 'Nought'. Nothing. Nothing but their children's deaths could stop the older generation feuding and infecting subsequent generations with their rancour.

There is so much more to explore in these simple fourteen lines:[1] the sound of the words; the way you really have to chew a line like 'From ancient grudge break to new mutiny', as the consonants clash against each other; how you need to finish the final 't' in the word 'ancient' before you can begin the next word 'grudge', the same with the final 'k' of break, before continuing 'to new mutiny'. How that line is stacked with so many different vowel sounds. They echo and mimic the grunts and thumps, squeals and cries of a violent fist fight.

What's the effect of the alliteration in 'From forth the fatal loins of these two foes'? Is the intention to sound portentous, highlighting the ominous significance, the almost mediaeval tone of morality, set against the airy lightness of the next line 'A pair of star-cross'd lovers take their life'? Those in the Rose audience who knew Arthur Brooke's original 1562 poem, from which Shakespeare takes the story, may well have been expecting a morality tale in which the young are shown the consequences attendant upon 'unhonest desire' and 'wicked lust' and warned to obey their parents. Perhaps the contrast in these two lines expresses how Shakespeare himself travels away from such heavy-handed polemic to a greater sympathy with the struggles of the young – and a distaste for the greed of their parents' generation who fail their children.

If the whole text of *Romeo and Juliet* were actually to be performed in the much quoted 'two hours traffic' of the stage, then this prologue would have to be delivered in just over 33 seconds (believe me, I have done the maths).

I ask for volunteers and somebody pulls up a stopwatch. If nobody is brave enough, I gallantly accept my own challenge. I normally manage it with two or three seconds to spare, but we all agree that if you did the whole play at that pace, you would run the risk of exhausting your audience very quickly.

But it is thrilling.

If you observe all those clues, where the verse stress and the word stresses don't coincide, the rhymes, the caesuras, the architecture, the pacing, the character in the lines, the onomatopoeia, then you can build pace and excitement. If you know the map you can run through the maze.

*　*　*

I arrived at the RSC essentially not knowing my iambic from my caesura and imagining that there was some divine panel sitting in judgement upon my ability with the verse, ready to leap on any errant stress or missed beat. But I met instead with kind encouragement and gentle provocation and learnt pretty much everything I know from legends like Cicely Berry, the RSC's voice guru for over forty years, and the director and teacher, John Barton.

---

[1]　If you want to continue with this Shakespeare Gym and read about how the use of caesuras increases the pace and excitement of the prologue, turn to Appendix A.

That is not to say that I had no experience with Shakespeare. In fact, I had done quite a lot.

I missed out on Ophelia, in the second form at the Preston Catholic College (it went to 'Gags' Ronson in 2A) but in my third year I landed the part of Lady Anne in *Richard III*. My Jesuit grammar school put on a Shakespeare play every year in the autumn half term. Being an all-male establishment, the women's roles were played by the younger boys. My twin sister attended the Convent of the Holy Child Jesus just across the street in Winckley Square, but the girls were never invited to take part.

I have a vivid memory of rehearsing the wooing scene between Lady Anne and Richard, Duke of Gloucester, on the stage in the school hall after classes, the din of a football game rising from the dark wet schoolyard below. Richard was played by a tall and strikingly handsome young man called Rory Edwards, in the second year sixth. As this was the early seventies most of us had haircuts like the Osmonds, but Rory had a dark glitter about him, a dash of Marc Bolan and T. Rex. I thought he was incredible. He was a sprinter, and the high-jump champion and I was nervous at the thought of acting opposite him.

We were rattling through the keen encounter of their wits, the breathless rally of praise and insult, backwards and forwards, as Richard extols Anne's beauty, and she vents her anger in a torrent of rebuke.

GLOUCESTER	Fairer than tongue can name thee, let me have
	Some patient leisure to excuse myself.
LADY ANNE	Fouler than heart can think thee, thou canst make
	No excuse current, but to hang thyself.

They match each other phrase for phrase:

LADY ANNE	He is in heaven, where thou shalt never come.
GLOUCESTER	Let him thank me, that holp to send him thither;
	For he was fitter for that place than earth.
LADY ANNE	And thou unfit for any place but hell.
GLOUCESTER	Yes, one place else, if you will hear me name it.
LADY ANNE	Some dungeon
GLOUCESTER	Your bed-chamber.

Now Richard pulls the carpet from underneath Anne's feet, by the outrageous suggestion that having killed her husband, he now deserves a place in her bed.

As we rehearsed the scene, the 14-year-old boy I was began to feel light-headed. The rapid stichomythia[2] meant that both of us were breathing fast, and getting faster, leading to the provocation that prompts Anne to spit at the hunchback murderer before her.

---

[2] A sequence of single alternating lines, or half-lines given to alternating characters.

Chest heaving, brain swimming, I threw my head back and lobbed a gob of spittle at my poor fellow actor, who reeled back in shock. For a moment I thought he was going to clobber me. This seemed to break all the rules. Standing there in my school blazer, and polished lace-ups, I was both channelling and, at the same time, suppressing all the complicated emotions I felt.

Richard takes Lady Anne's hand and places his ring on her finger. As Edwards reached for my hand, I could hardly breathe. Beyond jostling in the playground or on the pitch, touch was a rare occurrence between Catholic College boys in the early seventies. I felt faint.

'Doran,' came a shout from the back of the hall, 'don't roll your eyes.' Mr Malone, the English Master, and producer of the annual play was having none of this simpering display, and the rehearsal came to an abrupt halt.

The play went ahead for its three performances. The *Lancashire Evening Post* reported that despite what seemed 'an out-of-date tradition' of having the boys play the girls, 'Lady Anne was fetchingly played by G. Doran'. My first review.

Whenever the subject of what it must have been like in Shakespeare's company when the boys played the girls, I have a particular insight. If no 'divine perfection of a woman', I probably looked quite convincing in my widow's weeds. I may have been 'fetching', I may not have been any good. But for me, at any rate, the scene was deeply charged. Just by speaking it out loud, together, it produced a crackle that if not erotic, was certainly electric.

As a quietly spoken, polite, sports-averse teenager, I had been bullied in the dark playground of the 900-strong Lancashire school. After *Richard III* however, instead of getting worse, the bullying suddenly stopped. It was as if the mere fact of standing up in front of an audience and remembering lines of Shakespeare commanded respect among my peers. And whatever else I have to thank Shakespeare for in my life, I will always be grateful to him for that.

'Jock' Malone also ran the school theatre trips, ferrying the boys to plays at the Duke's Playhouse in Lancaster, the Octagon in Bolton, and the newly opened Royal Exchange Theatre in Manchester. Occasionally we got taken to Stratford-upon-Avon.

In early 1974, we saw Richard Pasco and Ian Richardson in John Barton's celebrated production of *Richard II*, in which they alternated the roles of Richard and Bolingbroke. I remember so many things about that production: the horses on which Bolingbroke and his followers appeared from Ravenspurgh; the flashing gold sunburst of Richard's pleated cape as he appeared on high at Flint Castle; and the unexpected laugh that Northumberland managed to get on hearing who accompanied the king, when he drawled wearily 'O, belike it is the Bishop of Carlisle'.

The great abdication scene was enthralling. Pasco (who was on as Richard that afternoon) in a highly fissile state, ricocheted from reckless self-pity to preening arrogance, playing capriciously with the court, teasing Bolingbroke bidding him seize the crown, 'Here, cousin', as if he were coaxing a shy kitten. And of course, the moment Richard calls for a looking glass, stays with me still, and the way he smashed it shocked me with its abrupt violence. I also wondered how they smashed a mirror every night

That autumn, Jock decided that we would do our own production of *Richard II*, and that I should play the volatile king. This was quite a departure for the school, as they had largely repeated a cycle of the same seven Shakespeare plays for well over forty years. But it meant I got to tackle that great lyrical flush of language at fifteen years of age. Our mirror was made of clear toffee.

I couldn't get enough of Shakespeare. And by now I was old enough to make my own way to Stratford whenever I could. I persuaded my best mate Richard Sharples to hitchhike down the M6 from Charnock Richard service station, with a tent in a rucksack. We would camp on the racecourse just outside town. But even that did not satisfy the itch.

One wet Spring weekend, Richard and I were kicking around his local park in Chorley. We decided to duck the rain and look round a stately pile in the centre of the park. Astley Hall is a Jacobean House with a long gallery running along the length of the house on the first floor. There are some later additions to the house, including some rather overpowering stucco ceilings. But at the centre of the house is a half-timbered inner courtyard which reveals its Elizabethan origins. Carved in the lintel over one of the doorways you could make out the date: 1600.

Somehow, I was surprised that here, near my own home, was something that survived from Shakespeare's day. I decided we should mount our own Shakespeare production and perform it in that evocative courtyard. I persuaded my friends to form an acting troop. We called ourselves, with not a trace of irony, The Poor Players. In fact, we had managed to secure the grand sum of £12 from Chorley District Council towards the costs of the show. We would present *Twelfth Night*.

I, of course, would play Malvolio (as I had the previous year in the school play), but this time the cast included girls from the Winkley Square Covent.

We raided jumble sales and dressing-up boxes and borrowed from the school wardrobe. And we made many of the costumes ourselves. On one visit to Stratford, I had been inspired by an exhibition in the Swan Gallery, which demonstrated how the costume department had transformed an ordinary felt hat, through a process called 'gunking', with dribbles of glue and metallic spray paint, into a dazzling copotain hat.

We had also all been avid fans of *The Six Wives of Henry VIII* with Keith Michell on the BBC. An exhibition of the costumes had arrived in Liverpool, which we trooped off to see: fascinated by the richly encrusted jewelled collars, made of sprayed fruit pastilles, and old washers mounted on felt.

As a result, Malvolio, despite his relatively lowly status as a steward, and his distinctly puritanical outlook, had in the Poor Players production, a grey velvet doublet (made from an old curtain with a brocaded effect achieved by dabbing Humbrol paints through a plastic doily), a crushed black velvet lady's evening coat (*c.* 1969), and a ruff the size of a cartwheel, made of an old tulle petticoat. The early seventies fashion for chunky gold jewellery made his chain of office very easy to source.

Later during that long-parched summer of 1976 (the second hottest summer since records began), I got my first taste of theatre in the West End. My parents decided to drive the caravan down to London for a week, staying at a camp site in Crystal Palace. My mate, Peter 'Ibi' Ibison, who, with his tall gangly frame and mop of flaxen hair, had been natural casting as Sir Andrew Aguecheek, came along. The Number 3 bus would take us all the way into the city, through Brixton, across Lambeth Bridge and drop us in Trafalgar Square.

Ibi and I saw everything we could: Janet Suzman as Masha in Chekhov's *Three Sisters* at the Cambridge; Glenda Jackson in Webster's *The White Devil* at The Old Vic directed by Edward Bond; Shaw's *The Devil's Disciple* by the RSC at the Aldwych; and *Love's Labour's Lost* at the Open Air Theatre in Regent's Park. The gorgeous Clive Arindell played Berowne and made my heart stop in the speech 'But love, first learned in a lady's eyes', which I was convinced he delivered entirely to me. I was in love . . .

And when Love speaks, the voice of all the gods
Makes heaven drowsy with the harmony.

And not just with Berowne, but with Shakespeare.

My parents mostly did their own thing, but we all went to the Theatre Royal Drury Lane one night to see the original American cast of *A Chorus Line*. We loved it. Though sitting between my parents as someone sang about gonorrhoea was about as challenging as it could have been for any good Catholic 17-year-old boy; made all the more excruciating by the smash-hit number 'Tits and Ass' about the benefits of silicone breast enhancement.

One morning, in our heady sight-seeing trip to the capital, Ibi and I visited St Paul's Cathedral. We clambered up the 257 steps to the Whispering Gallery. We had been told that the gallery gets its name from a weird quirk in its construction. If you whisper into the wall, it can be heard all the way across the other side. We had both been cast as the Macbeths in the next school play that autumn term, and already had most of our lines under our belts, so we waited until the gallery was clear of other tourists, ran round to opposite sides, and whispered the dagger scene to each other:

MACBETH	I have done the deed. Didst thou not hear a noise?
LADY MACBETH	I heard the owl scream and the crickets cry.
	Did not you speak?
MACBETH	When?
LADY MACBETH	Now.
MACBETH	As I descended?
LADY MACBETH	Ay.
MACBETH	Hark! –
	Who lies i' the second chamber?
LADY MACBETH	Donalbain.
MACBETH	This is a sorry sight.

It was so tense, so intimate, so dangerous. But then one of the minor canons appeared, giving us a suspicious look – we were clearly up to no good – and we scuttled away.

*   *   *

The following summer, on one of our hiking trips to Stratford, my best mate Richard and I queued for tickets for *The Comedy of Errors*, Trevor Nunn's glorious musical version, with music by Guy Woolfenden, and a sparkling cast including Judi Dench,

Michael Williams and Roger Rees. It was set in a sunny bustling Mediterranean market square. Our seats turned out to be on stage in a balcony overlooking the action.

Inspired by that production, and in my last school summer after A-levels, The Poor Players would put on our own *The Comedy of Errors*.

I would play Antipholus of Syracuse and Ibi would play my twin. But as Ibi had blonde hair and I was dark, I decided to write to the wig department at Stratford and ask if they could lend us two wigs. I got a very sweet letter back from Brenda Leedham, the head of wigs, saying she wouldn't be able to supply us with wigs, but we might think of using a temporary hair dye which could be purchased relatively cheaply. And that is what we did, and that is how the Antipholi twins in this production turned out to have rather weird mulberry-coloured locks.

We toured the show around various grand houses in the North West: opening back at Astley Hall, then Borwick Hall near Carnforth; Smithills Hall on the edge of the West Pennine Moors near Bolton; Turton Tower, a mediaeval 'pele' tower outside Blackburn; and Holker Hall in Grange-over-Sands.

At a post-performance charity reception in one particular stately pile, a rather imperious county lady complimented the production by saying: 'And do you know, the villagers understood every word.'

I was most excited to discover at Hoghton Tower, about 12 miles from Preston, that Shakespeare may have spent some of his 'lost years' here in Lancashire. It is possible that in the summer Shakespeare left King Edward School, in Stratford-upon-Avon, around the age of fourteen or fifteen (and sometime before he married Anne Hathaway, in 1582, at the age of eighteen), that he travelled to Lancashire. Tradition has it that he followed his old schoolmaster John Cottam here to Hoghton Tower and worked as a tutor and actor in the household of the Catholic grandee, Alexander de Houghton.

We were shown a copy of Alexander de Houghton's will. Following the bequest of some musical instruments and 'play clothes', there is a specific request that two men, Fulk Gyllom and William Shakeshaft, should be looked after.

Might they have been players? Was Shakeshaft a code name for Shakespeare? If the name is intended to be a disguise, you have to admit, it's not a very good one, but to this impressionable bardolatrous teenager, it seemed entirely plausible. And this evidence coupled with the news that John Cottam originally came from Preston and that his family were tenants on the Hoghton Estate, and his brother was a Jesuit priest (executed for his faith in 1582), to me turned possibility into probability.

It's a much disputed theory of course, but as everyone casts Shakespeare in their own image, I wanted to find some kind of connection with him, too. Standing in the great sloping courtyard of Hoghton Tower, I tried to think of Shakespeare in my own image, as he might have stood on this same spot at my age, here in Lancashire, a young man with Catholic proclivities, wondering what the future held, and who maybe like me was gay.

At the end of that summer, I left school, and prepared to head to Bristol University to do a degree in English and Drama.

But I did not leave The Poor Players behind. Now I would concentrate on what it meant to be a director. *Romeo and Juliet* would be our first production. It was the first Shakespeare play I directed without being in it as well. And it was a baptism by fire.

* * *

With my friend Chris Grady (a maths student) at Bristol, we set about raising money to tour *Romeo and Juliet* around the UK during the summer holidays. The company would be drawn from students from universities and drama schools all over the country.

Chris was a hard-working and ambitious administrator and had quickly set up a tour that would rehearse in a stately-home-turned-school, in Suffolk; open for a single Sunday night in London, and then travel the length and breadth of the country from Sterling to York and Bury St Edmunds, from a barn in Cranfield to a replica of Shakespeare's Globe in Abingdon. Chris also pulled together a rather impressive if eclectic board of patrons including Dulcie Gray, Paul Scofield and Lord Michael Birkett.

This was 1979, and that May, Mrs Thatcher had come to power. In her first spending review the Arts were cut by 4.8 per cent. Her emphasis on reducing public subsidy for the arts but increasing the opportunity for private sponsorship and corporate investment meant that every arts organisation around the country suddenly began looking for support. Very few knew where to start and most companies had little idea of how or where to donate their cash.

Through Chris's tireless efforts we secured a huge sponsorship deal from an international computer company. It was a ridiculous amount, about thirty thousand pounds. We could not believe our luck, and laughed that we would have to change the name of The Poor Players.

To begin with, things seemed to go quite smoothly. The firm's PR manager, responsible for the relationship was a short, bald man in his mid-forties, who flushed easily and spoke with a slurred public school accent. Let's call him Ivor.

Ivor asked if there was any punchy way we could link computers and Shakespeare on the poster. I jokily suggested 'Juliet would have found a better suitor, had she dated by computer', which to my consternation, he decided was a good idea.

We held a swanky press launch in London, which not unsurprisingly very few of the press attended. Afterwards, Ivor seemed unconcerned by the lack of journalists, and asked me if I had to head back to Bristol that night. 'It's just that I have a flat in Mayfair with some rather fine Hogarth engravings that you might enjoy.' I couldn't believe it. Had he actually just asked me to come up and see his etchings?

When I declined, as politely as possible, he suddenly turned quite red, and growled, 'See me in my office, tomorrow morning. Nine o'clock.'

Chris hadn't been able to attend the launch. He was suffering from glandular fever and was confined to his bed, in hall, back in Bristol. So ill was he that I had been unable to tell him what had happened or to seek his advice. Ivor said his firm was no longer able to support my company and would be withdrawing its entire sponsorship of the tour. The poorly attended press conference was merely one badly mishandled event in a catalogue of mistakes that had lost the confidence of his firm in my company.

I reeled out of the building wondering what on earth to do. Overnight I had lost the entire funding for the production, the tour, everything. Rehearsals were due to start in a month and my business partner was on his sickbed over a hundred miles away.

I ran to a phone box, pulled up the telephone directory, and looked up the number for the London office of what I imagined was the computer firm's biggest rival, IBM. I rang the number. I asked to be put through to the chairman's office and requested a meeting. I have no idea what I was hoping for, but with naive optimism I thought perhaps they would see this as an opportunity. When I described the reason for the urgency of my request as being a matter of some personal delicacy, the assistant rather graciously agreed to fit me in to meet their head of personnel.

A couple of hours later, I was sitting in the offices of IBM, laying out the story of how I had come to lose this substantial sponsorship. It quickly became clear they were not in a position to bale me out but were anxious that I relay my sorry tale to the director of a newly-formed charitable organisation called the Association of Business Sponsorship of the Arts (ABSA).

Later that afternoon, I found myself in an office in a Georgian mews called Pierrepont Place in Bath, addressing the director of ABSA, Luke Rittner. He listened attentively, eventually sending me back on the intercity 125 to London, to attend a hastily organized meeting with one of our board of patrons, Lord Birkett, in his town house, a stone's throw from Kensington Gardens.

I was shown into Lord Birkett's study, and waited. The room was full of shelves of classical music and populated with toy pigs of every description. As I wondered what the significance of the pigs were, the noble lord finally arrived. Birkett, a producer of Peter Brook's film of *King Lear*, had been persuaded to lend his name to our little troop out of a charitable fondness for our small but ambitious Shakespeare adventure.

He interrogated me rigorously on every detail of our relationship with the computer firm, and with Ivor in particular. I supplied everything we had, detailing the negotiations and the agreement to sponsor. Finally, he seemed satisfied with my account of what had happened and offered me a sherry.

'I am sorry I took so long to come in here,' he said, 'but I've just had this Ivor on the phone. I believe everything you tell me, but we now have a cornered man to deal with. He is going to restore the entire sponsorship deal. It is frankly far too much money to give a company of students in my opinion, however good you may be, which is as yet unproven. However, that is not the point. They agreed to it, for whatever reasons. But you are going to have to go and see him, now.'

The thought of facing Ivor again made me feel sick. We met in the Star and Garter pub by Putney Bridge.

'Gre-gory,' he drawled. 'What on earth were you thinking? There was no need for that. I was testing your mettle, that was all. Of course we are going to sponsor your little company.'

And so they did.

Business sponsorship of the arts was an enticing but perilous playing field for unscrupulous patrons ready to spend their company's money to buy them access to potentially vulnerable young people. Companies like ABSA (now Arts and Business) were set up to encourage sponsorship opportunities but also to regulate the industry. Ivor, however, was not an isolated bad apple, and over the course of the running the company we met others like him.

The computer firm ran into a financial crisis in 1981 and was eventually taken over by a Japanese multinational.

*   *   *

The tour of *Romeo and Juliet* had convinced me that if I was to pursue a career in the theatre, I needed further specific training. The *Romeo and Juliet* company had been made up of students from universities and drama schools all over the UK. But I had noticed a trend.

The actors from drama schools tended to regard the university students as too cerebral. They thought too much about it all, instead of jumping in and trying ideas out. Whereas the university students felt they were missing out on something called technique, which the drama school actors apparently knew all about: breath control, posture, character motivation. Both sides were suspicious of the other, and anxious that they were missing out on something that would be important later on, in the business.

At Bristol University, the English Drama degree course was pretty much 80 per cent of both the joint English and Drama degree courses, and perhaps inevitably I spent most of my time in the Vandyke Theatre of the drama department. I had the opportunity to dip my toe into all aspects of theatre, with an emphasis on the practical. I performed in plays like Christopher Hampton's *The Philanthropist*, and Ibsen's *The Lady from the Sea*. I directed a production of Goldoni's *The Servant of Two Masters*, and I designed a production of Steve Gooch's play *Female Transport*, about women prisoners being transported to Botany Bay, which involved designing three decks of a convict ship. *Female Transport* was directed by Professor Martin White, who would become a lifelong friend.

Bristol University then had two bursaries with the Bristol Old Vic Theatre School, which were available for students who wanted to train further and managed to secure a place. I was lucky to get one of those bursaries. Although I intended to become a director, I still hadn't got acting out of my system, and had decided that the directors' course, still in its early days back then, would not give me the inside knowledge of what an actor's technique actually involved.

I left the university and headed up to the theatre school which was (and still is) right at the top of Pembroke Road, as it meets the Downs, to start formal classical training as an actor.

*   *   *

As it turned out during my time at the school, I did more directing than any of the students on the directing course. But, best of all, I got to meet someone who would become a mentor in my life, and a friend: Raphael 'Rudi' Shelley.

Rudi was a legend. He had worked at the Bristol Old Vic Theatre School since it opened in 1946. He taught me about Rule Number One, the best piece of advice I have ever been given as a classical director.

Generations of graduates from the school can recall his memorable advice to 'pull down your bolero'[3] or 'squeeze your lemons'.

Rudi would tell everyone in the class to close their eyes. They then had to imagine they had a small lemon. It had to be small, maybe Sicilian. They were then to place the lemon in between their buttocks, Rudi said, just at the top of the crack. As you can imagine, most of the class would be busy suppressing giggles at this point. Then, you had to squeeze the lemon very gently, until it dribbled down your inner thighs. If you try this at home you may understand Rudi's brilliance. The exercise immediately identifies and activates the place in the body where you need to find support for your breath, right down in the abdominal lower back muscles.

Like all great teachers, Rudi knew that for students, in order to make something stick, it had to be expressed in a memorable way.

Rudi would arrive each morning immaculately dressed, his small frame decked out in a natty tweed jacket, with a dark shirt and a flamboyant line in batik cravats. He had large expressive hands, and always wore a ring on his right index finger, with a enormous stone.

In the summer term of my first year, we did a tour of *The Winter's Tale* around arts centres in the South West. My friend Tony Mulholland and I decided we would direct it together. And he pushed me to be innovative about the way we presented the play. It would be done as if a group of Victorian children were performing the story in a crowded attic.[4] I can't recall a great deal about the production, although the bear involved a game of hide and seek and an old fur coat. And I remember one performance of our barnstorming tour in an actual barn, during which a lamb walked unsteadily onto stage in the sheep-shearing scene, and that by the time Leontes reached out to the statue of Hermione and declared 'she's warm' the audience were so cold, they burst into laughter and a jovial round of applause.

The night Rudi saw it, at Clifton College in Bristol, we were all nervous and excited to hear his reaction to our radical interpretation of the play. He wagged his heavily-ringed finger at me and said in his much-imitated nasal twang, 'Greg, remember Rule Number One: don't want to be clever'. I say that is the best piece of advice I have ever been given as a classical director, because it is a reminder not to get in between the audience and the play, that is not your job. You have to reveal its greatness, that's all.

Rudi was old enough to be Prussian. He had trained at the Vienna Conservatory, and moved to Berlin, but after the rise of Hitler, things became too uncomfortable to stay. Rudi had been left alone in a large house. The Nazis would sometimes throw arms or ammunition over the wall into the courtyard. The soldiers would then pretend to search the house before discovering the evidence that they themselves had planted. You would then be arrested, convicted and your property confiscated. So, accompanied by his beloved Great Dane, Rudi would scour the garden for bullets at night. 'I knew,' he

---

[3] A note about posture. You had to imagine you were wearing a bolero jacket, like a matador's chaquetilla, and that it had a peak in the middle of your back. If someone were to pull that peak down, you would automatically pull back your shoulders and open out your chest.

[4] The idea was inspired by Dennis Potter's Play for Today, *Blue Remembered Hills* with Colin Welland, Michael Elphick and Helen Mirren, all playing 7-year-olds in the Forest of Dean.

said, 'that if I left even one undiscovered it would cost me my life.' He decided to flee to Palestine.

Rudi used to tell us that he had nearly missed his train out of Berlin. But as it happened the train was delayed because a group of Jewish children were being parted from their grieving parents and were taking a while to board. He caught the train and left, along with the last transportation of Jewish children to be allowed to leave Germany. The near-miss had given him a life-long horror of being late.

And at the Old Vic School, he never was late, and consequently we rarely were.

His teaching was infinitely practical. If someone was acting with their arms folded, he would say 'Ducky, let your arms hang' or 'don't hug yourself, hug the audience'. Or if students were being too cerebral, he would say 'You must learn to work from your guts not from your brains' or more simply 'It's called a play, so play.' 'Your task,' he would say, 'is to develop your craftsmanship to the degree that you can forget that you ever learnt it.' And if a student was being too eager to put all that they had learned on display, he would say 'Darling, your technique is showing.'

He would talk about what he looked for in a good actor (or at any rate in someone who wanted to train to be a good actor). He looked for the 3 Cs: the love of <u>C</u>raft; the desire to <u>C</u>ommunicate; and not being afraid to <u>C</u>lown, to fall flat on your face.

He had a precise approach to Comedy, which to Rudi was a very serious business. ('If something is not serious, it cannot be funny.') He would bring a red nose into class. He would hand it to different students and tell them to put it on and make us laugh. Generally, people immediately started goofing around, attempting to clown about and getting less and less funny, despite the weak laughter of their supportive classmates.

Then Rudi would put the nose on, and just carry on talking about anything at all. It was hilarious. In moments as he continued to speak, the class would be in fits. His point? Don't play the red nose. Don't be self-conscious or aware of the joke, or it won't be funny.

And he would recall his old Great Dane back in Berlin. 'That dog was a comic,' Rudi said. 'He had ears that stood up like a bat, and from him I learnt how to play farce. The dog didn't want to be funny. He was a perfectly serious dog, but everyone who saw him couldn't help but be amused. If a character knew that he was funny he would not be doing what he is doing. Comedy has to be played like that Great Dane.'

Everyone lucky enough to have come into Rudi's sphere has an anecdote about him. Actor Nick Farrell tells of coming to the end of his training, and completing his final show, when a friend complimented him on his performance, but said he had to do something about his hands. He was moving them around too much. Nick was distraught and went to seek out Rudi. 'I've just spent two years training, Rudi,' he wailed, 'and apparently I don't know what to do with my hands!'

'Nick,' Rudi shrugged, 'your hands! What about your feet!'

I loved him.[5]

I took Rudi with me when, towards the end of the Bristol Old Vic Theatre School course, I was invited to direct *A Midsummer Night's Dream,* in a community college in

---

[5] Many years later, at the end of May 1999, as I was preparing to direct *The Winter's Tale* for the RSC, I heard the news that Rudi Shelly had died at the age of ninety.

Jamestown in Upstate New York (famous as the birthplace of the comedienne Lucille Ball). The work of The Poor Players had been noticed by its entrepreneurial Head of English, Bog Hagstrom. It was, as it turned out, my first professional job as a director.

I took out a number of my fellow Brits, young actors I had worked with at the school and elsewhere, to play Puck, Oberon and Titania, and to help work with the students. The rest of the company was made up from the student body.

On the first day one of them came up to me brandishing his copy of the play, and said 'Mr Doran, this play, *A Midsummer Night's Dream*? It's by William Shakespeare?' 'Yes,' I replied warily. 'Why?' 'Well, it says on the cover it's by Pelican Shakespeare!' Presumably Penguin Shakespeare's American cousin.

Rudi's mantra about comedy needing to be played seriously proved itself to me, during that rehearsal period. The students had assumed that being Shakespeare, British, and four hundred years old, that (a) it couldn't possibly have much to do with their lives in Chautauqua County, and (b) that it must be deadly serious. And that is how they played it.

The quartet of lovers brought their own teenage anxieties about falling in and out of relationships with honest, earnest truthfulness. The rude mechanicals tried their utmost to make *Pyramus and Thisbe* as good as possible, terrified of the consequences if they failed, and relieved when they succeeded. As for taking Bottom and the fairies seriously, I was asked to come and address a group of staff at what was called the Human Potential Center, who grilled me about why I thought it was appropriate to be presenting a play where a husband drugs his wife and makes her submit to bestial intercourse with a donkey. (I guess they had a point!)

The result in performance was that instead of straining for laughter the company strove for truth and were overwhelmed and delighted when the audience welcomed their efforts with laughter and applause.

*   *   *

I applied for a regional theatre trainee directors' scheme at the end of my course at the Bristol Old Vic School. I got an interview at Nottingham Playhouse and managed to secure a job as assistant director. As it didn't start until the autumn however, I was offered a role in the acting company in the meantime. I had my first proper job, an equity card, and £96 a week.

I played half a troll, a ball of yarn, and a wanking lunatic in *Peer Gynt*, and my sister Jo (ever present at my press nights, then and since) said if Marius Goring as the Button-moulder had come on once more and said, 'I will meet you at the next crossroads', she would run screaming from the theatre.

When the cast list for *Antony and Cleopatra* went up, I discovered that I would be playing both the messenger – who gets pulled around by his hair by the furious Cleopatra (played in this production by the fabulously sultry Kate O'Mara) – and Pacorus.

Pacorus has, without doubt, the distinction of being the smallest role in Shakespeare. Pacorus is the son of the Parthian king, Orodes. And he is dead.

I was carried on stage by two of my fellow actors. They dropped me onto the floor, had a few lines of conversation about not upsetting your superior officers by out-performing them, and then picked me up again and carried me off.

The set was a simple, steeply-raked floor with a carpet against a huge reproduction of an engraving by Piranesi. Unfortunately, there had been a series of industrial disputes with the backstage staff at Nottingham Playhouse, so our technical rehearsals had been cut short. Our first time on stage was a dress rehearsal, in front of a large party of what were then described as ESN children. ESN stood for 'educationally subnormal', and was the appalling label used at the time.

The director didn't help matters by appearing in front of this restless group, tucking his hands together like an opera singer about to deliver an aria, and declaring that this was a very, very difficult play and they were all going to have to concentrate very, very hard.

All went fine, until the Pacorus scene. On we came, down I dropped, but as we had never rehearsed on a rake, like a good method actor, I did what any self-respecting dead body would do: I went with the momentum and rolled . . . right off the front of the stage. This really got the attention of the school parties, who all yelped out. When I got up, climbed back up, and resumed my dead body position however, the yelps turned to guffaws and the play never really recovered.

I spent a couple of years at Nottingham graduating into assistant director and then was given my own productions of *Waiting for Godot* and *Long Day's Journey into Night*. But after I left, things seemed to drift. I moved to London and returned to acting, being cast in a series of BBC sitcoms. I was truly awful in all of them.

But then one day I got a letter from Siobhan Bracke, the casting director for the RSC, and my life turned around.

2

Titus Andronicus

– 1995: The Market Theatre, Johannesburg; West Yorkshire Playhouse;
National Theatre (Cottesloe); Almagro Theatre Festival, Spain.
– Filmed by the South African Broadcasting Corporation.

Language most shows a man: speak that I may see thee
Ben Jonson: Timber, or Discoveries (1640)

You are how you speak in Shakespeare.

The second in the series of Shakespeare Gyms we do in Stratford tends to be on *Titus Andronicus*. And it's an exploration of how our house playwright packs the text with character clues.

The play opens with two short speeches of similar length. The object of the exercise is to try and derive from what Shakespeare has written, as many hints as to the identity of the speakers as possible. The advantage of the relative obscurity of the play is that actors are mostly unfamiliar with it, and therefore come with no preconceptions about the story, or the characters. Because the speeches open the play, they require no extra knowledge of what has happened, and the actors have to pick that up from the text before them. Here they are:

SATURNINUS   Noble patricians, patrons of my right,
                Defend the justice of my cause with arms,
                And, countrymen, my loving followers,
                Plead my successive title with your swords:
                I am his first-born son, that was the last
                That wore the imperial diadem of Rome;
                Then let my father's honours live in me,
                Nor wrong mine age with this indignity.
BASSIANUS   Romans, friends, followers, favorers of my right,
                If ever Bassianus, Caesar's son,
                Were gracious in the eyes of royal Rome,
                Keep then this passage to the Capitol
                And suffer not dishonour to approach
                The imperial seat, to virtue consecrate,
                To justice, continence and nobility;

> But let desert in pure election shine,
> And, Romans, fight for freedom in your choice.

We read it out loud. Half the group read Saturninus and the other half Bassianus. Then we put it into our own words. The language is pretty straightforward. 'Patricians' might need defining, and usually 'continence' takes a bit of glossing. But the situation becomes clear. Saturninus is the oldest son to the late emperor of Rome, but his younger brother Bassianus is challenging his right to succeed to the imperial diadem. I ask the group who they think is the most effective speaker. At this stage they are generally divided.

We slowly unpick the meaning of both speeches. Saturninus and his younger brother Bassianus rally their respective supporters. But by the end of the session, from the analysis of their different use of rhetoric, armed with Sharpie felt pens, we fill two large sheets of paper with adjectives describing their characters.

It's fair to say that in performance these two opening speeches often go by in a welter of shouting, as the two sides bark at each other, in an angry exchange of heckling. But when we do this exercise what becomes clear is just how many indications of character Shakespeare has given the actor.

Rhetoric, the art of persuading people through language, was an art familiar to Shakespeare because he had been taught it at school where the curriculum was essentially the three R's: reading, writing and rhetoric. He knew his Cicero. Following exercises in his Lily's Latin Grammar he would have been tasked with writing a speech in Latin in which he had to imagine he was Brutus defending the assassination of Caesar. That would have stood him in very good stead a few years later when writing *Julius Caesar*.

He would have known all about what Sam Leith[1] calls the three musketeers of rhetoric: Ethos, Pathos and Logos.

Pathos is how you use emotion to sway the crowd. Crack a joke, get them on your side. Move them if you can, stir them with a rousing climax perhaps.

And Logos, actually from a rhetorical point of view, the least important musketeer, is what you have to say. In oratory, it's not so much what you say, but how you say it that matters.

But let's take the first musketeer, Ethos. It's how you put yourself into the speech or why the audience should want to listen to you. Whether it's a celebrity endorsement ('Hi, I'm George Clooney, I'm really cool, and I am going to talk to you about coffee capsules'), or political advocacy. I guess I have made just such an appeal. 'My name is Greg Doran, I am the Artistic Director of the RSC, I have done every play in the First Folio, and I am going to talk to you about Shakespeare.' If I had said 'My name is Greg Doran, Director of the RSC and I am going to talk to you about upper intestinal endoscopy', you might have chosen not to listen.

And you can get Ethos wrong. As in the apocryphal story of Peter Mandelson campaigning in Sunderland and turning up for a photo op at a fish and chip shop. He

---

[1] In his entertaining book about rhetoric, *You Talking to Me: The Art of Rhetoric from Aristotle to Trump and Beyond*.

orders cod and chips and then, pointing to the mushy peas, says 'and I'll have some of the guacamole'. Ethos shot to pieces in one go.

In *Titus Andronicus*, Shakespeare makes good use of Ethos.

Saturninus appeals to the patricians to take up arms on his behalf and defend his right to become emperor as the oldest son. I get one actor to read the speech and whenever he says I, me, my, or mine, I get everyone else to repeat the word. It's a constant stream of self-interest.

We try the same with Bassianus' speech and soon notice that he uses the possessive adjective only once, in the first line, and refers to himself only one other time, by name, and therefore only in the third person, in the second line.

We try another exercise, saying the speech as we walk around the room, changing direction on the punctuation marks, and stopping dead when the character reaches a full stop. This reveals something interesting. We notice that Bassianus' speech develops and grows in one long sentence.

And speaking it out loud also reveals Saturninus' use of alliteration involves lots of plosive Ps, he splutters with them. Whereas Bassianus, by contrast, subtly strokes his audience with soft and friendly Fs in the first line, 'friends, followers, favourers', but builds to his climax using the same letter F, to entirely different effect with 'Fight for freedom in your choice'.

We beat out both of their first lines.

'Noble patricians favourers of my right' says Saturninus. 'No-ble' pings out. It's his priority, he wants to ensure the patricians, the posh nobs, are on his side.

But beating out Bassianus' first line produces a surprise. 'Romans, friends, followers, favourers of my right'. It all goes to pieces, it's disarming. It's like John Major's so-called Val Doonican Sessions in the 1992 election campaign, when he took off his jacket and put it on the back of his chair to indicate he was just an ordinary bloke. Bassianus is doing the same. 'I'm one of you', he is saying.

We try two different approaches to the speeches: doing them as if in public, as part of an election rally; and then as a party political broadcast in front of a television camera. To start with, we get the actors to deliver the speeches, as if they are out on the hustings, and get the rest of the group to surround them and heckle. First time round is a lot of fun, but usually just a lot of noisy yelling. But then we impose the rule that they can only heckle when the speaker comes to the end of a sentence or says something controversial provoking a response.

Saturninus gives lots of opportunity to heckle, either in support or to shout him down.

Bassianus, on the other hand, provides his audience with almost nothing to disagree with, leaving his controversial proposition until right at the end of the speech. He is, after all, proposing something deeply subversive and radical, nothing less than overthrowing the whole political system, and replacing monarchy with democracy. And this performed in the reign of Queen Elizabeth I, where even to question the succession was illegal, and could attract a sentence of imprisonment.

In the rehearsal room, Bassianus proves much more effective on TV than his brother. It's a bit like contrasting Kennedy and Nixon in the first televised presidential debate in Chicago in 1960. JFK looked relaxed and confident, while tricky Dicky looked shifty, and sweated profusely.

Here, in our TV exercise, Bassianus' quiet control contrasts with Saturninus' petulant insistence on his right to be emperor.

At the end of the exercise the list of characteristics the actors come up with might include for Saturninus: paranoid, impulsive, narcissistic, entitled, angry, goaded, petulant, and even psychotic. Whereas Bassianus often gets described as honest, rational, thoughtful, caring, patriotic, radical and subversive.

The lists are, of course, subjective, and often contradictory, as the actors' differing interpretations depend on whether they are persuaded by Bassianus, or suspicious of his use of rhetoric. Is he manipulative, perhaps? Might we resist his radical appeal for change or suspect the real motives behind his smooth delivery. Is it mere rhetoric?

We finish the session by casting the role from the group according to which actor everyone feels best expresses the characteristics we have identified, and we hear the speeches one last time.

At the end of the session, I ask the group whom they would vote for. Mostly they choose Bassianus. Then, of course they want to know what happens next in the play. And I have to inform them that the old reactionary soldier Titus, when asked to choose, supports the status quo, and despite his evident lack of leadership potential, Saturninus is crowned emperor, and Bassianus ends up stabbed to death at the bottom of a pit, by the end of Act Two.

*   *   *

After auditioning seven times for the RSC, I was cast in four plays in 1987. The first two productions were in the main house, and the latter two in the Swan (in only its second season). I was Octavius Caesar in *Julius Caesar* directed by Terry Hands, with Roger Allam as Brutus; Solanio in *The Merchant of Venice*; Don Mathias, the floppy-haired romantic interest in Marlowe's *The Jew of Malta*, played by Alun Armstrong; and in Ben Jonson's *The New Inn* directed by John Caird, I played a rake who elopes with a girl, who is in fact a boy dressed up as a girl, and who ultimately turns out to have been a girl all along.

During the rehearsals of *The New Inn*, the company found the play hard-going. We don't have the same familiarity with Ben Jonson's language as we have with Shakespeare's. Why should we? Jonson hasn't been a permanent part of the repertoire for four hundred years. So, there is delicious texture to lines like 'They'll be punching puck-fists' or 'He'll outswagger all the wappentake', but they have limited currency in clarifying a dense, one might even say impenetrable, text.

Director John Caird was determined to prove the hidden potential of this neglected play, which had been a flop, when it was first performed and had not seen the light of day since. Ben Jonson himself, wailed in despair about the play's poor reception:

Come leave the loathéd stage,
And the more loathsome age[2]

---

[2]   In his 'Ode to Himself' (1629).

What is the point, he declares, of writing such elevated stuff if the audience can't appreciate it?

'Twere simple fury, still thyself to waste
On such as have no taste.

And in a rare jealous swipe at his fellow playwright (who had in fact been dead for over a decade) he writes, that no doubt the crowd prefer 'a mouldy tale, / Like Pericles'.

Our rehearsals were interrupted when John had a car accident dashing back up to Stratford one morning for rehearsal. In those days the M40 only went as far as Oxford, and the road from there was perilously windy. The company decided to continue with the rehearsal. It was a scene in which Lady Frampul (Fiona Shaw) dresses up her maid Prudence (Deborah Findlay) as queen for the day, and they preside over a mock court of love.

I suggested that all the strange assortment of characters who inhabited the New Inn, servants and guests, might contribute to an improvised entrance for this queen for the day. I was encouraged to show my fellow actors what I meant and by the end of our rehearsal, as everyone pitched in, we had a rather lively moment of staging. Luckily on his return, John Caird approved, and kept this new business in the show.

At the end of the season, after the shows had transferred to the Barbican, I was asked in to see Siobhan Bracke, for a sort of end-of-term chat.

This was the conversation at which every actor hoped they would be invited back the following season, and that their progression through the company would be marked by being assigned better (and probably fewer) roles. So it was with some trepidation that I went into the meeting.

'We've all been chatting about you,' Siobhan said, 'the associate directors and I, and we all think that you should come back next season'.

'Yippee!' I thought.

'But we all think you should consider directing. Terry is going to shake things up a bit next year so the contract would be for six months in Stratford (as opposed to the usual year), followed by six months in London. We'd like to offer you a post as assistant director. What do you think?'

Fate seemed to be stepping in. I had already been given the title of Associate Director at Nottingham Playhouse, but this was the RSC, and I would be able to work much more closely with some of the talents I really admired. I said yes.

Flaubert says that most people end up in life doing what they do second best. What did I do best? Where did my heart belong? The RSC helped me decide.

The following spring, I started assisting, and quickly learnt some of the pitfalls and challenges associated with that difficult job. I also learnt how important it is as an assistant director to keep your own counsel. You may dislike the production or what the director is doing, but you must keep schtumm.

On one production that season, I had scrupulously kept my own thoughts to myself throughout the rehearsal period. Once we had opened, my parents came down to Stratford to see me and took me out to lunch at the Kings Arms in Chipping Campden. As we finished, my mum said:

'Greg, you haven't said what you think about the production.'

At which the floodgates opened. Out came my pompous objections to the production, to the whole approach, to some of the performances. When I was done, I felt a hand on my shoulder. Unbeknownst to me the director of the show had been having lunch at the table behind me. Whether in fact they had heard my rant over the hubbub of the noisy dining room, I shall never know. He was certainly gracious enough never to mention it if he did.

Assisting Terry Hands on his production of *Romeo and Juliet* in the Swan Theatre, I learnt the most valuable lesson about how Shakespeare works in front of an audience. The production was set to tour the UK and Mark Rylance was playing Romeo. At this rehearsal, on the stage of the Swan Theatre itself, Terry was rehearsing Juliet in the speech where she has to decide whether to take the potion Friar Laurence has given her.

Juliet began: 'What if it be a poison which the friar / Subtly hath minister'd to have me dead,' she mused, quietly to herself. Terry interrupted her.

'Who are you talking to?' he asked.

'Myself,' Juliet replied.

'And who are all these people?' Terry asked, gesturing round the galleried auditorium.

'The audience?' Juliet muttered.

'No, they are your friends, your confidantes, your sounding board. Try it again and talk to them.'

She did. She was urgent, direct, frightened, really asking the question.

> What if it be a poison which the friar
> Subtly hath minister'd to have me dead?

And I, sitting there watching, wanted to shout out 'I don't know!' Suddenly I felt complicit. Instead of sitting back in the dark, pondering about the dilemma facing this poor young girl, I was being implicated, asked my opinion, forced to think what I would do in her place.

That is how Shakespeare works. The traffic goes two ways. It's a conversation between the actor on the stage and the audience around them.

There is a contemporary account of what it was like to watch an actor on stage, in Shakespeare's period. 'An Excellent Actor' appears in a book of essays by Sir Thomas Overbury, called *Characters*, and probably describes Shakespeare's leading man, Richard Burbage:

> Sit in a full theatre, and you will think you see so many lines drawn from the circumference of so many ears, whiles the Actor is in the centre.

The actor in the centre of a circle of ears. That is theatre.

*   *   *

As you set out for Ithaka
hope your road is a long one,
full of adventure, full of discovery.
Laistrygonians, Cyclops,
angry Poseidon—
Ithaka by C.P. Cavafy
(Translated by Edmund Keeley)

On a sweaty night in 1993, I found myself chipping around Port of Spain at the Trinidad Carnival, among a crowd of other revellers all dressed as pigs. What am I doing here? I thought to myself.

The answer is to be found in the poem quoted above. The Greek poet Cavafy suggests in this beautiful poem that life is an odyssey, and that you should be careful not to be so focused on your destination that you miss out on all the adventures and possibilities on the way. Odysseus took ten years to reach his final destination, his home island of Ithaka, but concludes Cavafy, if your only goal is getting where you think you want to be, you will be disappointed. Ithaka is in reality just a stony little island, all it can give you is your journey to Ithaka.

The poem was given to me by the Caribbean poet Derek Walcott. I had asked him if he would consider adapting Homer's *Odyssey* for the RSC. Adrian Noble, who had just taken over from Terry Hands as Artistic Director in 1990, listened to my pitch to adapt this great epic, admired my ambition, and as it coincided with his own plans to stage a trilogy of the plays of Sophocles in the Swan, agreed to let me workshop some ideas.

For the next two years we worked our way through this extraordinary poem. Our first workshop was in Stratford, another took place in London, and then Derek said to Adrian, 'Right, I have done two workshops with you, now you must send Greg to me.' 'Great,' said Adrian 'where should he go?' 'St Lucia,' said Derek, 'my home island.'

I spent ten days on St Lucia, much of it sitting with Derek on a beach in the shadow of the Deux Pitons, the twin volcanic spires that dominate that beautiful island. I found myself worrying that we were not doing enough actual script work to justify my visit, until I realized that I was being taught a lesson, in listening to the waves, in waiting for the story to land and the words to arrive. Derek's work is suffused with the pull of the sea, a sort of tidal undertow that sucks you in.

The production eventually opened at The Other Place (TOP) in 1992. Derek was the first Black writer ever to be produced by the RSC, and he admitted at one point to being overwhelmed at being on the same bill as Shakespeare and Marlowe.[3] But he wanted the same attention to be paid to his verse as the company prided itself in paying to Shakespeare's text. He wrote me a note, which I have kept.

Derek asked me to ensure that the company preserved the metre, the quatrains, the rhymes and half rhymes. 'They,' he said, 'are the beams of the poem on which we are all passengers, they must be sound and watertight, without the chuckle of leaking syllables, or the ship would founder.' I think we discovered the truth of that and allowed ourselves

---

[3] Terry Hands's production of *Tamburlaine the Great* with Antony Sher was in the same season.

to trust that the ship was true and steady. I have used his phrase 'the chuckle of leaking syllables' many times in directing Shakespeare.

During the run of the production Derek was awarded the Nobel Prize for Literature. When I heard, I realized there was a matinee that afternoon at TOP, and dashed backstage just before the show. Ron Cook, playing Odysseus, was warming up backstage, and looked a bit irritated to see me, as it is customary for the director not to give notes after the half has been called. 'Derek's just won the Nobel Prize,' I said. Ron's face beamed. 'Go out and tell the audience,' he urged. I did, and it killed all the laughs in the show. The audience seemed suddenly to treat the play with a reverence that had not been evident before. I thought that instead of applauding at the end, they were going to genuflect.

Derek invited me to direct the play again at the Trinidad Theatre Workshop. The show was attended by Derek's friend, the 'mas-man' Peter Minshall, the great carnival designer. Minshall had designed the opening to the Barcelona Olympics in 1992. He decided immediately that he would 'do the Odyssey' the following year for his Mas band. And so it was that I found myself among about a thousand people dressed as Circe's pigs, as fancy sailors with spangled triremes on their heads, as Cyclopean monsters or lazy lotus-eaters, and of course presiding over it all, on that most Caribbean of deities, the goddess Calypso, presented by Minshall as a sort of sublime dancing mobile in fuchsia and lemon.

The Odyssey had taught me to relax a bit and follow my nose. The production transferred from TOP to the Pit where it sold out immediately. But it did not lead automatically to another RSC production.

I think Adrian felt I had not distilled the storytelling sufficiently. There were too many ideas. The simplest were the most effective: the moment, for instance, when Odysseus heard the sirens. How do you create the most enchanting song in the world? We had been playing a soundtrack of the sea from the moment the audience arrived in the theatre, quietly, almost subliminally. When Odysseus' sailors crammed wax into their ears, we cut the soundtrack. It was just like that moment when the air-conditioning suddenly cuts out and you hear silence. In that sudden shock of emptiness, we watched Odysseus ravished by the siren song.

After *The Odyssey*, Adrian suggested that I should go and do a few more productions elsewhere and then come back to Stratford. I wasn't sure he meant it. I began my own odyssey, travelling around the world, following my nose.

At the invitation of Derek Walcott, I became a director of the Trinidad Theatre Workshop, and did a production of his musical adaptation of the Don Juan story, *The Joker of Seville,* with music by Galt MacDermot (the composer of *Hair*). The show had in fact originally been commissioned by the RSC in 1974, but it was decided there were not enough Black performers with the requisite experience or ability to produce it back then. Our production played in Boston and Port of Spain.

I began a relationship with the World Wide Fund for Nature (WWF) and directed the premiere of a short play they had commissioned from playwright Edward Bond. *September* was performed in the crypt of Canterbury Cathedral. I worked for WWF again in Lagos developing a sort of Muppet Show series about the environment for Nigerian TV and went to Brazil to research a show about the rubber tapper, rainforest campaigner and martyr, Chico Mendes.

On the recommendation of Cicely Berry, I went to Philadelphia to direct a production of *Twelfth Night*, and I worked with John Caird on the Stephen Schwartz musical *Children of Eden* at the Prince Edward Theatre, which had the misfortune to open on the same day as the Gulf War.

But undoubtedly the most thrilling, and life-changing, of all these globe-trotting adventures was a production of *Titus Andronicus* at the Market Theatre in Johannesburg, conceived just as Apartheid ended, in 1994.

The role of Titus was played by Antony Sher who had by that point been my partner for seven years. We wrote an account of that roller coaster production, published as *Woza Shakespeare!*

The production came out of a visit by the National Theatre Studio to the Market, involving all sorts of theatre practitioners: actors, writers, directors, voice coaches, mime artists. We shared ideas and practices over two weeks, visiting schools, in both black and white areas of the city. As a result of the week the inspirational Barney Simon, one of the founders of the Market, asked Tony and I if we would consider coming to do a Shakespeare in their theatre. Tony had never performed professionally in his home country, and the invitation was irresistible.

We chose to do Shakespeare's early play *Titus Andronicus*. A controversial choice as it turned out.

In a country that had endured decades of violence, that had witnessed state-sanctioned atrocities on an unimaginable scale, and invented 'necklacing' (the process of forcing a rubber tyre over someone's head, dousing it with petrol and setting it alight), the violence in the play seemed horrifyingly familiar to many of the company.

If you do the play in the UK, it's likely that only a very few of the company will have experienced any significant violence in their lives. But in South Africa, the actress playing Lavinia, for example, was able to research first-hand the effects, not only of gang rape, but of having your tongue severed from your mouth, and indeed the reality of having both your hands chopped off with a panga. Another actor recounted witnessing the crime scene after his grandmother had been raped and murdered in her own bed by men who broke into her house. The actors playing the Goth boys, Chiron and Demetrius, practised with butterfly knives, which became extensions of their own hands, the blades fluttering with lethal intent. Somehow, we had to honour that violence, not exploit its pornographic voyeuristic appeal.

The play transformed from a gory blood-fest to an appeal for a way to break the cycle of violence, or as Marcus Andronicus says at the end of the play:

O, let me teach you how to knit again
This scatter'd corn into one mutual sheaf,
These broken limbs again into one body.

It seemed like a cry directed at the rainbow nation itself

However, the South African press didn't like our production. They wanted their Shakespeare in starched vowels and wrinkly tights. It wasn't until we got to the UK, playing at the West Yorkshire Playhouse and the Cottesloe of the National Theatre, that we received the reviews we had hoped for.

*   *   *

Our Market Theatre production of *Titus Andronicus* started to get invitations from around the world. We visited the Almagro Festival in Spain, and negotiations started about the possibility of taking the production to New York. I kept myself free, hoping this interest would turn into a reality, but alas in the end it fell through.

A friend sent me a cutting for an advert for an Artistic Director to run the 1996 summer season at the Century Theatre in Keswick. I knew the Century well. My parents were now retired, and living in nearby Cockermouth, twenty minutes from the theatre. To spend a summer, at home, working in what must surely be one of the most spectacular locations for any theatre in the world, on the edge of Derwent Water, nestled among the fells of Borrowdale, would be a joy, particularly after travelling around so much in recent years. So, I applied.

The season would be the last in the old Blue Box, the trucks that had toured the North of England for nearly a quarter of a century after the war, bringing plays to so many theatre-starved communities. I had seen them when they visited Preston and parked on the market square in the centre of town. The old mobile theatre was to be retired, and a splendid new 'Theatre by the Lake' built in its place.

On the interview panel was the tall imposing figure of Wilfred Harrison, one of the last actor-managers, in the tradition of Donald Wolfit. He had been an original founder of the Century and opened the theatre in 1952 playing Othello. He ran the Octagon Theatre in Bolton, throughout my school days in Preston, and mounted Shakespeare seasons in the autumn. I saw this admirable man play Macbeth, Falstaff, King Lear, and Prospero. I think we spent most of the interview talking about those seasons and the early days of the Century. He told me he had played in every county in Britain, from the Hebrides to Land's End. They offered me the job.

I spent a happy summer with a terrific company of actors, doing three plays back to back: *The Importance of Being Earnest*, *An Inspector Calls* and *Bedroom Farce*. Halfway through the season I got a call from Adrian Noble. 'Would I like to direct *Henry VIII* in the Swan?'

It felt as if my odyssey was about to bring me back home . . . to Stratford-upon-Avon.

3

Henry VIII, or All is True

– 1996: Swan Theatre, Stratford-upon-Avon;
Majestic Theater, Brooklyn Academy of Music, New York; Young Vic, London.

On Sunday 7 June 2020, during a Black Lives Matter march in Bristol city centre, cheering crowds hauled down the statue of the philanthropist and slave trader Edward Colston. They flogged it, sprayed 'BLM' and the word 'Prick' on his frock coat in blue paint, then rolled it to the harbour and dumped it in the Avon.

The Mayor of Bristol said it was 'undoubtedly a significant day in Bristol's history and had a profound impact not just in our city but also across the country and around the world'.

It took me back thirty years to another significant day in the city's history. On April 2 1980, when I was still at university in Bristol and living in Cotham Brow, riots broke out in St Paul's, at the bottom of our road. The Black and White Cafe in Grosvenor Road sold great Caribbean food but had a reputation as a drug den.

That April morning, about 20 police officers carried out a raid on the cafe. Tensions between the Black community and the police were already very high, in part because of the draconian use of the SUS laws, to stop and search kids from St Paul's largely Caribbean community. The raid sparked a riot which lasted for hours causing widespread damage and a number of injuries.

In July, an article on the front of *The Observer* caught my eye: 'Computer discovers new Shakespeare play'. Apparently stylometric analysis applied to an untitled handwritten manuscript in the British Library had proved that at least 90 per cent of it was by William Shakespeare. The manuscript was in five different hands. One of those hands had long been acknowledged to be Shakespeare's.[1] The play had been published in 1908, along with other disputed plays in the *Shakespeare Apocrypha*, edited by C.F. Tucker Brooke. Intrigued, I hurried up to the University Library on St Michael's Hill to see if I could find a copy.

I was not expecting to read anything more than a creaky old Elizabethan drama, but *The Booke of Sir Thomas More* (as the editor of the *Shakespeare Apocrypha* refers

---

[1] Perhaps the fact that the play is in so many different hands suggests the hasty submission of a rewrite, which, in order to reach a rehearsal or scheduling deadline, Shakespeare (if he was indeed the sole author) had pulled together the other writers in the stable of the Lord Chamberlain's Men: Munday, Chettle, Heywood and Dekker.

to the play) opens with a race riot. The angry aftershocks of the riots that had taken place just a mile away from where I was sitting were still being felt in St Paul's. I read on.

The citizens of London, aggrieved at the abuse they are suffering at the hands of 'aliens and strangers' (foreigners) determine to get their own back, under the cover of the May Day Festivities, and 'make it the worst May Day for the strangers that ever they saw'. The Londoners prepare to 'tickle their turnips' and the ringleader, a broker called Lincoln, excites the crowd to burn down the houses of these immigrants from Lombardy, and Picardy, 'and many more outlandish fugitives'.

His cry 'Shall they enjoy more privileges than we in our own country?' seemed to echo the shouts of the far-right National Front, who were on the rise in the early eighties. During clashes between the NF and the Anti-Nazi League the year before in Southall, one of the anti-racist campaigners, Blair Peach, had been killed. The play in my hands seemed to be a play for today.

The scene that followed was even more surprising, and it was the one in the British Library manuscript that was said to be in Shakespeare's hand. Thomas More himself arrives, in his role as Sheriff, to quell the riot and delivers a speech of compelling humanity and compassion, urging the rioters to put themselves in the shoes of the immigrants they are so keen to deport:

> Imagine that you see the wretched strangers,
> Their babies at their backs, with their poor luggage,
> Plodding to th' ports and coasts for transportation
> And that you sit as kings in your desires,
> Authority quite silenced by your brawl,
> And you in ruff of your opinions clothed:
> What had you got?

The play needed to be seen urgently, I decided, and I set about persuading my fellow students at the Bristol Old Vic School (who included actors Samantha Bond and Sophie Thompson) that we should present it.

The British Library copy of the play has scribbles in the margin signed by E. Tilney. Edmund Tilney was the Master of the Revels, and consequently the censor of all plays presented publicly in Shakespeare's day. In the margin to the left of the play's opening lines he insists, 'Leave out the insurrection wholly', concluding ominously 'at your own perils'. There is no record of the play ever being performed in Shakespeare's day. Is it possible that Tilney's demand for rewrites, and other prohibitions, prevented the play from happening?

It was certainly a dangerous subject to present in the reign of Queen Elizabeth I, to write a play in which the hero effectively challenged the monarch's right to reign – the story of the man who had denied the right of her father to divorce Katherine of Aragon and marry her mother, Anne Boleyn. It would be hard to think of a hotter potato to rake out of the embers of recent history. Perhaps it was no wonder that Tilney's objections were so fierce.

We decided to present it not only as a 'new' Shakespeare play, but as Shakespeare's 'banned play'.

We opened at the Vandyke Theatre of the university drama department on Shakespeare's birthday. And then in something of a coup, Frank Dunlop invited us to the Young Vic in London (which he had co-founded). Frank had the distinction of having directed the play at the Nottingham Playhouse in 1964, with Ian McKellen as Thomas More, possibly the first-ever professional actor to play him.

In the debate the play ignited, McKellen described More's eloquent plea against enforced repatriation, as 'vintage Shakespeare'. Quoted in *The Guardian*, he pointed out that the problem with literary analysis was that it never began to assess how the play worked in the theatre. 'I would rather these textual scholars spent more time in the theatre and less in the databank,' he said.

I met the man responsible for *The Observer*'s claim. Thomas Merriam, a lecturer at Basingstoke Technical College, and I were both invited onto a local TV programme, in Bristol. He explained at baffling length to the bewildered interviewer the process of his computer analysis: his exhaustive study of style, word order and sentence structure; the recurring frequency of unexceptional combinations like 'and so' and of the commonest prepositions and conjunctions, and all accompanied by detailed charts.

In truth, after the excitement of the riot scenes, the play becomes episodic, drifting through scenes involving a pick-pocket called Lifter, a man who refuses to get his hair cut, and a visit by Erasmus to More's house in Chelsea. But the play lifts again as the writers tackle the 'matter of the King's conscience', the annulment of Henry VIII's marriage to Katherine, and the demand that More sign the Act of Supremacy, which he refused to do.

The writers cleverly use the device of a play-within-a-play to dramatize More's essential dilemma. A group of actors (My Lord Cardinal's Players) appear at Chelsea to present a moral interlude called *The Marriage of Wit and Wisdom*. More agrees to step in to play the role of Good Counsel, as one of the actors, Luggins, has had to 'run to Ogle's' for a beard and has not returned.

In the course of the action Inclination, the Vice, tries to deceive Wit, the Everyman figure, into believing that Lady Vanity is in fact Lady Wisdom. So, More is faced with the challenge of distinguishing Vanity from Wisdom. According to the players, he acquits himself admirably. 'Did ye mark how extemp'rically he fell to the matter' one of them exclaims.

It foreshadows More's own moral choice. His family think his decision to refuse to sign the King's bill (which will eventually lead to his imprisonment and execution at the Tower), is vanity. More believes in the wisdom of his actions, for the spiritual good of his everlasting soul. Whether you in the audience agree with More's wife that his course is motivated by vanity or that his conscience is morally justified and his silence wisdom, will depend on your individual viewpoint. It is a tactful way of presenting the predicament without the writers taking sides.

We got more national coverage than might normally be expected for a student production. James Fenton in *The Sunday Times* called it 'a really surprising play partly about London xenophobia', while Ned Chaillet in *The Times* said, 'With what is a genuine literary controversy, it is a bit shaming to see the proof of it left to students' and commended us for our 'unusual serious intent in a student production'.

A fortnight before we opened, riots erupted in Brixton. The worst violence occurred on what was dubbed 'Bloody Saturday' resulting in over 300 injuries to both police and members of the public. Over a hundred vehicles were burned and shops looted. The St Paul's riot in Bristol ignited a trail of similar protest disturbances in that year, in Brixton and the Toxteth area of Liverpool. The Thatcher government commissioned an inquiry, which resulted in the Scarman Report.[2]

*   *   *

My obsession with the Thomas More play erupted again, fifteen years later, when I had the crazed idea of mashing it up with Shakespeare's *Henry VIII*, and thus telling the stories of Henry VIII's two troublesome Lord Chancellors, Thomas More, and the previous occupant of that office, Cardinal Wolsey.

Wolsey sums up the factors that have brought about his fall in his final speech in Act Three:

> Had I but served my God with half the zeal
> I served my king, he would not in mine age
> Have left me naked to mine enemies.

More's fall is precisely the reverse. He defied the king and prioritized his conscience above his duty to the crown.

In 1996, a year before the reconstructed Shakespeare's Globe opened on the Southbank, the director of education, Patrick Spottiswoode, invited me to direct a reading of the play at the Bear Gardens Museum, close by. We assembled a great cast, including Barbara Jefford as Katherine, but the script was far too long, and the idea proved flawed. Nevertheless, the event piqued Adrian Noble's interest. When he rang to discuss me directing *Henry VIII* at Stratford, I wondered if he meant my mash-up. Luckily, he did not.

*   *   *

Friends warned me not to be flattered by Adrian's offer to direct *Henry VIII*.

'It's a poisoned chalice,' one of them said. 'Nobody has ever really made that play work.'

A recent production had been described as 'A narcoleptic historical pageant', and that the play was widely regarded as an exceptionally tough nut to crack. So, was the play just a blatant piece of sycophantic propaganda, or a misunderstood, neglected masterpiece? Should it be counted along with the late plays as a culmination of a lifetime in the theatre, or, as one critic put it, 'An ill-advised comeback with a poor supporting band'.

---

[2] The Scarman Report highlighted problems of racial disadvantage and inner city decline, warning that 'urgent action' was needed. It stated however that 'institutional racism' in the Metropolitan Police did not exist, a claim challenged by the Macpherson Report, two decades later, in 1999.

Once popular for the opportunity it afforded for grand spectacle, *Henry VIII* was by then a very unfashionable play.

Director Howard Davies told me the story of how he came to direct the last RSC production in 1983. The associate directors had met together to divvy up the next season and determine who should direct which plays. Howard had nipped to the loo and returned to discover that he had drawn the short straw: *Henry VIII*.

Adrian Noble's advice to me was to assemble the best cast possible, and to 'get people who are better than you', who would stretch and challenge me. Jane Lapotaire agreed to play Katherine of Aragon; Ian Hogg would play Cardinal Wolsey; and Paul Jesson took on the role of the young King Henry.

Rob Jones designed. And we were blessed with the choice of the Swan Theatre for the production. The Swan acts like a film camera which can open out and accommodate the epic and zoom in for the intimate close-up: perfect for the play's mixture of public spectacle and closet privacy.

We were joined in the rehearsal room by academic Gordon McMullan, who was preparing a new edition of the play for Arden. The two-way process of his in-depth contextual knowledge and the actors' rigorous textual analysis was invigorating, and not unsurprisingly produced one of the thickest Arden editions in their canon. The introduction runs to just under 200 pages.

One of the intriguing factors about the play is why Shakespeare should return to the subject of the divorce of Henry VIII right at the end of his career. The date of the Thomas More play is unclear. It may have been written as late as 1600, but certainly in the reign of Elizabeth. We can date the *Henry VIII* play more precisely, as it was during a performance of this work that the Globe Theatre burned down, on 29 June 1613. Sir Henry Wotton,[3] King James I's ambassador to Venice, wrote a letter to Sir Edmund Bacon describing the incident. He referred to the play not by the title, *Henry VIII*, but as *All is True*. We decided to follow suit.

All is True, unlike other enigmatic titles in the canon, is freighted with irony. By apparently asserting that everything in the play is accurate, verifiable fact, it immediately makes you want to question it. Might there be some element of whitewashing about to happen? Or is he putting the audience on alert that there is no such thing as objective truth? The title implies (at the very least) that historical facts are always open to a variety of interpretations.

The title reminds me of a comedian, beginning his joke: 'I was coming here tonight, this is absolutely true . . .'. You know it isn't.

We emblazoned the title on the set, underlining the dubious propaganda of the phrase All Is True. We opened with a tableau: great doors, fretted with gleaming metalwork, swung open in a blaze of gilded pomp, to reveal a casket from which Henry's court cascaded; the king himself was mounted on a golden horse, flanked by Katherine on one side and Wolsey on the other; the court all dressed in glittering brocades paraded forwards carrying processional poles topped with royal heraldic beasts; the wardrobe and prop departments excelled themselves. It was spectacular.

---

[3] Famous for saying: 'An ambassador is an honest gentleman sent to lie abroad for the good of his country.'

But the splendour was deliberate. In the Tudor period, the concept of 'Magnificence' was regarded as an essential attribute of majesty, a conscious, lavish, public expression of status and power. This was never more clearly on show than at the summit conference known as The Field of the Cloth of Gold and described by the Duke of Norfolk in the first scene of the play. In a research trip to Hampton Court Palace at the start of rehearsals we had seen the great painting of this event hanging in the Great Hall.

In June 1520, Henry crossed to France to meet his fellow monarch Francis I outside the town of Guisnes. For Henry, showmanship was a necessary brand of statesmanship. The young kings vied with each other to outdo the sumptuousness of their display. Norfolk, picturing the scene to the Duke of Buckingham, who was not present, says the French 'were all clinquant', and then, as if he is interpreting the phrase, says 'all in gold', while on the English side they 'Made Britain India: every man that stood / Showed like a mine'.

'Now' he declares, 'this masque / Was cried incomparable'.

But Buckingham knows better. The money thrown at this extravagant event, he says, was wasted, and Cardinal Wolsey is responsible. 'This last costly treaty, the interview, / That swallow'd so much treasure', he protests, 'like a glass / Did break i' the rinsing'. You don't expect an image about washing up in a Shakespeare play – but reducing the result of this international summit conference to the simple domesticity of breaking a glass in the sink, is absolutely precise in its derision.

Now it could be argued that by staging the scene described by Norfolk, we could be accused of falling into the same trap as those nineteenth-century productions that used the play simply as an excuse for indulging in a lot of showy pageantry and spectacle. Some staged not only the execution of the Duke of Buckingham but his final journey to the tower by barge; whole streets of cheering crowds following the coronation of Queen Anne, and spectacular flights of angels appeared in the dream of Queen Katherine.

Other productions at the RSC had attempted to eschew the play's reputation for empty pageantry. Howard Davies, for example, staged the coronation of Queen Anne as a rehearsal with dummies standing in place of the courtiers. We tried to demonstrate the relationship between gilded triumphs and brutal realpolitik. But we wanted to underline the point that for Shakespeare the magnificence of the display matched the scale of the propaganda.

*   *   *

In rehearsal one day, as we ran a few scenes in Act Two together, I realized a feature of Shakespeare's writing I had not noticed before. Henry has just determined that Katherine's case will be tried at Blackfriars and Wolsey is to arrange it. He exits, lamenting the inevitable consequences:

KING HENRY   O, my lord,
    Would it not grieve an able man to leave
    So sweet a bedfellow? But, conscience, conscience!
    O, 'tis a tender place; and I must leave her.

And Anne enters for the next scene, mid-conversation with the Old Lady, saying:

Not for that neither. Here's the pang that pinches . . .

It sounds shockingly as if Anne is rejecting the king's claim that he is forced to divorce his wife, by implying that it has nothing to do with his conscience. Generally, in contemporary performance we are so used to creating different environments for each scene, and accompanying scene changes with music cues, that we might miss the way one scene is intended to respond to the next. But I know of no example in the canon as dangerously subversive as this.

The character of the unnamed Old Lady is very important in providing a balancing note of cynicism in the play. There's a hilarious moment when she has to tell Henry VIII that Anne Boleyn has given birth, although not to the boy that Henry so hoped for. She so wants to impress the king, and to gain from the opportunity, that when asked if the queen has given birth she says, 'Ay, ay, my liege, / And of a lovely boy'. Henry in our production started whooping and dancing for joy. The Old Lady has to backtrack quickly ' 'Tis a girl / Promises boys hereafter'. Cherry Morris as the Old Lady caught that wry edge to perfection.

*   *   *

Perhaps the greatest scene in the play is the famous Blackfriars trial. One of the most revelatory pieces of research I read about the play made me rethink this scene.

My old Bristol tutor, the Shakespeare scholar Professor Glynne Wickham, had proposed that although we know (from Wotton's letter) that the play had been staged at the Globe, it was also possible that it had been performed the previous winter at Blackfriars Theatre. If this was indeed the case, then the scene of Katherine's trial would have played in the very hall (formerly known as the Parliament chamber) in which the trial had actually taken place, eighty years before. The chamber was converted into a theatre by Richard Burbage's father, James, in 1596. Witnessing that scene played in that space must have been not only poignant, but an astonishing piece of site-specific theatre. It was an intensely political act.

Is it possible that the reason Shakespeare returns to this particular subject (after having his fingers burned with the Thomas More play) was that his patron, King James, was eager to restore the reputation of the Spanish queen, Katherine? One of his first acts as monarch was to forge a peace with Spain, and he had been eager to marry his son, Henry, the Prince of Wales (a staunch Protestant) to a Catholic princess.

The depiction of Katherine is immensely sympathetic, particularly in the trial scene, where she defends herself so robustly, that her husband's trust in his closest advisor is shaken, and Cardinal Wolsey's fall becomes inevitable. And she is, after all, virtually canonized in her final scene, and dreams of being assumed into heaven. If Shakespeare and Fletcher set out to rehabilitate her reputation, they do a pretty good job.

*   *   *

I learnt an important lesson about what directing demands during rehearsals for *All is True*. Jane Lapotaire married a raw emotional truth in her performance as Katherine, with a precise technical awareness. She required a process in which she could chart the arc of each scene, a structural map that she could define and then fix. Ian Hogg as Wolsey needed to continue to explore the scene afresh each time and resisted being tied down to a particular blocking, which he found restrictive.

It was my job to create an environment in which both could flourish, but it was challenging to accommodate their widely differing approaches to performance. Both found profound emotional truth in each moment of their journeys yet reached the destination of that truth via different routes.

I will never forget the moment in Ian's performance when, at the end of Act Three, Wolsey realizes his career is over. The lords have conspired against him, and (in one of the play's best scenes) have confronted him with the evidence they have collected against him. They surround him like mastiffs cornering a wild boar.

As part of our research for the play, we had been granted access to the office of the Lord Chancellor to learn more about the Great Seal of the Realm, of which he is formally the keeper. The props team had made a copy of the Great Seal, so that in this scene Wolsey could pull it from the purse and shake it in the faces of his detractors, who are determined to wrest it from his custody. Eventually Wolsey is forced to yield to their demands, and they leave him to lick his wounds. There follows one of the great speeches of the play:

> So farewell to the little good you bear me.
> Farewell! a long farewell, to all my greatness!
> This is the state of man: to-day he puts forth
> The tender leaves of hopes; to-morrow blossoms,
> And bears his blushing honours thick upon him;
> The third day comes a frost, a killing frost,
> And, when he thinks, good easy man, full surely
> His greatness is a-ripening, nips his root,
> And then he falls, as I do. I have ventured,
> Like little wanton boys that swim on bladders,
> This many summers in a sea of glory,
> But far beyond my depth: my high-blown pride
> At length broke under me and now has left me,
> Weary and old with service, to the mercy
> Of a rude stream, that must for ever hide me.
> Vain pomp and glory of this world, I hate ye:
> I feel my heart new open'd. O, how wretched
> Is that poor man that hangs on princes' favours!
> There is, betwixt that smile we would aspire to,
> That sweet aspect of princes, and their ruin,
> More pangs and fears than wars or women have:
> And when he falls, he falls like Lucifer,
> Never to hope again.

Ian's approach to character, delving into Wolsey's humble Ipswich origins (the 'Ipswich butcher') and investigating precisely what motivated this ambitious man, produced a shocking moment as surprising as it was truthful. Just as Wolsey cried 'Vain pomp and glory of this world I hate thee' Ian suddenly roared with laughter, as if immediately relieved by the weight of the office and the years of fighting in the king's service, now lifted from his shoulders. 'I feel my heart new opened' rang with unexpected joy, and always moved me.

Jane's most revelatory moment for me came in the final of the queen's four seasonal appearances in the play, her winter scene, if you like (Act Four Scene Two), as she prepares for death at her home in Kimbolton.

Katherine has just been told that Wolsey has died at the Abbey in Leicester. She somewhat uncharitably rails at her old enemy's short comings:

> He was a man
> Of an unbounded stomach, ever ranking
> Himself with princes.

Her servant, Griffith, reminds her of the good things that Wolsey accomplished in his life, saying:

> GRIFFITH   Noble madam,
>   Men's evil manners live in brass; their virtues
>   We write in water.

And Katherine chastened by his charity, learns to forgive the Cardinal:

> After my death I wish no other herald,
> No other speaker of my living actions,
> To keep mine honour from corruption,
> But such an honest chronicler as Griffith.
> Whom I most hated living, thou hast made me,
> With thy religious truth and modesty,
> Now in his ashes honour: peace be with him!

Freed from the purgatory of her hatred, heaven opens its doors to receive her. Katherine is left to sleep in her chair. The script then calls for a masque of white-robed angels to appear in golden vizards presenting the queen with a vision of heaven.

In the Swan, we decided that no such vision was needed. Jane merely opened her eyes and, filled with transcendental radiance, raised her hands to the dream as it appeared in her mind.

*   *   *

In the stage history of the play, the last act has often been severely curtailed. To begin with I thought that the potential downfall of Cranmer was one episode too many and felt that I should cut Cranmer from the story. But, as we rehearsed and grew to know the play, I realized that his inclusion demonstrates a learning process for Henry himself: he learns how to trust and whom to trust.

He trusts Wolsey and then the Lords gang up against the Cardinal, plot against him, and bring about his downfall. The Lords also conspire against Cranmer, and yet this time Henry, knowing Cranmer to be a good man, gives him his backing and his blessing. There is an arc to the story in terms of Henry VIII himself learning how to deal with the people around him.

When our RSC President, Prince Charles, came to see the play, just months after his divorce from Princess Diana, he found the scenes of Henry's rescue of Cranmer particularly potent. 'One realizes,' he said to me afterwards, 'how difficult it can be to establish which of those around you, one can really trust.'

*   *   *

Cranmer's final speech at the christening of the king's baby daughter is really challenging. It is absurd if you think of it in literal terms: there is Cranmer taking the baby who will become Queen Elizabeth I and projecting not only her future but also her death and the fact that King James will succeed her. At root, it's a plea for the security of the state.

There is a no doubt apocryphal RSC story of a row between directors Trevor Nunn and John Barton after John saw a preview of Trevor's production of this play in 1969. Cranmer lists a series of attributes, 'servants' to monarchy, which he deems necessary for good government: 'Peace, Plenty, Love, Truth, Terror.'

Trevor had cut the word 'Terror' and John objected. Terror is required, not only as a deterrent to your enemies, but as a policy to keep order.

Perhaps in 1969, in the era of anti-war protests, and peace demonstrations such as the moratorium to end the war in Vietnam, 'Terror', as part of a nation's armoury seemed inappropriate, or even unacceptable. In the year our production opened, terror was updated. It was developed by the US military as a strategic policy: the use of over-whelming displays of force to destroy your enemies' will to fight. Terror was redefined as Shock and Awe.

At the very end of our production, as the baby Elizabeth was being celebrated, Anne Boleyn appeared at the back, and slowly put her hand to her neck, just before the lights went out. It would frequently elicit gasps from the audience. Somehow it allowed the aspirational quality of Cranmer's speech to exist but then added a health warning at the end of the play.

Henry VIII succeeded his father Henry VII, who, as Richmond, is crowned on the battlefield at Bosworth, at the end of *Richard III*. That coronation is intended to heal division and signal an age of peace and stability after the chaos of the Wars of the Roses, the conflict described in Shakespeare's first history tetralogy.

If you see *Henry VIII/All is True* as the last beat of that story – as the very next king to reign – then you understand the context in which that monarch is determined to provide an heir for the country, and stability for his kingdom.

In 2020, we had planned to present Shakespeare's first history tetralogy, and to place *Henry VIII/All is True* as the final production. Unfortunately, the Covid-19 pandemic put paid to that. It closed all our theatres.

4

The Merchant of Venice

– 1997: Royal Shakespeare Theatre, Stratford-upon-Avon;
Barbican Theatre, London; Theatre Royal, Newcastle-upon-Tyne;
Plymouth Theatre Royal.

I have a framed company photograph on my bookshelves of all the actors in my first season at Stratford, in 1987. It's a heady line up. There's Fiona Shaw, Brian Cox, Deborah Findlay, John Shrapnel, David Bradley, Estelle Kohler, Alex Jennings, Barrie Rutter and Antony Sher.

The first play I was in was *The Merchant of Venice.* Antony Sher was playing Shylock. I was cast as Solanio. He is known as one of the Salads, along with Salerio (and sometimes even Salarino, who is surely one 'salad role' too many).

In Bill Alexander's production, Solanio and Salerio had an important function. They became representative of an attitude within the whole community. The Salads routinely spat upon their Jewish fellow-citizens and acted as a funnel for the bile of anti-semitism flooding through that society. The theme of racism was one this production brought right to the fore. If we forced the audience to witness the violent and unholy racism of the Christian Venetians, with the apartheid regime they imposed on its Jewish community, we might adjust that perspective. After all, Shylock is frequently spat upon, spurned and kicked as a matter of course.

Antony Sher had chosen to play Shylock as a Levantine Turk. There were apparently three different racial types among the Jewish population in the Ghetto: German/Italian Jews; the Ponentine Jews, who had escaped the Inquisition in Portugal; and the Turks. Making Shylock an Ottoman Turk allowed the two opposing communities to have distinct cultural differences, which the production could heighten.

Thus, the segregated Jewish quarter might resemble a Byzantine bazaar, with the money-lenders squatting in the street clicking abacuses; the Christians meanwhile strut about in doublets and lace collars, with swords strapped to their thighs. Here were two societies, irreconcilable opposites.

A shrine to the Madonna was juxtaposed with the yellow Star of David daubed on the back wall of the set, underlining this tension.

For a young actor, being on stage with Tony Sher was a revelation. I was witnessing great acting at close quarters, every night.

Tony gave a volcanic performance. I particularly remember the scene in which the Salads taunt Shylock with the loss of his money and his daughter. They have assisted in the elopement of Jessica, Shylock's daughter. It is partly their attack on him that provokes this grieving father into pursuing his impossible demands for justice. Suddenly Shylock turns on them. I wrote about it at the time.

Solanio is confused; he keeps the Jew at bay with his stick – at once a weapon and a defence.
   Sher began to grow; stalking the sycophants, his anger began to rumble and rise, ravelling out the injuries that Antonio has done him. And for what reason? Suddenly, with flashing eyes, Shylock erupted: 'I am a Jew.' He blasted his anger, white-hot, into the air. He seemed to tower with ferocity, fuelled with all the suffering of the Jewish nation.
   Exasperation hit 'fed with the same food' and tears of frustration seemed to well in his eyes, checked as suddenly with furious contempt. The salads quiver; there is silence and with chilling irony, Shylock pushed his bleeding hand into Solanio's face: 'If you prick us, do we not bleed?'; with icy derision – 'If you tickle us, do we not laugh?'; with outraged impotence – 'If you poison us, do we not die? And if you wrong us . . .' with a terrible howl – 'Shall we not revenge!'

One wet Thursday matinee, I was clearly 'phoning it in' as they say in the business (basically not concentrating properly). Before I knew it, Shylock had grabbed my stick and was chasing me around the stage. That taught me a lesson: to be in the moment. One of Tony's great gifts as an actor was to be completely there, utterly present on stage, and thus mesmeric, with the compelling quality of compression, of always having more power held in reserve.
   That year, *The Merchant of a Venice* was chosen as 'the birthday play'. The production would be attended by all the ambassadors, and high commissioners attendant upon the Court of St James, all of whom had been invited by the town of Stratford-upon-Avon for the celebrations marking the 423rd anniversary of the birth of its most famous son.
   But to the acting company's distress, among those eminent guests was the South African cultural attaché, who would therefore be in Stratford representing the Apartheid regime. Along with Tony there was another prominent South African actor in the company that year, Estelle Kohler.
   A fraught company meeting was held in the Ashcroft Room to determine a course of action, which included a possible boycott of the performance if the cultural attaché was allowed to attend. In the end, it was decided that it would be preferable to perform and to allow the play to speak for itself.
   As Hakeem Kae-Kazim strode to the front of the stage as the Prince of Morocco and declared 'Mislike me not for my complexion', the play began to crackle with racial static. That charge only increased as the play progressed.
   In the trial scene, as Shylock argued his case before the Doge ('What judgment shall I dread, doing no wrong?'), Tony Sher suddenly grabbed one of the court attendants (played by Akim Mogaji) and pulled him down to the front of the stage. Everybody on stage held their breath. What was he going to do? Then, having found out where the South African cultural attaché was sitting, he addressed the following speech to him:

You have among you many a purchased slave,
Which, like your asses and your dogs and mules,

You use in abject and in slavish parts,
Because you bought them: shall I say to you,
Let them be free, marry them to your heirs?
Why sweat they under burthens? let their beds
Be made as soft as yours and let their palates
Be season'd with such viands? You will answer
'The slaves are ours': so do I answer you:
The pound of flesh, which I demand of him,
Is dearly bought; 'tis mine and I will have it.

As Tony himself has written, 'I'll never forget his look of fright as he flattened himself against the seat. Theatre's magical fourth wall had suddenly shattered, and someone was talking to him. And that someone was the man whose birthday he was here to celebrate.'

The play's depiction of anti-semitism broadened for us, to include all racism.[1]

The Merchant of Venice is certainly a play that has been hijacked by history. After the Holocaust, it is impossible to view the play's depiction of anti-semitism as anything other than the insidious prejudice it is. Tony Sher argued in rehearsal (as many successive Shylocks have) that Act Five should be cut, that it is impossible to tolerate these obnoxious Christians and their trivial squabbling about rings, after the shocking humiliation of Shylock. He's not the first to argue this. I happen not to agree with him.

*   *   *

I had two further particular experiences of the play, and the challenges it presents, which deepened my own perspective. The first was a decade after that production, when Adrian Noble invited me to direct the play, my second Shakespeare production for the company, after *Henry VIII (All is True)*, and my first in the RST.[2] My second experience of the play was directing it in Tokyo, in Japanese, ten years later.

In 1997, Philip Voss played Shylock. Philip had joined the RSC in 1960, in *The Merchant of Venice* with Dorothy Tutin as Portia, and the 27-year-old Peter O'Toole as Shylock. Philip played a series of 'unnamed parts' alongside Diana Rigg and Roy Dotrice.

Philip had a rigorous approach to rehearsal. His very first question was about his opening line. Bassanio is outlining the loan he requires and for how long. Shylock says: 'Three thousand ducats, well.' Philip wanted to know exactly how much 3,000 ducats would have been worth? What is it worth today? And what would it buy you? Our best

---

[1] After the murder of George Floyd in May 2020, Adjoa Andoh and I discussed a Shakespeare response, which the RSC put on our virtual platform. Some key Black actors, who have appeared with the company in the last few years, created a very powerful recording of Shylock's 'Hath not a Jew eyes'.

[2] I had directed a production of *Cyrano de Bergerac* in the Swan, that summer. Just after press night, Adrian invited me to become an associate director for the company. I was overwhelmed by the honour.

guesses at the time were that it was indeed an inordinately large amount of money, certainly more than one young man would need to get himself a ticket to board the tranect, the ferry that apparently connects Belmont to Venice.

We hear that Bassanio is hiring new staff, ordering them new liveries, so that his arrival in Belmont won't betray his actual sham status, and it seems he makes a pretty splendid first impression, described in a speech that I think contains one of the loveliest images in the canon, and is entrusted to a servant:

> A day in April never came so sweet,
> To show how costly summer was at hand,
> As this fore-spurrer comes before his lord.

This 'ambassador of love' also brings Portia some 'gifts of rich value'. What do you give the heiress who has everything? Our calculations suggested that in modern terms 3,000 ducats, in today's money might be as much as £450,000 and would kit out Bassanio and his entourage in Armani suits, buy him a Porsche, and even hire him a yacht, with some spare change left over. No wonder Shylock repeats the figure '3,000 ducats' seven times in the first scene. Each time Philip reiterated it, the scale of the loan seemed to increase in absurdity.

With this extravagant and fraudulent hustle, underwritten by Antonio, Bassanio's unwilling, even masochistic, sugar daddy, the gold-digger pitches for the prize. My view of Bassanio's morals is, as you can probably detect, a rather dim one.

When news arrives in Belmont that Antonio's ships have been lost at sea and that his bond is therefore forfeit to Shylock, Bassanio is forced into the humiliation of admitting to the woman he just won by lottery, that he is indeed a sham. But as money is no object to Portia, she breezily offers to pay the sum twice over. Bassanio's luck keeps holding out.

When we came to stage the trial scene, having researched the size of the loan, we decided to try and demonstrate the scale of the temptation laid out to this Jewish money lender (who apparently dreams of money bags – a line that is often cut) by presenting the doubled offer of 6,000 ducats in real coins, which Bassanio and Gratiano cynically then empty out from two large chests, they have brought with them.[3] They are certain the money will trump Shylock's sense of Justice, by appealing to his greed.

The gold coins rang across the stage, spinning and rolling, taking minutes finally to rattle to a stop.

Philip Voss as Shylock then bent to examine one of the coins before coolly declaring:

> If every ducat in six thousand ducats
> Were in six parts, and every part a ducat,
> I would not draw them, – I would have my bond.

---

[3] I think the props department baulked at 6,000 coins and we finally settled for 1,000 but they made a pretty impressive sound nevertheless.

In rehearsal, when Balthasar, the young lawyer, can find no other course of action other than to allow Shylock to take his pound of flesh, Philip made a heart-stopping discovery. Some Shylocks have confidently marched forward, dagger in hand. Others have prepared their butchers' knives with clinical precision. Philip realized his Shylock had achieved his objective: to be granted the pound of flesh, his legal right. He had thought no further than that. Though he had come to court equipped with the means to do so, the balances and the knife, he had not anticipated *how* he would actually extract that pound.

There followed an agonizing improvisation as he attempted to work out which angle might be most effective. Just as Shylock alighted on his preferred option and was about to make his first incision, the lawyer draws attention to the stipulation that he can have his flesh – but in cutting it he must not spill one drop of Antonio's blood.

As Shylock realizes he is in a trap of his own making and as the Christians circle like vultures at a kill, he is told to kneel before the duke for mercy. In our production, Gratiano (John Dougall) man-handled him to the floor.

Then, as Shylock is told that the only mercy he would receive would be dependent on him becoming a Christian and making out a will, leaving all his wealth to the daughter who has abandoned him, he asks for permission to leave. As Philip's Shylock started to get to his feet, he slipped in the 6,000 ducats, and fell and tried to rise again and fell again. It was deeply painful to watch.[4]

After Philip Voss's death in 2020, the actor John Heffernan (who struck up a friendship with Philip in the 1990s) wrote beautifully of this performance:

> It was his sheer passion and intensity that to me as a hungry schoolboy, looking to Shakespeare as a way to understand the world and probably myself, knocked me for six. His cry to the heavens as Venice and his entire life swirled around him and then at the trial, his pitiful attempt to get back onto his feet as he slipped on the ducats are moments I will remember forever. For me, they cut to the centre of what Shakespeare and theatre can be, exposing and bonding us together in our shared humanity.

*   *   *

In my career through Shakespeare, I have rarely revisited a play. There have always been opportunities to do ones I haven't done before instead. However, when I got the chance to direct *Merchant* again, in Japan, I jumped at the opportunity.

The play was to be produced by someone who has played a very special role in my life, the redoubtable Thelma Holt, in co-production with a Japanese media giant called HoriPro. I would be directing two of their greatest stage stars, Masachika Ichimura (known to everyone as 'Ichi') and the young rising talent Tatsuya Fujiwara.

---

[4] As a happy coincidence of the scattering of the gold ducats in the Trial scene, when Lorenzo and Jessica sit in the starlight, at Belmont in the next scene, and he describes 'the floor of heaven is thick inlaid with patins of bright gold', the gold ducats seemed like tiny reflections of the stars he describes.

I had thought that the play I wanted to do in Tokyo would be *Measure for Measure*, which seemed, to me at any rate, to fit aspects of Japanese society rather perfectly. It was Thelma who persuaded me otherwise:

> Darling, believe your mother, you don't speak the language (though God knows, neither do I, in all these years), so for your first experience directing in Japan, you need to do a play you know very well indeed. And apart from that, Ichi is desperate to do Shylock, so you're doing *Merchant*.

*   *   *

On a previous tour to Japan, I had sought out the home of the first man to translate the whole of Shakespeare into Japanese. Tsubouchi Shōyō lived near Atami, on the Izu peninsula.

Our journey on the bullet train, the famous Shinkansen, took 43 minutes exactly, followed by a long taxi ride. The road seemed like an endless series of hairpin bends and even steeper inclines, until suddenly and unexpectedly, making a spectacular entrance like a seasoned Kabuki actor, Mount Fuji appeared. The sacred mountain seemed to float in ethereal blue. It looked as if a child had drawn a mountain in sugar and could blow it away on a whim.

When we arrived at the home of Shōyō, in an unprepossessing back street, a neat little lady in a crisscrossed, grey pinny met us at the gate. She took us through a wet garden, over little bridges and carp ponds, past lush pillows of bright green maple, to a pagoda with a kingfisher weathervane, where Shōyō used to work. Here on the second floor, he completed his canon in 1927. The room smelled of cedar wood and tatami matting. Visitors are not normally allowed up here, but as we were from the Royal Shakespeare Company, the lady said she was very pleased to show us up.

Around his desk, there were some little ceramic souvenir models of Anne Hathaway's cottage and Shakespeare's birthplace in Henley Street, which must date back to the 1920s or 1930s when he had visited Stratford. Above his desk was a 'brass-rubbing' of the gravestone from Holy Trinity, with its famous malediction. All around, the windows opened to the four points of the compass.

I began to think about all the options a translator has in trying to capture a text as rich as Shakespeare's. Do you translate for the poetry and rhythm of the original? Do you translate purely for the meaning of the text? Or do you try and capture a sense of the pace of the original? Generally, I was told, Japanese as a language takes one and a half times longer to speak than English. So, pace is a significant element in the translation.

Here in Shōyō's study, I reflected that he had been famous for the elegant lyricism and beauty of his translations, but would they work for a modern audience today?

Before we left, I recited 'Fear no more the heat of the sun', in Shōyō's honour.

As it happened, HoriPro were to commission a new translation for this production of *The Merchant of Venice*. I was asked what sort of translation I was looking for. Thinking back to Tsubouchi Shōyō, I said I would like a translator who combines all four elements: meaning, poetry, rhythm and pace, and I was lucky to find exactly such a one in the person of Professor Shoichiro Kawai. 'Sho' was a very hands-on translator, ready and excited to discuss not just the text of the play but the themes and how they might land differently in Japanese society.

I realized in talking to Sho that the play's focus on the conflict between Christian and Jewish communities would be less immediately understood here. But, more importantly, due partly perhaps to the fact that Japan and Nazi Germany were allies, the whole history of the Holocaust was less well known here. This lack of an immediate shared Eurocentric view of the world, in a sense, released the play from that particular burden of history.

During the Japanese tour of *Othello* in 2004, I had participated in a Q&A event, and was asked about the Venetian prejudice to the Moor's race, and how it resonated today. In reply I asked the audience what the equivalent racism might be in Japan today. Everyone continued to sip their drinks politely. In the interval, a gentleman approached me to say, the question had met with silence, 'because there is no racism in Japan today'. It was, he said, the result of being such a monocultural society.

Asking the actors of the Merchant company the same question (with regard to the Christian/Jewish antipathy in the play) met with a similar reticence. Only later, in a bar, did an actor confide in me. 'Doran-san,' he said, 'nobody spoke up about racism, because the assistant director is part Korean.'

I soon realized that the actors rarely expressed their own opinions. When challenged, Tatsuya told me that the Japanese for a director 'giving notes', translated as 'saying No'. It took some time for the rehearsal room to open up and for debate to flourish, but when it did the actors began to feel a sense of ownership of their work, which they confessed they had rarely felt.

5

The Winter's Tale

– 1999: Royal Shakespeare Theatre, Stratford-upon-Avon; Barbican, London.
– Heritage films.

10 April 1998: Good Friday.
I sit down to read *The Winter's Tale* in one go. Outside, it's wet, and the world seems rude with spring. It has suddenly thrust forward, bursting, budding, blossoming everywhere.

> Daffodils
> That come before the swallow dares and take
> The winds of March with beauty.

The meaning of Easter, of regeneration and resurrection, of hope, of renewal, seems almost palpable this year. Politically, the desire for regeneration is as strong – and yet as fragile – as the stray grass stems I can see pushing up through the concrete, by the railings at our front door.

At Stormont, all the delegates at the Irish Peace talks have been battling to produce an agreement by today. According to the breakfast news, they were still toiling past the midnight deadline and into the early hours. They hope to declare a lasting peace, so that Easter could be celebrated once again in that divided country, by Catholics and Protestants alike, with a true sense of regeneration.

So, it feels a particularly potent time to be reading *The Winter's Tale*. It feels like an Easter play. I am struck by how powerfully it describes the cycle of life and death, as it rolls round 'in earth's diurnal course', and the process of the seasons, achieving a hard-won spring after a fierce, bitter winter. 'Welcome hither as is the spring to the Earth' says Leontes to the young runaways, Florizel and Perdita.

As I finish reading, I want to burst. Bach's St Matthew Passion is playing on the radio: piety and passion, suffering and redemption. Overwhelming.

I am so lucky to be doing this play.

* * *

Adrian Noble has asked me to direct *The Winter's Tale*, to be staged in repertoire with a new production of *The Lion, the Witch and the Wardrobe* in an adaptation by Adrian Mitchell, which he would direct, and which would play over Christmas. The first major family show in the RST.

I am having some trouble. I can't find a Leontes.

Tony and I had been together for twelve years by this point and had worked together as leading actor and director twice, in *Titus Andronicus* in Johannesburg, and in *Cyrano de Bergerac*, in the Swan and on tour, in 1997. But somehow Leontes didn't attract him. He felt he had done it before ('the crazy psycho ranging around and frightening everyone') and though I respected his view, I could not change it, and had moved on.

Suddenly, there was a crisis. Tony had been cast in a production at the National Theatre (NT). When he got into rehearsal, he felt that what had been agreed beforehand, between him and the director, had altered. Mutually, they agreed to part company, citing those artistic differences. It had never happened to Tony before in his professional career. It left him bruised and reeling.

We went away for a few days' break to cocoon ourselves in a small country hotel outside Bath and walk for hours through the woods and fields. I knew I had to be sensitive about my timing, but I was also getting desperate about casting Leontes. And I had had an idea, which might move the offer on from the one Tony had so firmly rejected before. What if we were to double the jealous king Leontes with the rogue Autolycus?

It was possible, and to my knowledge had never been done. Autolycus is almost completely irrelevant to the plot. He parachutes into the play in the Bohemia scenes in Act Four, and though he follows the action back to Sicilia, has no real narrative effect on the action.

Tony was intrigued and suggested we drive into Bath and buy a copy of the play so he could read it again. I phoned Adrian Noble, in case he vetoed the idea. Adrian was over the moon about the possibility of getting Tony back, and Tony finally agreed.

I was blessed with a dream cast, three of whom (including Tony) had been in my first Stratford season: Estelle Kohler returning to the company to play the White Witch and Paulina; and Geoff Freshwater as Mr Beaver and Camillo. Ken Bones, who had been a silkily saturnine De Guiche in *Cyrano*, played Polixenes, and Alexandra Gilbreath, the Roxane in that same production, would play Hermione.

So we began rehearsals in Clapham. At the end of the second week, after detailed text study, we finally got to a read-through. The Sicilia scenes already crackled with violent static. But the Bohemia scenes were strenuous. Tony had proposed that for the character of Autolycus, the 'snapper-up of unconsidered trifles', he could channel his Jewish Lithuanian grandfather who had landed in South Africa and travelled the country as a 'Smous', a pedlar. But in these scenes he just seemed to bury his head in the script.

But then, when the read-through reached the final scenes as the action returns to Sicilia, it became clear almost immediately that I had made a terrible mistake.

Leontes must be left behind to endure the great gap of time, in regret and self-recrimination. But now as Tony swapped back to play Leontes, instead of re-emerging as the penitent king, he seemed merely to be another of Autolycus' multiple disguises.

I asked Tony if we could go for a stroll on Clapham Common in the lunch break. After walking for a while, wondering how to broach the subject, suddenly it was Tony who said:

'It doesn't work, does it.'

'What doesn't?' I asked.

'Autolycus,' he said, 'you need a great comic. And that's just not me. And however we get round it . . . the bastard's got five songs, and I can't sing!'

But he admitted that, even in the short time we had worked on the play, his admiration for the complexity of the writing of Leontes had bowled him over.

'Then let's just recast Autolycus. You can't leave a second show in as many months. You'll get a reputation.'

Very relieved, we agreed to recast Autolycus, and I made a swift decision to upgrade the inventive Ian Hughes from young Shepherd to Autolycus, and his lofty understudy Christopher Brand took on the young Shepherd.

The Winter's Tale is a play about domestic violence, the male abuse of their power – in this case magnified by his royal position – and the effect on those who get caught up in that violence.

We had cast Emily Bruni as both Perdita, and her brother, Mamillius. She played Mamillius, in our Romanov setting, as a sickly young tsarevitch, confined to a wheelchair. The chair had been redesigned with a lower seat which made Emily seem diminutive.

When Hermione is arrested on a charge of adultery, frail little Mamillius falls sick.

Tony felt that Leontes' jealousy was a disease. He consulted a number of different psychiatrists and concluded that he was suffering from a form of psychosis called morbid jealousy, which could descend rapidly, and particularly struck men in early middle age. What this meant in performance was that rather than just rage out of control, he shared his sense of self-justification with us. It wasn't the king who was mad, it was everybody else who simply seemed to refuse to accept the reality of the situation. This painful self-delusion made us pity Leontes.

Rob Jones's set was a long gallery of wintery grey, with roiling clouds above it, represented by acres of silk. The walls, disappearing upstage in perspective, could slide giddily closer together enhancing the intensity of Leontes' claustrophobic obsession.

We also noted, as with so many characters in Shakespeare (Macbeth, for example), that Leontes suffers from insomnia, and the lack of sleep only increases his delusion. 'Nor night, nor day, no rest' he says in Act Two Scene Three, as he paces, waiting news of his sick child. And he begins to contemplate the horrifyingly illicit thought that if Hermione were to be disposed of, he might be able to sleep again:

> Say that she were gone,
> Given to the fire, a moiety of my rest
> Might come to me again.

When the doctor tells him the boy's sickness seems to be passing, it is as if Leontes doesn't hear. He is so consumed with the belief that the child's malady is a mark of his nobility (unable to tolerate his mother's shame) that the king determines to convince a mere servant of his theory. Note how Shakespeare has Leontes describe the symptoms his son displayed:

> To see his nobleness!
> Conceiving the dishonour of his mother,
> He straight declined, droop'd, took it deeply,
> Fasten'd and fix'd the shame on't in himself,
> Threw off his spirit, his appetite, his sleep,
> And downright languish'd.

The detail is obsessive. In one rehearsal, Tony played it as if Leontes was trying hard to focus, struggling to keep awake himself, wearied and bewildered by the effort to make others see what is so apparent to his sick mind.

As he reached the word 'languish'd', he suddenly fell over backwards from standing.

It seemed to happen in slow-motion. Everyone in the room caught their breath. Actors in the scene rushed forward to help. At which point, he continued with the speech, angrily dismissing them all, with Leontes' next line 'Leave me solely, go.' And then tetchily reminding them of their duty to his heir: 'See how he fares.'

As the scene ended, I walked over for a quiet word with my leading actor. 'Can you warn me next time you are going to do something as dangerous as that?' I said, 'Are you sure you're OK?' 'Fine,' he said rather dismissively, 'fine.' 'Can you do that every night?' He did.

Estelle Kohler as Paulina avoided the trap of making this fine woman strident, and preserved an unhurried sense of dignity, which made her infinitely stronger. Paulina takes a huge risk in bringing Leontes newly born baby daughter from the prison. Striding through all the stressed courtiers clucking around the king, she refuses to be put off. There was a great moment when Estelle executed a swift false-exit, with the baby in its cradle, only to break back through and leave the child at the king's feet, relying on some inevitable paternal instinct to be roused in the father.

Leontes storms about, furious at being disobeyed and to have been bested by this woman. But then we noticed an exciting little crossroads. Leontes seems exhausted, a victim of his courtiers' selfish pestering: 'I am a feather for each wind that blows.' He sighs. A death sentence now is surely the more reasonable option. Then he seems to give up, relent, and reprieve the death sentence he has placed on the baby:

> Shall I live on to see this bastard kneel
> And call me father? better burn it now
> Than curse it then.

Then in a short half-line he gives up:

> But be it; let it live.

Tony slouched off up stage to the audible relief of the court, only to sweep back round, snatch a sword as he passed one of the guards, and pile back down stage towards the cradle, sword raised to stab it, crying, 'It shall not neither.' A tense shocked beat, until he switches his focus to Antigonus, telling him to take the baby and destroy it.

By the trial scene, Leontes' sickness, exacerbated by his lack of sleep, is painful to witness, as he enters tottering and unstable in an enormous purple cloak and spectacular Romanov crown. The pomp he has insisted upon, the height of the throne from which he presides over the court, served to make the entrance of his accused wife Hermione all the more pathetic.

Alex Gilbreath, not yet by that stage a mother herself, had done extensive research among her maternal friends. This led to some very detailed work in Hermione's early scenes of pregnancy, but to a shocking image of her arrival at her trial, having been denied the child-bed privileges she might have expected, either by virtue of her status as queen, or as a mother who has just given birth. Alex arrived slowly, face tear-smudged, hair shorn, barefoot, and her prison-issue night dress, stained not only with the filth of the cell, but the seepage of the milk her breasts had produced to feed her new baby.

Meanwhile the baffled Leontes cannot find his spectacles to read the indictment.

Later in the trial, Hermione is cleared by the oracle of the charges of adultery brought against her by her husband. But Leontes refuses to abide by the judgement. A servant hurries in with news:

> O sir, I shall be hated to report it!
> The prince your son, with mere conceit and fear
> Of the queen's speed, is gone.

Mamillius has died.

When the decision of the oracle was pronounced, the clouds started to darken and billow ominously. And as the scene ended, they fell, covering the entire set. This produced a snowy mountainous landscape for the coast of Bohemia, as Antigonus arrives with the baby he has sworn to abandon to its fate.

Any audience watching *The Winter's Tale* is likely to be waiting to see how the production is going to tackle the most famous stage direction in Shakespeare: *Exit, pursued by bear*. In my opinion, the problem is not so much *Exit, pursued by bear*, as *Enter bear*. The audience immediately see how you are trying to do it, whether it's a man in a bear costume, a large puppet, or some metaphorical ursine representation, and they are unlikely to be very frightened by the terrifying ordeal the poor old man endures.

Our snowy landscape provided us with an excellent solution. A huge puppet polar bear head, and paws, was concealed beneath the silk, and could rise up unexpectedly, towering over Antigonus, as if it was erupting from its den. When it worked, it was awe-inspiring. When it didn't, it looked like '*Exit, pursued by avalanche*'.

*   *   *

The sheep-shearing scenes in Bohemia can be delightful but are challenging. Adrian Noble had directed a luminous production four years before, which had set them at a sort of village fête à la Stanley Spencer's Cookham. When Adrian had entrusted me with this play, he had urged me not to make it too 'literal'. He had combined the very specific and recognizable social context of the fête with a little madness: Autolycus, exuberantly played by Richard (Bill) McCabe, had come floating in on a cloud of balloons.

We decided to locate them in a rural but more industrial setting, in a huge wool shed. With the bales all stacked, and work over for the season, we created a sense of a hard-working community ready to party. Ian Hughes had embraced the opportunity of playing Autolycus with both hands and retained something we had devised to get round Tony's inability to sing, a sort of Edwardian karaoke machine, with the ballads being phonograph discs, which he tried to flog to the working folk.

The scene is essentially a party with lots of different acts, including the dance of twelve Satyrs, which our choreographer, Siân Williams, realized with the aid of a joyous cast and a considerable number of very rude vegetables. When I became Artistic Director, I proposed a tour of *The Winter's Tale* in which Act Four was played as an extended interval, outside the theatre, in a nearby park, or community hall, with local amateur groups joining in, and returning to the theatre for Act Five.

Somehow, however it is achieved, the Bohemia scenes must blow fresh air through the play.

We must be prepared for the experience of Act Five, surely one of the most powerful and moving final scenes in all of Shakespeare. It's holy. It comes as close to an act of worship as any play I know. And it creeps up on you. Because if you are coming to the play, having never heard or seen it (oh happy state!), you can enjoy the working out of the story as Perdita is discovered to be the baby left on the beach, with a fardel by her side, which reveals she is the king's lost heir, and she is reunited with her father, and Leontes and Polixenes recover their childhood friendship, and see their children engaged. And if you haven't seen the play before you will be intrigued when all those happy reunions happen off stage, only to be recounted by a group of courtiers we haven't met before.

But magic is in store, because you then hear about a statue of Hermione (who died sixteen years ago), which Paulina keeps in her art gallery. Only by the time we get there, everything is hushed, and Paulina is referring to the gallery as a 'chapel', and like some sacred icon, this statue is preserved behind a curtain. And in order to conjure her magic everyone must be still, or leave, and music must be summoned as Paulina insists, 'It is required you do awake your faith.'

In our production, Hermione's statue stood in the dock in which she was tried. The dock is arranged with votive candles like a shrine, with the processional monstrance, used in the entrance of the oracle, creating a halo behind her head.

As Leontes reaches out to touch the statue of his dead wife, Shakespeare manages again to create the most powerful of moments in the simplest language: 'O, she's warm' he whispers. Magic and religion fuse. Sin, repentance, Easter resurrection, and impossible second chances (ached for often, but seldom achieved) are realized.

Hermione has no words to her husband but turns to see her lost daughter.

> You gods, look down
> And from your sacred vials pour your graces
> Upon my daughter's head!

We are all included in the benediction, we feel blessed. As Emily Bruni (Perdita) had also played her brother Mamillius, somehow the doubling allowed the family reunion to include the lost boy.

Redemption, renewal, re-creation.

6

Timon of Athens

– 1999: Royal Shakespeare Theatre, Stratford-upon-Avon;
Theatre Royal, Newcastle-upon-Tyne; Barbican Theatre, London.

Time's glory is to calm contending kings
To unmask falsehood and bring truth to light

The Rape of Lucrece

In the deserts of northern Morocco stand the ruins of the ancient Mauritanian capital. It became an outpost of the Roman Empire and was called Volubilis.

In 1995, Tony Sher had been asked to be one of the presenters for a travel series for BBC Two called *African Footsteps*. The cricketer Viv Richards was already slated to do South Africa, and I guess Tony, as a prominent gay man, had been selected to explore Morocco's reputation as a hedonistic destination for gay writers like Jean Genet, Tennessee Williams, Joe Orton and the Beat Generation author William Burroughs. So, celebrating our credentials as an out gay couple, I went along as well.

The programme focused on Tangier (once nicknamed 'Sodom-on-Sea') and we discussed its reputation for drugs and sex, back in the fifties and sixties, with those who were there, like the Honourable, and by then rather ancient, Lord David Herbert. But we were also able to travel. We visited the souks, and tanneries of Fez, with their amazing dye vats, and journeyed to a tiny village in the Southern Rif Mountains, to hear the master drummers of Joujouka, a group of Sufi trance musicians whom Timothy Leary once described as 'the 4,000 year old Rock'N'Roll band'.

And we went to Volubilis.

To ruinate proud buildings with thy hours
And smear with dust their glittering golden towers.

The most famous of the ancient Roman remains is the great arch of Caracalla, an awesome sight in the setting sun.

As we followed the outline of these quiet ruins with their grid of streets and low walls, we came across the remains of a house with a preserved dusty mosaic floor depicting Jupiter and his lover Ganymede. This seemed at best a rather tenuous link to the theme of gay life in Morocco. 'We've already got too much material for the programme,' said Tony, 'Not sure this is going to make the cut.' Then our guide did something miraculous.

'Here,' he said, handing us some water bottles, 'dash the water on the tiles.'

As we did, dazzling colours appeared: ruby and sapphire and malachite. The tiny square tesserae of enamel and glass seemed to flash in the dying desert sun, and history shimmered into life. We tried the same with other mosaics: one of Bacchus surprising Ariadne; another of Diana startled by Actaeon while bathing; and in a third, the Twelve Labours of Hercules were all depicted.[1]

This is what my job is all about, I thought, refreshing stories that were told many years ago, and making them vivid and bright and immediate, now.

No more so perhaps than with a play as apparently dusty and dry as *Timon of Athens* is reputed to be.

*   *   *

I started rehearsal with one Timon and ended with another.

Alan Bates had agreed to play Antony opposite Frances de la Tour's Cleopatra for Stephen Pimlott, and in order for him to play something else in the season, I was lucky enough to land him as Timon of Athens, which I was to direct in the RST. It was the first time the play had been done there since John Schlesinger's 1965 production with Paul Scofield. In fact, it was only the third time the play had been performed by the RSC, the second being Ron Daniels's Other Place production with Richard Pasco in 1980.

As we began rehearsals, Alan seemed engaged and excited at creating a role for which there was not such a huge weight of precedence, as there inevitably is with other Shakespeare protagonists. And we began to explore what made the man tick. A clue might be in the introduction of Alcibiades into the story, a character not present in any of the potential source material.

In Plato's *Symposium*, Alcibiades arrives late and drunk to the party, where the discussion is about the true nature of love. Socrates is deeply attracted to the devastatingly handsome Alcibiades. Alcibiades knows it. But he finds it frustrating that Socrates, whom he compares to a fat old ugly Silenus, never tries it on with him. In fact, Socrates' continence and self-restraint maddens Alcibiades so much that he finds himself obsessed with the older man, and determines to be his lover.

I felt sure that Shakespeare had the relationship of Socrates and Alcibiades in mind when he wrote *Timon of Athens*. I explained to Alan that I had detected a very strong homosexual element in the play. This seemed to me clearly to reflect Jacobean society and the scandals of King James, as a homosexual man, openly declaring his obsession for Robert Carr (who became Viscount Rochester and then the Earl of Somerset) and later George Villiers, Duke of Buckingham. His adoration of those frankly unsuitable men and his willingness to give them huge amounts of power and money drew considerable censure.

The entertainment that Timon puts on for his guests consists of a masque of Amazons: a really potent homoerotic image. Masques were a feature of Jacobean court life and Amazons frequented the drama of the period. John Marston's *Antonio and*

---

[1]   The Volubilis section didn't make the cut in our episode of *African Footsteps*.

Mellida has a central male character who dresses as an Amazon. There is an ambivalence to the sexuality of Amazon warriors; they're either fighting women or they are feminized men. When Timon invites all these single men to his extraordinary banquet and has Cupid introduce a masque of the Amazons, it's the equivalent of a decadent drag rave.

The idea reminded Alan of the drag ball in John Osbourne's stage play *A Patriot for Me* in which he had starred as the repressed Alfred Redl, blackmailed for his homosexuality: an acclaimed performance.

Alan had played a number of other roles where the character's sexuality is ambiguous, such as Rupert Birkin in Ken Russell's *Women in Love* with its famous erotic naked wrestling match with Oliver Reed, and while he was generally very reticent about his own private life, he was fascinated by the idea of exploring the root of Timon's philanthropic lifestyle, his sycophantic followers, and why there was no Mrs Timon.

If Alan's Timon was a spiritual brother to Antonio in *The Merchant of Venice*, then the performance would certainly be balanced by the machismo of his Antony going down every night on Cleopatra, like a 'cunning linguist', as *The Guardian* critic was to point out.

The company included Rupert Penry-Jones as Alcibiades.

The homoeroticism of the production also highlighted the play's misogyny, albeit in the context of a mass misanthropy. The only women in the play are the whores, Timandra and Phrynia, who follow the slime trail of parasites to the wilderness when rumour spreads that Timon has uncovered gold.

I know of no more violent line than when Timon says to the whores 'Paint till a horse may mire upon your face / A pox of wrinkles'. It is also full of self-loathing. It seems as though Shakespeare himself has jumped into a very black abyss.

Alan began to find rehearsing during the day and performing in the evening, a real strain. Timon has 30 per cent of the lines in the play and is virtually never off stage. Alan was 65, and suffered, amongst other things, from diabetes. The company decided to give him a few days' rest, from both rehearsal and performance to recharge his batteries, and put him up in Buckland Manor, a country house hotel in the Cotswolds, about half an hour from Stratford.

I went down to see how he was getting on. After lunch we took a walk around the rose garden. It was a beautiful July afternoon. He was apologetic about missing rehearsal, and anxious to build up his strength. He kept repeating how much he was enjoying rehearsals, but with every protestation, I realized what he really wanted was for someone to let him off the hook. I told him that I thought it was important that he continued to play Antony, and in order to do so I would release him from playing Timon. His shoulders dropped immediately. 'Thank you,' he said. 'And I am so sorry, I have never done this in my life, but thank you.'

I drove back to Stratford, wondering when my weird sense of calm would turn into panic.

We had just over two weeks to go before the first preview.

Back in Stratford, I made an emergency phone call to Michael Pennington. I had tracked him down to a dressing room at the end of a performance of *Les Misérables*.

'What would you say to playing Timon of Athens with two weeks to go?' I asked. And held my breath. And I have never forgotten his answer. 'Not impossible,' he said.

Michael arrived in rehearsal the following Monday astonishingly almost word-perfect.

Michael had been in the Schlesinger production of *Timon of Athens* in 1965 as an unnamed beggar (along with Frances de la Tour) in a company of forty-five actors. He remembered Paul Scofield arriving into rehearsal each morning, as the younger members of the company padded in, hugging coffees and finishing cigarettes. Scofield would go quietly to the back of the room, take off his jacket, and run through the great speech as Timon rejects the city and turns his back on Athens.

> Let me look back on thee. O thou wall,
> That girdlest in those wolves, dive in the earth,
> And fence not Athens!

I took Michael through the production, explaining my thoughts about how and where we were setting the play.

Tackling uncharted territory like *Timon* can prove liberating. Having by this point in my career done both *Titus Andronicus* and *All is True/ Henry VIII*, I found it very enjoyable to look at those Shakespeare plays that didn't have a huge back-catalogue of performances.

I had seen Trevor Nunn's production at the Young Vic with David Suchet as Timon. The genius of that version was to place the play very directly in the world of eighties London and to point up its relevance to the prevailing obsession with banking and money. As with so much of Trevor's work, every scene was precisely located; in the changing room of a City squash court, or a swanky reception, and most cleverly, the second half was set in a junkyard of crushed cars.

But by making a production so specific, do you run the risk of denying the play's application to the universal? By pointing out the parallels with today, might you deny a more general resonance? I wanted to retain the play as a metaphor.

It is a very bleak, dark play with all the snarl of Thomas Middleton, and the rage of Ben Jonson. The characters represented, like the Poet and the Painter, are types. And like Jonson with his characters, the writer(s) of *Timon of Athens* are entirely critical of them. They represent a whole spectrum of sycophancy and flattery and the sick society of Athens. Having identified that tone of the play, it allowed us to explore some of the themes of this society, the 'dream of friendship' that Timon is lost in.

Our design, by Stephen Brimson Lewis, took its cue from Wilson Knight's precise elucidation in *The Wheel of Fire*.[2] He describes the parable-like nature of the play as having 'massive ... and fathomless simplicity'. Not just simple, but massively simple. We took our inspiration for that massive simplicity from the work of artist Richard Long, and in particular his mud paintings. The paint shop created a splashy terracotta setting

---

[2]   G. Wilson Knight loved *Timon of Athens* so much he played the part twice, stripping down to a flesh-coloured jock strap for the famous 'Wall' speech.

sun eclipsed by a dark moon against a background of intense velvet black. It hovered ominously over the ellipse of the season stage.

And with Beckettian restraint Timon's dwelling was a grave-sized hole in the middle of the stage.

Michael was very excited about my choice of music for the play.

When the Shakespeare Theatre in Stratford, Ontario, got round to doing *Timon of Athens* in 1964, they decided the play needed jazzing up, and asked none other than jazz-legend Duke Ellington to write the score. Ellington had first shown an interest in Shakespeare when he visited Stratford-upon-Avon (and dropped in to Anne Hathaway's cottage) on his first tour of England in 1933. Then in 1957, he had been performing with his band at the Ontario Jazz Festival and had snuck into the back to watch one of the Shakespeare performances. Determined to stay for only a few moments he sat in the aisle but ended up watching the whole play. He was completely overwhelmed and went on to write a jazz suite called *Such Sweet Thunder* based on individual studies of Shakespeare characters (like Hank Cinq, Lady Mac, and Sister Kate).

When I started preparing our production in 1999, John Woolf (then the RSC's Head of Music) and I contacted Stratford, Ontario to ask if they still had a copy of the score. A couple of hours later they rang back to say they had found the score in a cardboard box in the cellar. John re-constructed the music and adapted it for our band.

Ellington's music caught the clamour of the twentieth century. It could be very funny; the brass would sometimes guffaw, and sometimes it would sob, sometimes scorch, and that seemed to me to fit the parable/moral fable nature of the play. It really helped to release and enhance the elusive sardonic tone of the play.

Michael was very pleased to find some old friends in the cast. His English Shakespeare Theatre accomplice John Woodvine was playing the loyal steward Flavius and giving real backbone to the character's integrity. Richard (Bill) McCabe was the coruscating Apemantus.

We threw ourselves into rehearsals with renewed energy.

What I most remember of Michael's excellent performance was the encounter with Apemantus in the second half, and in particular the viperous exchange of insults. It's a wonderful articulation of revulsion and disgust. Apemantus says at one point, 'The strain of man's bred out / Into baboon and monkey.' Timon returns, 'Were I like thee, I'd throw away myself.' It's a resplendently contemporary line, there's nothing complicated or 'Shakespearean' about it. Then Apemantus, with a lucidity that no one else possesses, expresses Timon's essential dilemma. He says:

The middle of humanity thou never knew'st, but the extremity of both ends.

Another uncannily modern line; it makes you think of so many people who have found fame fast, or become rich quick, who don't know what it's like to just live in the middle like most of humanity.

We opened at the end of August. Michael's performance as Timon was justly lauded. *The Times* declared he was 'magnificent' and one reviewer claimed, 'Pennington delivers the long tirades as if from some inner sense of musical notation, his incredibly flexible voice weaving the words into patterns in which sense, clarity and even subtlety form a seamless whole.'

He made the audience question Timon's motives. Is Timon changed by misfortune, or revealed by it? He has always had these fabulous riches and is held as a great man, a loved and a generous man, but a man who has been blinkered by his wealth. And perhaps we should be suspicious of that generosity. Michael's Timon seemed to use his wealth as a front to insulate him from emotion, to hide his loneliness, his isolation, and his inability to connect. It seemed inevitable that this man would swing so completely in the opposite direction. That made the moral fable in the end quite moving.

For me, Michael Pennington brought the play flashing vividly to life, like the mosaics at Volubilis.

There is probably no finer diatribe on the moral degeneracy of mankind than *Timon of Athens*. It stands as a statement on the corruption of mankind: there will always be Flavius characters who have essential goodness and integrity; there will always be the Apemantus malcontent characters who have a clearer perspective on what is really going on in the world; and there will always be delusional characters like Timon. But that doesn't necessarily make it a play to love: the imagery is so crowded with a menagerie of animals, from asses to flies to apes, so rotten with disease and infection. It is not a comfortable play to live with for very long.

*   *   *

Four years later, I slipped in at the last minute to a house-seat in the stalls at the National Theatre. It was a matinee of David Mamet's play *Edmond* with Kenneth Branagh, directed by Ed Hall. As I stowed my coat under my chair, the man sitting next to me said, 'Mr Doran, you either don't recognize me, or you are trying to ignore me.' As I turned to look at the man beside me, he removed his dark glasses and smiled. It was Alan Bates. But he was right. I could easily not have recognized him. His hair was now white, and his face was a little red and puffy, but he was still a very handsome man. 'Have you forgiven me yet,' he said, 'for letting you down?' As the auditorium lights went down, I gave him a hug.

Alan sadly died a few months later of pancreatic cancer.

7

Macbeth

– 1999: Swan Theatre, Stratford-upon-Avon; Japan.
– 2000: New Haven Tour.
– Filmed for television.

'Macbeth, Macbeth, Macbeth! There you are I've said it, and not been struck down.'

That's how I began our first day of rehearsals for 'Macbeth'. The so-called curse of this play has nothing to do with hocus-pocus. It is just very difficult to make the production match up to the audience's own imaginations, and the effect the play had on each of them when they read it for the first time. So I banned the use of the silly phrase 'the Scottish play'.

We recently had a production of *Twelfth Night* that was beset with challenges: serious illness, stage fright, etc. No one called it 'the Illyrian play'.

But we examined our individual reactions to a word that appears most frequently in *Macbeth*. The word 'fear'. I asked everyone to tell me when they had genuinely experienced fear. The accounts differed widely: one told of losing their child at the beach and fearing he had been swept away; another of slipping whilst rock climbing; another of lying in bed and listening to an intruder break into their house.

My own experience involved the re-emergence of a childhood phobia. Tony and I were on safari in South Africa. We were sitting high up at the back of the open-top jeep. I was wearing a singlet, shorts and flip-flops. We were in pursuit of a leopard and had come off road and into a stand of acacia thorn trees. The leopard had disappeared into a dense thicket, and all eyes were down and focused for any movement. Silence.

After a few minutes, I noticed something twitch in my peripheral vision just to my left. I turned my head slightly to discover a large spider, hanging like a clawed hand, just inches from my face. I held my breath. The giant spider's legs were tiger-striped black and orange and it seemed to pulse in a huge yellow web, but as I followed the web up with my eyes, I realized it was not the only one. We had crashed into what seemed like a colony, draping the entire grove with saffron webs and at the centre of each of them another pulsing spider. I started to suck the air in rapid pants. Tony by my side noticed my silent panic and asked if I was alright. I pointed to the spider but found myself unable to speak.

He called to the ranger sitting in the driver seat.

'Oh, OK,' he said, 'yeah, don't worry. They are golden orb spiders they are actually quite interesting. They all co-ordinate their mating at this time of year, which is why ...'

'Do you think we could just go?' Tony said, realizing that I was by now hyperventilating badly.

The ranger cranked the jeep into reverse. But as he pulled back, the jeep hit the trunk of the tree, dislodging spiders which fell onto my hair and bare shoulders. I curdled. I began to feel light-headed, and my hands had stiffened into involuntary claws.

'Don't worry, mate, they're not poisonous.'

I pulled a waterproof poncho over my head, and, like Kenny from South Park, I pulled the cord tight.

Each of the stories the company told produced fascinating physiological effects on the listeners. People started to hold their breath, or to breathe faster. Scientists tell us that this innate fast breathing response has an effect on our brain, and in particular to the amygdala, the part of the brain that processes emotions. It may be that by providing more oxygen to the amygdala it prepares us to think more quickly and prepare our flight response to fear.

Our job as a company, now we had noticed this, was to tap deep and prepare our audiences to engage, and to find ways of allowing Shakespeare's account of terror to pull them to the edge of their seats and grip their breathing.

The previous year, I had directed a double bill of Tom Stoppard's *The Real Inspector Hound,* and Peter Shaffer's *Black Comedy* for the Donmar, at the Comedy Theatre in the West End. Shaffer's play opens in total darkness. You hear the characters on stage chattering breezily away. Suddenly, brilliant light floods the stage. The characters on stage freeze. One of them says, 'God! We've blown a fuse.' The rest of the play takes place in full light while the characters flounder around in the dark. Peter told me he had had the inspiration watching the Peking Opera, which uses this same convention.

At a preview, on tour at the Yvonne Arnaud Theatre in Guildford, I was watching from the back of the auditorium. We had ensured that we had a total blackout for the necessary first few minutes. We had even covered over the little red bulbs on the lanterns and been given permission to conceal the green exit-signs briefly.

Within moments, I heard someone shuffling quickly up the aisle towards me. A woman in deep distress bumped into me. 'I can't bear it,' she gasped, 'I can't bear the darkness. Where is the door?' I tried to calm her by pointing to the lamps in the lighting box behind me. She continued to grip my hand tightly. As soon as the stage lights came back up she returned, still flustered, to her seat.

Now if that level of sensory deprivation can have that effect in a sixties 'light' comedy, I thought, how might it work for *Macbeth*.

We had the good fortune to be doing the play in the Swan. The first scene presents the same challenge I described in a previous chapter with the stage direction '*Exit, pursued by bear*'. Only this time it is '*Enter three witches*'.

So, we had a simple solution. Suddenly strike the light and plunge the audience into the dark. And make sure it's really dark. No ambient light. And as the scene lasts barely more than half a minute, we were even allowed to have the front of house team briefly hold cards over the exit-signs. So there really was no light at all. The sound effect of some huge industrial switch being thrown – CLUNK.

The audience let out a yelp of shock. And when the nervous laughter and whispers subsided you heard Noma Dumezweni as the first witch begin:

When shall we three meet again
In thunder lightning or in rain?

As the audience's eyes attempted to adjust to the dark, they focused their ears on the voices in front of them. They assumed they were coming from the mouths of three actresses standing on the stage just yards away. In fact, immediately after the blackout happened, in cahoots with the sound designer, John Leonard, we had flown in three tiny speakers, which relayed the witches' words. The actresses themselves were backstage in front of a microphone.

As the incantatory scene reached its conclusion and the weird sisters chanted

Fair is foul, and foul is fair:
Hover through the fog and filthy air

we pulled the tiny speakers out over the audience's heads. The audience had invested in the sound as the genuine voices of live actors standing in front of them, so they believed that somehow these women must now be actually hovering over their heads. The spooky effect produced squeals and gasps and even screams on the first preview we tried it.

But the knock-on effect on the next scene was more worrying. King Duncan's encounter with the bleeding sergeant was held up as the audience simply could not settle down. So reluctantly we cut the effect, and merely did the scene in darkness instead.

One of the principles of stage magic is to cheat the expectation of the audience: to make them confidently believe one thing, only to pull the carpet from under their feet.

The play may start with the witches, but ideas about the production should not. Any decisions about how to stage the play can get hijacked by working out how to do the witches first. They are parasites, they don't exist without the host animal they depend upon. They are the product of that society. Discover what the society is, what obsesses and motors it, and you may understand what has produced them. It's not a society terrorized by the witches. It's a society that has produced the witches and made them scapegoats.

The greatest witch persecutions have happened at times of civil crisis, during the English Civil War for example. At such times we require these targets to give vent to our national fears. The weird sisters became for us a product of the fear already existing in society. The strangeness of the witches kept the play ticking with a terrible undertow of fear.

We looked at them from their point of view. In rehearsal we never called them witches. Other people did, but they referred to themselves as the weird sisters. We took their own personal agendas very seriously, so that they were real people, with real appetites.

I rehearsed them separately from the rest of the cast, so that whenever their scenes were scheduled, I would work with the weird sisters beforehand and we would decide how they would play the scene but wouldn't tell the other actors.

We explored different aspects of them: their vindictiveness; or perhaps their heightened sexuality; or we would try investigating the idea that they were high on drugs. But the other actors would never know what route the weird sisters had taken; to them, the weirdness of the way they performed was all that was apparent. That meant that they remained this outside group.

We came to the conclusion that the weird sisters couldn't speak uninvited. They needed Macbeth to ask them a question. Then when he addressed them, they could reveal their understanding of the future to him. He would not only be made Thane of Glamis and Cawdor, but King hereafter. The problem was that Banquo then wanted to know his fate, too. So they had to reveal that Banquo's heirs would be kings, which messes up their plan.

The weird sisters would make one or two extra appearances in our production. At the murder of Banquo, as he and Fleance are attacked while out riding, the sisters were silently watching. At the end of the play, remembering that the weird sisters have told Banquo that his offspring will become king, we had Fleance appear silently, as Malcolm is declared king. He is clearly thinking 'My time will come'.

The cycle of violence and retribution will be endless.

Tony Sher was playing Macbeth, and we were lucky to secure Harriet Walter to play Lady Macbeth. It was an immense privilege to watch them both rehearse. They had an immediate chemistry and spent many hours discussing the nature of their co-dependent relationship.

Lady Macbeth has clearly had a child.

> I have given suck, and know
> How tender 'tis to love the babe that milks me.

Tony and Harriet decided that, rather than being the child of a previous relationship, this was a child that the Macbeths have had together, and who had died.[1] The couple had each suppressed the loss; the child had become a taboo subject, never discussed. Thus, at the vital moment when Macbeth decides that he can no longer go ahead with their proposed plan to murder the king, she brings up the subject of their child, and demonstrates her resolve with one of the most violent images of the play:

> I would, while it was smiling in my face
> Have plucked my nipple from his boneless gums,
> And dashed the brains out had I so soon as you
> Have done to this.

In our production, the shock slapped Macbeth, and aroused them both into a passionate sexual embrace.

We wove this child-haunting thread back through the production. When Lady Macbeth welcomed King Duncan to Inverness, Macduff was there in the party, with his

---

[1] Later, after Macbeth has slain his entire family, Macduff cries 'he has no children'.

young family. As Lady Macduff, this pregnant woman with all her pretty children, passed Lady Macbeth, Harriet gave her a very wan smile. Children were something this woman had desperately wanted, but now, perhaps because of her dead child, she was unable to have.

One evening, in the small kitchen in the corner of the rehearsal room in St Anne's, Venn Street, we rehearsed the Macbeths' dagger scene. In preparing for the rehearsal, the stage management had applied extra blackout on the windows, sourced some very sharp knives for the daggers, and, courtesy of the local butcher, four pints of pig's blood. The actors wore old clothes, and I sat out of the way on a Formica worktop. Then, having set out some very particular ground rules beforehand, Tony went outside, plunged his hands in the bucket of blood, and Harriet began the scene:

That which hath made them drunk hath made me bold . . .

It was of course electric, at any rate from my position perched up on the counter: the heightened sense of any sound in the darkness, the acrid metallic smell of real blood, the danger of the sharp knives slipping, the tense whispered urgency. The scene is written in such a modern idiom, it's like a film script, capturing the natural, almost overlapping, dialogue.

The dagger scene resolves in the sound of knocking, which gets louder and louder. Who or what is about to arrive? Unexpectedly, at this moment of hyper-tension, Shakespeare introduces a risky device, a comic turn. The Porter.

Stephen Noonan played the Porter in our production. He crashed out of a trap on the stage, an inebriated, unpredictable creature, both intimidating and hilarious.

It is notoriously difficult to make his speech funny today, because the jokes, about Henry Garnet and Jesuits, the Gunpowder Plot and equivocation, which would have been very topical then, don't make much sense now. We tried to translate the topical allusions and the weird freshness of the wit whilst using as much of the text as possible. Steve happened to be a very clever stand-up comic, so I allowed him a bit of leeway.[2]

Steve did use the Hell Porter's text, but he would talk directly to the audience. When it came to the line 'What are you?' occasionally people replied, saying 'I'm a lawyer', for example, which gave Steve licence to say, 'Well, you're going straight to hell.' It caught the mood of the scene precisely.

One night, when he directed the line 'What are you?' to a lady on the front row, she replied, 'Is this in the play?' and Steve said, 'Well, *I'm* in the play.' A moment worthy of Pirandello.

Once the Porter has finished his riff, and we return to the plot, Macduff and Lennox are admitted to the castle. But an almost feverish tone of hysteria persists. Lennox describes at length the freakish weather they have come through, with toppled chimneys, ominous screeches in the air, persistent owl cries and earth tremors; Macbeth replies with laconic bathos, ' 'Twas a rough night'.

---

[2] Our playing time was 1 hour 58 minutes, but it could stretch to 2 hours 7 minutes depending on how long the Porter went on. 'And let those that play your clowns speak no more than is set down for them.'

As the murder is uncovered, the guests all emerge from their rooms. So much for Lady Macbeth's suggested plan that she and her husband make their 'griefs and clamour roar' upon the discovery of Duncan's death. All she manages to say when she hears Macduff tell of the murder, is 'What, in our house?' like a society hostess, affronted at the inconvenience.

Then Macbeth compounds the confusion by admitting he has killed the drunken grooms, who are the chief suspects. It's an odd and potentially catastrophic decision, which throws suspicion on him immediately. There follows a much-discussed, pivotal moment in the play. Does Lady Macbeth faint? I believe she does. I don't think it's a ploy to distract attention from her floundering husband. And if it is a deliberate decoy, it doesn't work. It doesn't rescue him from his mistake, as suspicion is still clearly focused towards him.

The horror of what they have just done suddenly hits her. Perhaps the enormity of the crime as it is described brings back the image of her dead father.[3] She isn't able to deal with the tension, with the accumulated pressure. Momentarily, she shuts down and passes out. It is a crucial pivot. From that point Macbeth ceases to trust her or confide in her.

Macbeth imagines everything. Vividly. Lady Macbeth will not allow herself to. She will pay for that later. Lady Macbeth's capacity to compartmentalize and shut away in her brain things that are inconvenient, or that might distract her from the single aim of advancing her husband's ambition, is her downfall. She thinks she can just pack it away ('What's done is done'). She can't. And it will lead to her sleepwalking and, ultimately, to her suicide.

Lady Macbeth is certainly not a 'fiend like queen'. She is driven to do something that she doesn't allow herself to think through; she has a kind of emotional myopia. Whereas Macbeth thinks rather a lot (analysing all the deep spiritual consequences), she suppresses her imagination. Lady Macbeth has only one very short soliloquy in the entire play, two spare rhyming couplets, when she realizes that she has become queen at the cost of having blood on her hands:

> Nought's had, all's spent,
> Where our desire is got without content:
> 'Tis safer to be that which we destroy
> Than by destruction dwell in doubtful joy.
>
> Act Three Scene Two

She realizes that her husband no longer has any real use for her.

Nevertheless, her loyalty towards him, and her initiative, are sorely tested in the banquet scene. She has to improvise wildly as her husband apparently experiences a mental breakdown, both seeing the ghost of Banquo, and unintentionally revealing his own part in the murder – a plot Macbeth has kept from his wife.

---

[3] 'Had he not resembled my father as he slept, I had done it.'

At the end of the scene Lady Macbeth apprehends that Macbeth has left her, he has moved on, and is going to continue to secure himself as king and eliminate his enemies. She no longer has any knowledge of his plans.

In our production, as Macbeth stalks away, Lady Macbeth suddenly realizes she has been left alone. She picks up one of the candles from the table to light her way to bed. As she exits, she pauses briefly as if having heard something. As she left the stage, all the candles suddenly snuff out by themselves, leaving only trails of thin smoke.

And then a chair falls over.

Suddenly, a match is lit under the table. Crouched in silhouette against the tablecloth, frantically jabbering spells, and ripping or shredding with their fingers, the weird sisters appear. (They had in fact pulled the wicks through the candles from underneath the table, making them seem to self-extinguish.)

As Macbeth re-enters, demanding answers, the witches suddenly throw the tables over, sending the crockery crashing to the floor. The weird sisters ask Macbeth if he'd rather hear their replies from them or from their masters.

The apparitions are some of the hardest moments of this play to realize. But with designer Stephen Brimson Lewis, we had prepared for this from the very start of the play. As the audience came in to the familiar brick surrounds of the Swan Theatre, they perhaps did not realize that the back wall of the stage had been brought forward by a number of feet. A fake brick wall, painted to look as old as the Victorian brick walls of the original 1879 Memorial Theatre, stood in its place. I would guarantee that most of the audience took it to be the original wall. So, when the witches hurled an unidentifiable sludgy gloop at the wall, and the wall seemed to melt, and tortured faces emerged from the solid brick, the effect was, at the very least, unsettling.

We achieved this by constructing some sections of the wall, not on canvas, but from neoprene (the same material wet suits are made from), and painted to look like brick. Then, from behind, actors pushed their faces into the neoprene and apparently through the wall itself.

* * *

Shakespeare is very good at lighting his plays. And he does it all with words. *Macbeth* is his darkest play.

If the tragedies each express some elemental force – wild storm for *Lear*, brain-boiling heat for *Othello*, nipping cold for *Hamlet* – then *Macbeth* is characterized by its lack of light. Even when a scene takes place in daylight, characters comment on how preternaturally dark it is, as Ross says to the Old Man:

> By the clock, 'tis day,
> And yet dark night strangles the travelling lamp:
> Is't night's predominance, or the day's shame,
> That darkness does the face of earth entomb,
> When living light should kiss it?

Darkness entombs, light lives and kisses. In Macbeth, 'light thickens'. It is in the darkness that our imaginations play tricks on us, filling the shadows with nightmares.

In the welcome relief of daylight, in the England scene, Malcom nevertheless suggests that he and Macduff 'seek out some desolate shade, and there weep our sad bosoms empty'.

* * *

Somebody once said that, in *Macbeth*, if anyone had time to think, the events wouldn't happen. The furious pace of the text is crucial; things happen in this terrible whirlwind.

We were able to play *Macbeth* in the Swan very fast without an interval.[4] Shakespeare didn't have intervals. The imposition of an extra twenty-minute break, though no doubt good for bladders and bar sales, frequently alters the dynamic pacing of the play. There is often a change of pace or tone in Act Four, which acts as a mental break, or shift, and allows the leading actor a short break before the stamina required for the final act. The actor playing Macbeth has the England scene 'off' to prepare for the fight with Macduff.

In the England scene, Shakespeare debates what it is that we require our rulers to be.

In Scotland in Macbeth's time, kings did not succeed through primogeniture. Therefore, although Malcolm becomes the Prince of Cumberland it isn't an automatic choice that Duncan would choose his son as the next king. Indeed, at that point, because Macbeth has performed in such an extraordinary fashion in routing the enemy, everybody expects that he will be rewarded and perhaps nominated as the next king. In his mind, he was robbed of the crown, which of course he then seizes through devious means.

But then we are asked to consider whether Malcolm himself is fit to be leader of the country. The trick that Malcolm plays on Macduff of pretending he is a deeply flawed character forces Macduff to decide whether a man of such low morals should indeed accept the throne. That shift of perspective is important for the audience to see a larger canvas; not just to involve themselves in how Macbeth has hacked his way to the throne, but to enquire what it is that we want our monarch, our rulers, to be. It's about good governance.

* * *

The murder of the Macduffs is a perilously difficult scene. Partly, of course, because it relies on having an exceptional child actor to be able to play the bantering conversation with his mum and to deliver the most difficult line in the play, which (along with the murderer's 'What you egg! Young fry of treachery') is, without a doubt, 'He has killed me mother.'

We domesticated the scene as much as we could. Diane Beck as Lady Macduff played her with simmering fury and no shred of sentimentality. Here she is left alone, trying to cope, looking after all her children (she has at least three of the 'pretty chickens'). We set the scene amidst her washing: laundry hanging out to dry, a clothes horse, a basket of folded sheets. And it's bath time. Her son is still in his damp towel, his hair is wet. The sound of other children splashing in a bath in the next room. She keeps

---

[4]   We cut very little (apart from Hecate and old Siward).

working, in angry conversation with Ross, and then the unknown messenger, until they've gone. Then shadows appear behind the washing lines.

As the Murderers arrive, she corrals her little boy behind her. He's kneeling in the fold of the clothes horse. She is focused on the man she can see ahead of her. She doesn't notice the one who has crept up behind the clothes horse. The boy shouts out, calling him 'a shag-haired villain'. He laughs. Both men laugh. She is alert, prepared to fight, like the wren, 'the most diminutive of birds', she says, which will fight if she has 'young ones in the nest'. Where will the first attack come from? Then her little son says quietly, 'he has killed me mother'. As he slumps forward on to her lap, we see from the stain on the white towel hanging on the clothes horse. They have stabbed her child in the back. She screams. Blackout.

Macbeth is undoubtedly a merciless 'butcher', but the experience of watching the play is that you don't feel Macbeth is just a ruthless tyrant. That's partly due to how the play's imagery supports that. He says, 'O, full of scorpions is my mind, dear wife' and 'They have tied me to a stake; I cannot fly', as if he is a bear chained to a stake and attacked by dogs. The imagery supports his own perception of his victim status. You get a sense in performance that once he has realized the sin he has committed, his struggle to carry on living makes him worthy of our pity.

Lady Macbeth, too, is haunted by her conscience. Her sleepwalking scene is a devastating portrayal of a human soul in disintegration.

By this point in the play, our fading hope for some remaining flicker of human integrity in the world resides in the character of Macduff. Nigel Cooke's rough-cut Macduff was not from the same military background as Macbeth and Banquo. When he comes to prosecute his revenge on the 'hell-hound' who murdered his family, instead of fighting with standard military weaponry, he will use whatever he can find on the field of battle. Macbeth is way out of Macduff's league.

The first we hear of Macbeth is that he has unseam'd the merciless Macdonwald 'from the knave to the chaps'. Macbeth believes he leads a charmed life, relying on the witches' riddling prophecy, 'No man of woman born shall harm Macbeth.' He has already despatched young Siward with one deft, ruthless cut, callously joking as the young man dies, 'Thou wast born of woman.'

But when Macduff reveals that he was:

>   from his mother's womb
> Untimely ripp'd.

Macbeth first refuses to fight, and then defies the weird sisters' paltering riddles and throws himself into this final battle.

>   Lay on Macduff
> And damned be him who first cries 'Hold enough!'

One day, I popped in at the end of a fight rehearsal for this scene. Nigel and Tony had been exploring this climactic battle with fight director Terry King. Tony's invention had created a moment of breathtaking inspiration.

At the end of the fight, Macbeth suddenly freezes. Macduff watches as he claws at something above him but just out of reach. It is, of course, the air-drawn dagger, and while it distracts Macbeth, Macduff seizes his opportunity and deals the tyrant's death blow.

I could almost hear a screeching slice of sound in the air. The moment was a revelation. Tony had questioned me about the meaning of the elusive dagger, when we were rehearsing Act Two. Was it a warning? Or a provocation? Was he just hallucinating because he was drunk, or pumping with adrenaline? Now it seems clear: as if the beguiling, enigmatic appearance of the dagger, before the murder of Duncan, had led inevitably to this point. The 'dagger of the mind' as Macbeth had called it, pointed towards his own destruction.

The day after the press night, I was called up to Adrian Noble's office. He was holding the papers with the reviews in.

'These are what we want!' he said. 'Fantastic! Congratulations!'

The reviews were, indeed, universally excellent, and they secured the production's future. We toured to Japan, and were invited to the International Festival of Arts and Ideas in New Haven, Connecticut, where we got a stark reminder about just how precarious it can be to rely on reviews.

We happened to open at the same time as Frasier (Kelsey Grammer) was playing Macbeth an hour and a half up the road, in New York. That production had evoked lots of references to the curse of the Scottish play and was closing at the Music Box Theatre after just ten days. Ben Brantley, the influential critic of *The New York Times*, alongside pretty much every other critic, had given that production the thumbs down. Now he had booked his ticket to see us.

I wasn't in New Haven. I was 6,000 miles away, in York, directing the Mystery Plays.

In the middle of the night, I was awoken to receive an international phone call. It was Tony. He was hoarse, and distraught.

'I think I have just destroyed my career,' he croaked.

'What's happened?'

Before the show, Tony had realized that his voice was going. The heatwave, combined with the ravages of brutal American air-conditioning, had strained his vocal cords. He had struggled on until the company manager insisted that he was going to do permanent damage if he continued with the show and pulled him off. His understudy completed the show. But Ben Brantley had left as soon as the announcement was made.

Tony was inconsolable.

Astonishingly, two days later, when Tony was back on, Brantley returned to see the show. And he gave us the best review we had received so far.

After New Haven we returned to London and a sell-out run at the Young Vic, in the last week of which Chris Smith, the then Culture Secretary, suggested that the production should be filmed by Channel Four and managed to persuade its then Chief Executive, Michael Jackson, to schedule it. John Wyver's company Illuminations were invited to film it.[5]

---

[5]   If you want to see a list of Shakespeare productions that have been filmed and are available on DVD or online, turn to Appendix B.

I had never directed a film before, though we had recorded *Titus Andronicus* with the South African Broadcasting Corporation (SABC) in 1995. This was different. This was re-conceiving an existing production for a different medium, and we had less time and less money than Orson Welles had to film his *Macbeth* in 1948.

Our location was the Roundhouse in North London. We would choose a site around the old railway engine shed to play the different scenes each day. Our director of photography was Ernie Vincze, who filmed pretty much the entire piece on a single heavy Digibeta camera on his shoulder, with the help of his son. It gave the film the gritty urgency of a war correspondent filming in a war zone.

The Roundhouse was constructed in 1846, as a turntable for locomotives. In order to support this considerable weight, the floor was underpinned by an undercroft constructed like a bicycle wheel with spokes made up of brick walls radiating from a central circular hub. This created strange long spaces between the spokes which tapered in giddy perspective in a sort of surreal Escher-like way.

And so, we ended up on the last morning of filming in the undercroft, filming Harriet Walter performing the 'Unsex me here' speech in a bath of rapidly chilling water. In a break, as I apologetically poured in a kettle of hot water, she said, her teeth chattering a little:

'Do you realize, today is exactly a year since we started rehearsals?'

I hadn't spotted the coincidence.

'You know, if at the start you had asked me to play Lady Macbeth for a whole year,' she went on, shivering more openly now, 'I would have had to say no. But the journey has been so organic somehow, growing from the Swan to the international tour, to the Young Vic, and now to this, and I wouldn't have missed a minute of it. What are we doing next?'

*   *   *

20 March 2018.

I dashed up to Stratford this evening from *King Lear* rehearsals for the press night of Polly Findlay's production of *Macbeth* with Chris Eccleston and Niamh Cusack. Arrived at about five to seven, and Jane (my trusty PA) was waiting for me with my ticket, and a sandwich. I nipped upstairs to the RST gallery to take my usual place in A39.

The first half seemed to go well.

As the lights came up for the interval, Michael, the Front of House Manager, appeared at my side, and whispered in my ear. He apologized for disturbing me but said they had had a phone call and the house alarm at our home, O'Cahans, was ringing.

Stage door rushed me a 007 taxi and we sped up Welcombe Road in the dark. As I approached the house everything seemed pretty normal, except for the alarm clanging away. I unlocked the front door and unarmed the system. In the sudden quiet, the house seemed to hold its breath. I listened.

The alarm panel registered that there had been an intruder in three different zones. I turned on the lights and went into the front room. No smashed windows, no forced door. The same in the studio. Then I heard a noise. Upstairs. It sounded exactly like someone was flapping open a black plastic rubbish bag, presumably to stash the contents of our sock drawer. I called out, but I don't remember what I said.

The sound stopped.

I started to climb the stairs, keeping my eyes on the bedroom door. As I reached the landing, a huge coal-black crow exploded from the room, flew across the landing in front of me and disappeared into the dark of the spare bedroom. Swallowing hard, I followed it in and shut the door. I turned on the light. The panicked crow flailed about, trying to perch on top of the wardrobe door. Finally, it landed on the patchwork quilt and pinned me with the jet-black bead of its eye. For a moment I remember thinking how beautiful it was, glossy and satin sleek. I reached for the velux roof window, tugged it open, and the crow made wing to the rooky wood.

I closed the window.

Downstairs, as I reset the alarm, in order to head back for the second half, I realized that the panel recorded the time of the intruder's arrival: 7:00pm, exactly the time the play had been due to start.

During the second half, my wild encounter kept haunting my thoughts, intrigued and bewildered by the coincidence of this play and that bird, by the almost shocking brevity of the event, and the inevitable desire to attribute meaning to it. One thing I determined: I would make it an anecdote, not an omen.

The following morning Bill, one of the porters, popped round to check on any possible damage and to see if we could cap the chimney to prevent any further drop-ins. He pointed to the chess board. 'Did you knock all the pieces down, Greg?' All the white pieces were strewn across the board. All the black were still in place. Except for the black king. The crow must have picked him up in his beak, and he now sat alone in the middle of the board.

8

As You Like It

– 2000: Royal Shakespeare Theatre, Stratford-upon-Avon; The Pit, London.

O wonderful, wonderful, most wonderful wonderful, and yet again wonderful,
and after that, out of all whooping!

As You Like It (Act Three Scene Two)

The approach of the millennium made every institution up and down the country – and, indeed, across the world – consider how to mark it. The city of York had decided to combine their two greatest assets in one great jubilation by presenting the York Mystery Plays in the Minster for the first time in seven centuries. City and cathedral would present their civic and spiritual pride in these mediaeval masterpieces.

I was asked to direct.

'It's the three Ms: Millennium, Minster, Mysteries,' the ebullient Dean Ray Furnell enthused when I visited York to discuss the idea in the autumn of 1997. This Middle English cycle of plays had been performed annually in York on pageant carts around the city since at least the mid-fourteenth century. The traditions started up again when they were revived in the ruins of St Mary's Abbey, for the Festival of Britain in 1951 (with a young local girl called Judi Dench as 'the forgetful angel').

I felt an instant connection. Corpus Christi (the day on which the cycle was performed in mediaeval times) was a holy day of obligation. At the Preston Catholic College I attended it was the occasion for an annual school trip to York, to walk around the walls and visit the Minster. The idea of returning to York and making this my Millennium project felt, somehow, spiritually just right.

I accepted the offer to direct what became called The Millennium Mysteries.

Back at Stratford, it took a little longer to decide what the company's response to the turning of the millennia would be. Adrian Noble finally proposed that all the Associate Directors should plunge in and mount the two history tetralogies, through-cast but with different theatres and different approaches. It came to be called *This England*. Stephen Pimlott would direct Sam West as Richard II in TOP (The Other Place), Mike Attenborough would do both parts of *Henry IV* with Des Barrit as Falstaff in the Swan. I was slated to direct *Henry V* in the RST (Royal Shakespeare Theatre). Then, with a bit of help from an American University, Michael Boyd would do the *Henry VI* trilogy and *Richard III*, back in the Swan. A great idea.

But I told Adrian that I couldn't do it. I knew that this event would dominate the RSC's focus and suspected I would regret not being part of it, but nevertheless I was already committed, and I could not pass up the once-in-a-lifetime opportunity. Ed Hall was asked to direct *Henry V*, which he did with roaring gusto, with Will Houston mercurial as the young king.

But what would I do that season? During *The Winter's Tale* I had suggested to Alex Gilbreath that she should play Rosalind one day. I know of few actresses who can match the illuminating joy she brings on stage with her. It is radiant and irresistible. So, I proposed directing *As You Like It* in 2000. 'Deal,' said Adrian, 'we'll open the season with it in the RST.'

As You Like It was the first Shakespeare production I had ever seen at Stratford-upon-Avon. I still have a Letts schoolboy diary for 1973. On 11 August it says rather laconically 'Went to Stratford, saw As You Like It. Wonderful. Set made of bars'. We had a French student called Vincent Durlach staying with us at the time, and my mum clearly thought we had better show him some proper British culture. So, she packed us into her beige Mini, and we set off down the M6 from Preston for the matinee.

As the show ended, Eileen Atkins as Rosalind danced with her Orlando (actually the understudy Orlando according to the programme – his name was David Suchet). I wanted to jump up and dance with them. I apparently turned to my mum as we headed back up to Lancashire and said, 'that's what I want to do when I grow up'.

I still have the poster for that production on the wall of my study. It shows Eileen Atkins from behind, in her jeans and stetson, with a quotation from Martin Luther in 1531:

Men have broad shoulders and narrow hips, and accordingly they possess intelligence.
Women have narrow shoulders and broad hips. Women ought to stay at home; the way they were created indicates this, for they have broad hips and a wide fundament to sit upon, keep house and bear and raise children ...

The production was directed by Buzz Goodbody, the first woman to direct a main house show for the RSC.[1] Her rigorously feminist approach was probably not apparent to my 14-year-old self. But the bar set I refer to in my diary certainly seemed radical and ingenious. Designed by Christopher Morley it was a series of hanging metal poles, which were set in rigid formality for the court and in a canopy for the forest, all at different heights, and lit in dappled gobos.

Sitting down to read the play, I knew that the experience of watching it, certainly in the second half, has to be like sitting in deckchairs on a sunny afternoon, watching these engaging young people play endless variations on the game of love. It is motored by love, and you need to be at least a little in love with all of them.

I began to wonder just what the Forest of Arden was meant to represent. What was this apparently most English of landscapes with sycamores, fallow deer and shepherds'

---

[1] A number of women had directed at Stratford before, including Dorothy Green and Irene Hentschel, but Buzz was the first in the dozen years since the formation of the RSC.

cots? And why was it also apparently so effortlessly inhabited with predatory lionesses and boa constrictors?

During my time as a student in Bristol I became friends with an extraordinary woman who influenced the way I looked at the world. Her name was Dawn Pavitt, and she was a quilter. She had worked in the costume department in Stratford in the late fifties and used to tell me about the work of the legendary designer Lila di Nobili. Dawn's passion for needlework was infectious. She introduced me to many of the social and historical aspects of her craft, and how important it was in the history of women. How the needle, like the pen, could be mightier than the sword. We would take trips to Bath, where she invited me to look closely at heirloom quilts in the American Museum, Victorian patchwork and seventeenth-century stump work.

Among the embossed embroidery in colourful silk and metal threads, among the very English flowers, and birds, snails and butterflies that populated the margins of caskets and samplers, were leopards and lionesses. So, the imaginations of the women sewing these craft works were not confined to the literal. In this respect, they resembled the imaginative landscapes of Shakespeare's forest in *As You Like It*. Perhaps the Forest of Arden should be how Rosalind imagined it.

I pursued the idea, inviting the Californian textile artist Kaffe Fassett to design the production. Kaffe was by then a superstar in the world of textiles, the Mick Jagger of knitting, with sumptuous best-selling books of his gorgeous sense of colour applied to needlepoint. When we met at his home in West Hampstead, I described an image in my mind of Rosalind in a monochrome court, sublimating her rage into her needlepoint, rebelliously stitching a technicolour tapestry, which would then translate into her own forest in Arden.

Kaffe said yes immediately and, assisted by designer Niki Turner, produced a beautiful design: black and white for the austere court bursting into kaleidoscopic colour when the winter thawed and the spring arrived in the forest. Kaffe would sit in rehearsal happily embroidering cushions in long stitch. These enormous scatter cushions were mossy velvet green on one side, and when flipped over flashed with brightly embroidered flowers.

He knitted a great baggy coat for Adrian Schiller's deadpan Touchstone in a dazzling motley of rainbow colours. He knitted a beautiful jumper for Rosalind and sewed a floral patchwork skirt for Phoebe. The wardrobe team loved Kaffe's boundless energy and enthusiasm, and the opportunity to work with such an exuberant palette, and they were all, I think, immensely proud of the work they had produced.

At the tech, I noticed the entire team, assembled at the back of the stalls. When Hymen descended at the end and Rosalind returned in a cloud of tulle painted with lilies and roses, the wardrobe team burst into a round of applause. I don't think the RST stage had ever enjoyed such a riot of colour.

At the first preview, audiences seemed to enjoy the production, in particular Alex Gilbreath's heart-bursting Rosalind, tempered by Nancy Carroll's Celia, surprised by love; and the delirious score by jazz composer Django Bates.

But then we opened. My *As You Like It* was definitely not how they liked it. And the critics gave the production a resounding thumbs down. Although Alex's Rosalind received great plaudits, with Michael Coveney in the *Daily Mail* saying she came as close to Vanessa Redgrave's near definitive 1961 performance as any he had ever seen.

But I had to think again.

Shortly afterwards, Michael Billington interviewed me about what had been quite a lucky streak, a run of successful productions at Stratford: *The Winter's Tale*, *Oroonoko*, *Timon of Athens*, and particularly *Macbeth*, which had garnered the best reviews of my career.

'So, what happened with *As You Like It*?' he said.

What did happen? I had cast it well. Superbly, in Alex's case. The production was sumptuous, perhaps too self-consciously so, and despite my own reasoning, a needlework-inspired design just baffled some.

When the season transferred to London, I asked Adrian Noble if, instead of playing on the main stage of the Barbican, we could downscale into The Pit. We would retain the costumes but perform in a simple white box. I felt that perhaps the truthful performances by the cast had somehow been disguised by the exuberance of the design, that the critics had been distracted by the sheer beauty of the production and had distrusted that aesthetic.

I am making excuses, of course, though the reviews of the production in The Pit were, thankfully, much improved.

The Celia in Buzz Goodbody's 1973 production was Maureen Lipman. When I, as a young actor, worked with her years later and shyly confessed what a seminal experience that show had been for me, she groaned and told me how unhappy it had been for her. The cast and director did not see eye to eye. The critics had panned the show. Later still, Eileen Atkins herself confirmed that impression. She called it 'a disastrous modern production', and said that when Peggy Ashcroft came to see it she had told Eileen, 'My dear, you can't be expected to play Rosalind without a tree, and a hat.'

But none of that was remotely apparent to my young self, dizzy with the spell the production cast: I didn't know about reviews or critics. I just saw *As You Like It* and was inspired.

Within two years of that production, Buzz had committed suicide. Every press night I do in Stratford, I visit the cherry tree planted for her in the theatre gardens. It's usually in that tense half hour when the cast are all busy preparing backstage, and the director is the last person they want to see in case s/he gives them yet more notes. It's a little ritual, and a moment of silent thanks for what she gave me.

*   *   *

That summer I did direct the York Mystery Plays.

They were adapted by playwright, Mike Poulton, the first of many happy collaborations together. There was original music by the Minster Chamberlain, Richard Shephard, a cast of 250 local amateurs, and Ray Stevenson as 'the actor who plays Christ', as tradition had it. Joseph O'Connor, who was playing King Duncan in our *Macbeth*, at the age of 90, had played Christ in the 1951 Festival of Britain production of the Mystery Plays. He told me that the presentation of God on the stage at that time was still prohibited by the Lord Chamberlain, so he was credited in the programme as 'the actor who plays Christ'.

King Richard II saw the Mystery Plays in York in 1398 and they survived until the late sixteenth century. Shakespeare might have seen the Mystery Plays at Coventry as they were performed there until 1579, when he turned fifteen. Perhaps his memory of the actor playing Herod (and wildly over-acting – 'out-heroding Herod') stayed with Shakespeare when he came to write *Hamlet*.

Reading the plays for the first time, I was immediately struck by what I mistakenly thought Shakespeare himself had invented: the shared line. When Eve meets Satan in the garden of Eden, in play three (The Coopers' and the Armourers' Play), after very long speeches by God, by Adam and by Satan himself, suddenly come the lines:

SATAN   In a worm's likeness will I wend.
       Eve, Eve . . .
EVE   Who's there?
SATAN   I, a friend.

It's a jolt, something snaps and cracks, given even greater impact by the fact that it's a rhyme, as if the serpent has already caught Eve in his coils. It must surely qualify as the first shared line in English dramatic literature.

The Millennium Mystery Plays were staged on a massive scale, all effortlessly managed by Steve Rebbeck, whom we later appointed as Technical Director of the RSC. A huge bank of seats ran from just below the west window descending down the nave, to meet the stage which in turn climbed in a series of steps and platforms to just beneath the top of the rood screen, so that when Christ was crucified, his cross was erected in the same position as the Rood (as pre-reformation crucifixes were known[2]) would once have stood.

When the flood waters rose around Noah's Ark (in the Shipwrights' and the Fishers' and Mariners' Plays) two huge pieces of watery silk were pulled down from the top and up from the bottom of the steps, enveloping the ark and its freighted cargo of animals in an ocean of billowing blue.

Designer Rob Jones and I were initially stumped as to how to achieve the rainbow, until I realized staring down the nave, one morning, that behind the rood screen, the choir consisted of seven great arches, receding towards the great east window. If, I thought, we up-lit them in red, orange, yellow, green, blue, indigo and violet, we could create a gothic rainbow to fill the cathedral. Lighting designer Michael Gunning pulled off what was perhaps the production's greatest coup and a magnificent realization of God's covenant.

Thus God of mickle might
Sets His sign full clear
High in the air –
The rainbow, there –
In all men's sight.

---

[2]   In Shakespeare, characters often swear 'by the rood'.

The whole production was a joy, made more so by the involvement of the 250 or so local amateur actors, pretty much all of them Yorkshire folk. Everybody who auditioned of course got in, including those who had just come along to support their partners. One elderly gentleman demurred, 'Oh, no I'm not an actor, she's the actor,' pointing to his wife, 'but I suppose I could shout "Crucify him Crucify him", if push came to shove.'

The plays were one of the great experiences of my life and career.

9

King John

– 2001: Swan Theatre, Stratford-upon-Avon;
Newcastle Playhouse, Newcastle-upon-Tyne; The Pit, London.

On the front of the Swan Theatre in Stratford there are three terracotta bas-reliefs depicting Shakespeare's Histories, Comedies and Tragedies. The plaques were designed by the German sculptor Paul Kummer. The theatre's architect W.F. Unsworth paid for the History plaque, and the American actress Mary Anderson paid for the other two, earning the right for herself to be represented as Rosalind, which she played as a benefit to raise funds for the new theatre. Mary Anderson was perhaps the first actress to play both the roles of Hermione and Perdita in *The Winter's Tale*, a double repeated by Judi Dench in 1969.

Not unsurprisingly, Tragedy, on the right, is represented by *Hamlet*. The graveyard scene. Hamlet contemplating Yorick's skull. Comedy, on the left, shows a scene from *As You Like It*. Ganymede flirting with Orlando, who leans languidly against a tree with 'Rosalind' carved into its bark.

The plaque in the middle is more of a puzzle. It's a sinister scene. In the centre is a young boy on his knees. He is appealing desperately to a man who looks sternly away, one fist raised. His other hand reaches out for a poker protruding from a smoking brazier, held out by a soldier who has just entered from behind the arras. Another soldier, with chains slung over his shoulder, holds back the curtain. A pair of manacles hangs on the wall behind them.

You might have expected that History would have been represented by a young soldier king rallying his troops, or a man with advanced scoliosis wooing a woman over a coffin. But this is a scene from *King John*. It shows poor young Prince Arthur begging Hubert for mercy as the soldiers present the red-hot pokers intended to burn out the child's eyes: a mix of sentimental pathos and melodramatic cruelty that must have directly appealed to a Victorian audience. Certainly, the choice of this scene and this play suggests that when the plaques went up, in 1885, within six years of the theatre being built, it was regarded as an extremely popular play.

And indeed, it was. So much so that the spectacular production by Herbert Beerbohm Tree at Her Majesty's Theatre in 1899 warranted a trailer showing three silent scenes from the play. Tree himself plays King John. It is regarded as the first Shakespeare film.

The play fell out of favour in the twentieth century. When George Orwell saw it during the Second World War, he described it as 'a play which isn't acted very often' but acknowledged in a talk he gave to the BBC Overseas Service in 1942, that seeing the play performed made him change his mind about it.

'When I had read it as a boy it seemed to me archaic, something dug out of a history book and not having anything to do with our own time. Well, when I saw it acted, what with its intrigues and double-crossings, non-aggression pacts, quislings, people changing sides in the middle of a battle, and what-not, it seemed to me extraordinarily up to date.'

The play increased in popularity at Stratford in this century,[1] though when I came to direct it in 2001, there had still only been four productions in the forty-year history of the RSC. But our experience of working on it had much the same effect on us as seeing the play performed had for Orwell.

Buzz Goodbody's 1970 production for Theatregoround was heavily cut, playing mostly in schools and community centres. In 1974, John Barton's production included some of his own writing and sections of John Bale's 1538 play *King Johan* (a thoroughly Protestant piece of propaganda) and an Elizabethan history play called *The Troublesome Reign of King John*. Michael Billington described it in *The Guardian* as 'one of the best new plays we've seen this year'. Only Deborah Warner, at TOP in 1988, used an uncut text.

I was glad that the play didn't have such a significant past-production history; it meant that I could see it afresh. With *All is True* (*Henry VIII*) I had gone into rehearsals weighed down with research material and historical references. With *King John* I just went in with the script.

I was no more interested in the historical King John than I was in A.A. Milne's version of the bad king with this big, red India-rubber ball.[2] I was barely interested in the significance of the character in the period in which Shakespeare was writing. We needed to take the play on its own terms, with its corrosively ironic view of power politics, and see how it spoke to us now. I have to say that we understood it in a completely different way by the time we came to perform it than we had done at the beginning of rehearsals.

By casting Guy Henry as King John, I knew I had an exceptional comic talent who could spin in a moment from deep insecurity and vulnerability to camp petulance and vicious self-regard. His versatility, witnessed by his creepy Mosca in *Volpone*, and morally certain Octavius in *Antony and Cleopatra* in the previous season, would allow us to explore contradictory aspects of this fragile king.

During those rehearsals, at the start of 2001, the political wrangling of the first three acts of *King John* seemed to speak directly to the moment. The country was preparing

---

[1]   There have been three Swan productions since my own, all directed by women: Josie Rourke's with Richard McCabe as John in 2006; Maria Aberg's with Alex Waldmann as John, which cast Pippa Nixon as the Bastard in 2012; and Eleanor Rhode's with Rosie Sheehey as John, in 2018.

[2]   'King John was not a good man
      –He had his little ways.
      And sometimes no one spoke to him
      For days and days and days.'

for a general election for which it had increasingly little appetite.[3] Not-so-New Labour were having problems shrugging off a reputation as a cynical spin-obsessed party. Spin may have helped Tony Blair win his first landslide victory in 1997, but as his press secretary and spinmeister Alastair Campbell later acknowledged, that spin had contributed to a growing distrust in our political system. And when, during the first week of rehearsals, the first Sultan of spin, Peter Mandelson, resigned for a second time it was no wonder that parallels were drawn between the so-called 'Prince of Darkness' himself and the slippery papal legate Cardinal Pandulph.

The character of Arthur is a reluctant pawn in a power game for the English crown. In the first scene Chatillon, the French ambassador, arrives to inform John that his late brother's son, this young Arthur, has a more secure claim to the English throne, and that his mother Constance has won the support of the French king, Philip, to prosecute that claim.

John and his redoubtable mother Queen Elinor, accompanied by the newly-ennobled Bastard (son of Richard the Lionheart), make their way to Angiers, which is being besieged by the French king, who is threatening to attack the city unless they support young Arthur's claim. John then demands that the citizens of Angiers declare who they think has the more rightful claim. The wily citizens suggest that once the kings have sorted it out among themselves, they will support whoever is chosen. Poor little Arthur wails:

I would that I were low laid in my grave
I am not worth this coil that's made for me.

An absurd battle then takes place to determine who is right, immediately followed by heralds from each side declaring in highfalutin terms with the most bombastic rhetoric, that their side claim victory.

The Bastard sums up the absurdity of the whole situation saying:

I was never so bethumped with words
Since I first called my brother's father dad.

He cleverly suggests that instead of quarrelling between themselves, the kings join forces and attack Angiers. This prompts some fast thinking from the citizens, who present an alternative proposal: that the French king's son, Lewis the Dauphin, should marry King John's niece the Lady Blanche of Spain. This then fortifies John's claim and gives Philip's family a direct line of succession. It also sidelines Constance (to her fury) and undermines Arthur's claim. The wedding goes ahead despite her protests.

In yet another deliciously absurd plot twist, the Vatican then intervenes and breaks up the happy new alliance by excommunicating King John for some minor disobedience. We are plunged back into battle, and it is now that Arthur is captured and falls into the hands of his uncle.

---

[3]　In fact the election was postponed until June as a result of the outbreak of Foot and Mouth disease.

The fate of Prince Arthur is sealed in what has to be the most audacious shared line in Shakespeare. King John tries to persuade his loyal servant Hubert that the life of the young prince threatens his position on the throne, and that the only solution to his problem must be drastic. Hubert must without hesitation demonstrate his loyalty to him.

KING JOHN   Death
HUBERT   My lord?
KING JOHN   A grave.
HUBERT   He shall not live.
KING JOHN   Enough.

In rehearsal we tried resisting the rigorous demands of the pentameter here. It is very hard to play the line right through, picking up the cues; much easier to yield to the naturalistic instinct to pause between each phrase, indulge in the opportunity to react and wallow in the implication of each deadly instruction. But be brave, be an iambic fundamentalist, and the effect is much more shocking. The chilling economy of the exchange, its very brevity is only enhanced by the length that King John speaks on either side of it. In a scene between the two men of fifty lines, Hubert speaks only five of them.

When Prince Arthur's mother, Constance, hears of her son's imprisonment her distraction is desperately moving. She tears her hair, lamenting the loss of her child:

Grief fills the room up of my absent child,
Lies in his bed, walks up and down with me,
Puts on his pretty looks, repeats his words,
Remembers me of all his gracious parts,
Stuffs out his vacant garments with his form;
Then, have I reason to be fond of grief?

Although Arthur is not in fact dead by this point in the play, Constance's grief is prescient. Some believe this speech reflects Shakespeare's own feelings at the death of his son, Hamnet, at the age of eleven in 1596.

The death of Prince Arthur in Act Four Scene Three is the pivot of the play. Having been spared his sight, and his life by Hubert, the young prince has managed to disguise himself as a ship-boy and escape his prison. He has clambered out onto the high walls of the tower, intending to jump down and run away. The irony that King John has changed his mind and now needs the prince alive charges the scene with added tension.

The reason I describe this scene as pivotal is that it changes not only the course of the play but its tone. At the start of rehearsal, I had emphatically decided to avoid generalizing the tone of the play. The first three acts have some very funny scenes where political agendas are ruthlessly exposed and satirized. The Bastard is the play's novice narrator. He begins to understand that the way to get ahead in this mad world is to understand what makes it tick: 'tickling commodity'. 'Commodity' could be happily and usefully paraphrased as 'expediency'. Everybody is out for themselves. Arthur is but a casualty in this war of rapidly changing allegiances. But for a moment at least his death seems to make people stop and think.

In September 2000, just before we began rehearsals, the Camp David summit failed to reach final agreement on the Israeli–Palestinian peace process. A series of violent protests broke out, known as the Second Intifada. During a gunfight in a street in the Gaza Strip, a young Palestinian boy called Muhammad al-Durrah was shot while he crouched behind his father. TV Footage of the incident was beamed around the world. The controversial episode suggested that the martyrdom of a child might finally do what the Camp David Summit had failed to do. People would be brought to their senses and somehow a way to peace might be found.

It had the power of the photograph of the naked 9-year-old girl severely burned from a Napalm attack and fleeing down an open road during the Vietnam war, or more recently, the shocking image of the drowned body of a Syrian toddler lying face down in the surf in southern Turkey. In each case, the death of the innocent provoked an international outcry. Ultimately, however, it didn't change anything: neither the Israeli–Palestinian conflict, the Vietnam War, nor the plight of immigrants and refugees attempting to reach safety.

The challenge for us was to stage the scene of Arthur's escape attempt in such a way that the audience fear for the child's life. We played the scene high above the Swan stage with the boy edging out along the ledge, the narrow handrail of the balustrade of the musicians' gallery. Suddenly one of the spindles of the railing seemed to crack, the handrail collapsed, and the boy fell backwards, crashing through the floor of the gallery, his body slamming on to the stage perhaps eighteen feet below.

In fact, of course, it was a piece of stage trickery. We had widened the handrail (which could not be seen from below) and put the boy in a harness attached behind to a safety wire, so he could not fall forwards. What seemed precarious was perfectly secure. The rest was acting, and good lighting. On cue, he fell backwards onto a thick mattress on the gallery floor, but his fall triggered a trap on the underside of the gallery to open, releasing a life-size wooden mannequin in an identical costume, which fell with a sickening thud onto the stage, in a mangled heap.

The effect on the audience was very powerful. They quickly realized that the boy had not actually fallen (as the limp puppet was scooped up by the Bastard), but not before his fall produced gasps of shock. When we transferred the play to The Pit at the Barbican (which, as it had been built in one of the old rehearsal rooms, had very little height at all), Prince Arthur had to jump off a box the height of a chair. It did not have the same effect.

The death of Prince Arthur had a really significant impact on the play, which only deepened in performance.

Our production of *King John* opened in March 2001. It was still running in Stratford in the second week of September when, unusually in RSC schedules, we had a Tuesday matinee. The show started at 1:30pm.

Sixteen minutes into the show, a plane crashed into a skyscraper in New York. It was 8:46 in the morning there. Some of the actors had joined members of the props team who were watching a small TV under the stage in the crew room. Seventeen minutes later, a second plane hit a second tower.

The company didn't know what to do, whether to stop the show or continue.

Just before the interval at 2:59pm, the south tower of the World Trade Centre imploded, like an Apollo space-rocket launch – but in horrible reverse. The Swan audience, of course, knew nothing. And as relatively few of us had mobile phones in 2001, few would learn what had happened until the end of the production. Backstage however, everyone was aware. Two minutes into the second half, the second tower fell.

Jo Stone-Fewings, playing the Bastard, was unsure how to carry on. The appalling news that people had been jumping or falling from the Twin Trade Towers coincided with the dramatization of Prince Arthur's fall. Then the Bastard had a line that precisely caught a global sense of anxiety:

Now ... vast confusion waits,
As doth a raven on a sick fallen beast.

And that's what we all feared, that vast confusion, like some terrible bird of prey, waited upon the world.

Perhaps Shakespeare is able to show the very age and body of the time, its form and pressure, because his society was living through its own 9/11: the Gunpowder Plot, when a terrorist attack nearly succeeded in smashing the whole machinery of state by blowing up the entire royal family, and all the Lords Temporal and Ecclesiastical who would have been present at the state opening of parliament, on 5/11 1605.

The world seemed to have lost its moral absolutes, to have loosed its moorings and be adrift in a sea of uncertainty. And this prevailing sense of doom, of futility, of apprehension is present in many of Shakespeare's plays. And perhaps that is why we recognize our own reflection in his work.

*   *   *

The Bastard is our caustic guide through the play. The character is made up by Shakespeare. He learns how the world works and shares his enjoyment at his discoveries with us, as he later shares his horror. He starts as an opportunist; is the cheerleader for jingoistic self-interest; gawps and reels at the stupidity of how the world runs; gets lost in the middle; and ends as the king's guardian angel, a political realist and the play's moral compass. Both he and Hubert try to operate as good men in a mad world.

In its daringly original conception, one scene between these two men genuinely surprised us in rehearsal. It's Act Five Scene Six. The English lords, who in disgust at King John's involvement in Arthur's death had defected to the Dauphin, have now returned. The Dauphin's long-awaited supply of reinforcement has been lost on Goodwin Sands. And half the power commanded by the Bastard has met a similar fate in the Lincoln Washes. It is night. Hubert has come to find the Bastard in the 'eyeless night', to tell him the king has been poisoned at Swinstead Abbey. But as the scene begins, they cannot see, cannot recognize each other, in the dark. These two men have earned our respect in the play. They have both been tempted by self-interest but have risked their own skins for the good of others. Now, stumbling around in the dark, they try to find their ethical route through a very complex political quagmire. It seems a metaphor for how lost the country itself is.

In the final scene that follows, the tormented king is brought to his relief into the open air.

'Ay marry', he says, in one of the most moving images in the play, 'now my soul has elbow-room'.

As the king dies, and his young son Henry accepts the allegiance of his lords, the Bastard speaks the last lines of the play. England, he says, has never been – nor ever shall be – conquered except when it has weakened itself with internal bickering and division.

At the Old Vic in 1917, in the midst of the Great War, they were performing *King John* despite the Zeppelin raids dropping bombs on Waterloo Station nearby. One night, although there were only eight people in the audience (according to the great actress Sibyl Thorndike), the actors carried on. As the bombs fell, Ben Greet as the Bastard spoke the lines:

Some airy devil hovers in the sky
And pours down mischief.

And at the end of the play, that closing speech

This England never did, nor never shall,
Lie at the proud foot of a conqueror

elicited such cheers from the eight-strong audience, that the words were hung over the proscenium arch for the rest of the war.

In 1940, as the Nazis threatened the invasion of Britain, and George Orwell found new meaning in the play, I am sure these lines had obvious resonance too. At the start of 2001, however, we were ambivalent about what this speech implied.

Come the three corners of the world in arms
And we shall shock them.

By the end of the year, as George W. Bush announced the War on Terror had begun, and British Troops joined our American allies, determined to hunt down Osama bin Laden and seek retribution on Al-Qaeda, we told ourselves a different story.

10

Much Ado About Nothing

– 2002: Royal Shakespeare Theatre, Stratford-upon-Avon;
Haymarket Theatre, London.

Wednesday 8 May 2002.

I am sitting in the office of the Artistic Director of the RSC. It's on the north-west corner of the building, on the second floor, looking out over the Bancroft Gardens. Peter Hall once sat in this office. His Robin Day desk and heavy black leather swivel chair are still here. He bought them in the early sixties when he took over the job and secured the company its royal title. They have been used by all three Artistic Directors since: Trevor Nunn, Terry Hands and Adrian Noble. Adrian has just vacated the chair.

My fellow associate director, Michael Boyd, and I are sitting on the sofa, waiting. Last night he opened his production of *The Tempest* in London. Tomorrow, I open my production of *Much Ado About Nothing* here in the RST. Ten days ago, *Edward III* and *Eastward Ho!* launched the Jacobethan season in the Swan.

It's been a bloody couple of weeks.

A fortnight ago Adrian opened *Chitty Chitty Bang Bang* at the London Palladium. Last week he announced his resignation as RSC Artistic Director. By his own admission, the timing isn't great.

In the last eighteen months, Adrian initiated a programme involving some pretty profound changes to the company's direction, a radical restructure, which accelerated significantly in the last year. He decided to pull the company out of a ten-year deal at the Barbican, and cancel its annual six-month residency there, effectively losing the company's London home and putting backstage staff out of work, which prompted calls for industrial action.

He and then Managing Director Chris Foy, certain that the RSC brand could be more lucratively exploited, announced Project Fleet, to make the company, well, more *fleet*. Adrian was unapologetic for wanting to be more commercial, more aggressively entrepreneurial, and employed Andrew Wylie, the literary agent known as The Jackal, to assist that process. But Adrian's plans faced hostile opposition.

He infuriated Stratford residents and many RSC stalwarts by proposing to pull down the beloved 1932 theatre and build a new theatre on the site designed by Dutch architect Erick van Egeraat, which would be the centrepiece of a much maligned 'theatre village'.

Meanwhile, The Other Place closed its doors as an operating theatre, to concentrate on 'intramural activities', development projects and the like. The argument was that the economics are unsustainable, and that every ticket at the venue is subsidized by the rest of the company's work to the tune of roughly £50 a seat.

But Adrian was responding to real challenges. It was getting harder and harder to attract actors to Stratford for long seasons, made longer by the subsequent transfer to the Barbican. By giving up the Barbican, Chris Foy asserted that instead the company could enjoy a sort of 'Caravanserai' around the West End and other London venues.

In the RSC's new London presence, sans Barbican, Michael Boyd's *The Tempest* is part of a series of late plays at the Roundhouse in Camden. Matthew Warchus's production of *The Winter's Tale* opened first, and Adrian Noble's *Pericles* will complete the season.

Meanwhile, once we have finished the run of *Much Ado* (which is cross-cast with Michael Attenborough's *Antony and Cleopatra*, with Sinead Cusack and Stuart Wilson) both productions are to transfer from the RST straight into the heart of the West End to the gilded plushness of the Theatre Royal, Haymarket.

I fear the headline writers, busy describing the state of the RSC this year, are going to have a field day with the title *Much Ado About Nothing*.

Today Michael Boyd and I are the only remaining associate directors appointed by Adrian. Mike Attenborough is taking over the Almeida in July, and two days ago Stephen Pimlott resigned over the closure of TOP.

'How do you feel?' I ask Michael.

'Like one of only two green bottles left hanging on the wall,' he says. It's typical of Michael's wit: down to earth, original, precise.

That afternoon, I am wandering around the Antiques Market in Ely Street, looking for the odd first-night present. I come across two green glass bottles. They were made here in Stratford-upon-Avon for R.M. Birds, which was a wine merchants at the bottom of Bridge Street at the turn of the century. I buy them both, keep one, and leave the other for Michael at the stage door, with a note saying, 'With admiration, whichever one of us may accidentally fall'.

*   *   *

The phrase 'much ado about nothing' suggests an almighty kerfuffle which in the end turns out to have been caused by something trivial which is blown out of all proportion: a storm in a teacup. But as with many of Shakespeare's idiomatic titles there is also an implied irony here.

The Beatrice and Benedick plot, for which the play is famous, is, in fact, a subplot, much as Malvolio's gulling is the subplot to the story of the twins in *Twelfth Night*.[1] The 'much ado' is about Don John's revenge on his brother, the chaos it causes, and his determination to destroy the happiness of others. But the means he relies on for success involve a whole series of societal elements that are crucial to explore in creating the world of the play. They include the extremely patriarchal nature of that community: the way men, particularly army men, will close ranks when one of their number is attacked; and that society's attitude to women, underpinned by the church, against which Beatrice is in constant rebellion.

---

[1]   Charles and Mary Lamb's retelling of *Twelfth Night* leaves Malvolio out completely.

So, where to set *Much Ado*? We need a domestic environment in which the two gulling scenes will thrive, and the social status and hierarchy of the characters can be understood. But we also need to find a world that might intensify the issues at the heart of the play: when Claudio decides not only to reject but to humiliate his bride at the altar, for example. Too often, the positions that are adopted and maintained in that scene, and the values that are cruelly exposed, get softened or sanitized. This reduces the power and the impact of the play and makes the reconciliation at the end less potent.

I realized that although I had seen many productions of *Much Ado*, set in very specific locations, in very particular time periods, from the British Raj to the Antebellum Deep South, I had never actually seen the play set in Sicily. It is too easy just decorously to graft a particular period or place onto a Shakespeare text. But in Sicily, I began to have a strong sense of how locating *Much Ado* where the author sets the play might allow some of the values inherent in his world in the 1590s to be somehow more recognizable to a twenty-first-century audience.

In September 2000, just after completing the film of *Macbeth*, Tony and I had taken ourselves off to Taormina in Sicily for a break. From the balcony of our hotel, Mount Etna could be seen, smouldering. One morning we were walking through the Piazza Duomo and saw a plump little man in a grey suit and dark glasses, nervously smoking at the open side door of the church. He kept glancing at his watch and peering inside. Tony was sure some Godfather-like assassination was about to take place. As we drew closer the man took a last deep drag of his ciggie, flicked it away, took off his shades, did up his tie and strode inside.

As we walked up, we saw that a wedding mass was in progress and had reached the nuptial blessing. It was like peering into a stage set from the wings. The bride and groom knelt to receive the communion host, and the man we had seen was standing to the side. A cello began to play, then a harp and the soft-pedalled organ. The little guy opened his mouth and began to sing *Panis Angelicus* in the setting by César Franck. His astounding voice filled the crowded chamber of the church.

Later that day, we saw a group of the wedding guests: the men, against a great sun-kissed terracotta wall, ties undone, laughing and drinking, while on a balcony above all the women in their glad-rags, toasted the bride.

Sicily suggested a whole series of associations to a modern audience, which I thought would be helpful in amplifying the themes of the play. There is the strict Sicilian code of honour, Omertà; the influence of the Catholic Church; the role of women in that patriarchal society. I chose a very specific date, 1936, as Mussolini's soldiers returned triumphantly from their Abyssinian campaign through Messina on their way home to Italy. It was a period that would both seem close enough for us to recognize, and far enough away not to be distracted by elements that might intrude as archaic in a completely contemporary setting.

Harriet Walter, after a year of playing Lady Macbeth, was very keen to do some comedy. She leapt at the chance to play Beatrice, and we found her perfect match with the droll Nick Le Prevost.

Stephen Warbeck, then the RSC director of music, had just composed the score for the film of *Captain Corelli's Mandolin*, which was also set in the Mediterranean, in the

Ionian Islands, during the Second World War. He suggested a young composer I might like to meet who had just worked with him on the film. His name was Paul Englishby.[2]

Paul agreed to compose the music. And we employed a marvellous operatic tenor called Julian Jensen, who could delight us with 'Sigh no more ladies'; could move us with the dirge 'Pardon, Goddess of the Night', and inspire us with a beautiful setting of 'Ave Maria', to accompany the arrival in procession of a statue of the Virgin Mary wreathed in flowers, carried by soldiers, at the start of the church scene.

Paul provided a marvellous, tinny, town brass band to welcome the army into the town square, and who played for the masked ball that night.

Our inspiration for the men's masks in the ball were the Sicilian marionettes Tony and I had seen in Palermo. I had brought home a rather dashing marionette of Orlando Furioso, with a fine helm of plumes and some very shiny embossed armour. The Sicilian marionettes are an ancient tradition of puppetry, telling the tales of knights of old, and the battles between the good Christian paladins and their evil Saracen foe. The brass armour is designed to make as much clash and clatter as possible in the fights.

Our wardrobe department reproduced the visored helmets and glittering cuirasses, and the appearance of the menfolk in the play, dressed as these knights, produced a lot of fun. And albeit as merely a grace note, it did also perhaps suggest an exaggerated ideal of chivalry and the male crusading zeal to protect the chastity of every fair damsel, reinforcing the long-cherished but now outmoded nature of that gender role-play.

One of my favourite moments in rehearsal came in the ball scene when Beatrice has infuriated Benedick by calling him the prince's jester, and he refuses to stay in her company. Beatrice seems to let her guard down for a moment and pity her spinster state. At which point Don Pedro asks Beatrice if she would accept him. Harriet did one of those reactions in the moment that are so unexpected but so entirely accurate they reveal new aspects to character.

As Don Pedro asked 'Will you have me lady?' Harriet, caught off guard, burst into hysterical laughter, only to realize that the prince was serious. The embarrassment at having potentially offended their royal house guest prompted a swift exit from Beatrice. But not before the prince tries to compliment her when Beatrice delivers one of the great lines in the play. He says she was born in a merry hour, and she replies:

No sure, my lord, my mother cried, but then there was a star danced and under that was I born.

---

[2]   It was a couple of plays later when Paul was composing the music for the double bill of *The Taming of the Shrew* and *The Tamer Tamed* that I discovered we had something in common.
    'Where did you grow up, Paul?' I asked one day. I knew Paul had a light Lancashire accent but had never found out where he was from. 'Preston,' Paul said. 'No!' I said, 'I was brought up in Preston. What school did you go to?' 'A Catholic College in Winckley Square,' he replied. 'I went there,' I said, 'where did you live?' 'A little place outside Preston called Longton.' Longton was the village where I grew up. 'What parish church did you go to?' 'St Oswald's.' 'No. I went to St Oswald's!' The likelihood of discovering someone you worked closely with had gone to the same school, church and grew up in the same village as you, was surely remote, and might in other circumstances have led to charges of nepotism.

A line packed with a whole history of psychological complexity and exhilarating simplicity.

Don Pedro's plan to bring Benedick and Beatrice together 'into a mountain of affection, the one with the other' leads to the two gulling scenes. The men come first. Benedick has come out into the orchard intending to read and sends a boy to fetch his book. He hides on the approach of Don Pedro, Claudio and Leonato – just as well, or the whole plot would have collapsed.

The gentlemen have asked Balthasar to sing for them. 'Sigh no more ladies' is an odd song for a man to be singing to men. Unless it is a covert warning to Benedick that his men friends are about to set about deceiving him. However, the song draws from Benedick a whole philistine diatribe. It initiates the pattern of the scene: with Benedick providing a running commentary on the conversation, interjecting at regular intervals, and trying to get closer to hear when their discussion moves to Beatrice.

Nick Le Prevost, a master at the very serious business and conventions of comedy, would point out that Benedick cannot talk directly to the audience unless his line of communication to them is clear. He cannot address them from upstage centre for instance, if the others are mid-conversation across the stage on either side of him. That would not be credible to the audience.

The curious joy of the scene involves Benedick trying to remain hidden, and the others *not* trying to find him, or they cannot lay their plot. Nevertheless, there was much fun to be had as they executed short perambulations of the garden, forcing Benedick to scramble around on his knees.

We realized we could enjoy a moment of tension in the scene for both parties if the little boy, whom Benedick had sent on an errand for his book, should return with it. Where is he, after all? As the child arrived and went straight over to Benedick behind his bush, both sides held their collective breath. Benedick's attempts to shoo the boy away, without the gentlemen hearing, while the gentlemen tried equally hard not to notice, introduced an element of comic tensity into the scene, which was as delightful as it was unexpected. When Benedick managed to grab the book, the boy, instead of departing, then held his hand out demanding his tip. This would regularly bring the house down.

The scene in which Hero and Margaret attempt to convince Beatrice that Benedick is in love with her is written very differently. And it is vital to recognize that difference. Too often you feel in performance that the two scenes are competing, as if the girls, having watched a rehearsal of the boys' scene getting lots of laughs, have got together and demanded some gags.

Beatrice runs in 'like a lapwing, ... close by the ground', to hear the women's conference.

One of the primary differences with this scene is that, unlike Benedick, Beatrice does not speak until the end. We decided that her lack of interjections would prompt her friends to get more ardent in their attempts to flush her out. Ordinarily, Beatrice is never short of a response, so with her now unable to speak, they get more and more provocative. Are women more direct in their conversation with each other than men are? If so, would that account for the way Hero and Margaret seem to relish the opportunity, which they seldom get, to tell Beatrice some of her faults.

They seem frustrated, however, at her lack of response. So, in our production we decided (as this was a garden after all) that they would do a little watering. With a spray can they hosed down the pleachéd bower behind which Harriet's Beatrice was hiding. It was not until they departed that she emerged, soaked to the skin.

But surprisingly, Harriet seemed not to notice her bedraggled state, for she had fire in her ears. Here is a crossroads if ever there was one. It is possible that Beatrice might emerge from her hiding place in a rage that Benedick is claiming to love her, or suspicious that this is all a trick, and plot a counter offensive.

But no.

Beatrice is shocked to the core. And for the first time in the play she speaks in verse, delivering a foreshortened sonnet, ending (maddeningly) with a rhyming couplet that no longer rhymes:[3]

> For others say thou dost deserve, and I
> Believe it better than reportingly.

Harriet nevertheless took full advantage of the breathless possibilities of the personal pronoun's heady position at the end of the line 'and I . . .'. What is she going to say, this woman who has resisted love for so long, been hurt by it, defended herself against it with a carapace of barbed wit? When she continues 'and I . . . Believe it . .' the audience must hear not only that the ruse has been successful, but that they are witnessing a true, deep, vulnerable heart opening to love.

The hosing down of Beatrice also had the unexpected advantage of explaining why Beatrice, speaking 'in the sick tune', has a streaming cold in her next scene.

* * *

Gary Waldhorn, playing Leonato, seized on the opportunities the Sicilian setting brought. In the first three acts, he had played the head of this household of women with charm and bonhomie, graciously welcoming the prince, Don Pedro and soldiers into his home; slightly bewildered by what was expected of him in the gulling scene; and all beams at the church, as the proud father about to match his daughter into Florentine aristocracy.

Claudio and Don Pedro chose to make their declaration of Hero's disloyalty as public as possible, on the very steps of the altar. Instead of immediately defending his child, the humiliated father believes them. As Claudio ripped off Hero's veil and the soldiers closed ranks, Leonato was only too aware of the violent connection between chastity and family honour.

Once the prince and Claudio had made their exit, Gary's Leonato remained very still. His silence held the tension and terror of suppressed emotion. His question 'Hath no man's dagger here a point for me?' seemed in this context a real possibility, as if every male present had a stiletto hidden discreetly about his person. He began quietly at first, attempting to work out what had just happened and what must happen now.

---

[3] Although, in a Black Country accent, it can.

'Death is the fairest cover for her shame'. But then Gary rumbled to an inexorable crescendo, as Leonato threatens to kill his own daughter:

> Do not live, Hero; do not ope thine eyes:
> For, did I think thou wouldst not quickly die,
> Thought I thy spirits were stronger than thy shames,
> Myself would, on the rearward of reproaches,
> Strike at thy life.

The climactic shout released him from his frozen state. The prince and count could not possibly be wrong. Leonato tore at the women around his daughter, screaming: 'Hence from her! let her die.' It was like Etna erupting in grief.

He would not listen to the friar's attempt to unravel the mystery, for he had made up his mind. At the end of the scene, before his exit, Leonato adds a chilling warning. The groom and his companions may have underestimated his influence in the city of Messina. His threat is made all the more terrifying by being marshalled into a single relentless sentence building slowly with insistent repetition over eight lines:

> Time hath not yet so dried this blood of mine,
> Nor age so eat up my invention,
> Nor fortune made such havoc of my means,
> Nor my bad life reft me so much of friends,
> But they shall find, awaked in such a kind,
> Both strength of limb and policy of mind,
> Ability in means and choice of friends,
> To quit me of them throughly.

The friar makes his strange proposal to conceal Hero, and Benedick persuades Leonato to accept the plan. Shakespeare manages our feelings towards this dangerous, angry, selfish father with enormous pathos. Witness Leonato's exit line to Benedick:

> Being that I flow in grief,
> The smallest twine may lead me.

Our Sicilian setting allowed the scale and ferocity of the emotions described in this story. It might be a cliché to describe them as 'Latin'; it might be more accurate to understand them as Elizabethan, for we have evidence in letters from foreign ambassadors at the time that the English were an emotional bunch. Men frequently kissed each other, and 'it is common for a number of them that have got a glass in their heads,' reported Paul Hentzer, a German jurist, 'to go up into some belfry, and ring the bells for hours together for the sake of exercise.' Not the stereotype of the English character we expect, with our tightly-held emotions and stiff upper lips.

But if the scene has been gripping, and emotionally distressing, it now becomes almost overwhelming as Beatrice and Benedick are left alone. These two bruised, defensive wits. How astute of Shakespeare to decide to place their much-anticipated encounter now. We, the audience, know they believe each is in love with the other, and have been waiting for them to meet to see if the trick to bring them together has worked.

The delirium of their mutual declarations of love rises to the simplest and most beautifully eloquent protestation by Beatrice: 'I love you with so much of my heart that none is left to protest'. But it is swiftly followed, when asked by her new beloved to demand of him anything, by Beatrice's shocking 'Kill Claudio'.

It's a famous line. And in our Sicilian setting seemed horribly feasible. It is also frequently regarded by Beatrices as their Waterloo. Certainly to begin with, Harriet would find herself very irritated if the audience laughed at that point. But eventually she accepted that the suddenness of the line – it's very shortness, it's abrupt arrival into a giddy love scene – catches the audience unawares. Both Harriet and Nick learnt that whatever reaction the line got they simply had to wait until the shock settled before Benedick's refusal.

Harriet's fury as Beatrice, her anger that as a woman in this society she was helpless to exact the revenge her cousin deserved, was incandescent. Her passion, matched by the simple generosity of Nick Le Prevost's Benedick, a man who has ducked commitment all his life and is now forced to confront the imperatives of love, made me realize that the church scene, Act Four Scene One, is surely one of the supreme highlights in all of Shakespeare's comedies.

In Act Five, we meet Leonato again, still overflowing with grief at his daughter's catastrophe. Old Antonio is trying to counsel his brother to be patient, but Leonato, still clutching his daughter's bridal veil, will have none of it, insisting his words 'fall into my ears as water in a sieve'.

It's a beautiful speech, about grief and about anger, about injustice and empathy. He argues that unless you have experienced the same trauma, your attempts at giving conciliation can only 'Charm ache with air and agony with words'. He ends, 'My griefs cry louder than advertisement'.

*   *   *

Gary Waldhorn performed that speech as part of the Sunday service at Holy Trinity that birthday weekend. But the sombre tone of that birthday service intensified as Adrian Noble stepped up to the lectern.

Adrian had been under siege by the press for months, and speculation about his departure had deepened since the opening of *Chitty Chitty Bang Bang,* a couple of weeks prior. He had attended the various birthday celebrations the day before with his young family, wearing dark glasses. The reading he had chosen was the 'bowed but not beaten' verses from St Paul's letter to the Corinthians, where the apostle attempted to calm division within the Church. The packed congregation listened in silence. Adrian, as he read, looked around the packed congregation with a steady gaze.

We are troubled on every side, yet not distressed;
We are perplexed, but not in despair;
Persecuted, but not forsaken; cast down, but not destroyed.

The following morning, Adrian sought a meeting with Lord Alexander, the Chairman of the RSC's board of governors, at which he informed him that he would not be seeking to renew his contract when it expired in March the following year. I was in the bath on Wednesday morning when Adrian phoned to tell me. He asked if it would be alright to call a meeting in my rehearsal room and delay the rehearsal call by half an hour.

In the theatre, I went straight up to the office. Adrian came out. He was red-eyed. He had been phoning all the associate artists. He asked me if I could get hold of Harriet Walter before the meeting, and then told his PA Jude that he was going out for some air. I tracked Harriet down in her dressing room, and gave her his mobile number. She was unruffled, cool even. 'I don't know whether to congratulate or commiserate,' she said.

In the Ashcroft Room, sitting on the floor, in the window bays, on the steps, everyone was gathered – ushers, stage management, prop-shop, box office, green room, stage crew. One of the ushers whispered, 'Either we're bankrupt, or he's resigning.'

Adrian was no longer red-eyed. He was pale. And calm. He used the same words he had said to me on the phone. 'I sought a meeting with Lord Alexander at which I informed him . . .' He was not resigning. He was just not going to renew his contract. He briefly mentioned some of the factors that had led to that decision and revealed that a powerful factor was the toll on his family. Jo had been verbally abused and spat at.

He then smiled quietly, as he talked about his twenty-two years with the company, how he had known some of them for all those twenty-two years. I could only think of all the incredible shows he had directed in that time: *King Lear* with Gambon, then again with Robert Stephens; *Henry IV* with Robert Stephens; *Macbeth* with Jonathan Pryce; *A Doll's House* with Cheryl Campbell; *The Cherry Orchard*; *The Winter's Tale* with Bill McCabe as Autolycus floating in on that cloud of bright balloons; *The Plantagenets*. So many productions.

Adrian said he would remain in post until March the following year and announced that he would be reviving his hit production of *The Lion, the Witch, and the Wardrobe* for Christmas, and would then be mounting a new production of Ibsen's *Brand* with Ralph Fiennes in the Swan in April, which would transfer to the Haymarket.

As Adrian left, collecting his wife Jo at the door, there was applause. It wasn't tumultuous. It wasn't mean. It was polite. But the room was conflicted about what they have just heard.

I was shaken by the pain Adrian and Jo had been through. Was that what being an Artistic Director was about? Not only enduring hostile abuse from the press, but attacks on your family in public? That's unacceptable.

25 April 2002.

I am in the final day of my technical rehearsal for *Much Ado*. Tonight is the double press night for the Jacobethan season, and I am standing front of house, when *The Times* critic Benedick Nightingale approaches for a brief chat about the choice of plays for the season, and then says, 'Oh, one more thing, Greg. Are you going to run the RSC?'

The Guardian critic Michael Billington is talking to our chairman, Lord Alexander, and breaks off to wish me well with the season, and then asks if I am thinking of applying. I brush it off again.

At the after-show party, Bob Alexander grabs me. 'I know you're horribly busy, Greg, but I'd love to talk. What about breakfast. Can I boil you an egg?'

The speculation about who will take over is already rife. Last week Michael Billington in *The Guardian* wrote:

the RSC has always thrived on continuity. Peter Hall was nurtured by the 1950s Quayle-Byam Shaw regime. Since then, Nunn, Hands and Noble have all grown up within the organisation. The temptation now, with so much talk of crisis, will be to look for a total outsider. My suspicion is that the next director of the RSC is already lurking inside the organisation. But who is the natural custodian of a great tradition? I'd put my doubloon on Gregory Doran.

In contrast, in a spiteful piece in the *Evening Standard*, Nicholas de Jongh sniped, 'Anyone other than Lady Sher.'

26 April.
At 9am I ring Lord Alexander's bell in the house he has in Avonside. He ushers me in. He talks about Adrian, and the reaction to his resignation. There is shock, sadness and some sense of betrayal.

Michael Boyd has put his name forward for the job. Bob wants to know if I will put my hat in the ring too. But I am reluctant to do so. Almost as soon as I open *Much Ado*, I go into rehearsals for Fletcher's *The Island Princess*, the fourth play in the Jacobethan season. It's a fascinating and challenging play and we have a month to rehearse it. Then it opens in July.

Then I have agreed to spend a week on location with Michael Wood filming his new series *In Search of Shakespeare* for the BBC. Then *Much Ado* opens in the West End. In the same month the board intend to announce Adrian's successor, so I would have little or no time to think properly about how the company should move forward. But I tell Bob I will consider it seriously.

Over the weekend, as reviews start coming out for the Jacobethans, the press speculation continues. Some point out that the Jacobethan season precisely demonstrates what the RSC should be, an ensemble doing challenging work and demonstrating exactly what the Swan was built for.

Susannah Clapp in *The Observer* writes that the season is a model of how the company might be run, and that it looks like an impressive job application.

Wednesday 8 May.
Press photo call for *Much Ado*. The phalanx of cameras seems larger today, and they don't all seem to be focusing on the actors. The first set-up is the opening scene: a soldier arrives at Leonato's household to announce the arrival of the prince and his party. We play him as a despatch rider on a motorbike. During the course of the scene, Harriet Walter, in her Katharine Hepburn slacks and blouse, sits astride the motorbike and interrogates the soldier.

Once the photographers have got their shots, one of them shouts 'Come on, Greg, let's see you on the motorbike!' 'Hmmm,' I think to myself, as I decline the offer with a smile: I can just see the headlines. Either 'Doran ready in the driving seat' or 'On yer bike, Greg!'

Wednesday 8 May.
Press night of *Much Ado*.

Friday 10 May.
Ian Charleson Awards at the NT. Set up by John Peter, the drama critic of *The Sunday Times*, to honour the memory of the actor Ian Charleson, who died tragically young in 1990 at the age of forty. Ian was the first celebrity death in the UK to be openly attributed to AIDS. These awards are for the Best Performance in a Classical Role in Britain, by young actors under thirty. The RSC are well represented with half of the dozen nominees: two are from the *Much Ado* cast, John Hopkins and Kirsten Parker (Hero), with another four from other RSC productions, so very important to be there.

I nip into the NT shop to scan the *Evening Standard* if I can find one. It's a rave from De Jongh, despite his bitchy remark earlier. As Tony and I never considered for a moment making a joint application for the job, it's odd that some of the press assume we have. I did get taken out to lunch by Simon Russell Beale who wanted to float the idea of a joint ticket. He appears now, in the Lyttelton Foyer, and congratulates me on the reviews in *The Guardian* and *The Daily Telegraph*. And Samantha Bond comes up and does the same, but for the *Daily Mail*. It's twenty years since we were at the Bristol Old Vic School together, and she is just as radiant now as she was then.

Nick Hytner says he's heard great things, but studiously doesn't mention the job. Others do likewise: Michael Grandage air-kisses from across the room; Trevor Nunn comes in for a quick hug and evaporates; then Judi Dench grabs my hand and says we've got to save the RSC and asks if we can arrange to meet.

Friday 17 May.
Judi Dench radiates a special kind of grace, both merry and melancholy in the same moment. She has invited me to accompany her to a cocktail party to celebrate the 70th birthday of the Open Air Theatre in Regent's Park, and we swing in, with me on her arm, as it were. We find a moment to slip into the auditorium. Judi directed *The Boys from Syracuse* here in 1991, which won the Olivier for Best Musical Revival.

I tell her that I have decided to put my hat in the ring for the RSC. 'Good,' she says definitively, so I run through some of my ideas.

'I can't tell you how relieved I am to hear all this,' she says giving my arm a squeeze, 'I feel so much better.'

As the event finishes, Judi walks out with me. I ask her if I can persuade her to come back to the RSC.

'You'd better be quick, I'll be in my wheelchair soon,' she chuckles. 'Give my love to Stratford, won't you, and keep in touch. Please. I mean it.'

Monday 3 June.
I start rehearsals for *The Island Princess*.

It's a play about the mercantile enterprise of colonial expansion, set in the Spice Islands of the Moluccas, during the Portuguese occupation of the 1590s. But it was written at the same time as the Pilgrim Fathers were setting out across the Atlantic on the Mayflower, to form the Plymouth Colony in what is now Massachusetts.

Not only are the company rehearsing the play, but they are all participating in composer Adrian Lee's exquisite gamelan orchestra. I need to get my head down for the next month.

Tuesday 3 July.
Press night of *The Island Princess* last night. Very buoyant company, growing in confidence with each play.

This morning to Bob Alexander's for toast and Marmite. He reveals his opinion that Michael Boyd and I are 'the two genuine contenders for the job'.

Sunday 21 July.
At home in London, while Tony is in rehearsal for *The Roman Actor* in Stratford. He writes me a sweet postcard ahead of the interview for the job tomorrow:

> There are times in the creative arts when a job comes along that is so right for you, that fear and doubt have no place. You only have to respond through love. You love Shakespeare. You love the RSC. Tomorrow at the interview you will communicate that love, I know you will. And then, if you don't get the job, it won't matter, for you will have given of your best, you will have offered a piece of your heart.

Monday 22 July.
The interview took place at Lord and Lady Alexander's house in Little Venice. Sinead Cusack was there and Susie Sainsbury smiling encouragement, and Richard Eyre was on the panel. News of this had thrown me a bit as I can't remember Richard ever having seen any of my work. I think I acquitted myself honourably. I hope so.

Wednesday 24 July 7:50pm.
There is a board meeting going on in Stratford, and no word either way. But Tony has just phoned to say the company manager Jondon has rung to tell him there is to be a company meeting at 9:30 tomorrow morning. So, they have made a decision and, as I suspected, it isn't me. I feel exhausted, and empty. And angry that no one has had the courtesy to let me know. I need to move on.

10:30pm.
Bob Alexander phones to tell me that after an eight-hour board meeting they had decided to appoint Michael Boyd. He was gracious enough to say it was the hardest phone call he had ever had to make.

Tony says, 'You must ring Mike.'

'I will. Not just now.'

'Yes, now.'

I snap at him. And then phone. It's an answer machine. And I leave a message congratulating him on getting the job.

I ring Mum and Dad. Mum answers. I tell her that I didn't get the job. 'Ah,' she said, 'Never mind, love. Are you disappointed?' I love my mum's no nonsense Yorkshire sense of perspective.

'Oh, I'm fine,' I lie.

I pour myself a large tumbler of Laphroaig single malt.

Am I disappointed? Yes. But it is mingled with an intense relief too. But what happens next?

25 July 2002.

Michael Boyd is announced as the fifth Artistic Director of the RSC.

I pick up a message Michael has left on the answer machine, thanking me for mine, saying how lucky he felt. And 'not to fly away'.

Two days later, at the Haymarket Theatre in the West End, I open *Much Ado About Nothing*.

11

The Taming of the Shrew

– 2003: Royal Shakespeare Theatre, Stratford upon Avon;
Eisenhower Theater, John F. Kennedy Center, Washington, DC;
Queen's Theatre, London.

Michael Boyd had proposed to the board that he would not programme his first season as Artistic Director for eighteen months, opening in 2004, and the board had agreed. The 2003 season would therefore be an interim season, and I, now in my new job as Chief Associate Director, would contribute to its development.

I made three proposals: pairing *The Taming of the Shrew* with a sequel which was written in Shakespeare's lifetime, and the return of Judi Dench to Stratford (after twenty-five years) to play the Countess in *All's Well That Ends Well*.

Directors do not so much direct *The Taming of the Shrew* as try to solve it. Still an immensely popular title, the play had fallen out of favour. It is thought by many to be irredeemably misogynistic. But in 2003, I thought I had found the solution.

John Fletcher, the author of *The Island Princess* (which I had just directed as part of the Jacobethan season), had written a sequel to *The Taming of the Shrew*. Fletcher was fifteen years Shakespeare's junior, and in order (I suspect) to attract the attention of the older playwright, he had attempted something rather daring. He had written a follow-up to Shakespeare's early play. In *The Tamer Tamed*, as we chose to call it (its other title is *The Woman's Prize*), Petruchio's first wife, Katherina, has died, and he has married again. His second wife, Maria, turns the tables on the 'madcap ruffian' and tames him.

To me, the play indicates that even in the few years since Shakespeare wrote *Shrew*, attitudes towards women had shifted. And Fletcher's proto-feminist play suggests that he felt it needed a response. This had been suggested to me by Gordon McMullan, a passionate advocate for the plays of Fletcher, when he had sat in on rehearsals for the Shakespeare/Fletcher collaboration, *Henry VIII or All is True*. As far as we were both aware the plays had not been performed together since the Caroline period

Perfect, I thought, let's produce both together with the same cast. That way, if we failed to rescue the play from its reputation as either a heartless romp or as outdated and offensive, then with the Fletcher play we had an antidote at the ready.

And that was the plan I proposed to Jasper Britton and Alexandra Gilbreath, to play Petruchio and Katherina/Maria. Jasper, an immense talent, had joined the RSC in the 1992 season, in *Tamburlaine the Great* and Brome's *The Jovial Crew*, before playing Richard III at the Open Air Theatre in Regent's Park for Brian Cox, Thersites for Trevor

Nunn at the NT, and Caliban with Mark Rylance at the Globe. To my delight, they both accepted.

We prepared *The Taming of the Shrew* for the RST, and *The Tamer Tamed* for the Swan, with largely the same cast (although I adopted some of Shakespeare's names for the characters Fletcher had incorporated into his play). I was blessed with a crack team of comedians: Paul Chahidi played sly Hortensio; Chris Godwin was crusty old Gremio; Rory Kinnear as Tranio got more value out of a pair of tight-fitting shoes than can possibly be decent; Eve Myles was a canny Bianca; and Nic Tennant played a suitably grumpy Grumio.

Stephen Brimson Lewis designed an Elizabethan urban environment for both plays. For *Shrew*, it was a series of free-standing old oak doors. In the Swan, a rickety balcony jutted out into the space, like a precarious overhanging tenement.

The rehearsals for *The Taming of the Shrew* were to surprise all of us.

The first thing I had done was to cut the framing device called the Induction: the Christopher Sly prologue. I felt certain that Shakespeare had inherited the convention from an earlier play (*The Taming of A Shrew*[1]), and half-heartedly abandoned it. In *A Shrew* the convention is at least concluded as Christopher Sly wakes up in an epilogue and reforms his life. I felt that all the induction did was to place the play in inverted commas, suggesting that it was after all 'only a play', and had provided directors with the opportunity of distancing the play from reality. Without it, we would regard the characters as real human beings, revelling in all their flaws and contradictions.

And I knew Kate. I had grown up with her. She was in many ways like my older sister Jo, and her relationship to Bianca echoed Jo's relationship to my twin sister Ruth.

Let me digress for a moment. My parents had married in 1946, just after the Second World War, and for twelve years had tried but been unable to have children. In 1955 they adopted Mark, a bubbly, confident, gregarious baby boy who blossomed in their love. Two years later they adopted Joanna, my sister. Within nine months of Jo's first birthday, my mother gave birth to twins: me and my sister Ruth.

Whether Jo remembered the face of her birth mother, a young Irish girl who had travelled to Leeds to give birth to her daughter, 'born out of wedlock', and hand her over to the nuns, I can't know, but whereas Mark appears cheery and confident in all those black and white photos in the family albums, Jo looks shy. She must just have been adjusting to life in the Doran family, when suddenly an attention-grabbing pair of blonde babies usurps her place. One tiny photograph captures the problem. My mother, looking exhausted (she now has four children under four), holds my twin and I in either arm, in a froth of knitted lambswool. My brother kisses me on the head. Little Joanna is nowhere to be seen.

Ruth, golden-haired, rosy-cheeked, and blessed with a sunny personality, was always the apple of my father's eye. Jo, her light brown hair cut under a pudding basin, as often

---

[1] Some scholars believe that *A Shrew* is a muddled rewrite of *The Shrew*. But it feels to me that it is an inferior earlier play, which Shakespeare rewrote. The portrait of Kate in *A Shrew* is of a violent scold, who at one point screams:

'I tell thee, villain, I'll tear the flesh off
Thy face and eat it, and thou prates to me thus.'

as not made to sit at table until she had finished her food, and always scowling in family photos, was frequently sent to her room. I would be the one who crept upstairs to wipe away her hot, angry tears. And that was to remain a constant in our otherwise happy childhoods. All too often, her fists clenched, her heels dug in, and resentments grew.

So, I knew who Kate was. And I saw a young woman in pain. A woman struggling to get out of the box into which society had placed her. A box marked 'difficult'.

The first few scenes make this clear. Kate's father, Baptista Minola, is entertaining a string of suitors for Bianca, but insisting that he won't marry her to anyone, until a husband is found for her older sister. Kate, meanwhile, must endure this humiliation.

Enter Petruchio. Instead of the smirking braggadocio as he is sometimes presented, Jasper played him as a volatile neurotic, hiding his vulnerability and desperation behind a mask of anarchic self-confidence. He has arrived in Padua to find a wife. His father having just died (a casual detail that Jasper mined to reveal genuine grief), Petruchio has come into a huge estate but has no idea how to cope with that responsibility.

Clearly using alcohol to get through the day, and possibly steadily drinking his way through his inheritance, he seeks out his old friend Hortensio. He confesses to him that he is badly in need of money and needs to marry.

> I come to wive it wealthily in Padua,
> If wealthily then happily in Padua.

Hortensio, a suitor to Bianca, knows just the girl for him. Cut to the famous scene where Petruchio first encounters Katherine.

Petruchio tells us his one plan of attack is to contradict everything she says, turning any negative into a positive. Not necessarily a profound strategy, but straightforward enough.

In rehearsal we looked carefully at the pronouns: when a character used the 'You' form, or the more familiar (and to modern ears more archaic) 'Thee/Thou' form. It is just like the French use of 'Vous' or 'Tu/Toi'. The audience may not be aware of the distinction, but it can provide an indication of particular and changing attitudes within the scene. We could track the emotional graph of the scene.

So for example, Petruchio begins formally enough (despite the fact he uses the familiar form of Katherine's name, Kate, ten times in his opening gambit), addressing her with the more formal 'You' form (please note: I use the underlinings to point out the presence and frequency of the words, not to indicate emphasis):

> Good morrow Kate, for that's <u>your</u> name I hear.

But soon he gets into his stride and insists on their familiarity by frequent use of 'thy' and 'thee':

> Hearing <u>thy</u> mildness praised in every town,
> <u>Thy</u> virtues spoke of, and <u>thy</u> beauty sounded,
> Yet not so deeply as to <u>thee</u> belongs,
> Myself am moved to woo <u>thee</u> for my wife.

Kate on the other hand resolutely refuses to accept the invitation. She will only use 'Thou' once in the whole scene, thus amplifying its significance.

They rally quips about joint stools and buzzards, back and forth, like a pair of school children, for a bit, until Petruchio stops playing and suddenly reverts to 'You', to tell her a home truth:

> Come, wasp, <u>you</u> are too angry.

She picks up the wasp image, suggesting he beware of her sting, which initiates another rally leading to possibly one of the rudest cunnilingus jokes in Shakespeare. As Kate is about to sweep out, Petruchio says:

> What with my tongue in your tail?

In rehearsal this became a significant milestone in the scene, as Alex roared with laughter at the vulgar audacity of the joke. This seemed to imply some sort of potential plateau, a break in the keen encounter of their wits. Petruchio begins again:

> Good Kate, I am a gentleman.

At which she decides to test his resolve and slaps him across the face. She's pushed it too far. Petruchio immediately reverts to 'You'.

> I swear I'll cuff <u>you</u> if <u>you</u> strike again.

And so the scene progresses. In our production both of them attempted to walk out slamming the door behind them, but always returning for more until they ended up wrestling on the floor with Petruchio tickling her feet and breaking down her resistance to him. Exhausted and laughing she finally refers to him in the familiar form:

> Go fool, and whom <u>thou</u> keepst command.

This could, of course, be a deliberate attempt to demean her unconventional suitor, as the Thee/Thou pronouns are also used when addressing a servant or subordinate. Either way, this singular usage suggested to us some sort of crossroads in the scene, perhaps a thaw in their relationship, a chink in her defence. Petruchio exploits it and cuts to the chase. He adopts the 'You' form to make his proposal more formal:

> And therefore, setting all this chat aside,
> Thus in plain terms: <u>your</u> father hath consented
> That <u>you</u> shall be my wife; <u>your</u> dowry 'greed on;
> And, will <u>you</u>, nill you, I will marry <u>you</u>.

The full stop at the end of the verse line here might suggest a cue point for Kate to respond to this hijack. But Petruchio presses on, insisting they are meant for each other. This time his use of Thee/Thy and Thou is intimate, sincere, genuine. As Alex pointed out, it takes her breath away as he tells her how moved he is by her beauty (and even repeats the word, immediately, which Shakespeare seldom does) – a compliment she has perhaps never heard or expected to hear before.

> Now, Kate, I am a husband for your turn;
> For, by this light, whereby I see <u>thy</u> beauty,
> <u>Thy</u> beauty, that doth make me like <u>thee</u> well,
> <u>Thou</u> must be married to no man but me.

But now the whole road map for the scene indicated by the very specific use of the different pronouns fell drastically apart. We simply could not fathom why Petruchio's entire tone changed as he reverted bombastically to 'You'.

> For I am he am born to tame <u>you</u> Kate,
> And bring <u>you</u> from a wild Kate to a Kate
> Conformable as other household Kates.

Then one day, Jasper Britton came into rehearsal having made a discovery. He had gone back to the Folio searching for clues. He found that the stage direction '*Enter Baptista, Gremio and others*', had been moved from precisely that spot ('Thou must be married to no man but me') to the end of the speech where Petruchio says:

> Here comes your father: never make denial;
> I must and will have Katherine to my wife.

Perfectly logical, perhaps, but entirely missing the point. The whole reason why Petruchio suddenly adopts the wife-tamer pose is because his prospective father-in-law has entered the room. He is performing the role they expect him to play.

For us, the apparently innocent relocation of that single stage direction changed the meaning of the whole play.

That most erratically pedantic of Shakespeare editors, Alexander Pope, back in the eighteenth century, is responsible for this editorial intervention. It seems to have been automatically accepted, and universally adopted, by almost every editor since. Certainly, all of the many editions we had in our rehearsal room retained that position, even though the displacement unwittingly altered the whole play.

Alex Gilbreath, Jasper and I became convinced that this shifted the ground rules. Now they were complicit in playing a game together. Or at least that is the idea. By the time we get to the wedding however, Petruchio has got cold feet.

Kate cannot believe that she has arrived at one of those staging-posts in life that she never dreamed would be hers: her wedding day. And, imagining it to be impossible, and denied to her, she has in fact been complicit in making it unlikely. But now it's here. Alex arrived in the scene in what she described as her 'wedding meringue', a great pale-blue farthingale decked with ribbons and lace, which to Kate, is the perfect confection for the sweetest of days. However, her delight at being the centre of attention (for the right reasons for once) is short-lived as Petruchio has not turned up. Surely the bride's worst possible nightmare.

Kate cries:

Would Katherine had never seen him though.

Her use of her own name, referring to herself in the third person, suggests perhaps a self-protection technique, that she needs to disconnect herself from her own pain, a method she may have employed throughout her life to distance herself from the pain of rejection. Her exit weeping was very moving, a masterstroke of heartbreak.

Shakespeare is a genius in control of his tone. He follows Kate's tearful departure with the chaotic arrival of Biondello, heralding his master's appearance, with undoubtedly one of the most delicious (and longest) sentences in all of Shakespeare:

Why, Petruchio is coming in a new hat and an old jerkin, a pair of old breeches thrice turned, a pair of boots that have been candle-cases, one buckled, another laced, an old rusty sword ta'en out of the town-armory, with a broken hilt, and chapeless; with two broken points: his horse hipped with an old mothy saddle and stirrups of no kindred; besides, possessed with the glanders and like to mose in the chine; troubled with the lampass, infected with the fashions, full of windgalls, sped with spavins, rayed with yellows, past cure of the fives, stark spoiled with the staggers, begnawn with the bots, swayed in the back and shoulder-shotten; near-legged before and with a half-chequed bit and a head-stall of sheeps leather which, being restrained to keep him from stumbling, hath been often burst and now repaired with knots; one girth six time pieced and a woman's crupper of velure, which hath two letters for her name fairly set down in studs, and here and there pieced with packthread.

I once heard this speech held up (on Radio 4's *Today* programme) as an example of how Shakespeare needed updating, and why he was so difficult to understand. But this torrent of verbiage with its wealth of baffling and disgusting detail about horse diseases, and the sheer feat of memory it requires, earns the speech a sure-fire round of applause. In the hands of Simon Trinder in our production, it never failed to get one.

Then Petruchio turns up drunk.

The only way he can face the prospect of married life is to down a few in his local tavern. In church, he knocks down the priest and knocks back the communion wine. Then immediately after the ceremony, Petruchio says he has to go, and cannot stay for the wedding feast. It is not clear if he means to take his wife with him.

So Baptista entreats him to stay. Then Tranio adds his appeal. Finally, Kate adds hers.

He seems to relent, but then ducks it. So, she adds a plea that feels personal, and intimates intimacy.

Now if you love me stay.

At which Petruchio immediately yells for his horse. Is it love he is afraid of?

That commitment, that tentative unexpected affection they had both perhaps glimpsed by the end of their first encounter, she calls on now, and he is too frightened to sign up to. The public acknowledgement of having entered the establishment of marriage, or settling down, of leaving his selfish, self-willed bachelor life, terrifies Petruchio.

I don't believe Petruchio has planned any of this. I don't believe he knows what he is doing. He is improvising. Drink helps. He is on an almighty bender. He can perform and play-act but has no idea about the consequences of his actions or the pain he is causing others.

Petruchio implores his new wife not to be angry, at which she explodes:

I will be angry, what hast thou to do?

Whilst asserting her right to be angry for the treatment she is suffering, the humiliation and disappointment that the promised opportunity has been denied her, she repossesses her comfortable self-defence mechanism.

But the commitment-averse Petruchio (grabbing the priest's bible in our production, and quoting from it) reminds us:

I will be master of what is mine own –
She is my goods, my chattels, she is my house,
My household stuff, my field, my barn,
My horse, my ox, my ass, my any thing,
And here she stands; touch her whoever dare.

He is quoting from the book of Exodus, and in particular the tenth commandment. At which point in our production, Kate snatched the Bible from him and tore out that page in rage. Meanwhile Grumio bumped her into a trolley and whisked her off stage, throwing the biblical endorsement of her status as wife into the air, like ironic confetti.

The bewildered congregation comfort themselves by redefining this damaged pair as mad. 'Being mad herself she is madly mated.' To which one of them retorts:

I warrant him Petruchio is Kated.

*   *   *

We ended the first half, not at the end of the wedding as is usual, but one scene later, as Petruchio arrives home in the middle of the night with his exhausted bride, and yells at his newly inherited household. None of his actions seemed premeditated: whether the accidental tipping of a bowl of water over his new wife, or the refusal of burnt meat (which he has been told is bad for his temper, and therefore is surely so for her). But, once she has stomped off to the bridal chamber, Petruchio returns to share his thoughts with us.

Jasper's Petruchio took down a portrait of his deceased father, hawk on arm, draped in black, and began to formulate his plan. He would commit to the process of training his angry hawk, which would involve a lengthy commitment of watching and waiting.

It is the only way he knows. He asks the audience if they have any better ideas, but inevitably they are silent on the matter.

The 'taming' process, which takes up the next half, is inevitably at best mean, at worst sadistic, and no production can entirely excuse starvation, or sleep deprivation, as humane or viable strategies towards a happy married life. In his own hippy philosophy, however, Petruchio has a few precepts. His appearance at the wedding in his outrageous outfit provokes him to the quite legitimate argument: 'To me she's married, not unto my clothes'. When he now demolishes the haberdasher's cap, or the tailor's gown, he concludes:

> What is the jay more precious than the lark,
> Because his feathers are more beautiful?

And they now determine to head back to Baptista's house for Bianca's wedding, dressed as they are, which in Kate's case is in an old cardigan, her petticoat tucked into a pair of breeches, and the rescued haberdasher's cap.

When Janet Suzman played Kate, she told me that when she contradicted Michael Williams's Petruchio about whether the sun was shining or the moon, suddenly the penny dropped, and she realized it was all a game, at which she began to roar with laughter, which sometimes went on for a good three minutes.

We found a similar beat of mutual understanding, as Kate plays along with the befuddling of the old man (who turns out to be Lucentio's father, Vincentio).

In the last scene, Kate and Petruchio were to us by far the happiest couple in the room. Hortensio has married for all the wrong reasons. He is unlikely to be happy with his wealthy widow. Lucentio, played by Dan Hawksford as a not too bright 'surfer dude', is unaware that Tranio is taking aim at his bride; lastly Bianca, spiteful in all her responses, is clearly already straining at the marriage leash.

So, when Kate delivered her famous speech it was a negotiation, an understanding of the status quo, and a willingness to play by its rules. But when she presented her hand, ready to place it metaphorically under her husband's foot, suddenly Jasper's Petruchio seemed to turn. 'Come on,' he beckoned, raising his foot, as if to say, 'go on then, humiliate yourself'; Alex's Kate hesitated in front of her family and neighbours, but moved forward to oblige, at which point Jasper scooped her up with the rest of line . . . 'and kiss me Kate'.

They left the stage, probably to bed. Happy – at least for that moment.

*   *   *

At the double press day, my sister Jo was as always at my side. I was anxious to know what she thought of *Shrew* in particular. Had it tugged at any painful shared family memories? At the after-show party, Jo was glowing. There was a bubbly sense that with this theatrical pairing we might all have achieved something quite special. Jo and Alexandra Gilbreath were busy catching up, when I overheard Jo say: 'You know Greg based the production on me and my sister, don't you?' As Frederick Fellini said: 'All art is autobiographical; the pearl is the oyster's autobiography.'

John Peter in *The Sunday Times* thought *Shrew/Tamer* 'a brilliant piece of programming'. And all the critics seemed united in hailing the strength of the ensemble, with Alastair Macaulay in the *Financial Times* declaring, 'With its new double-bill the RSC are back on form' and Susannah Clapp in *The Observer* suggesting, 'Suddenly the RSC looks as if it's got a point again.'

I read the Sunday reviews with breakfast in bed, on a sunny morning in the Palace Hotel in Torquay, where Tony was filming. He's playing Hitler in the Peter Richardson satire *Churchill: The Hollywood Years* with Christian Slater as Churchill. Luckily, the toothbrush moustache is applied in the makeup van, so when we go out for a walk on the cliffs I am not accompanied by the Führer.

It's a Hockney-blue day, and the air feels washed and clean. Tony says to me, 'Are you still sorry you didn't get "The Job"? All that fuss two years ago, now it all seems like *Much Ado About Nothing*, and what's next?' 'What do you mean?' I say. He chuckles. '*All's Well That Ends Well*, of course. You couldn't make it up.'

The pairing of *The Taming of the Shrew* and *The Tamer Tamed* travelled on to play at the Kennedy Center in Washington, DC, over Christmas, and then on the strength of the reviews, returned to the UK in the New Year for a season at the Queen's Theatre on Shaftesbury Avenue, courtesy again of Thelma ever so politely twisting Bill Kenwright's arm.

12

All's Well That Ends Well

– 2003: Swan Theatre, Stratford-upon-Avon; Gielgud Theatre, London.

I sent Judi Dench a postcard inviting her to play the Countess in *All's Well That Ends Well*. The following morning, I got a phone call. It was Judi. 'The Countess? *All's Well*? The Swan? This autumn? Yes, to all four questions.' A few days later, we were strolling around her garden in the Surrey Weald.

10 May 2003.
'I don't know the play,' she says, 'never seen it, read it, or been in it. You're going to have to tell me everything about it, please. The plot, everything.' She pours me a glass of Dom Pérignon and we walk about the garden. We sit by the side of the lawn and I tell her the whole story, with its fiendishly complicated ring plot, which I am quite sure I messed up completely. She smiles and cries with every turn of it. Sammy, her 5-year-old grandson, flits among the trees, looking for all the fairy kingdom like Puck, overhearing our conference.

I leave her the new Penguin edition, and some tentative dates, and pray she'll do it.
'Feel good?'
'Yes,' she says, 'it does.'
Judi hadn't performed for the RSC in Stratford for nearly twenty-five years. She had played Imogen in David Jones's production of *Cymbeline* in 1979, and it's ten years since she had appeared in Peter Shaffer's *The Gift of the Gorgon* in The Pit at the Barbican.

* * *

We were taking the cue for the play's setting from the intriguing fact that the King's Men performed for their new patron, King James I, at Wilton House near Salisbury in December 1603. One grey summer morning, our creative team, Stephen Brimson Lewis (set designer), Deirdre Clancy (costume designer) and Paul Englishby (composer), and I went down to Wiltshire for a visit. We wanted to absorb the beauty of the place and have the opportunity to discuss together how the play might be revealed by such an Arcadian setting.

The Double Cube Room at Wilton is one of the most beautiful grand rooms in England. On one side of the fireplace hangs Van Dyck's painting of William Herbert, 3rd Earl of Pembroke. I stand staring at the picture. Can this rather gloomy, scowling portrait really have once been the beautiful young man that Shakespeare adored? Is this Mr WH, the 'Lord of my vassalage', to whom he addressed intensely private sonnets? And was that same young man perhaps also the person on whom Shakespeare based the character of Bertram in *All's Well That Ends Well*?

We have no record of the original performance of *All's Well*, but scholars usually place it as having been written in 1604. If this is true, then Shakespeare may have used his experience of visiting Wilton House, the home of the Pembroke family, a few months earlier in December 1603.

James I had fled the plague that was ravaging London and arrived for an extended stay at Wilton. His host, the recently widowed countess, Mary, invited Shakespeare's company to perform for the royal party.

It has been suggested that this was not Shakespeare's first visit to Wilton, and that the countess had invited him before to help sort out her troublesome son, William Pembroke. To celebrate his seventeenth birthday, she is supposed to have commissioned Shakespeare to write seventeen sonnets, urging the headstrong young heir to marry.

Two years earlier, a marriage had been negotiated with Elizabeth Carey, granddaughter of the Lord Chamberlain, then patron of Shakespeare's company, but William declared it 'not to his liking'. Then Bridget Vere, the granddaughter of Queen Elizabeth's great minister, Lord Burghley, had been chosen as a bride for him, but again he refused to obey his parents.

If Shakespeare did write those seventeen sonnets for Mary's son, they were not successful. William was not persuaded to give up his bachelor life.

I imagine the young 3rd Earl of Pembroke, in 1597, arriving at the court of the ailing Elizabeth and catching the eye of the 'it girl' of the moment, Mary Fitton. Mary was one of the Queen's maids of honour and had a wild reputation. They had an affair, Mary became pregnant, and William, perhaps by now predictably, refused to marry her. The Queen was enraged and jailed the reckless young courtier. Eventually released, he fled his disgrace and travelled to Italy.

In *All's Well*, the Countess of Rossillion is recently widowed (like Mary Herbert when the King's Men visited Wilton). She sends her young son Bertram as a ward to the ailing King of France. Despite the insistence of the monarch (and just like the marriage-averse William Herbert) he is reluctant to marry and runs away (like William Herbert) to Italy to fight the Tuscan wars. The coincidences seem too extraordinary to ignore.

But if Bertram is a portrait of William Herbert, the object of Shakespeare's infatuation, does that make Helena a self-portrait of Shakespeare?

Helena, a lowborn doctor's daughter, is obsessively in love with young Bertram, and bewails her idolatrous love in the knotty, tortured language of the sonnets, gnarled by the pressure of thought.[1] He is, she feels, too far above her for her love to become a reality.

> I am undone: there is no living, none,
> If Bertram be away. 'Twere all one

---

[1]   Indeed, she creates her own complete sonnet at the pivotal moment, when she determines on her plan to follow Bertram to court, beginning 'Our remedies oft in ourselves do lie.'

That I should love a bright particular star
And think to wed it, he is so above me:
In his bright radiance and collateral light
Must I be comforted, not in his sphere.

Nevertheless, she follows him to Paris, where she cures the king with one of her father's remedies.

Shakespeare himself constantly reiterates the difference in estates between himself and the beautiful young man he addresses in the sonnets, and, like Helena, feels privileged to move in elevated spheres by dint of his special gift. Can he be projecting his life into the character of Helena? I think the answer is probably yes – and into the character of Parolles, too, the play's delightful fantasist. What better name for Shakespeare to give himself than Mr Words (paroles being the French for 'words')?

However, if Bertram is a veiled portrait of someone that Shakespeare knew, William Herbert isn't the only possible candidate. Perhaps Bertram is based on that other striking young earl who had been Shakespeare's earlier patron, Henry Wriothesley, Earl of Southampton.

Southampton had also caused embarrassment by refusing to marry a granddaughter of Lord Burghley and had finally been trapped into marrying a girl called Elizabeth Vernon when she became pregnant by him. He too incurred the wrath of the monarch and went away to war; this time to the Irish wars where he was made a General of the Horse by the Earl of Essex – the title conferred upon Bertram in Act Three of the play.

Perhaps the ease with which I can apply Bertram's story to the biography of either earl is proof that it is finally a redundant, if diverting, exercise. After all, Shakespeare would surely not have risked the displeasure of either patron by exposing their private affairs on the public stage. On the other hand, why did he choose this particular story to turn into a play, if its subject matter is so close to the knuckle? Is he indulging his passionate obsession for either or both of these young men, by sublimating his feelings in the characters of this most bittersweet of plays – in the dangerous, if futile, hope that 'all's well that ends well'?

If William Herbert was the handsome young object of Shakespeare's adulation in the sonnets, that was many years before the portrait in the Double Cube Room was painted. Here he is a sober establishment figure. Now Lord Chamberlain, he has become, like his mother, a great patron of the arts. It was to their lordships William and his brother Philip 'the most noble and incomparable pair of brethren' that John Heminge (*sic*) and Henry Condell dedicated Shakespeare's First Folio in 1623.

Our first record of *All's Well* is its appearance in this collected edition. If William was the original for Bertram, and he was aware of it, what did he feel about that man Shakespeare two decades later? And what would his older self have made of his younger portrait? Perhaps, like the Countess in the play, he would muse:

Even so it was with me when I was young.
If ever we are nature's, these are ours: this thorn
Doth to our rose of youth rightly belong.
Our blood to us, this to our blood is born.

At the end of *All's Well*, Helena has become pregnant by Bertram (albeit by a bed trick), and he finally accepts her as his wife. We are left to wonder whether or not the young couple will find happiness together.

I have always thought that *All's Well That Ends Well* should have a question mark at the end of the title. Or is the definitive assertion, that everything will turn out all right, meant to be as ironic as *All is True*, as cockily presumptuous as *As You Like It*, or as optimistically determined as *Much Ado About Nothing*?

All's Well may have been presented in 1604, the year that William Herbert finally did get a wife. Perhaps that is why he seems to be scowling in his portrait. He married a wealthy heiress, Lady Mary Talbot, who (it was reported) was 'dwarfish and unattractive'. One waspish courtier wrote: 'He paid much too dear for his wife's fortune by taking her person into the bargain.'

All's well that ends well, indeed.

*   *   *

We began rehearsals for *All's Well* in October, in Clapham in the hall of St Peter's, often affectionately referred to as St Peter Hall. Judi Dench was finishing a film for the first week, so she missed the initial work of reading the play and taking the text apart line by line. But I deliberately waited to do any full read-through or any model-showing until her arrival.

On the Monday morning of the second week, I arrived at St Peter's awash with nerves. Judi arrived with a streaming cold. She put her bag down by the door, a ritual I had heard about. She never quite believes the part is meant to be hers, so she leaves her bag by the door in case a hasty exit is required.

I have a rule that if anyone's mobile phone goes off in rehearsal, they are charged five pounds (and twenty-five pounds if it goes off during a run, which I am glad to say has never happened). Within moments of her arrival, Judi's phone went off in her bag. She rushed at the bag, picked it up and flew out of the door, returning moments later in abject apology. We all immediately knew it was her phone. The ring tone was the James Bond theme tune.

Ice broken, we got onto the serious business of rehearsal, although I suspect laughter is never far away when Judi Dench rehearses. In the first scene, Bertram enquires, 'What is it, my good lord, the king languishes of?' and the Lafeu replies laconically, 'A fistula, my lord'. For some reason it took about a week for Judi and fellow culprits Charles Kay and Jamie Glover (playing Lafeu and Bertram) to get past the word 'fistula'.

George Bernard Shaw, in a coruscating review of a production of the play by the Irving Dramatic Club in 1895, castigated the actress playing the Countess for being unable to discover any of her 'wonderfully pleasant, good sense, humanity and originality'. It was, he wrote, 'the most beautiful old woman's part ever written'. I omitted the word 'old' when I recounted Shaw's description to Judi, or perhaps I softened it to 'older'. However, the character does make several references to her age, a fact that taxed Judi.

'She keeps on going on about her age,' she would say. '"My heart is heavy, and my age is weak", or she says she rejoices that she'll see the king before she dies. Is she about to pop her clogs? How old am I meant to play her?'

I said I thought the accumulated burden of grief at the loss of her husband, and now her son and the troubles he gets himself into, and the abandonment of Helena, all that make the Countess feel her age weighing upon her.

'So how old am I meant to play her?'

I urged Judi to play herself, at which she roared, 'Oh thank you very much! My director thinks I am decrepit!'

Throughout rehearsals Judi continued to explore and deepen the Countess's relationship with Lavache (Mark Lambert) her wise fool, a strange mystical 'woodland fellow', and with her surrogate daughter, Helena. She'd often surprise us with sudden flashes of feeling in the Countess, for instance at the point where the Dumaine brothers bring the news that her son has gone to war, she turned on them in a sudden blistering fury when they attempted to excuse his actions. She'd work tirelessly at focusing and refining the laughs. She delighted in the invention of giving Lavache a bath before he sets out to court to deliver a letter. But she was as rigorous at ensuring that every moment of the last scene, as revelation follows revelation, was given its proper shock weight and emotional significance.

The younger actors would often sit in on my rehearsals with Judi. To listen to her delivery of the text was to hear a masterclass in Shakespeare's verse. She would feel the verse line, beating out the iambic rhythm on her hand if in doubt where the stress lay. And in the early stages of rehearsal, she would not be able to remember the line if the pulse was wrong. She'd seek to release the easy natural effects of the line endings, never pausing so much as lifting and considering the end of the line before completing the sense with the next. For example, when the Countess (in Act One Scene Three) says to Helena as she dissembles her love for Bertram:

My fear hath catch'd your fondness; now I see
The mystery of your loneliness, and find
Your salt tears' head. Now to all sense 'tis gross:
You love my son.

At the end of the first line, where others might have run on, Judi would lift the word 'see', allowing the next phrase ('the mystery of your loneliness') to be considered precisely, and compassionately expressed. And lifting the end of the second line allowed her to land on the next four syllables with tough maternal love, leading to the confession that she wants to flush out of Helena: 'You love my son'.

If that sounds very technical it's because it is. Classical acting wouldn't be a craft if there weren't disciplines involved. The art is to hide the technique, to marry application with inspiration, and balance concentration with relaxation. Like a great master craftsman, Judi not only continues to hone her craft, but to pass it on.

When the Countess discovers that Helena loves Bertram, she realizes that she's gaining a daughter, and pours all her efforts and love into her young ward. That makes the loss of Helena in the middle of the play almost intolerable for her, and why her eventual recovery in Act Five can't be expressed in words.

The Countess says nothing when Helena returns, as if from the dead, at the end of the play. Her new daughter-in-law turns to the Countess with the line, 'Oh, my dear mother, do I see you living?' There is no reply. There can't be. Judi's choice was for the Countess to stare at Helena, almost unable to move, and finally, slowly turn her outstretched hands, palm upwards, to signal silent, welcome, acceptance, and profound relief. It was a moment to haunt you with its radiant stillness, and she created it with transcendent economy and truth. The effect was devastating.

I can watch what Judi does, study it, admire it, comment on it, but I can't tell you how she does it; how she makes silence eloquent, or humanity palpable. It's just her. It's why she's great.

*   *   *

The Countess is the beating heart of the play, but of course it is a relatively small role. The ensemble around her was packed with talent.

Claudie Blakley seized the challenging contradictions of Helena with both hands. Helena is a problematic heroine. She can seem an alarmingly manipulative character, tenacious, masochistic perhaps, certainly coercive in her pursuit of love. She is a mixture of calculation and passion; part nun, part stalker; a social victim and an iron butterfly. Why does someone so clever, so passionate, foist herself on the emotionally stunted Bertram? Claudie played her with disarming power, with a mischievous grace and a raw emotional candour that reconciled and resolved those contradictions by acknowledging that that is what make us human.

The bed-trick she plays on Bertram may be morally dubious, but from her perspective it acts as a sort of corrective for his bad behaviour.

Jamie Glover, as Bertram, also embraced the opposing sides of that character: spoiled immature brat, but with the valuable potential to prove himself an excellent soldier. Bertram doesn't want to be shackled by marriage or by the society of the French court. Going off and becoming General of the Horse is liberating for him; he wants to sow his wild oats and play the field. He has a kind of charisma that is irresistible to somebody like Helena. She firmly believes she is the one who can solve his problems; she is the one who will make him fall in love with her. His mother, the Countess, sees that this love is deeply felt, and does not object to it on class grounds because she sees virtue and integrity in Helena and therefore allows the sincerity of her love to prosper.

Bertram's accomplice is the congenitally unreliable Parolles, the moral negative to Helena's positive. Guy Henry played him not so much as the braggart soldier but as an insecure pretentious neurotic, with the desperate survival instinct of the self-deluded.

When he is captured and blindfolded by his fellow soldiers posing as enemy troops, they interrogate him in marvellously improvised Russian gibberish phrases ('boblibindo chicurmurco' being my favourite). His cowardice is soon exposed, but in Guy's revelatory performance, you realize that this humiliated, forlornly self-knowing figure achieves a little belated dignity. When he declares 'There's place and means for every man alive', it is with palpable relief that he no longer has to maintain his fake ID.

We tried to embrace the play's elusive ambivalence with an emotional integrity. The play is life-haunted, tantalizingly full of sorrow and joy, of cynicism and hope, a meditation on the sadness of age and the folly of youth, all fused into a life-enhancing whole. The plot may be fanatical, but the people who have to negotiate their way through it must be very real.

3 December: Technical rehearsal.
Reached the last scene of the tech. The perspex panels of Stephen Brimson Lewis's pewter set design look like etched glass, or tarnished mirrors, and Tim Mitchell's silvery lighting illuminates them like pale sunlight filtering through bare winter trees.

Then in Florence, as Helena implores the Widow and Diana to assist her, Tim creates a ravishing warm chiaroscuro glow, which makes the women, sitting around a small table, lit only by a candle, look as if they have stepped right out of a painting by Georges de la Tour.

Our costume designer Deirdre Clancy isn't happy with the pilgrim costume for Helena. It somehow needs to be humbler. The costume supervisor arrives with a whole rack of alternatives pulled from the store. A couple are chosen and Claudie disappears for a few minutes to try them on. She returns in the perfect outfit, a simple ankle-length black dress with long fitted sleeves. Judi comes over.

'Just a moment, can I have a look at the label?'

All RSC costumes have labels in the back saying which actor, which part, which play, and sometimes a date. Claudie turns round and Judi lifts the neckline.

'Judi Dench, Lady Macbeth, Macbeth 1976.'

Claudie is thrilled.

*   *   *

The day after press night I had to fly out to Washington, DC, to open *The Taming of the Shrew* and *The Tamer Tamed* at the Kennedy Center.

Sunday 14 December 2003.
The River Inn. Washington, DC.
The phone wakes me. It's Tony.

'Turn on the TV.'

'What? Why?'

'Saddam Hussein has been captured.'

'What!'

On the press night of *Shrew* and *Tamer* back in Stratford on 9 April, Saddam Hussein's statue was toppled in Firdos Square, in Baghdad. Jubilant crowds attacked it with sledgehammers and slapped the face with their sandals. It becomes the abiding image of the Iraq War. Now General Raymond Odierno is describing the spider-hole in which he has been found. There is footage of Saddam in his bushy grey beard being examined for hair lice, his mouth open wide with someone shining a torch and putting in a spatula.

Tony doesn't like me being in Washington, for fear of some sort of reprisal attack.

'How close are you to the White House?'

'Very.'

'Wrap up when you go out.'

'Why?'

'It's snowing outside.'

'What?'

Overnight, a blanket of snow has settled over the capital city. On the TV, everybody is waiting for President George W. Bush to speak to the nation at noon. Tony Blair is talking about how good this is for the world. So, all's well that ends well, then!

'Oh, and by the way,' says my Tony, 'the Sunday Reviews are fantastic.'

13

Othello

– 2004: Swan Theatre, Stratford-upon-Avon;
Japan Tour; Trafalgar Studios, London.

Tony and I had been thinking about *Othello* for years. Iago was one of those roles that he had been frequently asked to play. The part, as they say, 'had his name on it'. The question was who should play Othello.

In 1988, director Deborah Warner asked then Artistic Director Terry Hands if she could direct Brian Cox as Othello, with Tony as Iago. But the days when white actors would count Othello among their list of ambitions were already numbered. The last white actor to play the role at Stratford was Donald Sinden (with Bob Peck as Iago) in 1979/80.[1] Ben Kingsley, who is of Indian heritage, had played the role in 1985. Michael Gambon was probably the last white actor in the UK to play the moor, in Scarborough in 1990 (the first and last Shakespeare play to be directed by Alan Ayckbourn). Nevertheless, in 1992, Robert Stephens (who was enjoying a late blaze of glory at the RSC, playing Falstaff for Adrian Noble) proposed to Tony that he play Iago to his Othello. By the time Deborah made her request, Terry had already planned the RSC's next *Othello*; Trevor Nunn had cajoled the opera singer Willard White to play the title role the following year, with Ian McKellen as Iago. It would be the last production in the old TOP.

After Willard White, it was ten years before the RSC did *Othello* again, when the 25-year-old Ray Fearon became the first Black actor to play Othello on the Royal Shakespeare Theatre main stage.[2] This was not an Othello remotely 'declined into the vale of years', but Ray gave a very powerful, sexy performance. There followed a brace of other young black Othellos: David Harewood at the National and Paterson Joseph at the Royal Exchange.

An intriguing photo-negative production at the Shakespeare Theatre in Washington, DC, in 1997 saw Patrick Stewart as Othello in an otherwise African-American cast. Patrick had said that Othello was a role he had in a sense been preparing for since he was about 14. 'When the time came that I was old enough and experienced enough to do it,' he was quoted as saying, 'it was the same time that it no longer became acceptable

---

[1] At the same time, Paul Scofield played the role for the NT in 1980, recording it in 1988.
[2] Paul Robeson played it in 1959, before the company obtained its royal title.

for a white actor to put on blackface and pretend to be African.' He continued perhaps provocatively: 'To replace the black outsider with a white man in a black society will, I hope, encourage a much broader view of the fundamentals of racism.'

Interestingly, at the same time as white classical actors of a certain age might have been lamenting the loss of this great role from their potential repertoire, a prominent Black actor suggested, 'Of all the parts in the canon, perhaps Othello is the one which should most definitely not be played by a Black actor.' Hugh Quarshie delivered a lecture under the title 'Hesitations on Othello'[3] at the University of Alabama in September 1998.

In the preface to the printed edition of this lecture, Gary Taylor reminds us that, at that time, Hugh was best known for 'crossing the colour line' at the RSC. 'In the 1980s, he became the first Anglo-African actor to play major roles: Hotspur, Tybalt, Antony, Banquo, which had traditionally always belonged to whites.'

Hugh's contention was that in choosing the story of the jealous moor, Shakespeare was 'endorsing a racist convention'; that performance conventions 'had further reinforced racist views'; and that 'it may never be possible to avoid the conclusion that Othello behaves as he does because he is black.' He distils his nagging anxiety further saying, 'If a black actor plays Othello does he not risk making racial stereotypes seem legitimate and even true.'

In 2001, in our search to find Othello I felt I had at least to approach Hugh to see if his views had changed, or whether he felt, as he had indicated in his lecture, that 'a non-racist interpretation may nevertheless be possible, with careful editing of text, and a radical re-reading of key passages'.

We met to talk further. Hugh is the Oxford-educated son of a Ghanaian diplomat. His insistence was that if, in his descent into his jealous rage, Othello seems to revert to behaviour that could be regarded as innate to his African heritage, that just vindicates Iago's view of him as a savage.

He felt that the characterization of the Black general who, for all his military control in the field, loses it in his personal life – suggesting that he somehow reverts to an animal behaviour that is closer to his nature because of his race – is a dangerous racial stereotype, which Shakespeare has inadvertently perpetuated for centuries.

I argued that surely Shakespeare's genius is to be able to capture men and women in all manner of adversity, at all sorts of extreme moments of their lives regardless of their race or gender. Surely it is not that Leontes is King of Sicilia, that makes his fits of jealousy so violent. 'Oh, he's Sicilian! what would you expect?' It is a portrait of a man unbalanced by the disease of morbid jealousy. Or is it because Macbeth is Scottish, that he can 'unseam' a man 'from the nave to the chops', and 'memorise another Golgotha' in his bloody beserker onslaught of the Norwegian forces. Faced with a threat to our lives and families, that violent potential is perhaps there in all of us and underpinned with the unspoken ambition for potential advancement.

Because Lear is old and furiously curses his own daughter Goneril with sterility, should this imply that the behaviour is just typical of old people who have lived

---

[3]   Later called 'Second Thoughts about Othello' and given on behalf of the International Shakespeare Association.

privileged lives? Is it because Shylock is Jewish that he demands his impossible bond, or the fact that he has not only endured a lifetime of constant physical and mental abuse from the Christians, but suffered the loss of his only daughter? And of course, is it intrinsically because Richard III was born with scoliosis that he behaves in such a way, or is it the product of years of dealing with society's prejudice against him?

One of Hugh's inevitable concerns was about Othello not being just a foil to Iago. As we concluded our first meeting with an agreement to talk further, Hugh warned me about the distinct possibility of a TV series later that year.[4] Although our conversation did not lead to Hugh playing Othello opposite Tony as Iago, it did result, albeit many years later, in me persuading him to return to the RSC to play the role opposite Lucian Msamati as Iago in 2015. The debate over racism, anti-semitism, sexism and ableism in Shakespeare has only intensified since then.

Our search to find Othello took us to America. That July, we made a three-day trip to New York at the invitation of André Bishop at the Lincoln Center, to discuss the possible co-production of *Othello* at the Vivian Beaumont. Tony had had huge success with Pam Gems' play *Stanley* at The Circle in the Square in 1997, nominated for Best Actor at the Tony Awards.

I still have the typed list with scribbled notes of potential Othellos that the Lincoln Center, and their casting director Daniel Swee, had drawn up. It included Morgan Freeman, Samuel Jackson, Mahershala Ali and Denzel Washington.

Ultimately those negotiations stalled as the RSC entered a very rocky period in the early 2000s.

Tony published his autobiography *Beside Myself* in May 2001, and Random House invited us to South Africa to launch it there. They hosted a party at Exclusive Books in Cape Town. The guest list included a number of friends from the production of *Titus Andronicus* we had performed in Jo'burg in 1995. This list included Sello Maake Ka-Ncube who had played Aaron, now in his mid-forties, and with a successful television career.

Later that month back in the UK, we met up with Sello again in a joyous celebration that we helped to organize called *Freedom Too!* at the Festival Hall on the South Bank. The event was intended to promote the new South Africa in the UK. And the high commissioner, the exuberant Cheryl Carolus (who could get anyone to do anything), had pulled in a great line-up, with everyone from Hugh Masekela to the opera singer Sibongile Khumalo, Janet Suzman and Richard E. Grant. At the end of the concert, I danced on stage with Desmond Tutu, one of the happiest experiences of my life.

As part of the show, Sello and fellow actor James Ngcobo did an extract from *Sizwe Banzi is Dead*, which was written collaboratively by Athol Fugard with the original actors John Kani and Winston Ntshona. Sello's energy on stage was phenomenal, his charisma, his appetite for life. We were reminded of his performance in *Titus*. As Aaron, he seemed to walk on stage with the whole weight of Apartheid on his back, a huge burden. You understood Aaron's motive for revenge and his desire to get his own back.

---

[4] It turned out to be Holby City in which Hugh would become one of the show's longest running cast members, playing Ric Griffin for nineteen years until leaving in 2020.

As we watched in the wings, we both knew we had finally found our Othello. I caught Tony's eye:

'Do you think he could do it? Othello?'

'No idea. But I'd love to try.'

We asked Sello. He was thrilled. Then he was terrified. 'I'm just a boy from Orlando East,'[5] he said. 'English is not my first language. And Shakespeare's language is not even English, it's a 400-year-old whatever version of English.' When we had worked on *Titus*, Sello asked me one day what the word 'Thee' meant. And *Titus* had premiered in South Africa, where the audience could relate to a variety of different accents, languages and pronunciations. 'This,' as Sello cried one day, 'would be at the Royal Shakespeare Company, in Stratford-upon-fucking-Avon!'

Both Tony and Sello grew up in South Africa under Apartheid. How thrilling to view Shakespeare's play from those specific perspectives. As Tony said:

> Racism was just second nature. It was simply what you were brought up to believe: that black people were inferior. Now, I could simply play that. Othello as my senior commander was inferior just by virtue of being black. The fact that it's second nature doesn't make it any less ugly – it's far worse that people can be racist without even stopping to think about it.

Othello is a fight between heavyweights. Now we had found two who could enter the ring together. Or as Tony put it, 'It's about two men who tumble into hell together, each dragging the other along with him.'

*   *   *

Our production had been designed to play in the Swan Theatre. Like *Macbeth*, we wanted this chamber play to bake in that particular oven.

When Michael Boyd took over the RSC as Artistic Director, in 2003, he planned to do 'The Tragedies' for his first season and asked us to consider moving our production to the Main Stage. I was anxious that this would expose Sello to a much tougher challenge, but Tony was adamant. His conception of Iago required an intimate relationship with the audience which he argued was virtually impossible in the RST.[6] Michael understood but made it clear that we would have to find the extra costs involved in mounting the production.

In 2002, Adrian Noble had allowed me to mount a risky season of Jacobethan plays in the Swan. In the normal course of events these Swan shows might have expected to be seen in The Pit. But with the company's departure from the Barbican there was no obvious way of finding a London home for this ambitious season. Adrian, although officially still in office, was now too beleaguered, and financially under too much pressure to consider any thought of transferring the season. The Roundhouse season had cost too much, and the deficit stood at an estimated £2 million+. The fate of the

---

[5]   A suburb of Soweto.
[6]   Ironically, that intimacy is now eminently possible in the transformed theatre that Michael Boyd saw through to completion six years later.

Jacobethan season hung in the balance. We would need a generous, and possibly crazy, backer to invest in such a risky project. So, we went looking for angels. And one arrived.

We persuaded Thelma Holt to come up to Stratford.

'I knew exactly what he wanted,' Thelma said later in an interview. 'We sat in his garden. He gave me tuna. He knows I like tuna. They're such tarts, these directors.' Had the RSC approached her first, she says, 'I'd have told them, "Bugger off".'

She came to see *The Malcontent* and then *The Roman Actor*,[7] and by the time she had seen my production, *The Island Princess*, she had agreed to take all five plays into the West End. Thelma roped in her old ally, producer Bill Kenwright. He asked her one question. 'Why, Thelma, why take five old plays no-one has ever heard of onto Shaftesbury Avenue?' Her reply was simple: 'Because it's impossible! Now open your cheque book!'

Bill later joked, 'Thelma's like Einstein crossed with Bugs Bunny. There is genius, which she has in abundance. But there is also a touch of Looney Tunes. Every year she goes to the brink of bankruptcy and every year she bounces back. She lives like a hurricane.' There has been no one like Thelma in British theatre since that last great female crusader, Lilian Baylis. She is a true maverick, one of the country's most daring and visionary producers.

In December 2002, against all odds, and having successfully persuaded Bill Kenwright, Thelma opened the entire Jacobethan season at the Gielgud Theatre: the first time plays by Ben Jonson, John Fletcher, John Marston and Philip Massinger had ever been seen on Shaftesbury Avenue. We were extended by six weeks, and six months later Judi Dench presented me on behalf of the whole company with an Olivier Award for Outstanding Achievement.

But Thelma didn't stop there. When *The Taming of the Shrew* and *The Tamer Tamed* returned from its residency at the Kennedy Center in Washington, DC, over the Christmas of 2003, she and Bill Kenwright took both shows into the Queen's Theatre. Later, when she heard I had landed Judi Dench for *All's Well that Ends Well* in the Swan that winter (2003/4), they secured the Gielgud for a run of that.

So, on this more recent occasion, in 2003, when Thelma learnt that we hoped to produce *Othello* in the intimacy of the Swan, but that in order to do so we needed to find some extra funding, her eyes glinted with delight. 'Darling, it's simple,' she declared, airily wafting her hand. 'I'm sure we can persuade HoriPro to fund the production outright in return for a little tour of Japan. We'll do a couple of dozen performances: the Ginza, in Tokyo, then Kitakyushu, Biwako, and end up in Big Nina's[8] gaff in Saitama.' And then to dot the eye of the dragon, we would return to London and open a brand new theatre called The Trafalgar Studios, based in the old Whitehall theatre, the home to the Brian Rix farces of the early sixties.

We were on.

*   *   *

---

[7] Tony played Malevole in Marston's *The Malcontent*; and Domitian Caesar in Massinger's *The Roman Actor*, a performance he considered one of his best.
[8] 'Big Nina' was Thelma's infinitely affectionate name for her beloved Yukio Ninagawa, the world-renowned stage director.

Tony played Iago as a die-hard regimental sergeant major, right down to his square-bashing boots. His characterization was based on the men he knew and feared during his national service in the South African army, back in Walvis Bay: rough, humorous, popular with the lads, happier at work than at home. On the outside, absolutely trustworthy; on the inside, severely disturbed. Tony elaborated:

> Iago can't seem to open his mouth without some sexual allusion spilling out. You could argue that this is just the way soldiers talk, but there's something odder, more perverse in Iago's language. To him, having sexual intercourse is 'making the beast with two backs'. Why this savage image? Perhaps a clue comes in his speech about Desdemona: 'Now, I do love her too, / Not out of absolute lust – though peradventure / I stand accountant for as great a sin'. Why does Iago have to reassure us that he could be lustful if he chose? We wouldn't expect anything less of this supremely macho man. Is it that he's impotent, and physically incapable of making the beast with two backs? Or is he sterile? Could these things account for his strange energy, his appetite for chaos, his nihilism? I'm not sure. I certainly based my portrayal on the idea of a man with a severe sexual hang-up, though I rather liked leaving this undefined . . .

The fact that a large amount of Iago's dialogue is written in prose became very useful to our setting of the play, which was a military base on Cyprus, mid-twentieth century. In this context Tony's interpretation of Iago, as a master of barrack-room banter, was much more available in prose than it would've been in verse.

Iago is a great improviser. Tony really responded to this definition. Iago is intoxicated by the joy ride and is indifferent to his own fate. He loves bouncing on his tightrope.

It was during the rehearsals of *Othello* that I realized a key challenge in directing Shakespeare. How do you keep a sense of spontaneity? How do you make the actors approach the action as if they don't know what is going to happen next? They need to forget they have read the play and know how it ends. The challenge seems particularly acute in *Othello*. It is too easy for Iago's duping of Othello to seem effortless, and for the action to seem entirely in his control (one of Hugh Quarshie's main concerns).

One day, we were rehearsing the terrifying Othello/Iago encounter, in Act Three Scene Three. It starts with Iago meeting his wife Emilia who has just discovered the handkerchief spotted with strawberries that Othello had given to Desdemona. He wrests it from her and tucks it away for potential future mischief.

The encounter between Othello and Iago starts simply enough, with Iago enquiring if Othello knew Michael Cassio when he started courting Desdemona. But it very swiftly tilts into a terrifying match of wits as Iago begins to poison his superior officer's mind. Sello charted Othello's rage as he descends ferociously into jealousy. It suddenly felt as if Iago, the great improviser, might be exposed and his own malicious jealousy revealed.

Tony's Iago, sweating from the exertion of the fight with Othello, wheeled back from this encounter. He pulled his hanky from his pocket to wipe his brow, only to discover that he had pulled out the embroidered handkerchief. Swiftly pocketing it again, he enquired:

> Have you not sometimes seen a handkerchief
> Spotted with strawberries in your wife's hand?

It was an electric moment. The course of the scene was not predetermined but seemed, instead, to rely upon a chance event.

I now call these beats 'crossroads'. I have already mentioned a number of them. They occur when a character reaches a moment of choice and determines to go in one particular direction. The trick is to leave open the possibility that they will go in quite another direction, but, for whatever reason, does not.

I remember the moment in Trevor Nunn's production of *Romeo and Juliet* when Ian McKellen's Romeo, embracing Francesca Annis's Juliet in his arms, was about to kill himself, when suddenly behind his head, Juliet stretched out her arm as if she was about to awake, and the whole audience gasped. With what? With relief? With shock? With the possibility that just for tonight the story would end differently? It didn't. Of course. But for a moment it might have.

Tony wrote of these crossroads: 'Sello and I played the Act Three Scene Three crossroads for all they were worth, and each night it felt like a wild rollercoaster ride, without either of us quite knowing who would reach the other end safely or in command.'

*   *   *

When Laurence Olivier played Iago opposite Ralph Richardson, at the Old Vic in 1938, he and director Tyrone Guthrie were 'swept away' by the theory 'that Iago was subconsciously in love with Othello and had to destroy him'.[9] There was undoubtedly very little possibility of the straighter-than-straight Richardson entertaining this idea, but nevertheless Olivier pursued it.

> In a reckless moment during rehearsals I threw my arms around Ralph and kissed him full on the mouth. He coolly disengaged himself from my embrace, patted me gently on the back of the neck, and, more in sorrow than in anger, murmured, 'There, there now; dear boy; *good* boy ...

But it didn't end there. Olivier had one more trick up his sleeve. When Richardson fell to the floor, helpless in the clutches of an epileptic paroxysm, Olivier would fall beside him, and simulate an orgasm.

'Terrifically daring, wasn't I?' Olivier wrote years later in his autobiography.[10] But apparently, after one particular matinee, the comic actress Athene Seyler came round and said, 'I'm sure I have *no* idea what you were up to when you threw yourself on the ground beside Ralph.' That was the end of that. The business came out. Actor and director concluded that Iago just hated Othello because he was Black and his superior

---

[9]   The theory of Ernest Jones, biographer and friend of Freud, and first English-speaking practitioner of psychoanalysis.
[10]   *Confessions of an Actor* (1982), Simon & Schuster.

officer. And that Othello preferred Cassio as his lieutenant 'because he was a gentleman and Iago was not'.

Attributing Iago's motives to homosexual desire is interesting but problematic, perhaps as problematic as saying Othello is prompted to primitive violence because he is Black. It risks playing to the audience's prejudice that Iago's wickedness stems from his sexuality. He's sick, disturbed and therefore dangerous. If Iago is gay, doesn't that dangerously play into a notion of queerness being inherently equal to evil?

As a gay man I've personally never found any homoerotic strain in the play. I suppose the theory comes from the sequence when Iago tells of sleeping next to Cassio one night, and Cassio becoming aroused, and kissing Iago. I think this is just Iago in rabid, tabloid-journalist mode, trying to paint Cassio in the most salacious colours imaginable.

So what *is* Iago's problem?

Is it, as Samuel Taylor Coleridge famously scribbled in his copy of Shakespeare, 'motiveless malignity'? One day, after reading the play again, Tony said, 'Coleridge must have had too much opium the day he wrote that'. Iago's motives for corrupting the mind of his general are manifold: his anger at being overlooked by his superior officer, his hatred of 'the moor' because of his colour, and his belief that both Othello and Cassio have slept with his wife. Some argue that he is lying when he makes these claims. But as no other character in Shakespeare can be said to lie in a speech delivered as an aside to the audience, why should Iago?

Tony wrote,

> I don't believe that Iago lies to the audience in his soliloquies. When he suggests that both Othello and Cassio have slept with his wife, Emilia, he thinks it's true. Iago seems as much under the spell of the 'green-eyed monster' as is the Moor. I think the reason that Iago is so successful at duping Othello is that Iago knows about jealousy from deep within. 'O, beware, my lord, of jealousy' he says with real feeling. Earlier, talking of his suspicion that Othello has slept with Emilia, he says 'the thought whereof / Doth – like a poisonous mineral – gnaw my inwards'. Iago is like a man with a highly contagious disease, who is determined to pass on the germs. This aspect of Iago was crucial to my interpretation.

In fact, during the rehearsals we discussed a whole series of factors that might contribute to Iago's behaviour, but determined not to make any specific decisions, to prevent cutting off different options in the course of the performance run. One factor, however, that proved very intriguing was the possibility that Iago might be impotent.

This introduces the third member of the quartet, Iago's wife Emilia.

The instruments in a string quartet echo the register of the human voice – soprano, alto, tenor, bass. The four main characters in this play could be identified in the same way: Iago is surely the natural tenor and Othello the bass (though Verdi reversed this order in his opera *Otello*). The soprano is Desdemona; the alto, Emilia. The four must work together effortlessly, as together they carry three quarters of the lines of the entire play. Iago is the largest role in the canon next to Hamlet and Richard III. Together, he and Othello command over half the text of the play. Therefore, casting this play is particularly important to get right.

We persuaded Amanda Harris to play Emilia. Amanda brings her life with her on stage. And it's a colourful one. Born in Australia, brought up in Papua New Guinea, and coming to the UK when she was ten, Amanda joined the RSC in 1986 at the age of twenty-three in the first Swan season, playing Emilia in *The Two Noble Kinsmen*. Tony had worked with Amanda in Peter Flannery's *Singer*, and in Tom Stoppard's *Travesties*. I had first worked with her when she played Penelope in *The Odyssey*.

Amanda and Tony discussed the relationship of Iago and Emilia, proposing that perhaps at the start of their marriage things had been fine. There is no evidence of children, which might be through choice, of course, or the demands of his work. But if, for whatever reason, Iago had suffered from some kind of erectile dysfunction, does he avoid the problem that it might be him, by making the problem her. Might that be the reason that his language swills with sexual imagery, that rises to the surface like scum from a cistern of bitterness and unfulfilled desire? And knowing he can't satisfy his own appetite or his wife's, is that why he suspects her of infidelity?

As Tony said, 'The play is famously about one man possessed with jealousy. We're saying it's about two.'

Amanda relished the idea of taking a fresh look at the role of Iago's wife Emilia. Rather than characterizing her as a meek long-suffering soul who waits at home for her husband, enduring his meanness to her because, despite herself, she cannot help loving him, we saw Emilia as tough as a pair of military boots, an army wife used to an ever-shifting life, married to an NCO, moving to whatever base he is deployed.

As we worked, we questioned whether the fondness expressed between Emilia and Desdemona had necessarily been there from the beginning. Perhaps she is annoyed that her husband has been assigned the job of escorting his general's new wife on campaign, knowing that the responsibility of looking after this rich Venetian senator's daughter will inevitably fall to her.

Her husband abuses her with his lewd misogynistic banter from the very first time we see them together, on their arrival in Cyprus. Although Desdemona addresses Emilia in the scene, it is not clear that Emilia says anything directly to Desdemona.

At the party on the base that night, to celebrate the defeat of the Turkish fleet, we had Emilia showing she could not only hold her own but was capable of drinking any of the men in the unit under the table. Cassio, as Iago discovers, has no head for drink at all. He ensures that he exploits that information so that as the evening gets more drunken, and the fight breaks out, Cassio loses control and is disgraced.

The following morning the wretched Cassio comes to ask Emilia if she can arrange for Desdemona to speak on his behalf to her husband.

*　　*　　*

An aspect of Shakespeare's vocabulary that can be very easy to overlook is the language of faith. It is crucial to the understanding and development of certain key characters. The word 'soul', for example. For Shakespeare, the soul is what each character holds dear and must protect at all costs. It is a proof of what is eternal and will outlive them. There is no casual emphasis of intention when characters swear on their souls.

Desdemona demonstrates her total dedication to her husband, in front of the senate, by insisting she has not only devoted herself and her fortunes 'to his honour and his valiant parts' but consecrated her soul to him, a sacred act of devotion.

After Othello's elopement with Desdemona, Iago advises him to go back inside before Brabantio's men arrive. Othello insists that such evasion is not appropriate for a man in his position:

> I must be found. My parts, my title, my perfect soul
> Shall manifestly me rightly.

The phrase 'my perfect soul' surely suggests this man's certainty of the unblemished nature of his soul and his determination to preserve it.

Our human action can jeopardize the fate of that soul, as Othello is only too aware when he protests to Desdemona, 'Perdition catch my soul, but I do love thee.' He would risk utter ruin and perpetual damnation for her love, which he calls 'my soul's joy'. Iago shares with us his view that Othello's 'soul is so enfetter'd to her love', that Desdemona can do what she wants with him,

> Even as her appetite shall play the god
> With his weak function.

At the start of Iago's attempt to poison Othello's mind, by implying that Desdemona is dishonest, Othello rebuffs him:

> ... exchange me for a goat,
> When I shall turn the business of my soul
> To such exsufflicate and blown surmises,
> Matching thy inference.

Othello's priority, 'the business of his soul', will not be contaminated by such weak human frailties. For the audience perhaps, it is just this lofty, high-minded, principled approach to his life that will blinker him from what is about to happen and make him peculiarly vulnerable to a wily predator like Iago.

Iago reinforces Othello's trust in him, by using the same language of interior spirituality. He expands upon the precious nature of reputation telling his general:

> Good name, in man or woman, dear my lord, is the immediate jewel of their souls.

When that poison starts to work, Othello threatens Iago:

> Villain, be sure thou prove my love a whore,
> Be sure of it; give me the ocular proof:
> Or by the worth of man's eternal soul,
> Thou hadst been better have been born a dog
> Than answer my waked wrath!

As Othello's suspicions are aroused and his rage is unleashed on Iago, the ensign quickly challenges the very basis of Othello's self-belief and begins to undermine it. He yells:

> O grace! O heaven forgive me!
> Are you a man? have you a soul or sense?

Othello's deep religious convictions (perhaps deepened further by being those of a convert) are not the only aspect of his character to inform his language and separate it from Iago's simpler, direct, demotic speech. Roderigo has called Othello 'an extravagant and wheeling stranger / Of here and everywhere'. And as Othello loses his faith in the love of his wife

>   . . . Look here, Iago;
> All my fond love thus do I blow to heaven.
> 'Tis gone.

He summons revenge from the bowels of the earth and dedicates himself to vengeance, dismissing in one wild flourish his entire military career:

>   O, now, for ever
> Farewell the tranquil mind! farewell content!
> Farewell the plumed troop, and the big wars,
> That make ambition virtue! O, farewell!
> Farewell the neighing steed, and the shrill trump,
> The spirit-stirring drum, the ear-piercing fife,
> The royal banner, and all quality,
> Pride, pomp and circumstance of glorious war!
> And, O you mortal engines, whose rude throats
> The immortal Jove's dead clamours counterfeit,
> Farewell! Othello's occupation's gone!

He exchanges everything he had formerly held sacred with a global metaphor of his cataclysmic rage, in a single, propulsive sentence of seven breathtaking lines.

>   . . . . Like to the Pontic sea,
> Whose icy current and compulsive course
> Ne'er feels retiring ebb, but keeps due on
> To the Propontic and the Hellespont,
> Even so my bloody thoughts, with violent pace,
> Shall ne'er look back, ne'er ebb to humble love,
> Till that a capable and wide revenge
> Swallow them up.

In performance, Sello Maake came into his own here. Tony described being on stage with Sello in this scene as like experiencing 'a fire or a hurricane'.

Faced with the duke's casual prejudice, and in the teeth of Brabantio's vitriolic racism, Sello had negotiated the Venetian scenes with a measured calm. He adopted an abstemiously blank-eyed expression, eyes front, which suggested this was not the first time he has taken racists' flak. But now, as if the faith he held had constricted, or suppressed and kept in check a darker access to a more violent emotional capacity, Sello looked into his own cultural reference to express that.

At one rehearsal, he described how, back home, he had witnessed the inyangas, or sangomas,[11] summoning the spirits of ancestors, and he drew on his own Xhosa heritage and experience to echo the moment that Othello invokes the Furies:

Arise black Vengeance from thy hollow cell.

Suddenly, as if such things can only be expressed physically, Sello broke into a pounding dance, beating and slapping the floor. It felt as if Othello was unleashing his own spirit, something that all his years of attempted assimilation into the polite constraints of Venetian society had suppressed. Now he was throwing that away.

Later when, as a result of Iago's further provocation, Othello falls into a fit, Tony echoed Sello's powerful invocation, with a mocking racist monkey dance, over the semi-conscious body. Very disturbing, and yet probably the moment when the experience of these two South Africans, growing up on either side of the Apartheid divide, came most sharply into focus.

*   *   *

The fourth member of the quartet is Desdemona. We were lucky enough to attract Lisa Dillon to play the role. Lisa had recently made a cracking stage debut as Iphigenia in Sheffield, followed swiftly by her acclaimed performance as Hilda Wangel in Ibsen's *The Master Builder*, starring opposite Patrick Stewart.

She brought a tensile strength to Desdemona without diminishing her fragile position. That vulnerability was heightened in one particular scene, where we reached another of those crossroads. And it all happened by questioning the meaning of an empty half-line.

We imagined that Emilia has helped Desdemona improvise a dressing room, in a corner of the officers' quarters. It not only has a hairbrush, hand-mirror, jewellery box and perfume bottles neatly laid out on an army field table, but the steamer trunks, standing open and brimming with drawers full of the stockings and lingerie Desdemona has brought with her from Venice. It is here, in Act Four Scene Two, that Othello, once he has dismissed Emilia, interrogates his wife.

We must feel at least a possibility that the couple might just untangle the web in which they are caught now. Sello looks like an old giant among these feminine knick-knacks. He perches on a stool. She protests her innocence upon her knees. But the more she does so, the more Othello despairs, breaking down in tears.

[11] The highly respected healers among the Zulu people of South Africa.

Iago's ability to prey on Othello's trust in his young wife is based not just on the difference in their race, but in their ages. His insecurity stems surely as much from his perception that he is, after all, 'declined into the vale of years' and that her youth may inevitably tempt her to look elsewhere. Desdemona defends herself robustly from his charges that she is a whore, swearing her honesty by invoking heaven and her true Christian faith.

This seems to move Othello. The pace suddenly slows. In the next two lines, shared between husband and wife, we played it as if Othello had indeed been convinced by his wife's devout protestation:

OTHELLO   What, not a whore?
DESDEMONA   No, as I shall be saved.
OTHELLO   Is't possible?
DESDEMONA   Oh heaven forgive us!

In the empty half-line that follows, Desdemona tentatively slid into his bear-like embrace, relieved that her husband had finally seen sense. A breath of possible reconciliation. But then with icy cynicism, Othello growls:

OTHELLO   I cry you mercy then:
                I took you for that cunning whore of Venice
                That married with Othello.

It was a chilling moment. Lisa seemed so tiny in Sello's massive cold embrace. It served to reinforce our anxiety for Desdemona's safety, as Othello calls Emilia back in.

Moments later, with Othello gone, Iago joins the shell-shocked Desdemona. With childlike trust she falls into his arms and weeps.

This provided Tony with one of the most telling, disturbing and yet wordless moments in his performance. While Emilia is distracted, trying to work out who could be responsible for this abuse of her mistress, the culprit, Iago, says almost nothing. He is almost breathless, trying to suppress his excitement, sexually aroused by holding this beautiful young woman in his arms. When the women leave, Iago sniffs and fondles the silk stockings in her wardrobe trunk. Obsession transmuting into evil.

In the following scene, Emilia helps Desdemona prepare for bed. The conversation turns to Lodovico, who has just arrived in Cyprus with the duke's mandate that Othello should return to Venice. Why does Desdemona bring up Lodovico? Perhaps she wants to discover what Emilia made of the incident. If so, she doesn't pursue her enquiry. She just says she thinks Lodovico is a proper man and speaks well. Emilia describes him as not just 'proper' but as 'very handsome'. She then says:

I know a lady in Venice would have walked barefoot to Palestine for a touch of his nether lip.

Desdemona does not reply but begins to sing the sad willow song.

In one rehearsal, as Amanda delivered that line, we realized that perhaps Emilia herself was that lady. That she had been in love with Lodovico, would have done anything for him. Whether or not Lodovico returned that love, whether or not they might have had an affair, we were left to wonder as Desdemona sings her lament.

As so often happens with Shakespeare, little biographical details can emerge and allow a deeper complexity to exist. For me, the possibility that Emilia had a 'past' that did not involve her husband fed directly into the scene between the two women that follows.

Iago has told us that he suspects Othello of sleeping with his wife, and that knowledge gnaws away at him. And Emilia in conversation with Iago and Desdemona, discussing Othello's treatment of his wife, has already revealed that she is aware of her husband's suspicions:

> Some such squire he was
> That turn'd your wit the seamy side without,
> And made you to suspect me with the Moor.

*   *   *

Approaching Desdemona asleep in bed, Othello addresses his soul, his most intimate spiritual principle.

> It is the cause, it is the cause, my soul.

Why? Is he trying to convince himself that his motive for murdering his wife is justified? He will give her the opportunity to say her prayers, because he would not have her spirit unprepared for death:

> I would not kill thy soul.

Once he has murdered her and is made to realize what he has done he looks at her body, imagining meeting her again on the day of reckoning:

> ... when we shall meet at compt,
> This look of thine will hurl my soul from heaven,
> And fiends will snatch at it.

Iago has ensnared his soul and body.

As the plot unravels, and Emilia reveals her husband's culpability, Iago kills his wife. In our production, by stabbing her between the legs, a final demonstration of his violent misogyny. When he is asked to explain his actions, Iago famously remains silent. Why?

Tony described it as a very simple matter, arising from a very complex one:

> He himself can't explain what happened; any more than a psychopath can say, 'I did it because of that.' Whatever it is that Iago suffers from, the man has been on a tremendous drug rush, fuelled by weird chemicals in his own brain, and now it's over. The only appropriate response is his final statement: 'What you know, you

know: / From this time forth I never will speak word.' Shakespeare leaves a powerful mystery there, like he does in all his best plays – questions, not answers, about human behaviour.

* * *

The production opened to largely good reviews. Sello was highly praised in the *Financial Times*, 'as a case study in something rare: mature, dignified, virile innocence. He is both powerful and wide-eyed, like a lion stepping into a trap.'

Amanda was acclaimed by several critics including Benedict Nightingale in *The Times* who declared, 'Has there ever been a better Emilia than Amanda Harris, a hard-drinking army wife whose disillusion with Iago, with men, and sex has become a scarily sweeping cynicism?' Amanda won the Olivier Award that year as Best Supporting Actress.

The Sunday Times thought Tony 'one of the great Iagos', adding colourfully that he was like 'a cross between a bull and a ferret'. Ultimately, Tony justified the dangerous proposition that had haunted him, that the role was somehow tailor-made for him, in such reviews as the *Daily Mail*, which trumpeted, 'Antony Sher has fulfilled his destiny as Iago.'

But Tony was not comfortable in the production. Something happened during the run of *Othello* in Stratford. He described it as 'the fear'. It settled in on the press night, but continued right through the run. On stage, one night in Japan, he felt a strange moment of imbalance. He thought briefly that an earthquake had struck. He said, 'My performance became a question of survival rather than achievement.' It was stage fright.

He didn't tell me until much later. In fact, in order to exorcize the threat, he drew it. The image is of a strange rough sloping beast. 'It's a hyena,' he said, 'the ugliest animal in

creation with a snout permanently blackened with blood. This thing has its head in my guts, and I don't know what to do.'

The year after *Othello*, Tony confronted the hyena, in the most courageous way possible. He did a one-man show. It was about Primo Levi, the Auschwitz survivor. The subject was too important to allow the fear to interfere. In the drawing, the hyena is slouching away, never to return.

14

Venus and Adonis

– 2004: A co-production with the Little Angel Theatre; TOP.
– 2006: Revived in the Complete Works Festival.
– 2017: Revived as part of the Rome Season.
– Filmed by the V&A.

In the summer of 1999, I was asked to prepare an entertainment for an event that Prince Charles was hosting on behalf of the RSC at Highgrove, his home in Gloucestershire. I didn't want to put together the usual scenes and speeches from Shakespeare, so I hit on the idea of doing a reading of extracts from *Venus and Adonis,* Shakespeare's first great narrative poem, combining sex, comedy, tragedy and horses. There's even a wild boar hunt.

Alex Gilbreath lent her dusky voiced charm to the goddess of love; Toby Stephens brought out all the rugged austerity of the unwilling Adonis; and Tony, who read the connecting narrative, scored a particular hit as Adonis's randy stallion. The poem gets into quite a lather in its description of this handsome horse:

Round-hoof'd, short-jointed, fetlocks shag and long,
Broad breast, full eye, small head and nostril wide,
High crest, short ears, straight legs and passing strong,
Thin mane, thick tail, broad buttock, tender hide:
Look, what a horse should have he did not lack,
Save a proud rider on so proud a back.

At the end of the reading, Adrian Noble came up to speak to the special guests, stakeholders and potential donors attending. He began by ripping up his notes. He spoke instead, off the cuff, as only Adrian can, in response to what he had just heard, and distilled from it what made Shakespeare great and why we all spent our time at the RSC trying to do him justice.

This one gem of a poem, he said, encapsulated Shakespeare's genius, in miniature: vivid characterization, terrific storytelling and sublime poetry. The piece demonstrated how he could turn in a second from highly charged eroticism to profound human tragedy, expressing obsession one moment and grief the next, with such wit, extravagance and aching beauty.

Needless to say, he encouraged me to think about developing the half-hour entertainment into a full-scale production. It might make an excellent theatre piece, I thought – if only we could work out how to stage the horses and the wild boar.

* * *

Some months later, in March 2000, we were in Japan. Our production of *Macbeth* had been invited to visit Tokyo. One day, while the company had a matinee at the Globe Theatre, I made a pilgrimage to Osaka to see an art form that has been designated as one of the world's intangible cultural assets, the famous Bunraku puppet theatre.

Osaka is about 250 miles from Tokyo, but the bullet train, the famous Shinkansen, got me there in just two and a half hours.

I had no idea what to expect. The large auditorium was packed, not with children, but with adults. The stage was as wide as the RST proscenium, but not as high. On the right, on his tatami mat, knelt the *tayu* (reciter), who narrated the entire piece, speaking the voices of all the characters. On the left, a musician accompanied him on the shamisen, the three-stringed Japanese lute.

Each Ningyo doll, about a half to two-thirds human size, was manipulated by three puppeteers in black. The master puppeteer, who operated the head and the right hand, had his face uncovered. His apprentices, who operated the left hand or the feet, wore hoods. But the concentration of each on the puppet they were operating meant that they quickly became invisible, and you concentrated intently on the emotions expressed by the exquisite white doll faces.

When I arrived, the play had already started. (The performances sometimes last up to eight hours.) It was one of the most famous in the Bunraku repertoire, *The Love Suicides at Sonezaki* by Chikamatsu Monzaemon, known as the Japanese Shakespeare. The scene showed two traditional teahouses with paper sliding-screens, and long verandas surrounded by cherry blossom. The two houses were divided by a tumbling waterfall, ingeniously created by painted rolling cylinders. At the height of the story, one of the lovers floats the head of her beloved across the raging torrent.

I was lucky to be able to visit backstage during one of the intervals and meet the stars of the show.

Stagehands were busy changing the sets for the next instalment. We passed racks where the master puppeteers stored their high raffia buskins, which gave them extra height over their apprentices. I peered into a sort of puppet green-room where the Ningyo-dolls were waiting to go on. Finally, I was shown through an indigo curtain into the dressing room of a 'living national treasure'.

Yoshida Bunjaku is one of the grand puppet masters. This wise craftsman looked like a monk in his dark silk robes. He is an *omo-zukai*, a head puppeteer. His assistant handed him the gorgeous Princess, one of the puppets from that afternoon's repertoire. His deep-set eyes rested on the back of the Ningyo's head as he demonstrated how to make her quake with grief in her scarlet and gold kimono. Watching him manipulate the Princess, I was fascinated by how details of the headdress amplified her slightest head movements, how she could whip out a strand of hair on her otherwise immaculate coiffure to demonstrate her distracted grief or seem to grip the sleeve of her kimono in her teeth by means of a tiny pin projecting from the corner of her mouth.

To the master's right and left were his acolyte apprentices. The junior of the pair operated the feet: he might expect to do this for five or ten years at least, before graduating on to the left hand, operated by his companion.

Yoshida Bunjaku explained to me that Bunraku is a highly refined art form from the early Edo period, that marries poetry with puppetry and music. The three art forms are regarded as equally and elegantly balanced in importance.

The stories tell of divided lovers and suicide pacts, epic adventures and concealed identities – very much the stuff of Shakespeare's plays, and from about the same era.

On the Shinkansen back to Tokyo that evening, I began to wonder if the Bunraku could be the inspiration for how to stage *Venus and Adonis*, a fusion of Shakespeare's poem and this ancient Japanese art.

November 2002.

In Dagmar Passage in Islington, north London, there's a workshop where they make magic. Over the years I've peered through its dusty window, glimpsing a world of gentle craftsmanship. A knight in tarnished golden armour – a huge Sicilian marionette – hangs from the rafters among a little flock of cane-frame paper birds. There's a blush-faced rod puppet peering out, bewildered at the world beyond, and a grey goose hissing at him. There are empty coffee cups on the workbenches, shelves stuffed with drippy paint pots and varnishes, and wood chips cover the splashed floorboards. I've often wanted to open the green half-stable door and wander in to explore.

Now I can. This is the Little Angel, home of British puppetry. Its theatre, a converted temperance hall, stands next door. A few years ago, it was faced with closure, and a campaign was mounted to save it. In all the shop windows of nearby Upper Street there were puppets from the vast collection the Little Angel has made in the forty years of its existence. Even the video shop had a couple, and in one of the local estate agents little figures seemed to be checking out house prices.

Now the Little Angel is thriving again, and I've been introduced to some of the puppets and their makers. Lyndie Wright, widow of John Wright, who began the company in 1961, is the Little Angel's mum. Although she has officially retired, she and her elderly whippet Nellie live next door. Steve Tiplady is the recently appointed artistic producer. His mission is to broaden the appeal of puppetry while still providing a full variety of family entertainment – to explore the use of puppets in other contexts. And that's why I'm here.

I begin my pitch. 'I want to develop a production of Shakespeare's great erotic poem *Venus and Adonis* as a sort of puppet masque.' Steve looks surprised but interested, so I tell him a bit about the poem.

Venus and Adonis was Shakespeare's first bestseller. He wrote it in 1593, when the theatres were closed because of the plague, and it was an immediate publishing hit, running to 16 editions over the next few years. It's raunchy stuff, designed, no doubt, to appeal to the 19-year-old appetite of the Earl of Southampton, to whom it is dedicated. Not usual Little Angel fare at all.

It tells the story of the sex goddess Venus and her passionate obsession for the petulant pretty boy Adonis. 'She's Love, she loves, and yet she is not loved.' In the variety of tactics she invents, from alluring seduction to volatile temper tantrum, she feels like an early sketch for Cleopatra. However, Adonis repudiates her advances, rejects the offer of being her divine toy boy, preferring to go boar-hunting instead, although he finally gives in to her strenuous advances. He ends up gored by a ferocious wild boar, and Venus curses love for ever more.

Shakespeare's main departure from his source material, Ovid's *Metamorphoses*, was in the treatment of the hero. In the original, Adonis returns Venus' advances; in the Elizabethan poem, the hero becomes a bashful teenager.

Steve and Lyndie get excited, and we decide we need a workshop to try out ideas. It takes place at the Little Angel itself, and begins with a session in which I try and convey why I think the poem is so fine, funny and human, and how it manages then to become so moving.

The first decision, once we have confirmed the cast list, is to decide what form of puppetry the different characters should be represented in. So, Venus and Adonis, who have the majority of the action, will be table-top puppets, akin to the Japanese Bunraku Ningyo puppets. Each will have three operators: one on the head and right hand, another on the left hand, and one on the feet, rooting the puppet; though, unlike the Bunraku, the operators may change the limb they operate.

Then I get a crash course in the skills involved in creating puppets. Before committing to the labour-intensive crafts involved in constructing the finished puppets, which will be carved in lime wood and sewn in soft leather, we try out ideas in cardboard and gaffer tape . . . lots of gaffer tape.

The puppet maquette for Venus is made of foam, with a mop of hair made of shreds of cloth in ribbons. She needs to be very light because as a goddess she occasionally becomes airborne. Whereas for Adonis, we need the puppet to be earth bound, and we use one of the vast stock of puppets in the Little Angel's collection. It's made of wood, and it feels solid and clanks.

We know there will be a prologue involving a dance between Queen Elizabeth I and the Earl of Southampton, who will be long string marionettes, operated on a bridge from above, like the lonely goatherd in the film of *The Sound of Music*.

The animals represented in the poem are, of course, completely possible to create in this medium. The horses need to be in proportion to the puppet. Adonis has a lot of trouble controlling his frisky stallion. For the workshop they have mocked up a horse in cardboard and some calico and pieces of cut-out ply. It has articulated front legs, a segmented neck to suggest the volume it will ultimately need and a cardboard head.

Then we look at how the wild boar might appear and one of the puppeteers, Sarah Wright (Lyndie's daughter), suggests we could create an ominous sense of danger by seeing it first in shadow play, in the thicket or undergrowth of some dense forest. A few twigs are poked through a piece of cardboard. In what seems minutes a screen has been rigged up, and a light source found. When the lamp is lit behind the screen, and then moved slowly around the twigs, from my position out front, it looks like I am being guided through a nightmare forest.

We then discuss Death.

There is an extraordinary section of the poem when Venus goes in search of Adonis, terrified that he will be hurt in the hunt for the ferocious wild boar. She finds his hounds, one hiding in a brake, another bleeding and licking his wounds. Another begins to howl mournfully and is joined by another and yet another. Amid this dreadful cacophony she fears the worst and 'exclaims on Death'.

She chides and curses Death for attacking her beloved. And dissolves in tears.

But like a stormy day, now wind, now rain,
Sighs dry her cheeks, tears make them wet again.

Then suddenly Venus hears the halloo of a huntsman. She revives. She is sure it is Adonis's voice. She apologizes to Death for cursing him, and instead starts to praise him:

She clepes him king of graves and grave for kings,
Imperious supreme of all mortal things.

Now there is a tumble of ideas. Someone suggests a huge carnival puppet. Perhaps it can have been there all the time, hidden in the baroque architecture of the proscenium arch. And that it has long arms and huge hands which can cradle Venus and rock her when she weeps. And then we're off.

People start cutting up cardboard boxes and ripping tape to make the huge head, drawing great hollow eyes with a sharpie. Others are creating ropey arms out of some old sash cord. And it has hands, made from kitchen rolls for the metacarpal bones, and toilet rolls for the fingers, all manipulated by broom stick handles.

And there he is: the 'grim-grinning ghost' of Death himself, in all his macabre glory, a 'hard-favour'd tyrant, ugly, meagre, lean'.

He towers over little Venus as she chides him. The puppeteers play. Try things out. Improvise. Death can rock the goddess of Love in the palm of his bony hand, or she can climb up from hand to hand to whisper in his ear. 'Perhaps they can dance together,' says Rachel Leonard, one of the puppeteers, and soon Venus is swinging joyfully from Death's little finger. I'm captivated. It's an entirely original *danse macabre*, except of course that Venus herself is immortal, and Death has no power over her.

Venus laughing and swinging on Death's digit feels emblematic. Amor vincit omnia, perhaps, or rather 'Death cannot conquer Love'.

Venus and Adonis is by turns funny and tragic. It parodies the absurd behaviour that obsessive love can lead to, and which later in his career Shakespeare was to dramatize so powerfully. It is sometimes erotic, even bordering on the pornographic at times, but it is also profoundly moving as the grieving Venus laments the death of Adonis and curses Love:

Since thou art dead, lo, here I prophesy;
Sorrow on love hereafter shall attend:
It shall be waited on with jealousy
Find sweet beginning but unsavoury end.

Throughout that summer of 2004, some of the best known names in puppetry were very busy in the workshops at the Little Angel. The international team was headed by

Lyndie Wright, with her fellow South African, John Roberts, constructing the marionettes (for the prologue). Jan Zalud from the Czech Republic carved Venus and Adonis (Venus made of soft leathers, and her recalcitrant boyfriend made of wood); Stefan Fischert from Germany was hard at work making the horses and the shadow puppets, and Simon Auton made the wild boar.

Rob Jones, in charge of the overall design, created a magnificent, miniaturized baroque proscenium, which accommodated an ingenious appearance by Death itself, as the golden orb above the stage pivoted to become a skull, and huge hands with long fingers descended to clasp Venus in their bony grip.

Rob even persuaded the RSC wardrobe staff to sew the miniature costumes for the two marionettes. The wardrobe team were very excited when the puppets arrived in Stratford-upon-Avon to be fitted for their costumes. Queen Elizabeth was to be dressed in a miniature replica of the gown she wears in the Ditchley portrait. Here she appears arrayed in white, with a rose attached to her elaborate open ruff. The marionette of Southampton was modelled after the Hatchlands portrait.[1] He looked very dashing in his silver doublet. The wardrobe team had never worked on this exquisite scale before.

Elizabeth's dress was of course made in the ladies' department, and Southampton's in the men's. When the team came in one morning, they discovered a tiny love letter addressed to her majesty, sitting on the workbench. And spookily the following day they found a return love letter to the Right Honourable Earl.

*   *   *

With the workshops over, and the puppets made, we could begin rehearsals. I marvelled at the tranquil concentration of the puppeteers, their incredible dexterity and impeccable precision, and how serenely collaborative their work was, how generous and apparently free from ego. The puppets were what was important and breathing them into life.

I'm astonished at how nuanced the puppets' physical language can be, the slightest tilting of a head or lifting of a chin speaks volumes. There is no deceit in puppetry: the mechanics of the performance are entirely visible. Their clear sense of collective endeavour compounds the joy and creates a very special magic.

Actor Michael Pennington joined us as the narrator. He effortlessly shaped his mellifluous delivery to the puppets' actions accompanied by musician Steve Russell's opulent guitar chords. The whole production opened at the Little Angel in October 2004, before a short run at The Other Place in Stratford.

I have seldom seen an audience of adults remain open-mouthed with wonder; but that is what happened in performance when on the couplet:

---

[1] In 2002, while we were preparing our production, there was an exciting development. A portrait of the young Earl of Southampton was 'discovered' at Hatchlands House in Surrey. The oil painting shows a young Elizabethan with a Venetian collar and long hair. It was thought until very recently to be a picture of a young woman. Now scholars believe that this is a portrait of Henry Wriothesley, Earl of Southampton, in late teenage. If so, then we have a picture of Shakespeare's patron, and possibly the object of his obsession; certainly the young man to whom he dedicated *Venus and Adonis* in 1593.

Her arms do lend his neck a sweet embrace;
Incorporate then they seem, face grows to face.

In a moment worthy of Chagall, the lovers' long-postponed kiss caused Venus and Adonis to float up into the air. Surreal bliss, and a rich demonstration of puppetry's ability to suit the action to the word.

I was delighted when a young woman approached me after one show and asked me when and how we had swapped the puppet of Venus, from the voluptuous sultry two-foot temptress in low-cut chiffon in the first part to the tragic forlorn figure grieving over her dead lover in the second. She found it very hard to believe that there was only one puppet, and that she had projected onto its wooden features that whole gamut of emotion.

During its various outings since,[2] *Venus and Adonis* has also been narrated by actors Harriet Walter, John Hopkins, Suzanne Burden, and on a couple of occasions by me, as the understudy.

I was very pleased for the Little Angel when the reviews came out. They were a fitting tribute to their extraordinary craftsmanship. In the *Mail on Sunday*, Georgina Brown wrote:

> There's not a more original, more exquisitely beautiful, more entrancing show to be seen in London today, as spectacular, if in miniature, as *The Lion King*.

---

[2] When *Venus and Adonis* was revived during the Complete Works Festival in 2006, I was also able to produce a rehearsed reading of Shakespeare's next narrative poem, the 'graver labour' he had promised his patron, *The Rape of Lucrece*. Jane Lapotaire performed Lucrece.

15

A Midsummer Night's Dream

– 2005: Royal Shakespeare Theatre, Stratford-upon-Avon;
Novello Theatre, London.
– 2008: Revived at the Courtyard Theatre, Stratford-upon-Avon.

There are more instances of the word 'love' in *A Midsummer Night's Dream* than in any other of Shakespeare's plays. OK, except *The Two Gentlemen of Verona*.

I finally got to direct my favourite play at Stratford in 2005. It turned out to be a busy year.

Michael Boyd's first season of The Tragedies in 2004 was to be followed by The Comedies. Meanwhile, in the Swan, I would follow up the 2002 Jacobethan Season by curating another collection of rare Jacobean plays built around the 400th anniversary of the Gunpowder Plot.

The Comedy Season would open with my production of *A Midsummer Night's Dream*, and be followed by Michael's *Twelfth Night*, then by *The Comedy of Errors* and *As You Like It*. The two productions would cross-rehearse together for twelve weeks with an initial fortnight of workshops exploring different disciplines and physical techniques.

One of those workshops included a comedy session with theatre-maker John Wright and his team from Trestle, the mask and physical theatre company. The actors were asked to work out a simple mime routine to present to their fellow actors. Then they were asked to present the same routine, but halfway through to imagine they had accidentally stepped in a large pile of dog poo. They were to continue with the routine, making sure their audience did not notice their mishap. Different actors took it turns to try. They explored the growing embarrassment and rising stress as they imagined the smell of the excrement becoming all too obvious, and a trail of dirty footmarks all too evident. It became overwhelmingly funny. In a very short time, tears were rolling down my cheeks.

There is a key here to the Pyramus and Thisbe scene, I thought. Comedy often derives from a very human sense of panic, and of disaster narrowly averted. The company started sharing stories about their experiences on stage: how when things had gone catastrophically wrong, somehow, they had to continue. Often people referred back to their early experiences either in school plays, or in amateur theatre.

I vividly remembered one such occasion as a child in Lancashire, during the annual village pantomime in St Andrew's Church Hall, Longton. My mum was the 'producer'.

For some reason, the elderly vicar, the Reverend Fred Seddon, always played the demon king. Likewise, Harry Hunter, who lived close by in Birchwood Avenue, always played the Dame. During the front-cloth scene before the finale, they were on stage together when Fred's false teeth slipped out and fell to the floor. The dame tried to cover as the Rev stumbled about trying to retrieve them as inconspicuously as possible, fumbling to get them back into his mouth while still delivering his lines. Their hopeless attempts to continue and suppress both the dame's corpsing and the vicar's embarrassment produced waves and waves of helpless laughter, rising to near hysteria among his parishioners in the audience. I sat at the back of the hall next to my mum, watching her rocking with laughter, despite herself. There was nothing to be done, the subversive spirit of comedy ruled.

Saturday 8 January 2005.

I get a phone call from my sister, Jo. Mum has collapsed and been taken to hospital in North Wales. When I get there, hours later, my dad is confused. Mum lies rumpled on a hospital trolley. 'She hasn't spoken yet,' he says. Dad has suffered from progressive dementia over the last few years and can't compute what is happening. I know Mum's had a stroke.

Later, when it's dark outside and a bed has been found, Dad sits on the armchair and I perch on the bin. Mum has suffered paralysis all down her right side. Her mouth is lopsided, and her pupils seem to slip away to the side.

Dad keeps trying to get her to talk and wipes the hair on her forehead. She keeps lifting her arm. He's trying to work out what she means. Then quite suddenly she manages to grasp Dad's upper arm and pull him towards her. He bends over her, and her vital arm holds him in a tight embrace. His white head rests in the nook of her neck and shoulder. Mum's cheek pressed against his. After precious moments, they relax.

Tony's in Cape Town. About to open *Primo*[1] at the Baxter. It's his first professional appearance on stage in his hometown. I'm meant to be going out there next weekend for the press night. Doubt I will make it now. I ring and tell him about Mum, about the hug. I think she was trying to say goodbye.

On Monday morning, as I drive back down the motorway to get back to rehearsal, I realize that my dad is responsible for my introduction to Shakespeare. He used to belong to a record club, and one day, along with a box set of Beethoven symphonies, a 45 rpm record of Mendelssohn's miraculous incidental music to *A Midsummer Night's Dream* arrived with it. From the moment those first four evocative chords sounded, I was hooked. I could see the fairies rushing in on a breeze, like leaves being scurried across a lawn. I could picture Bottom hee-hawing, and the rude mechanicals thumping about in the earthy brass fortissimo.

But in between the musical sections, the little record had extracts from the actual play itself. And as Shakespeare instructs, I attended 'with patient ears', as this magical story unfolded. It was an American production, and the actress playing Puck sounded to my young ears just like Mickey Mouse. But when she squeaked 'I'll put a girdle round about the Earth in forty minutes,' I caught my breath.

---

[1] His one man show about the Holocaust survivor Primo Levi.

Just before I was born, my dad told me, the Russians had launched the first satellite, triggering the space race that obsessed my childhood. Sputnik, as this satellite was called, could orbit the globe in just over an hour and a half. So Puck was twice as fast as Sputnik!

A Midsummer Night's Dream has always had the ability to capture and tangle the imagination, like any good dream. It contains some of the most beautiful poetry in the English language, or I would vouch, in any language on earth.

On the car seat next to me is a pillowcase full of my sisters' old dolls that I have pulled from a cupboard at home. For toys that had inspired such love in the past, they now seem peculiarly repellent, with their matted hair, and missing eyes. I think they may come in handy in this week's puppet workshop, as we tackle how to realize the fairies.

As I head back down the A5, and south, a single magpie flies across the road.

'Good Morning, Mr Magpie,' I chant quietly, automatically, 'and how's your lady wife?'

Dad's much-loved lady wife could be in hospital for some time.

Week Two.

As a result of Mum's collapse, I missed welcoming the Swan company on the first day of the Gunpowder Season and caught up with them later in that week. We would be opening with Shakespeare's 'banned' play, *Thomas More*, and a black comedy about euthanasia called *A New Way to Please You or The Old Law* written by Thomas Middleton and William Rowley.[2]

Back in the *Dream* rehearsal room, Steve Tiplady from the Little Angel Theatre, who directed *Venus and Adonis* with me last year, is exploring the use of puppets in the play. He loves the bag of my sisters' dolls but wants to start with some basic skills. He has the actors using just their coats, fleeces or jumpers, holding the neck of the garment in one hand and the arm in the other hand. He demonstrates how to bring the piece of clothing to life, to make it breathe slowly, and then start to explore its environment.

Soon the room is populated with a quiet array of curious little creatures. Later he will explore how the mood can be changed and become threatening. We want to see what happens as Quince and his friends are chased out of the forest. Steve has pulled together the tool bags of these workmen, carpenters' and joiners' tools: saws, hammers and drills, which suddenly amalgamate to become nightmare snapping monsters.

We continue the workshop exploration to include shadow play. 'If we shadows have offended' says Puck. He refers to Oberon as the 'King of Shadows'. We experiment with actors in silhouette and play with scale. This is something Shakespeare does in the text.

---

[2] The Gunpowder Season boasted five plays: *Thomas More* directed by Rob Delamere; Middleton and Rowley's *A New Way to Please You* by Sean Holmes. I would direct Ben Jonson's exhilarating political thriller *Sejanus*, then Josie Rourke would direct *Believe as you List* by Philip Massinger, and *Speaking like Magpies*, a new play about the Gunpowder Plot by Frank McGuinness, would be directed by Rupert Goold.

The fairies seem capable of shape-shifting and changing size. Puck can transform himself into a joint stool, or a crab-apple. Titania and Oberon can make love to human beings, but when frightened their fairies can 'creep into acorn cups and hide them there'.

We improvise a projection screen with an old sheet and an angle-poise lamp. Some netting is found and draped over a garden cane (very useful having an ironmongers just a few doors down from the rehearsal room in Clapham). The net, tucked into an actor's belt while they stand in front of our screen, looks like fairy wings. Perhaps, just as you can't see vampires in mirrors as they have no reflection, you can only see fairy wings in shadow. A magical world of imaginative possibilities is emerging. Next week we will start on the text of the play itself.

Saturday 15 January.
Crazy dash to Cape Town to surprise Tony for his first night. Flew Friday night and arrived this morning. When I rang the doorbell to Tony's rented apartment, he answered the intercom, but when he heard my voice, was convinced he must have picked up the real phone by mistake. He couldn't believe I was just downstairs, outside his front door. We hug. For a long time. I have so badly needed this, since Mum's stroke.

When he goes in later to warm up for the show, I stare out at the bright blue scene before me, at Bantry Bay below the apartment, and the wide expanse of the Southern Atlantic Ocean. A man is floating among the glistening kelp. Perfectly still. His arms behind his head. Bathing in the sun and the surf. The tide turns his body slowly round.

I phone my twin sister, Ruth, who has flown over from her home in Colorado to be with Dad. She asks when I am back, and if I could come up for a family conference ... about Mum. About how long she has left.

My eyes turn back to the man floating in the sea. I want Mum to be able to plunge into that water and let the cool surf heal her sick brain.

Week Three: Starting on the text.
I start with the title. And some assumptions. What does 'midsummer' mean? Today, we associate midsummer with the evenings stretching out in the middle of June, with strawberries and Pimm's and Wimbledon. But what did midsummer mean to the Elizabethans?

I realized, re-reading the play before rehearsal, that there were a number of references in the text that were very familiar to me but of which I had little actual experience. What exactly was eglantine? Or love-in-idleness? What does wild thyme smell like? I had never heard Philomel, the nightingale, sing in full-throated ease, or seen 'the fiery glow-worm's eyes', and when Shakespeare stared up at the 'starry welkin', was he seeing the same thing we see today?

With the help of an expert guide in the amiable character of botanist and writer Richard Mabey, I made a documentary for BBC Four in 2004 in which he explained that, in Shakespeare's day, midsummer was a perilous and precarious time. The crops were in the field, but if they did not ripen, if the green corn did not attain a beard, as Titania suggests, and rain spoiled the harvest, then there would be corn shortages and rural discontent, as had happened in successive summers in the 1590s as Shakespeare wrote the play. Titania seems to be predicting climate change as she lists the litany of complaints against the warring Fairy King and Queen, which have caused the seasons to alter and all the devastation they could see around them, the floods, the disease and unseasonal weather conditions in the natural world.

Delightfully, Richard introduces me to the diminutive wild pansy (love-in-idleness), the heady resinous smell of the wild thyme, and points out that Titania's bower was provided with its own brand of Goldspot, as eglantine, a sort of briar rose with furry leaves, was used as a breath-freshener by the Elizabethans. I learnt that in Shakespeare's day they believed that between midsummer's night and the feast of St Peter and St Paul, a portal opened up between the fairy world and our own, and you needed to take especial care your children were not snatched away by sprites and replaced with logs; and to protect your cattle you hung their byres with garlands of vervain, marigold and mugwort.

I also got to discover that glow-worms don't fly (unlike fireflies, their continental cousins, which can), but the females climb a blade of grass and advertise their readiness to mate by waggling their bioluminescent bottoms around; and that if we cared to turn all the street lamps off for one night and witnessed the true glory of the Milky Way in the night sky as Shakespeare knew it, we would never turn those street lights back on again.

Sunday 23 January.
Mum's been moved. To the Gilliat Ward of the Maelor Hospital. When my sister Jo rang to tell me, I thought she said 'Gilead'. I find myself humming the old spiritual 'There is a balm in Gilead, to make the wounded whole'. They've taken Mum's teeth out. I spotted her empty gums as I helped the staff nurse insert her feeding tube.

My brother Mark, a neurologist, explains what has happened to our mother: 'an acute middle cerebral artery stroke'. The 'infarction' has damaged both the areas that review language and translate it into sense, and the area that translates thoughts into words. Both the receptive and the expressive areas of her brain.

I look around at the family I love, sitting around Mum's bed. Ruth massaging Mum's paralysed hand and quietly chatting to Jo. Dad holding Mum's other hand and scowling at a family laughing noisily on the other side of the ward, while Mark chuckles at him. And Mum slip slidin' away. And I realize quite gently and without any sense of panic that this is probably the last time we would be together as a family.

I take Mark's hand, and Jo's, and simply say, 'Let's join hands . . . make a circle' and we do, and we smile for a moment, not long enough to embarrass. And some sort of strength flows round. And then Jo reminds us of a joke-shop buzzer we had as kids which would deliver a shock if you shook someone's hand, and the laugh allows us to relax and separate.

Week Four: Four worlds.
There are four distinct worlds in *A Midsummer Night's Dream*: the court, the lovers, the rude mechanicals and the fairies, and they all collide. What is most hard in production is to get each of them balanced. In this most perfect of plays, Shakespeare juggles each

world with expert, giddy, delirious precision, never allowing any of the four balls to drop. And he introduces them each in order, in the first three scenes.

The Court

Theseus seems to bear very few of the traits of his mythological namesake, the serial adulterer and slayer of the Minotaur. Nor does Hippolyta seem to display many of the wild martial characteristics of the captive Queen of the Amazons, although she does some classical name-dropping in Act Four about the time she went hunting with Hercules and Cadmus in Sparta.

Are they in love? Theseus is certainly longing for the time to pass, and he can bed his new bride, promising that though he won her with his sword, he will wed her 'in another key'.

The solution in our production to the presence of this classical allusion in our contemporary Warwickshire Athens, was to begin the play with what seems to be two armed Greek warriors in desperate combat. They turn out to be the duke and his duchess, fulfilling a little bit of light role play, or possibly foreplay, as their classical forbears test each other's mettle. Hippolyta, of course, wins.

The Lovers

The Jamestown Community College experience had taught me to see the play afresh, not just as one of the funniest comedies ever written, but as a deep dive into the nature of Love: that is the true magic in *A Midsummer Night's Dream*.

Rebellious Hermia (Sinead Keenan) defies her father Egeus, and his choice of a husband, Demetrius (Oscar Pearce), and elopes with her beloved Lysander (Trystan Gravelle). We are experimenting with playing Demetrius as an ambitious hooray-Henry, determined to appeal to Hermia's father (the prime minister) and quite content to jilt his own girlfriend in the process. We're trying Lysander as a floppy haired bo-ho poet whose very sight would offend Egeus.

Lysander has serenaded Hermia at her window at night and showered her with knacks and trifles: bracelets of his hair and sweetmeats, which her father warns are 'messengers / Of strong prevailment in unharden'd youth'. They swear their love for each other in clichés 'by Cupid's strongest bow' and 'by the simplicity of Venus' doves'. You fear for the adolescence of their infatuation. But there is something wilful in Hermia, spoilt perhaps. You feel she has always been the object of affection and has always got her way, and perhaps she is using Lysander to escape her father, rather than commit herself to him entirely.

Helena (Caitlin Mottram), the girl Demetrius dumped, is humiliated and hurting. She is all too painfully aware how fickle Love can be. The more she loves Demetrius, she says, the more he hates her. And yet she won't let him go. It is an unhealthy obsession and potentially dangerously self-destructive. She decides to betray the confidence of her best friend Hermia, by revealing their plans to Demetrius.

But herein mean I to enrich my pain,
To have his sight thither and back again.

The experience of the four lovers in the forest is traumatic.

We find ourselves quite shocked by how Helena abases herself before Demetrius, begging that he treat her like his dog. Demetrius even suggests that she risks being raped if she doesn't leave him alone.

Puck's interventions with the drug juice reverses the current of affection, and the girls find themselves in unfamiliar territory: Helena receives the adoration of both the boys, which she assumes is deliberate mockery, while Hermia finds herself rejected and abused. When her beloved Lysander insists that he hates her:

What, should I hurt her, strike her, kill her dead?
Although I hate her, I'll not harm her so.

Hermia plaintively declares:

What, can you do me greater harm than hate?

The long quartet scene in Act Three is full of pain, which is why of course it is also so full of laughter. We recognize ourselves, our own experience of infatuation, or rejection, and the absurdities it can lead us into.

As the boys thrash away blindly at each other in the dark, and the girls wander desolately lost in the wood of their own entanglements, we watch as finally they all stagger in and fall asleep. Helena longs for sleep:

And sleep, that sometimes shuts up sorrow's eye,
Steal me awhile from mine own company.

It's one of my favourite lines in the play. Shakespeare must surely have been an insomniac; he is so obsessed with sleep.[3] Here, with such simple language, he knows how sleep can sometimes give you a little respite from your own worst enemy: yourself.

The four young people grow up in a single night. They learn about themselves. They learn how difficult love is. They mature.

When they are woken by the duke and Hippolyta, and Demetrius realizes that his true sight and affection has been restored and he proffers his damaged love to Helena, we feel a sense of relief.

But, as in health, come to my natural taste,
Now I do wish it, love it, long for it,
And will for evermore be true to it.

---

[3] Look at Macbeth's multiple definition of sleep, in the dagger scene.

The Rude Mechanicals

Bottom and his mates arrive in the second scene. They are described later as 'hard-handed men', and 'rude mechanicals / That work for bread upon Athenian Stalls'. We have decided to set their first scene as they all return from the Athenian market, in the rain, to park those stalls, barrows and carts in a city lock-up at the end of the day. It feels important to make these working folk as real as possible, so that when they encounter the fairy world it is as extraordinary as possible. Bottom sports a donkey jacket, and a builder's crack. Flute, the young bellows mender, has a welder's mask and arc lamp for mending whatever machinery he is paid to repair. Quince arrives on his bicycle, with the scripts, etc.

As we rehearsed, and fell in love with this crew of patches, we realized that there are a number of tensions within this amateur group, particularly between Bully Bottom and Peter Quince, which emerge once they arrive at the Duke's Oak, to rehearse. Bottom has already landed the eponymous role of Pyramus (having put in his bid for almost every other part in the show), but now seems to have contrived a way of enlarging his part. He suggests that the court audience won't tolerate Pyramus drawing a sword. His fellow actors agree this is a problem. So, Bottom proposes he gets a specially written prologue to explain.

But he has set off a cataract of anxiety among his fellow actors. Won't the court audience also be afraid of the lion? Long-suffering Quince agrees another prologue must be written. But he is perhaps being particularly accommodating because he wants to introduce his band to some new and innovative thinking. He poses them a problem. How should they suggest it is night-time when the lovers meet?

The literal-minded Bottom proposes that if the moon happens to be shining that night, they just have to leave a window open. Job done. But Quince has more radical thoughts in mind. What if someone represented Moonshine? Initially, the actors, baffled, make no response. So, Quince moves swiftly to his second directorial intervention, and asks them what they are to do about the wall through which they whisper? The largely unimaginative Snout immediately rejects the absurdity of the challenge: 'You can never bring in a wall!'

But Bottom has caught the spirit of innovative theatrical possibility and, impressed with the genius of his own imagination, proposes that someone comes in dressed as a wall. If Quince had proposed the idea himself, it is possible that it would have been rejected. But in the manner of many a director after him, he has employed reverse psychology, and made the actors think it is their idea, and only has to applaud it for the idea to be admitted.

The Fairies

The Fairies are introduced next.

Our initial idea for Puck came out of a meeting with the actor Jonathan Slinger, during the auditions. Puck is frequently cast much younger, with a spritely cheeky wit, and initially Jonathan couldn't see how he could play him. But as we talked about it and read the first scene, it seemed to us as if Puck was perhaps losing his touch. He was no longer able to make Oberon smile, because Oberon has been distracted by his obsession with the changeling boy, and Puck I think is jealous of that.

We felt that the First Fairy's line

Either I mistake your shape and making quite,
Or else you are that shrewd and knavish sprite
Call'd Robin Goodfellow.

was the equivalent of saying, 'Aren't you that guy off the telly? You used to be quite funny.' But Puck couldn't live up to that reputation anymore, and as he lists his hilarious repertoire – imitating filly foals, making old women spill their drink, or fall off their stools – the gags seem lamer and lamer. He's like some old comedian whose jokes no longer work; a glum Tony Hancock, who once was great but suddenly it just isn't working for him.

We have started work on a prototype for the changeling boy. He will be a toddler-sized puppet, manipulated by the Fairies themselves, who seem obsessed by humankind. His mother, we are told, was a votaress of Titania's 'order', and in the spicéd Indian air by night, would gossip by her side. But in the saddest of beats, we hear that she died in childbirth, and Titania has taken over control of the child. Oberon wants the boy as his plaything, as a 'knight of his train to trace the forest wild'. But Titania refuses him.

Oberon is one of Shakespeare's great depictions of jealousy, alongside Leontes, Othello and Iago, and Ford in *The Merry Wives of Windsor*. He and Titania have a tempestuous relationship, accusing each other of affairs with Theseus and Hippolyta, among others. They cannot meet but they start rowing, and the latest bone of contention is this little changeling child.

Oberon's furious reaction at being refused access to the child is to subject his wife to the ordeal of being doped so that she falls for poor old, transformed Bottom. Love soured, corrupted and cruel.

Week Five.

One of the important design decisions any production of this play must tackle is the donkey's head that Puck places on Bottom. Actors playing Bottom generally argue that they need to have their faces uncovered and visible for the scenes to be funny. But after some of the mask work sessions with Trestle, I could see other possibilities.

In the history of the previous fifty years of productions of the play at Stratford, most Bottoms had felt a long pair of ears would suffice. Charles Laughton added a pair of donkey-hoof gloves; David Waller in the Brook production added heavy cothurnae buskins; Des Barrit even added large buck teeth; and Darrell D'Silva in a quirky gothic Richard Jones production wore a sort of rubber gimp mask with phallic ears. Only David Troughton in John Caird's glittering production sported the full head, marvellously animated with fluttering eyelids and open drop jaw with teeth.

In discussion with Malcolm Storry (Bottom), we decide to try a full head. Stephen Brimson Lewis and I spend an afternoon on a Welsh hillside studying a particular donkey called Teddy. We notice how his ears swivel. They are, in the words of his owner, 'super-expressive'. You can tell when he is alert and inquisitive, as his long ears perk forwards. But they can swivel out to the side and back, if he is suddenly surprised, or register disapproval if he lowers his neck at the same time.

Stephen has in mind a special effects designer called Leigh Cranston to make the head. It needs to be light enough to wear, and both see and be heard through. The head, when it finally arrives, is a masterpiece. Built on a light frame, covered with wig lace (which the wig department will knot with tufts of hair), it also has a marvellous, wobbly rubber lower lip. When Mal nods his head even slightly, it makes the donkey looks as if he is speaking.

Steve Tiplady has been creating more magic. He turns his attention to the workmen's stalls in the lock-up. On the falafel/hot dog cart is a Pyrex dish of oil with saveloys swimming in the grease. Lit from below it throws an image of the tray on the roof. Steve experiments. He removes the saveloys and puts some ink into the dish. Suddenly a dense deep blue sky seems to be projected, and as the grease bubbles pop to the surface they look like a whole Milky Way of stars. Steve flicks his biro through the oily blue and there is a shooting star.

He tips the dish sideways, and the blue deepens at one end and lifts at the other like midnight yielding to dawn. Exquisite. He and lighting designer Tim Mitchell will explore how we might expand that across the proscenium.

Week Nine.
Travelling in and out of rehearsal during these last few weeks, I have been listening to a tape I made of Mum just before she turned 80 in 2001. It's a bittersweet experience. She laughs recalling the time during the war, when her father was nearly caught with a tray of black market eggs in the back of the car when a policeman flagged them down for a lift. And the first play she 'produced' for the St Patrick's Players in Huddersfield, called 'Sit Down a Minute, Adrian', and how she and Auntie Mary nipped over to Halifax to see a professional production to check out how it was done. And how she met Dad at a bus stop, and how they were married just after the war, sixty long loving years ago next July.

Saturday 5 March.
Fr Brignal has arrived to confer the sacrament of the sick upon my mother. Dad leans his arms against the high bedside rails and rests his white head on his wrists. Every now and again he raises his eyes to watch his wife lost to him now these two long months. The sacrament involves a blessing, prayers and an anointing ('a balm in Gilliat').

'The first grace of this sacrament,' Fr Brignal says, 'is one of strengthening, peace and courage to overcome the difficulties that go with the condition of serious illness or the frailty of old age.'

When it's over, Dad shuffles off to the loo and I have a few moments alone with my mum. I tell her how I have been rehearsing *A Midsummer Night's Dream* since she had her stroke, and that the play, with its magical verse, has a strangely healing effect. And quietly I recite to her some of my favourite passages:

> 　　　Thou rememberest
> Since first I sat upon a promontory

And heard a mermaid on a Dolphin's back
Uttering such dulcet and harmonious breath
That the rude sea grew civil at her song
And certain stars shot madly from their spheres
To hear the sea-maid's music.

It occurs to me that my own recitation paralleled the symbolic ritual as the sacrament Fr Brignal had performed. And that both fulfilled our human need for symbols to comfort and mark events. Sartre said that, in our secular age, man had 'a god-shaped hole in his consciousness'. Perhaps I have filled mine with Shakespeare. It doesn't seem too bad a fit.

Week Ten.
We are looking at the scene where the rude mechanicals have gathered back at their lock-up and are waiting for any news of Bottom. Flute keeps reminding everyone that had their play gone ahead they might have earned sixpence a day for the rest of their lives. Suddenly Bottom appears. He refuses to tell them what has happened. But he continues:

Get your apparel together, good strings to your beards, new ribbons to your pumps; meet presently at the palace; every man look o'er his part; for the short and the long is, our play is preferred.

In our first go at the scene, everyone cheered at this point. But as we have explored the tension of the occasion, the investment of the little band of performers in their play, and the terrors of what they have so far experienced, a different reaction seems called for. They all freeze in fear, until Flute lets fly a rather anxious fart. This seems to justify Bottom's next line:

In any case, let Thisbe have clean linen.

Wednesday 9 March.
I have just bought a single ticket to Coventry and am about to board the 5:40pm train to travel to Stratford for the first preview of *Thomas More*, when I pick up a message on the mobile. It's from Mark, saying Mum has deteriorated. She may not have long left.

Suddenly the forecourt at Euston seems very empty and then very full again. I head home, grab the car keys, and drive north.

The staff nurse has just given my mother an injection of diamorphine to calm her. She is tugging at her nightie. Her eyes, like grey pebbles dropping under water, search my face. Mum's hands are 'as pale as milk'. Sometimes she slaps my hand in light little pats, sometimes she squeezes it tightly as if she'll never let go.

I sit with her through the night.

The nursing staff have been fantastic, caring and generous. Tonight, the staff nurse changes Mum's wrist band. 'Oh, she's got a birthday coming up.' 'Yes,' I say, 'Tuesday. She'll be 84.'

I am sure she will go on her birthday. But death is not convenient.

By Sunday, I decide I will have to say my farewells. I hum her some of her favourite songs and wish I could remember the words to 'There's a balm in Gilead'.

And then I thank her. For being my mum, for always being there for me, for understanding. And I kiss her forehead, tell her I love her and leave.

She didn't go on her birthday. She went the following day, with family around her. I was on my way up the M40 to see the first preview of *A New Way to Please You*, when the phone shivered in my pocket. I pulled off the motorway just before it descends through a steep chalk cutting in the Chiltern Hills, where England stretches out before you.

Ruth said she and my father sat by the bed for a while afterwards, until it got dark outside. At which point my dad looked at his watch and said, 'It's dark early today.' 'It's seven o'clock, Dad,' Ruth replied. But his watch had stopped at ten to five. The moment she had died.

Week 11: TRUTH.

The Pyramus and Thisbe scene is surely one of the most joyful moments in all of Shakespeare.

Peter Quince (Paul 'Ghiv' Chahidi) introduced his radical new cutting-edge production:

Gentles, perchance you wonder at this show;
But wonder on, till truth make all things plain.

At this point he threw off his jacket, revealing his stretch Lycra leotard with the word TRUTH emblazoned across the chest in bold capitals. Keeping truthful is the hardest challenge ahead.

There are some 'Elizabethan' dirty jokes in the play-within-a-play, which tend to go by unnoticed, or get heavily underlined with graphic gestures, which resolutely and inevitably kills the gag. Our useful discovery was that perhaps the seemingly innocent script only reveals just how rude the jokes are mid-performance, and the resonance of the *double entendres* had never occurred to the poor amateur actors either in preparing the script or in rehearsal.

The trouble comes as the actors reach the moment that Pyramus and Thisbe kiss through the 'crannied hole or chink' in the 'vile wall'. Tom Snout, who was to play Thisbe's father, has now been entrusted with the radical and innovative idea of making the wall itself a character in the drama. He has presumably made his own costume. He is a tinker after all and probably good with his hands. We imagined he had really run with the idea of playing a wall, and adapted an old wicker laundry basket, punched out the base, turned it upside down, and painted it up with a touch of whitewash to look like wattle and daub. Now here he is, his head and bare legs covered in white slap to match the stone, a very proud wall, as he declares:

This loam, this rough-cast and this stone doth show
That I am that same wall; the truth is so.

But, as frequently happens, when a performance has had no sort of technical or dress rehearsal, suddenly things that hadn't been anticipated occur. In the play's first and possibly only rehearsal in the forest, the Wall was going to hold up his fingers to represent the chink. But what if, in his preparation of the wall-laundry basket, he had forgotten to make a hole for his hand to poke through?

Our resourceful Wall, in a swift piece of improvisation, decided that he could create the chink by spreading his legs apart, and did so, turning to face Pyramus and silently appealing to him to run with the idea. As Pyramus kneeled and peered through Snout's legs, the accommodating tinker lifted his laundry basket a little higher to give him more space, unfortunately revealing more than he had intended to in the process. Thus, when Pyramus delivered what had been a perfectly innocent line

O wicked wall, through whom I see no bliss!
Cursed be thy stones for thus deceiving me!

he found himself facing Snout's red Y-Fronts. And things only got worse when Flute entered as Thisbe, unaware as yet of the new chink. As she knelt and addressed the Wall, the Wall dutifully turned round to face her. Now her once innocent line

My cherry lips have often kiss'd thy stones . . .

. . . seems entirely inappropriate in front of the duke and his wedding guests. And it gets even worse, as faced with the bulge in Snout's pants, she has to say:

Thy stones with lime and hair knit up in thee.

Pyramus and Thisbe then have a fast piece of snappy dialogue to deliver, which in their embarrassment they decide to rattle through as swiftly as possible, with Wall trying to pirouette between them until Pyramus declares

O kiss me through the hole of this vile wall!

At which Thisbe lunges forwards as rehearsed only to discover she has kissed poor old Snout's bum, and then through gritted teeth has to deliver the now obscenely filthy line:

I kiss the wall's hole, not your lips at all.

The poor amateur actors' attempts to continue just got increasingly and helplessly funny.

And remember, in the earlier scene, they were all terrified that if the lion roared too loudly and frightened the ladies they would all be sure to be hanged. What might their punishment be for gross indecency?

The Interlude continues with the introduction of the Lion and Moonshine, and the death of Pyramus, but then something magical happened as Flute came to the moment when as Thisbe she mourns the death of her beloved, Pyramus. 'Her passion ends the play'. We noted that suddenly the snippy clever little interjections from the court audience become silent as Thisbe delivers her lament.

The text, though mostly set out in different editions as four-four-six beat lines, are in fact the thumping fourteeners of the drama that preceded Shakespeare, and the metre of Arthur Golding's translations of Ovid's *Metamorphoses* that Shakespeare would have read at school.

> Asleep, my love? What, dead, my dove? O Pyramus, arise!
> Speak, speak. Quite dumb? Dead, dead? A tomb must cover thy sweet eyes.

But as Flute embraces the tragic loss felt by the character he portrays, perhaps a genuine metamorphosis occurs and he discovers his ability to connect with Thisbe's grief and to express the depth of it, albeit in colloquial language. And his suddenly realized talent transcends the silly thumping fourteeners, and the absurdity and embarrassments of the performance.

> O sisters three, come, come to me, with hands as pale as milk;
> Lay them in gore, since you have shore with shears his thread of silk.

And the aristocratic audience (and we) recognize and are ultimately moved by that rare transformation.

> Tongue, not a word: come, trusty sword; come, blade, my breast imbrue:
> And, farewell, friends; thus Thisbe ends: adieu, adieu, adieu.

Perhaps my own personal experience of loss would not allow me to countenance any cheap laughs here, but that Thisbe's grief, and Flute's emotional engagement with it, needed honouring.

Cis Berry, the RSC voice guru, watching an early run, approved. 'It's so easy for the play-within-a-play to become too knowing,' she said, 'to lose its innocence. It's rude, it's crude but then it's true. He (Shakespeare) knows that laughter comes out of vulnerability.' Cis's wisdom becomes our watch word through the remaining rehearsals and previews. 'TRUTH.'

On Thursday 14 April, *A Midsummer Night's Dream* opened to great reviews.

I watched the production grow over the summer, as I moved on to direct Ben Jonson's *Sejanus* for the Swan Gunpowder Season.

The first weeks of December that year were hectic. We were opening an exuberant two-part adaptation of *The Canterbury Tales* by Mike Poulton in the Swan. On the Monday morning before press night, at nine o'clock sharp, as the doors of Islington Town Hall opened, Tony and I made our appearance at the registrar's office, to register our intention to become civil partners, after eighteen years together. Fifteen days later, on Wednesday 21 December 2005, we returned to the Town Hall to celebrate our civil union. It was the very first day on which same-sex couples were allowed to do so in England and Wales. (Ireland and Scotland were a day or two ahead.)

As part of the ceremony, Tony read a piece from Anthony Burgess' scintillating version of *Cyrano de Bergerac* (which we had done together a few years before) and I read Sonnet 29 'When in disgrace with fortune and men's eyes', and our hearts sang hymns at heaven's gate.

It was a happy day. Mum would have loved it.

And to all the couples who celebrated their unions on that day or since, Duke Theseus' words from the end of *A Midsummer Night's Dream*:

Joy, gentle friends, joy and fresh days of love
Accompany your hearts.

16

Antony and Cleopatra

– 2006: Swan Theatre, Stratford-upon-Avon; Novello Theatre, London.
– Filmed by the V&A.

Sometimes, in choosing where to go on holiday, I manage to persuade Tony to visit the setting of whichever play I am about to do, like the trip we made to Sicily before setting out to direct *Much Ado About Nothing*. When I knew I was to do *Antony and Cleopatra*, I persuaded him that we should go to Egypt. I had never been, and since queuing for hours at the British Museum on a school trip to see the fabulous golden mask of the boy king at the Tutankhamun Exhibition in 1972, I had always longed to travel there.

There is probably about as much point sailing down the Nile in order to understand Shakespeare's inspiration in writing *Antony and Cleopatra*, as there would be heading to Milford Haven to better comprehend the complexities of *Cymbeline*. I don't remember making it a priority to head for Elsinore when we did *Hamlet*, or Cyprus when we did *Othello*, or the seacoast of Bohemia before *The Winter's Tale*.

We were to begin our trip in Cairo. I was keen to explore the museum on Tahrir Square, to see if there was any evidence of Cleopatra's Egypt; but a week before departure, a suicide bomber in Cairo detonated an explosive device near the Khan el-Khalili bazaar, popular with both Egyptians and tourists. A subsequent attack, perpetrated by two veiled terrorists who opened fire on a tourist bus, was the first to be carried out by women in modern Egyptian history.

Consequently, wherever we went on our Egyptian tour, we were accompanied by a heavily armed police presence, frequently (and rather dramatically) on camel back. They were out in force at the pyramids, although, because of the recent bombings, the tourist numbers were low.

We had the subtle Sphinx all to ourselves.

I got up early one morning and sat on the deck in the prow of our boat to read the play again as we slipped silently down the Nile. The flat land to either side of the river is clumped with date palms and low-lying water meadows. White egrets flitted here and there, and occasionally a pied kingfisher would dart from a hole in the riverbank.

The barge she sat in like a burnished throne
Burned on the water, the poop was beaten gold,

Purple the sails, and so perfumed that
The winds were love sick with them.

The language of this play is more lush, more heady with sensuality, than any other Shakespeare play. This speech, where Enobarbus describes the first meeting of Antony and Cleopatra on the river Cydnus,[1] is one of those passages that Shakespeare virtually copies wholesale from *Plutarch's Lives*. So evident is this that you can picture him with a copy of Thomas North's translation open on his desk and writing it out, translating into pentameter as he goes. Nevertheless, the alliteration, unobtrusive in its simplicity, the incantatory phrasing, short phrases setting up a breathless expectation of the elemental climactic hyperbole, turns prose into unforgettable poetry.

*   *   *

There is a water buffalo, tethered and listless. Hooded crows on a village rubbish heap. A girl holding her red skirts up to her thighs in the water pauses to watch us as we glide by.

I am aware of how easy it is to indulge in tourist romanticism, that patronizes the East and glamourizes social division. What Derek Walcott once described to me, referring to a disadvantaged neighbourhood in his native St Lucia, as 'photogenic poverty'. And of course, the tourist industry is predicated on the sensuality of different experience: the sights, the smells, the beauty, the history of elsewhere.

And Shakespeare knew his audience: the appeal of being transported through time and space, out of themselves and their everyday lives. *Antony and Cleopatra* does all those things and much more. What it has to do with the real region of Egypt and her people is irrelevant. Though he is alert to the fact that Cleopatra's country was in revolt against its powerful foreign ally, with a ruler who uses her considerable intelligence to outwit them. But nevertheless, his conjuring of that world elsewhere and elsewhen is intoxicating.

Later, and further down the Nile, we drive in convoy through this biblical countryside with an armed patrol. As we enter one crumbling mud-brick village, with its donkeys and satellite dishes, there are soldiers posted at the end of every street, a precaution designed to make us feel more secure, but which makes the threat of attack seem not only constant, but imminent.

We searched for evidence of Cleopatra at Luxor and Karnak, Philae and Abydos. At the temple of Edfu the old guide ushers us around the site, and then gestures us towards the steps heading to the roof of the temple. We thank him and head on up. But he trots after us in the dark passageway with his torch. 'Here, here,' he cries, flash-illuminating one of the relief carvings on the limestone wall. It's Min, the god of fertility, with an enormous erection. The old guide chuckles and we jog on hoping to lose him if we walk fast enough. But we are foiled at the top of the stairs by a grille gate which is locked. We turn back to face our grinning pursuer in the beam of his torch.

'Look, Cleopatra!' he smiles. I ask him how he knows. 'Cartouche, cartouche!' he insists pointing to the carved oval next to her figure, but as I can't read hieroglyphics, I

[1]   Which is of course in Turkey not Egypt.

am none the wiser. She is holding a pair of sistrum, a sort of rattle, to ward off violence, both musical instrument and warning bell. Tony says he'll take a photograph of me with Cleopatra, and as he does so our jovial guide rests his head on my shoulder.

At Dendera, in ancient Upper Egypt, at the temple of Hathor, the goddess of love and pleasure, we finally and unmistakably came face to face with the Queen of the Nile. Cleopatra VII Philopator appears in a carved relief on the back wall of the temple. Her son Caesarion (fathered by Julius Caesar) stands next to her. It is the only genuine carving of the last active ruler of her country before it became a Roman province. I get a lump in my throat when I see her towering perhaps twenty feet above.

Cleopatra wears a tight-fitting sheath dress, and a headdress of cow horns supporting a sun disk. In one hand, she carries an offering to Hathor; in the other, as at Edfu, she holds a sistrum.

Our guide tells us that Hathor is not only a love deity, sensual and beautiful, but she is also celebrated as the mistress of music and myrrh, dancing and drunkenness. She can be both wild and dangerous, or benign and erotic. She is sometimes represented as a lioness, sometimes as a cobra, but she is also often depicted as a cow, symbolizing her maternal aspect. Hathor sounds like the divine patroness of infinite variety, an appropriate object of worship for our Egyptian queen.

My final hint of Cleopatra on our trip came in a little tourist trap called El Sultan Perfumes Palace. It's right next to the Nubian Alabaster Palace and the Al Fayed Papyrus Institute on the main drag out of Aswan. I had to bribe Tony, who was sceptical we would find anything of interest or worth in a tourist trap.

We sat on couches around a low table in a room with mirrored walls, lined with glass shelves lit from below, and sparkling with all the perfumes of Arabia, hundreds of dainty scent bottles, frosted and gilded, in pink, and green and blue glass. Our host detailed the process of distilling flowers into an essence that was then poured into alabaster jars and buried for forty days. He picked up a tiny perfume flask from the table in front of him, lifted the glass stopper, and dabbed a little kiss of lotus flower essence onto our out-stretched wrists.

Our host continued in full flow, how distilled sandalwood was great for rheumatism, that the musk oil is extracted from gazelles, and he suggested we sample the Attar of Roses, the Heliotrope and the Black Narcissus. 'But here,' he said, his eyes fluttering with pleasure, 'is one of our most especial blends. Number 14: Queen Cleopatra. The effect upon men,' he confided in the respectful tone of someone imparting a trade secret, 'well, let me just say, when you wear this, we call it Egyptian Viagra.' Sadly, we were his only audience that day. Tony rolled his eyes. I nodded appreciatively.

On our last night in Egypt, the air grew hazy and yellow. By sunset it was a murky mustard colour. The sun went cold like a dull penny, shedding pewter ripples over the muddy brown Nile. A sandstorm was brewing.

* * *

The success of *Antony and Cleopatra* depends upon the actors who play the title roles, and not just because they have two-thirds of the lines of the entire play. Their chemistry has to work. Harriet Walter had played both Lady Macbeth and Beatrice with me, which sounded like the perfect equation to play Cleopatra. Lady Macbeth's ferocious certainty yet tragic vulnerability, with Beatrice's acerbic wit and passionate nature. The greater challenge is to match your Cleopatra with an Antony, which, I discovered, is not a role actors have high on their list of parts they must play. They often dismiss the challenge saying, 'It's her play.'

So, I was really delighted when Patrick Stewart agreed to play Mark Antony. I had been talking to him about coming back to the company for a couple of years. We decided that he should also reprise Prospero (whom he called 'the old misery') in that season, which he had already played for George C. Wolfe in Central Park in New York in 1995.

Patrick had last appeared at the RSC when he opened the Barbican Theatre as King Henry IV in 1982. Since then, of course, he had found considerable fame and fortune in the United States, in the role of Captain Jean-Luc Picard in *Star Trek*, and in films like *X-Men*. Patrick is quoted as having said that his years playing kings, emperors, princes and tragic heroes at Stratford 'were nothing but preparation for sitting in the captain's chair of the Enterprise'. Oddly, I think the converse may also be true and the star status he achieved in Hollywood for that role contributed to his understanding of the difficult role of Mark Antony.

Patrick knew *Antony and Cleopatra* extremely well having played Enobarbus twice at Stratford, once in the 1972 Roman Season, and then again in 1978. I had seen that production in the rehearsal room or, at any rate, the first four acts of it.

It was as a student that I found myself in this room watching an open rehearsal of Peter Brook's production of the play with Glenda Jackson and Alan Howard. It was, of course, electric. The proximity of the actors, the immediacy of the performance, the willing suspension of disbelief, as they performed in tracksuits and jeans, and the emphasis placed on the words to deliver the story, all left me breathless. And one of the actors even came over to talk to us. He was playing the messenger, and his name was Richard Griffiths.

We made a special pilgrimage back to Stratford in October that year to see the production when it opened in the RST. All I knew was that something had disappeared. How often since have I mourned the loss of what can emerge in a precious final run in a rehearsal room, when the play is inflated into full production.

But perhaps the element that suffered most in that particular transfer was the intimacy. *Antony and Cleopatra* is a chamber play. Their intimate relationship might be carried out against a context of geo-politics and their actions may have world-changing consequences, but they act as if they are in a bubble of their own. The play defies the temptation toward epic design: rolling on pillars for Rome and pyramids for Egypt, which swamp the action.

Luckily our production would play in the Swan Theatre. So, if Cleopatra was on stage, the audience would know we were in Egypt (her people tended to lounge around on cushions); whereas if Octavius appeared we were likely to be in Rome (where they would sit upright on stiff-backed chairs).

The Swan Theatre itself had already cracked another challenging play, *All is True (Henry VIII)* for me, by allowing both the epic and the intimate. It's like a film camera, which can open out for the wide shot and shut right down for the close up, and it is capable of cinematic fluidity. It also shuns too much set. It is scenery-averse!

The Swan balconies (although the sight lines from some seats are not perfect) effortlessly allow all those scenes described in the Quarto and Folio stage direction as 'above', or 'aloft' and which can otherwise involve a lot of surplus structure. And *Antony and Cleopatra* famously requires a monument. In a sort of older parallel to *Romeo and Juliet*, Antony must reach up to Cleopatra for their most tender scene together.

Stephen Brimson Lewis's design incorporated a sort of *mappa mundi* on the back wall, accommodated musicians' positions under the side balconies and concentrated its major focus on the monument. Our then technical director, Geoff Locker, had a sound piece of advice for any director/designer team: 'What's your money shot?'[2] Well, for Stephen and me the money shot would be the monument.

I don't know how many productions of this play I have seen where the impact of this emotionally climactic moment has been severely diminished. Often as a result of bad sight-lines from the back of the stalls, the monument is barely the height of a tea-chest, affording Cleopatra and her women very little protection from Caesar's forces. Too often, instead of the poignant suspension of Mark Antony, 'the triple pillar of the world' between the elements of earth and air, the action involves some rather clumsy fumbling and bundling, and suddenly becomes more about soft furniture removal.

The scene has a very subtle balance of comedy and tragedy, which sit closely together. Unintentional laughs are not useful.

We wanted to play the monument scene, as the theatre seemed to dictate, high up on the musicians' balcony, but realized that not everyone could indeed see the action up there. Stephen's clever solution was to create a sort of lift, lowering the central section of the balcony floor, with Cleopatra and her women, into the centre of the space, the midway air, where everyone could see, and yet still a good twelve feet above the stage floor. As if the monument had a sort of hoist to lift goods, but now used to raise a precious cargo.

* * *

A key moment in Harriet Walter's creation of her alluring Cleopatra was when she came to tackle the reputation of her notoriously infinite variety. 'How on earth do I play that?' she asked one day. The answer was simple. You don't. You play those qualities she has one by one, not all together, and play each of them as fully and vividly as possible. If they seem contradictory, that is because we are all full of glorious contradictions. It's one of the greatest indices of our being human. The advice recalled something John Barton used to say. He described how Shakespeare's idea of psychology was pre-Freudian. He thought of character as beads on a necklace. In this scene you are a bright green bead, in the next a red one, a blue one in the next. But if you think that is somehow inconsistent, and that you should make the character a bit more red in the blue scene, or a bit more yellow in the green scene, instead of a vibrant necklace (a human portrait of subtle contrasts) you'll get a sludgy string of muddy colours. The audience supply the thread on which the beads are hung. You don't have to.

---

[2]   I don't think I was aware at the time that this useful term is derived from the porn industry.

But much in the way that Cleopatra has to investigate that myriad personality, and make it believable, so Antony has, in a way, a similar job. But the trap with him is not infinite variety, but infinite similarity, with every scene hitting the same note.

He has to balance the heroic with the old ruffian, the strumpet's fool. He must convey the man's reputation as a soldier beloved by his men, who once in dire straits, as Octavius says

> ... didst drink
> The stale of horses, and the gilded puddle
> Which beasts would cough at.

and marry that rugged capacity with his self-destructive side, his addiction for lascivious wassails, and gaudy nights ('I'the east my pleasure lies'). Antony makes some pretty anarchic and disastrous decisions: his insistence to fight at sea despite all advice and appeals, and his own common sense; his bragging challenge to fight Octavius in single combat astonishes everyone, and his sudden farewell to his servants, which makes them all cry, and baffles Cleopatra.

Patrick Stewart realized the opportunity for those contradictions and absurd choices to allow us to laugh, and to make us love Antony.

Mark Antony has always been a star. But, as the play progresses, he finds his stardom is beginning to lose its gilt. No longer able to live up to his own PR, or endure the spotlight of publicity, he expresses that in the most telling imagery.

'I have fled myself' he says after chasing Cleopatra on her departure from Actium, when she hi-tailed it from the sea battle; as one of his captains sneers 'the breese upon her like a cow in June' she had hoisted her sails and fled. 'I have lost command' Antony says in disbelief, at which point Patrick would fold himself up, as if he wanted to vanish.

Right at the end of Act Four when he thinks he has been betrayed by Cleopatra, Antony says to Eros:

MARK ANTONY	Sometimes we see a cloud that's dragonish,
	A vapour sometime like a bear or lion,
	A tower'd citadel, a pendent rock,
	A forked mountain, or blue promontory
	With trees upon't, that nod unto the world
	And mock our eyes with air: thou hast seen these signs:
	They are black vesper's pageants.
EROS	Ay, my lord.
MARK ANTONY	That which is now a horse, even with a thought
	The rack dislimns, and makes it indistinct
	As water is in water.
EROS	It does, my lord.
MARK ANTONY	My good knave Eros, now thy captain is
	Even such a body: here I am Antony,
	Yet cannot hold this visible shape, my knave.

Act Four Scene Fourteen

Laurence Olivier once dismissed the role of Antony as 'an absolute twerp' who 'doesn't have a lot between the ears'. Patrick's genius was to see that the character's tragic decline was both funny and poignant.

After this existential moment of identity crisis, Mardian arrives to tell Mark Antony that his threats to kill Cleopatra are in vain and that she is already dead. We know this is not true as Cleopatra herself has sent Mardian, and moreover she wants him to return so she can hear how news of her death went down.

Antony asks Eros to help him remove his armour and prepares to kill himself. There is a touching scene as Eros, rather than assisting his master with his suicide, kills himself instead. Antony has been tricked but learns from the lesson and falls on his sword … but doesn't die. He manages to botch his own death. In performance, Patrick would stab himself with the sword, collapse to the ground, and lie still. Then, as Antony realizes he has failed to do even that final act successfully, on the line 'How? Not dead. Not dead?' Patrick would surprise us by laughing.

It is often not in the thundering tragic speeches, but in moments of telling laughter where the audience fully understands a character and is most moved by them.

Antony then calls the guards to assist him, but in a further dangerously comic humiliation, the guards refuse to do so and run away, leaving the seedy Decretas to pinch his sword. When Diomed enters and Antony begs him to finish the job, Diomed has to tell him that he has been sent by Cleopatra. Another darkly comic moment, which highlights the strange hilarity that has been noted in the play.

Antony asks the vital question: 'When did she send?' Patrick, in perfect control of the tone, allowed the audience to laugh at this absurd situation. And he continued to judge this dangerous comic precipice into the monument scene which follows immediately.

As he is hauled up to the monument by Cleopatra and her women (an image of piercing vulnerability) and finally arrives in her arms, he gasps:

I am dying Egypt, dying.
Give me some wine and let me speak a little.

But Cleopatra won't let him speak, and her expiring lover has to insist – twice – that she shuts up and listens to his dying words. It's outrageously good writing, exceptionally human, and requires actors at the top of their game to recognize and then to handle the subtle comedy, understanding how it will intensify the emotional impact of what is to follow. Similarly with the clown who arrives with a basket of figs in the next act, allowing us the release of laughter deepens the grief and the majesty of Cleopatra's death – no botching there.

Harriet Walter's performance balanced Patrick Stewart's marvellous disintegration as Antony, with some of the most moving moments I have ever had the privilege to see on stage. Her fury at herself, her self-disgust, her compassion for her women, her dull resignation that 'This case of that huge spirit now is cold', and her pragmatic determination that

We have no friend
But resolution and the briefest end.

had heart-catching intensity.

But the briefest end it is not. In fact, after Antony's death there are still over 450 lines of the play left, a potential playing-time of about half an hour. The actor playing Cleopatra has to deal with some swift politicking from Octavius ('he words me, girls, he words me'), a side plot about her dodgy accountant, and an asp.

We auditioned a variety of snakes for the asp.

A snake enthusiast brought in a selection to our Clapham rehearsal room. There were a couple of corn snakes in a vivarium, a beautiful, red-banded milk snake and an enormous royal python with glittering coal-black scales, which he removed from a heavy canvas bag. The royal python supposedly gets its name because it was thought to be the species of snake which Cleopatra reputedly wore around her wrist. Harriet was thrilled by the corn snake. At least she wouldn't have to start manipulating a puppet at the climax of her performance. Golda Rosheuvel, playing Charmian, was less enthusiastic.

None of the snakes was venomous, indeed none would bite. Stage management took down a series of very strict instructions about when to feed our chosen snake, nicknamed 'Billy Snakespeare'.[3] Billy would need to be fed with tiny naked baby mice (known as 'pinkies' as opposed to 'fuzzies'), which came in frozen packs and could be kept in the fridge at the stage door. If he was fed too close to the performance he might regurgitate when handled, or worse, defecate over the Queen of Egypt, which would not have the required effect.

Meanwhile Charmian, who had struggled with the situation for weeks, finally admitted that her ophidiophobia had not abated; and the stage-door keepers were in a state of revolt over the frozen pinkies in the fridge.

Then the prop department came to our aid; they invented a cracking snake constructed of cast rubber around a piece of bicycle chain. The chain could imitate the way when a snake is held that it reaches out for its escape route, an action we had witnessed in rehearsal. Finally, the prop snake was substituted, and Billy was retired.

*   *   *

Our much-anticipated press night was an eventful one. Technical rehearsals and previews had been disturbed by a rogue fire alarm, caused by the use of some smoke effects in the RST. Even though we knew these pyrotechnical effects were what was triggering the alarm, we could not turn the alarm off (in case an actual fire happened to break out that particular night) and I was assured that the smoke effects had been sufficiently diminished to warrant no further concern.

The inevitable happened about five minutes into the show: the dreadful bell rang. I was incandescent. This was one of the most important productions I had ever directed. I was very proud indeed of what we had achieved, and now, we were effectively shooting

---

[3]   The runner-up in the competition to name him was 'Hiss-topher Marlowe'.

ourselves in the foot. So out trooped an audience of just over four hundred, all the major critics included, into the wet, dark April night.

When they returned ten minutes later, the culprit being the already-identified pyrotechnic, I decided to go on stage, to try and win the shivering audience back. 'Well, at least the critics will be able to say the actors set the stage alight,' I quipped. When the play resumed, the actors stormed it, determined not to allow the incident to spoil their play. Many shone: Ken Bones wry and sardonic as Enobarbus, initially cynical and finally deeply moving; and John Hopkins, not the usual ice-cold Puritan Octavius, but an unnervingly tormented neurotic, disappointed by Antony. And luckily the critics applauded their efforts.

Harriet (wearing the lotus blossom scent in the little bottle I had brought her from Egypt) gave a mesmerizing performance of restless volatility, vicious and capricious. From one moment to the next, she was hilarious and hyperbolical, playing the long adagio of the last act when, as Michael Billington said, 'Shakespeare's poetic genius overtakes his dramatic instinct' with consummate intelligence.

But, as the same critic pointed out, we have seen many fine Cleopatras, but very few great Antonys, which he described as Shakespeare's most demanding male role. He declared that Patrick had given us 'a magnificently wounded lion: one haunted by the memory he was once king of the jungle' and called him 'the best Antony since Michael Redgrave half a century ago'.

When Ian McKellen came to see his friend in the role, he told me that he had never really considered Antony as a great part, but Patrick had made it one.

17

Merry Wives: The Musical

– 2006: Royal Shakespeare Theatre, Stratford-upon-Avon.

When Michael Boyd first proposed the idea of a Complete Works Festival for 2006, I wondered about what a suitable Christmas Shakespeare offering might be. I suggested a musical version of *The Merry Wives of Windsor*. Michael liked the notion. As we still had two years before the festival there would be time to write, adapt and workshop the idea. I immediately rang composer Paul Englishby. We began work on it straight away.

Paul, working with choreographer Mike Ashcroft, had amply demonstrated their joint ability to create a showstopper, in the female power number in *The Tamer Tamed*: 'The women must wear the breeches'. The women of the town show solidarity with Maria (Petruchio's second wife) who has called for a Lysistrata-type sex strike by all the wives of the city, until their demands are met. This 'monstrous regiment of women' arrive in their clogs, banging an array of pots and pans and singing. The sex strike is averted when Petruchio finally reviews the women's demands, saying 'As I thought, money and clothes', which guaranteed a round of applause from the audience.

For that show, Paul had immersed himself in the music of John Dowland, Thomas Morley and others. He became addicted to writing catches and canons and had fallen for the sheer tunefulness of the music. With a fantastically wide range of interests as a composer, he is always curious, searching for something new.

His greatest love is jazz. This came through as he composed the music for *Merry Wives,* with long, melodic lines and the vivid colours in the orchestrations. What began to emerge was a very eclectic musical mix, including tangos, vaudeville and big band jazz, 'all sewn together' as Paul himself put it 'with Elizabethan twine'.

As Shakespeare's only domestic middle-class comedy, its themes and characters do seem to lend themselves to music. Certainly, we were not the first to have thought so. It's a romp, Shakespeare's sitcom, or as someone once said, 'It is the *I love Lucy* of the Shakespeare canon'.

Many of Shakespeare's plays have been given the musical treatment. And this particular play has enjoyed more adaptations than virtually any other play in the canon. In one supreme case the adaptation matches, if not surpasses, it.

A vogue for adapting Shakespeare took hold during the eighteenth century. Indeed, and rather bizarrely, *Merry Wives* was translated into Russian by none other than

Catherine the Great, with the snappy title *This is what it means to have buckbaskets and linen*. The only other Shakespeare she is known to have translated was *Timon of Athens*.

Within the eighteenth century, there were two French operas of *Merry Wives* and two German ones. The century ended with Antonio Salieri writing his own. He made a number of changes to the text, including the transformation of Mrs Quickly into a lively chambermaid called Betty, and the addition of a scene in which Mrs Ford pretends to be German.

When it was suggested to Otto Nikolai that he should write a Shakespeare opera, he said: 'Only Mozart is worthy of Shakespeare.' However, he overcame his reservations and produced *Die lustigen Weiber von Windsor*, in Berlin in 1849.

It was Verdi who, at the age of eighty, in creating his last great masterpiece *Falstaff*, produced the finest musical adaptation of this play. He and his librettist Boito fused the plot of *The Merry Wives of Windsor*, but fleshed out Falstaff with the best of his individual philosophy from the Henries. Boito wrote to Verdi about the difficulty of starting work on Falstaff, saying:

> To extract all the juice from that great Shakespearean orange without letting the useless pips slip into the little glass, to write with colour, clarity and brevity . . . to make the joyous comedy live from top to bottom . . . is difficult, difficult, difficult, and yet one must make it seem easy, easy, easy. Corragio e avanti!

The next step in our process on *Merry Wives* was to engage a lyricist. I asked Paul what he felt we needed from his point of view. 'It's a big ask,' he said, 'we want to keep the spirit of the Shakespeare text in the songs, retain the imagery and where possible actual lines from the original, while creating satisfying song forms, and heightening the comedy or emotion. It's got to be someone who can write hilarious lyrics and be an experienced adapter of dramatic text into verse, knowledgeable about classical literature, prolific and collaborative.'

We asked Ranjit Bolt. He turned out to be all of the above.

One of the challenges was to create something more for the young lovers in the play, Fenton and Anne Page. Paul thought their relationship had terrific potential musically, but they have very little stage time in Shakespeare's play. The same instinct occurred to Arthur Sullivan when he composed music for the play in 1851, when the actor-manager, Samuel Phelps, mounted his production of the play at the Gaiety Theatre. He commissioned the young composer to write a song for Anne Page, 'Love laid his sleepless head', with lyrics by Algernon Swinburne.

So, how did Shakespeare come to write *The Merry Wives of Windsor* in the first place?

The critic John Dennis wrote his own adaptation of the play in 1702. *The Comical Gallant* was a flop that only lasted two nights, but Dennis also wrote an accompanying essay, which is the source of the famous story that Queen Elizabeth I herself had ordered the play. Apparently, she had so fallen for Falstaff, in *Henry IV*, that she wanted to see another play about him. 'She was so eager to see it acted,' Dennis wrote, 'that she commanded it to be finished in 14 days.' Some critics have attributed the fortnight deadline to their sense of the play's inferiority to Shakespeare's other plays of the period. Nicholas Rowe, Shakespeare's first biographer, later amplified the details of the story, adding that the queen wanted to see 'Sir John in love', which is indeed the title Vaughan Williams chose when he wrote his opera on the subject.[1]

Some believe that Shakespeare wrote *Merry Wives* after *Henry IV Part One*, but before *Part Two*. But I now think he wrote it after the two *Henry IV* plays. If *Merry Wives* was written after *Part Two* it would also make some sense of the odd epilogue to that play, which promises 'If you be not too much cloyed with fat meat, our humble author will continue the story, with Sir John in it.'

It is possible that Shakespeare may have originally intended to put Falstaff in *Henry V*, as the epilogue also goes on to promise to 'make you merry with fair Katharine of France: where, for any thing I know, Falstaff shall die of a sweat, unless already a' be killed with your hard opinions', which might suggest the original plan for a third appearance for Falstaff, was not a play about 'Sir John in Love' but 'Sir John at War'.

If *Merry Wives* was written to entertain the royal court, then Shakespeare follows a by now familiar formula of transporting a set of characters that the audience recognize and placing them in a different setting. A bit like the cast of characters from *Eastenders* turning up in an episode of *Fawlty Towers*. And it only works if you know what to expect from them and have been introduced to them.

So, Shakespeare takes Falstaff and his cronies and transports them all from The Boar's Head in Eastcheap, twenty-odd miles up river to Windsor: sozzled Corporal Bardolph, with his bulbous nose; the firecracking swaggerer, Ancient Pistol; and Falstaff's tiny page, Robin. In our production they all exploded into Windsor, on a sort of half-timbered Harley-Davidson.

One other significant character who appears in both the *Henry IV*'s and makes her reappearance in *Merry Wives* is Mrs Quickly. Her previous life as the hostess of The Boar's Head tavern now forgotten, she has a respectable occupation as the housekeeper for the French Dr Caius and seems well-acquainted with the business of all the folk of Windsor. She has the same delicious linguistic invention as the hostess – she laments 'the frampold life' Mrs Ford leads, for example – but she has no knowledge of the fat knight, nor does he seem to recognize or acknowledge her.

I took this as a challenge. We decided to restore her temporary amnesia, and imagine that somehow she had finally left Eastcheap and settled in Windsor. She then finds herself face to face with the scoundrel who continually borrowed money he did not repay, ate her out of house and home and promised to marry her. That way, when she joins in the plot to fool him at Herne's Oak, she too can have her revenge.

In which case Mrs Quickly would need a song where she laments her infatuation and her frustrated affection for Sir John Falstaff. I suggested Quickly's description of Falstaff in *Part Two* as a 'honeysuckle villain' might be appropriate. Paul Englishby turned it into one of the show's best numbers.

In the dubious business of filling in loose ends, we then considered Mrs Quickly's status in *Henry V*, when we learn that she has married Pistol, whose very presence she could hardly tolerate in *Part Two*,

---

[1] Vaughan Williams had been composer in residence in Stratford-upon-Avon in 1913, and had already written incidental music for the play.

There comes no swaggerers here; I have not liv'd all this while to have swaggering now. Shut the door, I pray you . . . Your ancient swaggerer comes not in my doors . . .

But we decided to mark Quickly's shift of allegiance here, and having delivered 'Honeysuckle Villain', she would sail off into the sunset on Pistol's arm.

Having identified where the musical numbers should be, Ranjit Bolt helped develop the script and wrote the lyrics. Once we had the script and the score together, and workshopped it a couple of times, we all piled down to Surrey to Judi Dench's house and sang it through for her in her living room. She said 'yes' to Mrs Quickly immediately.

Rehearsals began in October.

By week three we were able to piece together a sort of sing-through with the musicians to see how everything was coming together.

I was really enjoying the whole experience of directing a musical. The onus is not so entirely on the director as with a straight play. Much of the responsibility lands with the musical director (Bruce O'Neil, in our case) and of course the composer, and indeed the choreographer and his team.

As we sat watching the run the room was full of laughter and excited expectation.

There was a great tongue-in-cheek opening number to introduce us to Windsor. Alexandra Gilbreath and Haydn Gwynne, as the two wives, were beginning to deliver the duet 'Letter for Letter' as Mrs Ford and Mrs Page compared their letters from Sir John, as if they had been singing opera all their born lives. The love duet between Fenton and Page's daughter Anne, sung by the impossibly handsome couple of Martin Crewes and Scarlett Strallen, brought a lump to my throat every time. Alistair McGowan, as well as having those talents for mimicry for which he was very well known, turned out to have a great voice, delivering Mr Ford's growing jealousy in 'The Hour Is Fixed' with real fury.

The first half closed with a fifteen-minute extended sung-through number, which took us through the search for Falstaff and the fat knight's escape in the buckbasket.

Mike Ashcroft and Paul had devised a rambunctious drinking number to open the second half. 'Sack' featured Simon Trinder, as feeble Abraham Slender, and the chorus; some of the lyrics borrowed from Falstaff's famous paean to sack in *Henry IV Part Two*.

Des Barrit had two major numbers as Falstaff. The first as he sets out his plot to his henchmen, and the second as he emerges from his dumping in Datchet Mead in the buckbasket and tells 'Mr Brook' (Ford in disguise) all about it.

The double-act of Hugh Evans (Ian Hughes) and Dr Caius (Ghiv Chahidi) made the most of Ranjit's very funny lyrics in a song about the relative merits (or otherwise) of Wales and France.

When Judi delivered 'Honeysuckle Villain' with that soulful catch in her voice, it broke your heart. Then she sailed off on the arm of Brendan O'Hea who was basing his hilarious performance as Pistol on Russell Brand, with a dash of Jack Sparrow.

Denise Wood, the RSC lead producer, turned to me and gave my arm a squeeze and said, 'Aren't we lucky, to do what we do!' And she was right. And then disaster struck.

I got in one morning to hear that Falstaff was in hospital. Des Barrit had damaged his ankle in a fall and would have to come out of the show. I went to see him in hospital in East London. He was distraught at having to give up the role.

As a proud Welshman with a fine singing voice, Des had been thrilled when I offered him a musical version of Falstaff. He seemed such a perfect fit for the role.[2] But now we had a problem: we needed someone with the comic chops to play Falstaff who could sing and who would be free to start rehearsals immediately.

Frantic conversations were had with some fairly original ideas being aired. Then someone said, 'Can Simon Callow sing?' 'He's very musical.' 'He's directed tons of opera.' 'He originated the role of Mozart in Amadeus.' 'Yes, but did he sing?' 'He played Emmanuel Schikaneder in the film of *Amadeus*; didn't he have to sing a bit of Papageno in that?' 'He must be a baritone.' 'He might have been dubbed.'

I rang Simon Callow.

He was on a Mediterranean island, playing Pliny the Elder in an episode of a children's drama series called *Roman Mysteries* about the eruption of Vesuvius for CBBC. But he only had a day left, and yes, he would love to do it.

I think this may have been my third time lucky as I had asked Simon to play a number of parts before and he had never been free. Simon had the advantage of knowing Sir John Falstaff rather well, having played the part in a stage production of the Orson Welles film *Chimes at Midnight*, in 1998. But nevertheless, this Falstaff had to sing. Simon began rehearsals the following Monday. We had just three weeks to go.

Saturday 2 December 2006.
Merry Wives: The Musical started previewing.
In the audience, as the overture began, Tony gave me a smile and bobbed his eyebrows.

The set looked magnificent, conceived in Stephen Brimson Lewis's design as a merry England suburb, on the edge of the countryside. There was even a row of gabled houses, which diminished in perspective along the road, providing the best Dench double-take of the evening as she caught sight of them and realized she was taller than the house.

Simon Callow, in (unbelievably) his RSC acting debut, had done an incredible job, not only having learnt the part but having made it his own. He inherited the rather opulent latex fat-suit worn by Bryn Terfel as Verdi's Falstaff at the Royal Opera House in Graham Vick's production a few years before. It worked particularly well in the scene where Falstaff is recovering from his dousing in the river, which we played with him taking a hot bath in a wooden tub.

There was a priceless moment as Sir Hugh Evans led his team of schoolchildren skipping around as fairies, and the smallest child, wearing a huge pumpkin-head, ran across the stage and crashed into the proscenium. Not sure how many of the audience realized that that had been rigorously rehearsed.

As we reached the end of the show there was one surprise bit of business as Mrs Quickly cart-wheeled across the stage. It was of course a double (Matt Cross in a

---

[2]   Des did finally play Falstaff in *The Merry Wives of Windsor* in 2012 directed by Phillip Breen.

duplicate frock) but as Judi staggered back on stage breathless, the house went up. At the end, as the audience leapt to their feet, Tony turned and gave me a kiss.

Press night followed a week later. It was a dizzy experience, full of flowers and gifts, and laughter and joy. Perhaps I should have kept in mind a few lines from the last play I had done with Dame Jude. In *All's Well* (Act Two Scene One) Helena says:

Oft expectation fails and most oft there
Where most it promises, and oft it hits
Where hope is coldest and despair most fits.

The following day, I walked through Old Town to the newsagents to get the papers. When I got back to our flat in Avonside, Tony was still in bed.

'Well?' he asked.

'It's a disaster. They all hated it.'

'Yeah, really!' he laughed

'No,' I said, 'it's true.'

And alas, it was true. The critics had simply not come to the party.

Luckily, it didn't seem to affect the audiences' enjoyment. We were packed for the entire run, with standing ovations every night.

Paul, Ranjit and I had spent two years trying, as Arrigo Boito said to Verdi, to extract the juice from this great Shakespearian orange. It had been difficult, difficult, difficult. The production's tough critical reception was hard, hard, hard.

18

Coriolanus

– 2007: Royal Shakespeare Theatre, Stratford-upon-Avon;
Eisenhower Theater, Kennedy Center, Washington, DC;
Theatre Royal, Newcastle; Teatro Albéniz, Madrid, Spain.

In 2005, I was asked by the British Library to select a series of extracts for a double CD of Shakespeare performances from its archive. I had not realized that a sound recording of every Shakespeare production at Stratford-upon-Avon had been lodged with the Library, going back before the founding of the RSC in 1960.

I went to the library on Euston Road, next to St Pancras Station, excited to think what might be there. I was amazed to discover that they held in their vaults not only RSC productions, but recordings going back to the late fifties. Here was not only the great Paul Robeson as Othello (with Sam Wanamaker as Iago), but Sir Laurence Olivier himself as Coriolanus, directed by Peter Hall in 1959.

Until then, I had seen only photographs of this legendary production, shot by Angus McBean. One in particular, of the most talked about scene, when Olivier, having fallen backwards from an upper level, hangs upside down, held by his heels, and is stabbed by Tullus Aufidius. We have the red breastplate and orange cloak worn by Olivier in that famous production in our RSC collection. And we also have the quilted dress worn by Dame Edith Evans as his mother Volumnia. Actually, seeing and even touching these items brings the production vividly to life. But nothing had prepared me for the shock of hearing Olivier play the part.

Listening to the tape of his performance, at the British Library, I was transported back to a July night in the Shakespeare Memorial Theatre, as Sir Laurence snarls his curses on the people of Rome. The immediacy of its impact was quite astonishing. There is a startling aliveness to the performance. This is not filtered. It's not a recording session in a muffled studio. You can hear it as if it's happening in front of you. You can hear their footsteps on the floorboards. You can hear the audience laugh and listen.

The scene I eventually chose for the CD was from the forum scene (Act Three Scene Three) as Robert Hardy, playing the tribune Sicinius Velutus, pronounces Coriolanus 'an enemy of the people'. Olivier's voice swoops octaves as he delivers Coriolanus' disdain: 'The fires of the lowest hell fold in the people.' It's grand acting, melodramatic, thrilling. But as the vicious tribune works the crowd and insists the Roman hero should be banished the city or be precipitated from the Tarpeian rock, and Coriolanus turns on them, promising to turn his back on Rome, Olivier finally declares, in an almost inaudible whisper: 'There is a world elsewhere.' Riveting.

Olivier was squeezing *Coriolanus* in between finishing filming *Spartacus* in Hollywood (directed by Stanley Kubrick), and John Osborne's *The Entertainer* for Tony Richardson, which was being filmed in Morecambe Bay. Olivier was ferried up to Lancashire after the show every night in an ambulance (in case of any emergency hold-ups), already dressed in his pyjamas so he could get an uninterrupted sleep and be ready for the next day's shoot.

At the end of the 2006 Complete Works Festival, the Royal Shakespeare Theatre was to be torn down in order to undergo its transformation from a proscenium house to a thrust stage with a galleried auditorium all around. We would keep the 1932 proscenium. It was my job to ensure that the ghosts of those many great actors who had appeared on this stage, like Sir Laurence, would be locked in the walls for all time.

My contribution to the Complete Works Festival had already included *Antony and Cleopatra*, *Venus and Adonis*, *The Rape of Lucrece* and *Merry Wives: The Musical*. For the final production in the old RST, and with some trepidation, I would tackle *Coriolanus*.

The designer Richard Hudson and I wanted to recognize that this would be the last production on this stage and take full advantage of that opportunity.

We employed the basic metaphor of Ancient Rome, filtered through the Jacobean period (so togas were worn over doublets). We didn't want Hollywood Rome; this is not the Augustan city after all, but a more primitive, volatile, war-mongering state.

We would rearrange the front of the stage, removing the apron and replacing it with a full set of steps which ran down into the auditorium and could easily accommodate a large crowd, without destroying the audience's line of sight to the action on stage.

The city of Rome would be a series of crowded corridors, of receding walls punctuated with doors, creating a sense of the bustling streets. The walls were metallic, striated with a sort of rusty red, echoing the bloody conflicts which Rome had undergone, scarred like Coriolanus' own body with the glorious wounds of battle.

For Corioli, we had two huge iron doors to represent the city gates. Then in the final act, on the battlefield, we would suddenly pull out all the scenery and play right to the back wall of the fly tower, an immense space that would be seen for the very last time. I remember at the technical rehearsal, when we first achieved that transition, there was a gasp in the auditorium. Normally during an ordinary summer season, sets for other shows are stored up stage, so no-one had seen the whole space completely empty. It was a very powerful image highlighting the lonely vigil of Volumnia and the women as they arrive at the Volsci encampment.

Janet Suzman was Volumnia. Perfect casting in the role. I had asked Janet to play Volumnia a few years before and was delighted that she kept her word. I was equally fortunate that Timothy West accepted my invitation to play that 'humorous patrician' Menenius Agrippa, 'one that converses more with the buttock of the night than with the forehead of the morning'. I can think of few other actors who could deliver the witheringly barbed speech to the tribunes ending 'what harm can your bisson conspectuities glean out of this character?' with more acerbic charm, more lethal asperity, or indeed who could make me believe they actually use phrases like 'bisson conspectuities' in their everyday speech.

I had directed Will Houston as Sejanus, the title role in Ben Jonson's Roman tragedy, in the Gunpowder Season in 2005. Will has a vulpine quality, a maniacal volatility on stage which is as rare as it is mesmeric. He captured the vaulting ambition of the narcissistic Sejanus with terrifying precision, a man for whom power is an addictive aphrodisiac. As with all good actors you work with, you busily think what they should play next. On the press night of *Sejanus*, I asked Will to play Coriolanus.

*   *   *

Coriolanus can be viewed from almost every political point of view. You can take a right-wing angle and side wholeheartedly with the patricians; a left-wing agenda and promote the play from the plebeians' angle – 'What is the City but the people'; or indeed from a sort of nihilistic perspective, and view both sides as absurd in their own ways. Shakespeare doesn't come down on any one side and is frequently satirical in tone. But the play is too complex, too multi-faceted to be reduced to a single political perspective. Shakespeare sees both sides, empathizes with both, and yet is critical of both. *Coriolanus* seems to me to be closely akin to *Troilus and Cressida* in that respect, in its dark humour and its cynical attitude to male posturing.

It's crucial in production not to take sides. Your political affiliations or prejudices are likely to emerge anyway. But it is too easy to send up the plebs as a stupid, fickle mob. They have genuine grievances and are starving to death. At the same time, it is very easy to be taken in by the warm affability of the apparently eminently trustworthy Menenius, whereas actually he is a wily, manipulative, reactionary old bastard. I think part of the success of Will Houston's performance as Coriolanus was his ability to marry the ruthless warrior on the battlefield with the temperamental child at home.

But whereas it is vital to see every character from their own point of view, we found that job hardest with the tribunes. Was there ever a more self-serving, cowardly, vicious, pusillanimous pair in all literature? They are right to defend the people from the man who would 'vent their musty superfluity' in battle; on the other hand, when they have secured Coriolanus' banishment from Rome, they realize that they have effectively dismantled their nuclear deterrent only to have that same weapon, doubled in power, pointed right at their walls. The play is power-driven in performance, high-voltage, a real thriller, if you engage passionately with the rhetoric and invest each side with real conviction.

Menenius' fable of the body is a total fraud. If the senators are the belly of Rome, then their job is to distribute the nourishment through the arteries of the body to the outer extremities – the plebeians – and they are palpably not doing that. By hoarding corn, they are depriving the plebeians of food and therefore threatening their survival. Unfortunately, Menenius doesn't seem to be aware that the story actually works against him. Nor does the crowd happen to notice that this elegant fable cannot be comfortably applied.

But what of Coriolanus himself? When Aufidius attacks Coriolanus and calls him a 'boy of tears' the effect is devastating, not only because it is insulting but because underneath it there is a truth. Caius Martius Coriolanus in the end is a mummy's boy.

He is childlike, naive in his belief that he can march over to the other side in a fit of pique and – for no genuine principle, out of hurt pride – prosecute war on his own people. Aufidius' charge is wounding too, because it comes from the man he loves, and it prompts from Caius Martius a vainglorious boast that 'like an eagle in a dovecote' he 'fluttered your Volscians in Corioles'.

Coriolanus may be capricious, and erratic, but Aufidius is even less stable: witness the violence of his mood swings. Trevor White as Tullus seized upon these with some relish. Aufidius doesn't realize that in his unequivocal welcome of his arch enemy he has, as one of his servants says, cut himself in the middle and 'is but one half of what he was yesterday'. In the very next scene that we see Aufidius, he is already disdainfully calling Coriolanus 'the Roman' and regretting his precipitous action, jealous of the man's charismatic effect on his own soldiery. 'And you are darkened in this action, sir', warns the lieutenant, 'Even by your own'.

The two men cannot truly be friends, as their characters demand that they are the sole champion, the holder of the cup, the leader, the best, and there can only be one of those. Rome ain't big enough for the both of them: 'the fall of either / Makes the survivor heir of all'. By Act Five, Coriolanus is already pushing his new ally around:

> My partner in this action,
> You must report to th'Volscian lords, how plainly
> I have borne this business.

Aufidius complains that though he took his enemy into his house and made him his equal, 'joint-servant with me', 'till at the last / I seemed his follower, not partner'. It is hard not to detect under his bitterness a profound sense of slighted affection. His determination that Coriolanus shall die 'And I'll renew me in his fall' is jealously neurotic. With its overtones of ritual sacrifice, it is also disturbingly revealing.

Volumnia has bred a monster. Her tragedy is that by finally persuading him to give up his attack on Rome, she kills him.

Her triumphal re-entry into Rome as its great patroness – 'life of Rome!' – is silent. But Janet and I chose to make her silence eloquent (like the silence of her son in the previous scene, when he takes her by the hand – possibly the most potent pause in Shakespeare). Her entry is heralded by the senator bidding Rome 'Unshout the noise that banished Martius.' We decided that a speech is expected from her, that she would silence the crowd in order to address them. After all, Volumnia is never lost for words. She has just delivered a fifty-line appeal to her son, surely one of the longest speeches in Shakespeare. But when it comes to it, she can say nothing. Even she cannot spin this personal disaster into a civic triumph. She has just killed her son and she knows it. Janet held the moment, trying to articulate some potent propaganda that will glorify her son. It was electrifying. Finally, she turned and walked away.

It would be very hard to ignore the theme of homoeroticism in the play, and wilful to do so. The language is full of it, and not only Coriolanus' and Aufidius' language. The comedy servants at Aufidius' house in Antium describe how extravagantly he treats his new guest: 'Our general himself makes a mistress of him.'

Each sees in the other a perfect male fighting-machine. They excite each other. Aufidius calls Coriolanus 'Thou noble thing' and admits when he sees him that his 'rapt heart' dances. Both declare how much they love their wives, but how much more they worship each other (Martius has embraced Cominius on the battlefield, declaring that he is as happy as when he took his bride to bed on their wedding night). Martius says of Aufidius when he is first introduced into the play in Act One, 'were I anything but what I am, / I would wish me only he.' That reflected vanity is deeply narcissistic. When Martius hears that the Volsci have regathered their forces, all he wants to know is if Titus Lartius has seen Aufidius and whether Aufidius spoke of him. In an urgent little shared line, he neatly expresses his obsession:

CORIOLANUS   Spoke he of me?
LARTIUS   He did, my lord.
CORIOLANUS   How? What.

They even dream of one another. When Caius Martius arrives at Antium in Act Four Aufidius, in his tumbling speech of obsessional adoration, admits

> I have nightly since
> Dreamt of encounters 'twixt thyself and me:
> We have been down together in my sleep,
> Unbuckling helms, fisting each other's throat,
> And waked half dead with nothing.

Even in a pre-Freudian world the analysis of that has to be pretty clear.

We chose, noting the extravagancy of that language, to make the narcissism evident in their characters, and barely sublimated in the fight between them in Act One. Male worship is a Roman obsession. Coriolanus admits he has always been 'godded' by Rome, and by Menenius in particular. And his mother has an unhealthy interest in the precise number of her son's scars.

The terrifying bloodbath at the end is pitiful, and Coriolanus helps to incite it, impaling himself upon Aufidius' sword. When the frenzy is over, the image of Aufidius standing on the body of his quondam partner is horrifying in its animal brutality. It seems to shock the lords of the city, who cry out for him to 'Hold, hold, hold, hold!' Sublimated sexuality or not, the hunting imagery that runs throughout the description of their relationship culminates in this brutal triumphing over his enemy's body. And it is replaced as suddenly with horror at what he has done. In our production, Aufidius was left trying to lift the body of Coriolanus by himself, as the lords and even his co-conspirators drift away, leaving Aufidius to howl the final word: 'Assist!'

On press night Professor Stanley Wells told me that Will's performance as Coriolanus was as close to Olivier's performance as he had ever seen. The following day, Patrick Marmion in the *Daily Mail* agreed, writing that Houston is 'possessed by the ghost of Laurence Olivier who once more stalks the stage and shakes the masonry with his voluble vowels'.

* * *

Coriolanus went on to tour. We visited Newcastle, and were also invited to perform in Spain, at the Teatro Albeniz, in Madrid. However, when the production managers checked the theatre plans they discovered not only could the set not fit in the theatre, it could not even get through the dock doors. But rather than be deterred by such things we decided simply not to take the set to Spain but to play just with costumes and props.

In Washington, *Coriolanus* was the final production in the RSC's five-year residency agreement with the Kennedy Center.[1] *The Washington Post* called the play 'Shakespeare's paean to monumentally inept public relations' and the production 'precisely in tune with the real-life political arrogance on display in Washington today'.

Zoe Caldwell came to see a matinee in Washington. This acclaimed actress and director had, among other great achievements, played Cleopatra (at Stratford Ontario) opposite Christopher Plummer, and run the Shakespeare Theatre in Stratford Connecticut in the mid-eighties.

I was expecting a rather sedate 'First Lady of the American Theatre'. I noticed her eyes first, very bright and glimmering with mischief and fun. This tiny figure, dressed in black trousers and top, approached our company manager. 'Who's the director? Who is the director?' She seized me with her grin. 'It's so exciting I'm on the edge of my seat, and oh! your Coriolanus!'

I asked her why she had never played Volumnia. 'I have been asked many times,' she said, 'but you see, in 1959, I was in Stratford-upon-Avon, playing Helena in Tyrone Guthrie's production of *All's Well That Ends Well,* opposite Edith Evans as the Countess. And of course, I saw her as Volumnia with Olivier. I thought it was a definitive performance. I couldn't improve on it, I could only copy it.' She was good enough to add that she thought her friend Janet Suzman had now joined Edith in the definitive stakes.

---

[1]   The other visits included: *The Canterbury Tales* in 2005; *The Taming of the Shrew* and *The Tamer Tamed* in 2003.

1 Titus Andronicus.
Photo by Donald Cooper.

2 Henry VIII, *or All is True.*
Photo by Zuleika Henry.

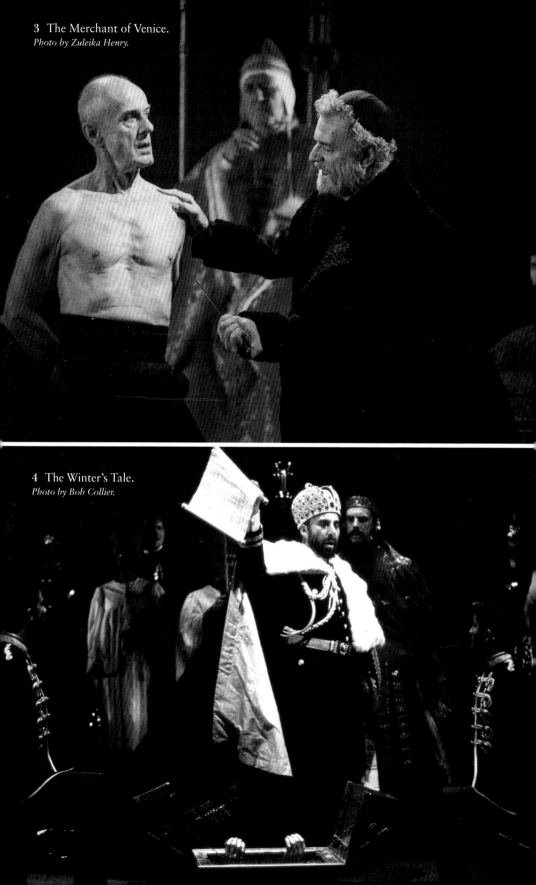

3 The Merchant of Venice.
Photo by Zuleika Henry.

4 The Winter's Tale.
Photo by Bob Collier.

5 Timon of Athens.
Photo by Willoughby Gullachsen.

6 As You Like It.
Photo by Jonathan Dockar-Drysdale.

7 Macbeth.
Photo by Jonathan Dockar-Drysdale.

8 King John.
Photo by Jonathan Dockar-Drysdale.

9 Much Ado About Nothing.
Photo by Jonathan Dockar-Drysdale.

10 The Taming of the Shrew.
Photo by Jonathan Dockar-Drysdale.

11 All's Well That Ends Well.
Photo by Manuel Harlan.

12 Othello.
Photo by Manuel Harlan.

13 Venus and Adonis.
Photo by Stewart Hemley.

4 A Midsummer Night's Dream.
Photo by Stewart Hemley.

15 Antony and Cleopatra.
Photo © RSC.

16 Merry Wives: The Musical.
Photo by Stewart Hemley.

17 Coriolanus.
Photo by Simon Annand.

18 Hamlet.
Photo by Ellie Kurttz.

19
Love's Labour's
Lost.
Photo by Ellie Kurttz.

20
Twelfth Night.
Photo by Ellie Kurttz.

21 Julius Caesar.
Photo by Kwame Lestrade.

22 King Lear.
Photo by Ellie Kurttz.

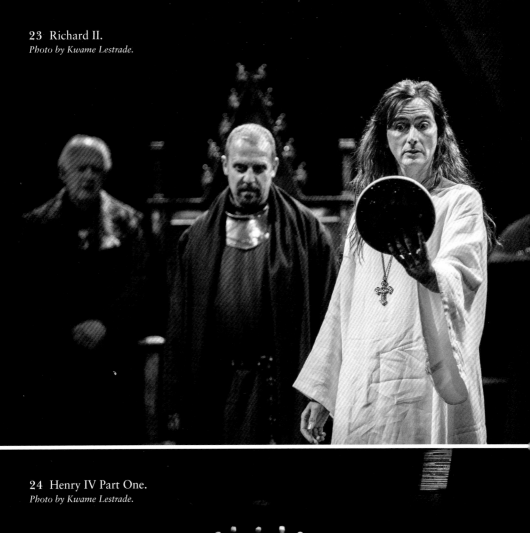

23 Richard II.
Photo by Kwame Lestrade.

24 Henry IV Part One.
Photo by Kwame Lestrade.

25 Henry IV Part Two.
Photo by Kwame Lestrade.

26 Henry V.
Photo by Keith Pattison.

27 The Tempest.
Photo by Topher McGrillis.

28 Troilus and Cressida.
Photo by Helen Maybanks.

29 Measure for Measure.
Photo by Helen Maybanks.

30 Richard III.
Photo by Ellie Kurttz.

Hamlet

– 2008: Courtyard Theatre, Stratford-upon-Avon; Novello Theatre, London.
– Filmed for the BBC.

At the start of rehearsals, I take the company up to the Shakespeare Birthplace Trust in Henley Street. Sylvia Morris, then the Head Librarian, brings out the RSC's own copy of the First Folio for the company to see.

It was given to us by the Flower family in 1889, although we nearly lost it. In 1964, on the quatercentenary of Shakespeare's birth, three RSC actors, Dorothy Tutin, Derek Godfrey and Tony Church, flew to Rome to perform some Shakespeare pieces in the Palazzo Pio, near St Peter's. The recital was performed before Pope Paul VI, and 2,000 dignitaries of the Catholic Church, including the College of Cardinals, attending the Second Vatican Council. It was said to be the first time a pope had ever attended a theatrical performance. The actors took our Folio with them, to be blessed by the pontiff. But when the treasured tome was presented, instead of blessing it, His Holiness, thinking it was a gift, nodded gratefully, and handed the book to a cardinal. It very nearly disappeared into the Vatican vaults, and only a little frantic diplomacy finally redeemed it.

I love the early page, which gives '*the names of the principal actors in all these plays*'. The list begins with William Shakespeare himself followed by Richard Burbage. Over two spectacular decades, for this one actor, Shakespeare wrote Romeo, Richard III, Henry V, Brutus, Shylock, Macbeth, Coriolanus, Othello, Pericles and King Lear – a lifetime's career of great roles. And of course, Burbage was the very first Hamlet.

Further down the list is Joseph Taylor. He joined the King's Men a month after Burbage's death and took over his roles, including Hamlet, which according to a later account, he acted 'incomparably well'. William Davenant, Shakespeare's self-proclaimed godson, saw Taylor perform it, and when the theatres reopened at the Restoration (after a period of eighteen years when they had been closed by the Puritans), Davenant passed on his knowledge of Taylor's performance to Thomas Betterton. Betterton continued to play the role until he was seventy-two. The play has never been out of the repertoire since, and the role has constantly been redefined, by Garrick, Kean, Macready, Irving, Gielgud, Olivier, right up to David Tennant in our production now. 'No pressure there then, David,' somebody quips.

And for any Shakespeare director too, *Hamlet* is one of the biggies. Presenting the play at the Royal Shakespeare Theatre in Stratford-upon-Avon, you are profoundly aware of being part of a long history. I discovered our 2008 version would be the 85th production of the play in the theatre's history (the Shakespeare Memorial Theatre, as it was originally called, opened in 1879) and we have thus been performing *Hamlet* on that site for 140 years.

So, what have I got to say about this play, now? Why is it that though I have often admired the play in production, I have seldom really enjoyed it? Why should I direct it? What is it that speaks to me, in this moment, now? Perhaps the answer lies in the very first line, 'Who's there?'

Before we know anything, we are asked to identify ourselves. As Barnardo, on the battlements of Elsinore, checks out his jittery fellow sentry Francisco, it's as if Shakespeare is checking us out too. Where will we put ourselves in this play? How do I identify with Hamlet, with his turmoil, his grief, vulnerability, sense of betrayal, instinct for revenge, but inability to achieve it?

William Hazlitt asked the same question. He answered, 'It is we who are Hamlet.'

The true answer for me is that in order to set out on this voyage of discovery, to risk exposure, to begin to measure up to this litmus test of one's ability, I need to know who my travelling companions are, and be confident that together we can let this 400-year-old play speak now, as if the ink were still wet on the page.

*   *   *

Eighty per cent of good directing, according to eminent theatre director Tyrone Guthrie, is casting.

I knew David Tennant could be a great Hamlet, having seen his RSC performances both as Romeo, and as Touchstone, the fool, in *As You Like It*. Anyone who can pull off both those difficult roles, one tragic, one comic, might have what it takes to play the 'Dane'. David had the added advantage of becoming one of the most famous actors in the UK having incarnated as the tenth Dr Who, which he played for three series on the BBC.

I had also had the special pleasure of working with David a decade before when I put together a double bill of Tom Stoppard's *The Real Inspector Hound* and Peter Shaffer's *Black Comedy* for the Donmar, at the Comedy Theatre in the West End. He played the embittered second-string critic Moon in the first play, and the flustered sculptor Brindsley in the second of these witty one-act comedies, so I knew what a virtuosic performer he could be. Nevertheless, I also knew there would be detractors who would complain that his casting was a cynical act intended only to pull in a crowd of young Dr Who fans. Would David himself prove them wrong?

I also wanted to make sure that the production grabbed that audience even if they knew the play well and would keep them on the edge of their seats. So how I prepared the text would be the next vital step.

To cut or not to cut?

Cutting is an art. In my experience Shakespeare goes at around 900 lines an hour, if spoken 'trippingly on the tongue', as Hamlet himself advises. Now *Hamlet* is Shakespeare's longest play, over 4,000 lines long. That equates to at least four and a half hours of playing time, and if you want a 7:30pm start and an interval (and bar sales these days demand it), then expect the curtain to be pushing midnight.

If you want to come down at 10:30pm then, by my rubric, you have roughly 2,400 lines to play with, which means cutting 1,600+ lines of *Hamlet*. It's a straightforward mathematical equation, but it's also a conundrum.

The play is unlikely ever to have been performed at its full length in Shakespeare's lifetime. We know that one of the few things the Lord Chamberlain did for the acting company he patronized was to write to the Lord Mayor of London in 1594, guaranteeing that when his men performed at the Crosse Keys in Gracechurch Street (an ancient coaching inn, then a banking house, now a noisy Wetherspoons pub), they would start by two in the afternoon and be over between four and five, a maximum of three hours playing time. He also adds that the actors 'will not use any drums or trumpets at all for the calling of people together'.

In fact, we think the first time the full text of *Hamlet* was ever performed was in Stratford-upon-Avon in 1899, by actor-manager Frank Benson. They played up to the closet scene as the matinee and then did the rest of the play for the evening performance. It was known as the 'Eternity *Hamlet*'.

When I began thinking about how to cut *Hamlet* for our production, I was aware of the fact that there was no definitive text of the play.

There are in fact three different texts of *Hamlet* extant, from the period it was written. The first published version we have of the play is a quarto edition (the small single paperback version, if you like) often referred to as the 'Bad' Quarto. It may have been rushed together by actors, perhaps when on tour, as many of the lines are mis-remembered, – with the exception, oddly enough, of the lines spoken by Marcellus, one of the sentries at the start of the play, which are rather accurate. Nevertheless, 'To be or not to be, that is the question' is rendered in the 'Bad' Quarto as 'To be or not to be, Aye, there's the point'. The text is short: about 2,200 lines. The next version, published in 1604/5, the Second Quarto, is almost twice as long at 3,900 lines. Shakespeare must have kept revising the play as it continued in the repertoire, because by the time his fellow actors published the Complete Works, after his death (the First Folio), the play had been cut and substantially rearranged.

I became beguiled by the idea of the length of the 'Bad' Quarto, which should deliver a playing time of 2 hours 20 minutes. I wondered what a tighter version of the play might be like. Once I had got over the disconcerting effect of the roughly approximated lines, and the renamed characters (Polonius is called Corambis), I realized that the play is essentially a thriller. It has a murder, a ghost, a revenge plot, a girl driven out of her wits to suicide, and a climactic sword fight. I pondered what a script that replaced the unfamiliar 'Bad' Quarto lines, with the more familiar Second Quarto or Folio lines would be like and set about preparing such a text. A tight, tense, packed two-hour version of the play might have a refreshing impact.

I showed my initial explorations to David Tennant. This is how 'To be or not to be' works out if you replace the mis-remembered lines with the good Quarto/Folio lines. It's roughly half the length:

> To be, or not to be, that is the question,
> To die, to sleep no more; to sleep,
> Perchance to dream, ay, there's the rub,

For in that sleep of death what dreams may come:
For who would bear the whips and scorns of time,
Th'oppressor's wrong, the proud man's contumely,
The pangs of despis'd love, the law's delay
When he himself might his quietus make
With a bare bodkin; who would fardels bear,
To grunt and sweat under a weary life,
But that the dread of something after death,
The undiscover'd country, from whose bourn
No traveller returns, puzzles the will,
And makes us rather bear those ills we have,
Than fly to others that we know not of?
Thus conscience does make cowards of us all.

David was intrigued, and we thought it might be interesting to explore the exercise a little further. I spoke to a member of the RSC board; the Shakespeare scholar Professor Jonathan Bate. He applauded the idea, adding, 'When have you ever left a Shakespeare play wishing it were longer?'

In the end, I rejected the idea of using a reconstituted 'Bad' Quarto text because it seemed like too much of an academic idea. I had by then secured a top-notch RSC cast including Patrick Stewart as Claudius (doubling with the Ghost), Oliver Ford Davies as Polonius and Penny Downie as Gertrude, wanting to take full advantage of their talents, and knowing these roles are severely diminished in the 'Bad' Quarto text (even though Gertrude actually gets an extra scene) I prepared a text with a potential running time of about three hours and ten minutes.

In rehearsal I am very happy for actors to negotiate the cuts I have made. And frequently we put lines back and remove others. But I have a rule: show me which lines you want to put back, but then show me which lines you are prepared to remove to replace them. This may seem draconian, but I have experienced too many previews of Shakespeare productions in which directors have discovered too late that their productions are running too long, and instead of refining the production, spend their time in previews cutting lines and upsetting actors who may have spent weeks learning them.

Apart from variations in the lines, there are significant other differences between the texts of *Hamlet*, which any director or producer must consider when preparing their version for rehearsal.

For instance, take that most famous speech, 'To be or not to be'. It appears in very different positions in each edition.

In the 'Bad' Quarto, this existential anthem comes at a point when the young prince has just been told by his father's ghost that he was murdered by his uncle. Hamlet rushes distraught into his girlfriend Ophelia's room, but finding himself incapable of speech, runs away in order to articulate his darkest thought to us, the audience.

In the Second Quarto and the Folio however, that same speech appears much later, after the players have arrived at Elsinore, and Hamlet has devised the plot to expose his uncle. He will spring 'The Mousetrap' (the name of the play, with his own lines inserted), which he hopes, when performed before the king, will prompt his uncle to reveal his guilt.

> The play's the thing
> Wherein I'll catch the conscience of the king.

Psychologically, the soliloquy is perhaps odder in this latter position. Hamlet is charged with adrenaline, no longer wallowing in abject despair, but focused on revenge. But perhaps those apparent contradictions reveal the violent mood swings the young man is experiencing. The actor and the director must decide on which position is more interesting to explore.

Thus, each production of *Hamlet* is unique, not just because each actor playing Hamlet is different, but because of the textual choices they make.

We even considered opening the play with this iconic soliloquy, as it seems to convey pretty well Hamlet's suicidal state of mind on his return to Denmark before any suspicions about his father's death have been presented to him. Ultimately Shakespeare does it better, opening his play by diving straight into the tense atmosphere and (as mentioned above) demanding 'Who's there?'

To enhance the sense of the play as a thriller, we chose to put the interval (a choice Shakespeare and his actors never had to make) as Hamlet raised his dagger to kill Claudius at prayer, going to a blackout at that point. To those young members of the audience who did not know the plot, this kept them guessing what might happen next. The second half began at the same point, as Hamlet changed his mind, and stole away.

Hamlet says Denmark is a prison. It is certainly a world of hyper-surveillance. Polonius, the first minister of state, seems addicted to spying. He sends Reynaldo to spy on his own son in Paris and sets up his daughter (virtually wiring her for sound), and then pushing her in front of the volatile prince, while he and the king watch proceedings in secret. Indeed, Polonius meets his end as a result of his obsession, hiding behind the arras in Gertrude's closet while eavesdropping on mother and son.

Designer Rob Jones and I decided that we would set the play in a contemporary European court, which would allow us to present a world that has remained pretty much unchanged for the last half-century. Now, but not quite now. The production would play on the thrust stage of the Courtyard Theatre in Stratford, the thousand-seater theatre built to accommodate the seasons while the Royal Shakespeare Theatre was being transformed.

Hamlet famously says that the purpose of playing is to hold a mirror up to nature. He tells his mother that he will set her up a glass in which she may see the inmost part of her soul. Rob's set would be dominated by a vast, mirrored back wall, which would reflect the audience as they arrived.

It could work as a two-way mirror, through which Polonius and Claudius could observe Hamlet and Ophelia. When Polonius hid 'behind the arras' in the closet scene, he would slide behind this mirror, and when Hamlet hears him cry out and shouts 'a rat, a rat', instead of stabbing him through the curtain, he would pull out a gun from Gertrude's bedside table and shoot him, smashing the huge mirror (a clever swivel of panels in an almost subliminally brief blackout coinciding with the pistol shot). This great cracked wall would then suggest the fractured state of Denmark, and of the minds of Ophelia and of Hamlet himself.

*   *   *

'Nowadays people sit through Shakespeare in order to recognize the quotations.' So said Orson Welles, and he may be right. *Hamlet* of course is full of quotations. Our job in the theatre is to fresh-mint some of those famous lines. But how do you do that? How do you 'look with thine ears', as King Lear says?

When he played Hamlet at Stratford in 1984, the late-lamented Roger Rees decided to try to surprise the audience one night with that most famous line: 'To be or not to be'. He would rush forward to the front of the stage with an urgent immediacy, as if the line had just emerged from the quick forge and working house of thought. The cue came. He hurtled down to the front of the stage, and promptly forgot the most famous line in the canon ... and if that wasn't humiliating enough, he was then prompted by a member of the audience.

When I began our production, we discovered a rather unconventional way of fresh-minting another of those lines whose fame transcends the play. As the gravedigger presents Hamlet with the skull of his father's old Jester, he declares:

Alas poor Yorick!

In 1982, a man had actually bequeathed his own skull to the RSC to be used in a production of *Hamlet*. His name was André Tchaikowsky. He was a Polish pianist and composer. The undertaker had baulked at the idea of removing the head from one of his customers as this was not regarded as normal practice, and quite possibly illegal. Permission had to be sought from the Home Office. Eventually, the local hospital removed the head, and accomplished the job that presumably the cold clay of the grave did for Yorick.

Whatever the process, one day the skull arrived in the prop department at Stratford in a Delsey tissue box, and when it was opened, Crusty, the prop-shop dog, went crazy. The skull still stank ('Pah!' as Hamlet says, 'My gorge rises at it') so it was put up on the roof in an onion bag, until the weather – and perhaps the birds – had done the rest. Then it was stored in a box on a shelf, where it had stayed ever since: no one had chosen to cast André as Yorick.

So, on the first day of our rehearsals, as usual, I welcomed the actors and announced the parts they would be playing, and then I said, 'Ladies and gentlemen, let me introduce you to the final member of our company.' Pulling on some purple latex gloves, I opened a cardboard box, and lifting out the skull, I said, 'This is André. He will be playing Yorick.'

A silence fell on the room.

I offered to hand the skull to any of the team who wanted to touch it. Some recoiled, some were drawn towards it in grim fascination. Cicely Berry was present, and declined the skull with a smile, saying she was close enough to that state herself. Many were disturbed by such a vivid *memento mori*. Folk don't generally keep death's heads on their desk-tops these days. Imagine, next to your calendar, between your laptop and your paperclips.

Whatever the reaction, that line, 'Alas, poor Yorick', never languished into cliché in our production. The skull never became just another stage prop. As Hamlet peered at the old comedian's skull, he stared into those hollow eye sockets and saw his own mortality staring straight back at him.

And so did we.

*   *   *

I never do a read-through of the play on the first day of rehearsal. You either get people mumbling through lines they don't really understand, or presenting a predetermined performance, and if you have very few lines in the play you suddenly become dispiritingly aware of just how small your role is.

Over the years of working on these plays I have developed a process. We spend the first few days, if not the first couple of weeks, working through the text line by line. We work around the table reading the play and putting it into our own words. There are a few rules: no one can read their own parts, or comment on the interpretation of their own character; and you are not allowed to explain what happens by reference to what transpires later in the play, so that we see that action as the characters see it, unaware of how things might develop. In this way the whole company develops a deep collaborative sense of what the whole play is about and how their character fits in to the story.

It may sound laborious, but it reveals how easy it is to assume you know what the words mean, and how hard it is to be specific. Sometimes it shatters preconceptions, sometimes confirms them. Occasionally someone provides a memorable 'translation'; Andrea Harris (playing one of the ambassadors) with admirable alliteration paraphrases the word 'Mountebank' as 'drug-dealing-dude', and (revealing her Arkansas roots) converts 'John-a-dreams' to 'Who-hit-John-and-run'.

We have every possible edition of the play open on the table and scour them for notes. Invariably the editors fall silent on the one point the actors want illuminating.

This analysis of the text demands that you unpick each image to ensure that you have really understood it, and in so doing are surprised by the originality, or pertinence, of the metaphor. We focused on the images as we worked out what Hamlet has to say about Rosencrantz and Guildenstern, and how Claudius abuses them:

He keeps them, like an ape an apple, in the corner of his jaw;
first mouth'd, to be last swallowed.

Just picture that image! It's so specific. I can imagine Shakespeare at the Royal Menagerie in the Tower of London, among the lions, wolves and porcupines, watching a baboon or chimpanzee, fed with apple pieces, do just that.

When he needs what you have glean'd, it is but squeezing you and, sponge, you shall be dry again.

It's a shocking, metaphysical, almost absurdist image.

As a little light relief from all the brainstorming, we watch an episode of *The Simpsons* in which Bart plays Hamlet. Above his bed is a sticker that reads 'Danes do it melancholy'. And assistant director Cressida Brown and some of the company present a rehearsed reading of *Fratricide Punished*, a seventeenth-century German version of *Hamlet*, which has a particularly funny account of how Hamlet got away from the pirates. This might be a fragment of the *Ur-Hamlet*, sometimes ascribed to Thomas Kyd, which some think Shakespeare re-wrote.

When we finally do a read-through with everyone playing their own parts all in one go on the Friday of the second week, everyone is excited and prepared. The result is a turbulent, thrilling ride. Cis Berry, who has been sitting and listening, shakes her head and says, 'It's all so human', but she puts her finger on the challenge ahead. Everybody might now know precisely what they are talking about, but it is not only literal meaning that is important with Shakespeare. His power is also conveyed through the rhythm and sound of the language; 'the sound must seem an echo to the sense'.

Rehearsals for *Hamlet* continued in Stratford throughout July in the rather brutal chilly white rooms at Arden Street.

One of the most refreshing features of David Tennant's Hamlet as it emerged over these weeks, was how funny he could be. It stemmed from examining his line to Rosencrantz and Guildenstern when he admits: 'I have of late – but wherefore I know not – lost all my mirth.' So the prince was a funny guy before all this happened. A strain of darkly glittering black humour emerged, and grew in performance.

Patrick Stewart's Claudius proceeded from his simple but incisive conviction that everything Claudius does is for the good of his country. His first act as king is to send ambassadors to Norway to negotiate a peace that his belligerent brother could never have countenanced. Hamlet's father has kept Denmark on a war-footing for years, liking nothing better than 'an angry parle' or two, or to smite 'the sledded Polacks on the ice'. In fact, we held back Claudius's own admission of guilt for the murder of his brother, until the scene where he tries to pray, and realizes that though his words go up, his prayers remain below. Patrick's performance distilled to a point where his self-containment had the terrifying intensity of an unexploded bomb.

The key to Penny Downie's Gertrude was revealed in four short monosyllables in the closet scene. When Hamlet kills Polonius, she howls 'O, what a rash and bloody deed is this?' Hamlet snaps back:

> A bloody deed! almost as bad, good mother,
> As kill a king and marry with his brother.

'As kill a king?' she repeats. This surely reveals that Gertrude knew nothing of Claudius' involvement in the murder. She tells her son his behaviour is 'ecstasy', at which he rounds on her, insisting she is not going to get away with pretending he is mad to distract her from her own guilt. As we rehearse the scene, it gets raw with an agonizing energy.

When Hamlet leaves, tugging the corpse of Polonius behind him, Gertrude is left alone. Penny howled in anguished despair. We chose not to play the scene break that editors suggest at that point, but had Claudius suddenly appear behind her placing his hands on her shoulders. Will he caress or throttle her? He says:

There's matter in these sighs, these profound heaves:
You must translate: 'tis fit we understand them.
Where is your son?

It's a chilling moment. Patrick's lethal Claudius would not allow even his new wife to get in the way of Denmark's future. And she, suddenly forced to choose her best course of survival, does the thing she has just promised her son she would not do, and insists he is in fact as 'mad as the sea and wind'. The way Penny is charting Gertrude's descent from society hostess to exhausted remorse-filled alcoholic is harrowing.

One July afternoon after rehearsals Mariah (Minnie) Gale, playing Ophelia, and I went for a walk along the Seven Meadows stretch of the River Avon, out beyond Holy Trinity Church. I wanted to show her how many of the flowers Ophelia weaves into her fantastical garland could still be found growing along the banks.

Here were certainly plenty of nettles and daisies. The crowflowers are probably ragged robin, and the purple loosestrife that bristle the banks of the river in a phalanx of magenta spikes could be long purples. Though scholars suggest that the long purples that Shakespeare describes:

That liberal shepherds give a grosser name,
But our cold maids do dead men's fingers call them.

are probably a kind of orchid, known as 'dogs' bollox', in Warwickshire parlance, because of its double bulbous tuber roots. There are also plenty of flowers Shakespeare would not have known including the giant hogweed that towers up to seven feet along the path.

Upriver at Tiddington, there is a footpath that leads down to the Avon. Here, when Shakespeare was fifteen, a young woman called Katherine Hamlet drowned when she fell in the water trying to collect water in her pail. Was she the inspiration for Ophelia? Minnie and I walk down the path and discover at the river edge that there is indeed an ancient willow growing aslant the brook.

Rosemary and pansies, fennel and columbine, violets.

I have seen Ophelia's flowers presented in so many different ways in production: as bare twigs, as stones, even as little swastika flags. After our walk through the lush chaos of summer growth, Minnie and I decided that Ophelia had run through the fields and scooped and torn a great swathe of greenery, and become muddy, scratched by brambles and red-raw with nettle stings.

The props department created a believable armful of grasses, weeds and wilting nettles.

*   *   *

The production opened on 5 August 2008. We had a number of celebrity guests during the sold-out run, including the prime minister Gordon Brown, who arrived a little late, reeling from the fatal Labour loss in the Glasgow East by-election. Hamlet's line about the politician's inability to 'circumvent God' went down rather well that night.

The local chippy meanwhile had a cut-out of David as Dr Who and a sign saying 'exterminate your hunger', but the reviews bear witness to the fact that David has banished all thoughts of his most famous role and proved his detractors wrong. If anyone thought that the Dr Who fans attending *Hamlet* would spend the time he was off-stage noisily rustling their sweet wrappers, they were wrong. They consistently remain rapt throughout.

We ran in Stratford until November, in repertoire with both a revival of my 2005 production of *A Midsummer Night's Dream*, and *Love's Labour's Lost* in which David Tennant played Berowne.

We then moved the production to the Novello Theatre on London's Aldwych. We sold out in a single day. Steve Haworth, then our head of sales and ticketing, dropped me this note:

> Last Friday at 10am the Novello received 2,000 calls per second = 120,000 attempted calls between 10.00 and 10.01. The call volume on the RSC number represented 10% of the national network capacity. Between 8am and 2pm they received 1.4 million hits on their website.

There were queues around the block for tickets from the very first preview.

But then disaster struck. After just two previews, David suffered a prolapsed disc and was admitted to hospital in Queen's Square. I went round to see him. 'I'm absolutely gutted,' he said. I didn't know what to say. I knew how devastated he was. He had only missed one performance in his entire career. I remember during *The Real Inspector Hound*, he got food poisoning and was vomiting backstage between shows, but still managed to pull himself onstage for the evening performance. It was clear that he would not be able to do the press night of *Hamlet*, nor indeed most, if any, of the run.

The RSC went into its hyper-efficient mode to deal with the emergency. Ed Bennett playing Laertes was David's understudy. He would go on as Hamlet on press night. But it doesn't end there. There are at least four 'knock-ons': Hamlet is understudied by Laertes, who is then understudied by Guildenstern, who is understudied by Lucianus, who is understudied by Reynaldo. Cressida Brown, the assistant director, had it all in hand.

Ed was fearless, although when the company manager rang to tell him the news that he was going on, he said his hands were shaking so much it took him ten minutes to tie his shoes. In his dressing room beforehand, I felt like the harassed producer in *Forty-Second Street* telling the understudy Ruby Keeler that she has to save the show: 'You're going out a youngster, but you've gotta come back a star.' Addressing the audience before the press night, I knew the reaction would be a dispiriting groan, but I told the house that they were very lucky, because this was the RSC and we invest heavily in our ensemble and that tonight they were going to see something quite extraordinary, a very special performance indeed.

And it was. The company were universally magnificent. They rose to the occasion and the audience rose to their feet, as Ed took his bow. He acquitted himself with great credit and vindicated the RSC's emphasis on ensemble work. By the time I got back into his dressing room at the end, a photographer from the *Evening Standard* was already there. The photograph, with Ed's enormous grin of relief, was destined for the front page the following day.

But going home, late that night, alone in a black taxicab, it hit me in the chest. Though the company had pulled off a significant achievement, this would now be the version of the play that the capital would see for the rest of the run. Selfishly, I realized that I was grieving for the production of this great play that I had thought about and worked on for so long.

In fact, astonishingly, David did return for the last week of the run and was even better than he had been in Stratford. Later that year, in June, as if to make up for the lost performances, we filmed the production for the BBC, with John Wyver's Illuminations company, in a derelict Jesuit seminary in Mill Hill. It was all done on a tiny budget, with everyone agreeing to travel on public transport. Except for André the skull, who was chauffeur-driven in his special box all the way from Stratford and back for his scene as Yorick in the graveyard.

The production was shown on BBC Two on Boxing Day that year, enticing 900,000 viewers to tune in. Prime Minister Gordon Brown wrote in *The Observer*: 'Like many people, I had my love of Shakespeare reawakened by David Tennant's TV portrayal of Hamlet over Christmas.'

David even appeared as Hamlet on a stamp published by the Royal Mail in 2011 to celebrate the fiftieth anniversary of the RSC.

And André's Yorick turned up as a question on 'Have I Got News For You'.

20

Love's Labour's Lost

– 2008: Courtyard Theatre, Stratford-upon-Avon.

Did Shakespeare write the role of Rosaline for a Black actor? Is it possible that there was a highly talented boy player in Shakespeare's company who was Brown or Black?

Shakespeare of course wrote several Black male roles, which we know were performed by white actors, with some sort of black makeup, possibly soot mixed with almond oil. Burbage himself created the role of Othello and it was one of his 'chiefest' roles (as an elegy written at the time of his death testifies).

Each of Shakespeare's major Black characters are the subject of racial abuse. Othello is referred to by Iago as 'the thick-lips'. Prince of Morocco's very first line ('Mislike me not for my complexion') invites Portia to see beyond his colour. And in *Titus Andronicus*, when Lavinia and her new husband Bassianus, while out hunting in the forest, come across Tamora, they berate the Queen of the Goths for her relationship with Aaron, the Moor, her 'raven-coloured love':

> ... Your swarth Cimmerian
> Doth make your honour of his body's hue,
> Spotted, detested, and abominable.

In each of these roles, their racial identity is essential to the story. Rosaline's is incidental. So incidental, you might argue that it has hardly been noticed, and to my knowledge no actress in the history of the theatre has ever considered blacking up to play it. Indeed until 1985, when Josette Simon played the role,[1] thus becoming the first Black actress to play a lead role at the RSC, I doubt that Rosaline's heritage was given much thought, and any inconvenient lines merely excised from the production.

But the lines are there. And some of them reveal such a disturbing trait of casual racism in the characters that they risk reinforcing any similar prejudices in the audience or causing offence by their continued inclusion. Or are we to assume that the audience are sophisticated enough to allow that the lines provide a glimpse into the otherwise benign character of these young men, and we should afford them an element of contradiction?

Berowne's first description of Rosaline is hardly flattering:

---

[1] In Barry Kyle's production with Roger Rees as Berowne.

And, among three, to love the worst of all:
A wightly[2] wanton with a velvet brow,
With two pitch-balls stuck in her face for eyes.

Pitch (or tar) is not the most complimentary comparison. But worse is to come. The squabble between the boys about their respective would-be girlfriends makes it clear that Rosaline is Brown, if not Black. Their banter contains language that may convey their societal prejudices about non-white members of their community (and suggest Berowne's and perhaps Shakespeare's open-mindedness in contrast). But the overt racism is troubling.

In rehearsal we debated the point of this banter and tried to consider what the effect of it might be. Did Berowne's defence of his beloved's skin colour make us side with him against his mates' unthinking racism, or were we inviting the audience to laugh along with their jackal cackles?

The king begins the rally, unequivocally, by pointing out that Berowne's intended is as black as ebony. To which Berowne's riposte is that if ebony is like Rosaline, then it is a 'wood divine'. He declares provocatively, 'No face is fair that is not full so black.'

Berowne here precisely echoes the argument of sonnet 127, the first of the so-called Dark Lady Sonnets, which begins:

In the old age black was not counted fair,
Or if it were, it bore not beauty's name;
But now is black beauty's successive heir,
And beauty slandered with a bastard shame.

Berowne's declaration produces a slew of examples of how black is traditionally used as a derogatory term: it is 'the badge of Hell, / The hue of dungeons and the suit of night'. In which case, counters Berowne, Rosaline 'is born to make black fair'. Longaville and Dumaine pile in to parody Berowne's assertion, laughing that in that case, chimney sweeps and coal miners must be trying to imitate her. Berowne sneers back that their girlfriends dare not go out in the rain for fear their complexions (powder and makeup) will wash off. The competitive baiting then escalates to new heights of puerility, as Longaville tops it all by pointing at his black leather shoe and saying, 'Look, here's thy love, my foot and her face, see?'

The king calls the bickering to a halt by stating the obvious, that all four of them are in love, and prompts from Berowne one of the most ravishing paeans to love in the entire canon – 'But love first learned in a lady's eyes'. But are we just to ignore the overt racism expressed by his colleagues, put it aside and revel in the language, washed away in the sparkling waterfall of words?

We have a simple choice of course, which is to cut the entire section. But should we automatically chose this option?

---

[2]   Might the choice of the word 'wightly', meaning 'nimble', also suggest 'white-ish', or 'tending to white', and be a clue to the identity of the original actor?

In *Much Ado*, when the chastened (but still priggish) Claudio has performed his penance for (apparently) bringing about the death of his betrothed, Hero, he is asked if he is still prepared to go through with the alternative marriage arranged for him. He protests defiantly:

I'll hold my mind were she an Ethiope.

Noma Dumezweni as Margaret (in our production back in 2002), standing right next to Claudio, was able to give him such a withering look at that point, it not only suggested how un-reconstructed, or un-rehabilitated the young man was, and besides getting a very good laugh in performance at Claudio's expense (for us then), it validated the decision to keep the reference in.

But perhaps the Quarto version of *Love's Labour's Lost* provides us with a hint. The frontispiece advertises several things that were clearly regarded as significant selling points: (1) that the play had been presented 'before her highness this last Christmas' (1597); (2) that the writer is William Shakespeare (the first time his name had appeared on any of his plays – the publisher Cuthbert Burby clearly thought it would help shift a few copies); and (3) that W. Shakespeare had revised the play from an earlier version, and it was now 'newly augmented and corrected'. Or in other words, Shakespeare rewrote his play, expanded it, and probably cut out stuff that didn't stand the test of public performance. Shakespeare was after all a pragmatic man of the theatre.

Let me double back.

Would it have been worth blacking up a boy actor to play Rosaline? Is Rosaline's complexion sufficiently significant to the narrative of the play to warrant the effort and the cost of elaborate makeup? It's a crucial role, albeit not a large one. Berowne for example has three times the number of lines, and the Princess of France has far more than her. And surely, she is sufficiently distinguished among the quartet of young women by her wit, with no need for any other feature to make her stand out. So, my argument presupposes the possibility that there was already a young Black boy actor so talented that Shakespeare accommodated his colour within the text, creating the role around him to some extent.

When we were working on his BBC documentary series *In Search of Shakespeare*, Michael Wood told me there were probably several thousand Black people in the London of Shakespeare's day, many of whom were baptized Christians. He had researched the records of the parish of St Botolph's in Aldgate. Among the 25 Black people that Michael found registered there during Shakespeare's lifetime, are the names of 'Suzanna Pearis, a blackamoore tenant to John Despinois, and Cazzangoe tenant to Mrs Barbor'. Later the name Anne Bause appears; she is 'a Black-more wife' to Anthonie Bause, a trumpeter. In Turnmill St, in nearby Clerkenwell, Lucy Negro ('Black Luce') who ran a brothel had once been a dancer in the queen's service.

It seems Queen Elizabeth maintained a group of ten Black performers (seven musicians and three dancers). In Act Five, 'Blackamoor musicians' accompany Berowne, Navarre and the boys when they enter dressed as Muscovites to greet the ladies. As the play was performed at court, before Her Majesty, it is surely likely that these were those same musicians. There had been a similar Masque of Muscovites at Gray's Inn in the Christmas of 1595, so they were probably building on the success of that appearance, and no doubt recycling the costumes, the choreography and the musical accompaniment.[3]

Is it not feasible that, among this significant Black minority city population, of servants, musicians, dancers and entertainers, the various marriages (interracial or otherwise) might have produced some sons who were gifted at singing and performing? If so, there were pretty unscrupulous talent spotters about. Like Nathaniel Evans who ran the Children of the Chapel Royal. Evans was master of the choristers,[4] and had a patent to impress those children he wanted into service, sometimes despite their parents' wishes. Or might such precocious ability have attracted the attention of the Lord Chamberlain himself, or members of his company, and prompted an invitation to become apprentice to one of the players?

Does this young man's complexion then warrant a reference when he takes on the role of Hermia in *A Midsummer Night's Dream* and is rejected by her beloved Lysander spurning her away with 'Thy love! out, tawny Tartar out!'?[5] And might the boy's talent and his wit have grown, among the five or six other boys in the troop? Might that have inspired Shakespeare to write a role specially for him? So, the boy's racial heritage is a noteworthy characteristic to feature. It provides an opportunity for some pretty low-brow laughs, but their inclusion can make the hero Berowne seem non-discriminatory in his choice of inamorata.

Or did Shakespeare make Rosaline Black in order to challenge the accepted norms of beauty, in a societal context in which such claims would be provocative? And is he doing this to amplify the arguments he made in some of the sonnets[6] (which we learn were distributed 'among his private friends'), in the public arena of the theatre, and even the more rarefied forum of the royal court? Is he attempting to create a greater sense of tolerance towards inter-racial relationships? Is he encouraging his own lover, the notorious Dark Lady, by celebrating the possibility of such dangerous liaisons, and extolling their very outsider status, in such an open way?

Or is there an even more provocative suggestion, that the Dark Lady herself played Rosaline? There was no actual law forbidding women from performing on stage in Shakespeare's day, it was just customary practice. There are accounts of women on stage.

---

[3] In the same way, the masque of satyrs suddenly appears in the middle of *The Winter's Tale*, having appeared at court in a masque to celebrate the wedding of the King's daughter Elizabeth, in 1613.

[4] Nathaniel Evans, the master of the choristers of the boys' company, the Children of the Chapel (who performed at Blackfriars in the winter of 1600–1), had been granted a patent to impress talented boys into his group. In fact, with two of his associates, he kidnapped a 13-year-old boy called Tom Clifton, en route from his lodgings near St Bartholomew's in Smithfield to his school at Christchurch. Even when his father turned up and demanded his son's release, they refused to let him go. It became a star chamber matter, which ultimately upheld Evans's right to impress talented children, but only as choristers, as it was deemed 'not fit or decent that such as should sing the praises of God Almighty should be trained up or employed in such lascivious and profane exercises'.

[5] It is possible that the term 'tawny' was used to denote dual heritage, which is precisely how Aaron describes the child that Tamora has born him. 'Peace, tawny slave, half me and half thy dam!'

[6] Such as sonnet 130: 'My Mistress' eyes are nothing like the sun'.

On 22 February 1582, one Richard Madox[7] saw a woman perform at a playhouse in Shoreditch. He wrote in his diary, 'went to the Theatre[8] to see a scurvy play set out all by one virgin, which there proved a freemartin[9] without voice, so that we stayed not the matter'. The remark is one of the very rare indications that a woman might appear on a regular professional stage.

In the autumn of 1629, the Master of the Revels, Sir Henry Herbert, allowed a French company, which included women, to perform a farce at three playhouses: Blackfriars, the Red Bull and the Fortune. The furious Puritan William Prynne fulminated, 'some French women, or monsters rather, . . . attempted to act a French play at the playhouse in Blackfriars – an impudent, shameful, unwomanish, graceless if not more than whorish attempt'.

The thought that Rosaline was performed by Shakespeare's Dark Lady is certainly interesting to contemplate, if even for a moment.

We were very lucky to land Nina Sosanya as Rosaline in our production.

* * *

Love's Labour's Lost would be the final production in a three-play season I directed in the Courtyard Theatre. *Hamlet*, the production described in the previous chapter, opened first. I then revived *A Midsummer Night's Dream* from the RST in 2005. We finished with *Love's Labour's*. The company were fully warmed up by that point, functioning brilliantly as an ensemble, and with the vocal dexterity required to get their mouths round this 'great feast of languages'.

Shakespeare enjoys creating some of his greatest language portraits in this play. Think of Don Adriano De Armado.

Armado is one of the great original speakers in the canon, like Pistol (in *Henry IV Part Two* and *Henry V*) or Mrs Quickly. His original command of English produces frequent double entendres, sometimes bawdy, sometimes scatological. As for instance when he demonstrates his closeness to the King:

. . . For I must tell thee, it will please his grace, by the world, sometime to lean upon my poor shoulder, and with his royal finger, thus, dally with my excrement, . . . with my mustachio; but, sweetheart, let that pass.

The princess at one point is moved to ask: 'Doth this man serve God?' 'Why ask you?' Berowne enquires, and the princess responds, 'He speaks not like a man of God's making.'

John Peter, then Chief Critic of *The Sunday Times*, commending Joe Dixon's performance as Armado, called the role 'Shakespeare's homage to lifelong immaturity'.

---

[7] Madox was an English explorer.
[8] The first successful public playhouse, built by James Burbage, in Shoreditch.
[9] A freemartin is an infertile cow, which acts like a bull, and has become masculinized in its behaviour. It is genetically female, but with the characteristics of a male. I guess Madox saw some sort of transvestite performer. A drag show circa 1582!

Equally charming, and sometimes equally impenetrable in their latinized disquisitions on the finer points of hunting, are the schoolteacher, Holofernes (Oliver Ford Davies), and the curate, Sir Nathaniel (Jim Hooper).

In Act Five Scene One, Shakespeare brings 'the pedant' and 'the hedge priest' together with the braggart Armado and his sidekick, the diminutive Moth. They discuss the pageant of the Nine Worthies, which they will present to the royal party 'in the posterior of this day' as Holofernes so eloquently describes the late afternoon. As they depart, Holofernes turns to the Constable, Dull, and points out that that he hasn't spoken a word throughout. 'Nor understood none neither, sir' replies the laconic Dull.

One critic pointed out that 'the flashy, abstruse self-regarding wit of Shakespeare' can make it 'an almost unstageable play for modern audiences' but that this ensemble transformed it into 'a crystal-clear stream'.

The final act of *Love's Labour's Lost* is the longest scene in Shakespeare. And it builds to the much anticipated Nine Worthies play.

Costard, the wily, smiley joker in the pack (Ricky Champ), comes on first as Pompey the Great. Costard has precisely the right attitude to their little production, not taking it very seriously, but apologizing when he forgets his name, and retitles the great hero of the Roman Republic 'Pompey the Big'. When the curate arrives as Alexander the Great (clearly very bad casting) the aristocratic audience are dismissive of his efforts. But Costard jumps to his rescue, declaring that Sir Nathaniel is 'an honest man, look you, and soon dashed'. He vouches that the curate is 'a marvellous good neighbour, faith', adding 'and a very good bowler', which is one of those little details that make me love Shakespeare 'this side idolatry', as Ben Jonson said.

The 'imp', Moth, represents Hercules in his infancy and strangles a snake with his bare hands. And then poor old Holofernes, appearing as Judas Maccabaeus, is mercilessly teased by the men. He is defiantly proud of his learning, and will not be put out of countenance by the rude interjections of his noble audience, who insist on supposing that he is not Judas Maccabaeus, the heroic Jewish liberator, but Judas Iscariot, the betrayer of Christ.

The baiting of the men becomes malicious, and unpleasantly clever:

BOYET   Therefore, as he is an ass, let him go.
           And so adieu, sweet Jude! nay, why dost thou stay?
DUMAINE   For the latter end of his name.
BEROWNE   For the ass to the Jude; give it him:– Jud-as, away!

The forlorn schoolteacher protests, 'This is not generous, not gentle, not humble.'

As Armado (trying to give his Hector of Troy) tells the gentlemen off, Costard suddenly turns on him, revealing that Armado has made Jaquenetta pregnant. 'The poor wench is cast away' he accuses, 'she's quick; the child brags in her belly already: tis yours'. Armado's Castilian pride is wounded, and he protests (with more of his deliciously invented English) 'Dost thou infamonize me among potentates?'

Costard has had a grudge with Armado throughout the play, for the attention he has paid to Jaquenetta. The scene now gets surprisingly ugly as the men leap in, trying to stoke a fight between Armado and Costard, and the women in turn try to intervene.

Costard gets ready for a fight, and strips down to his shirt. Moth implores Armado to follow suit, and sadly reveals that for all his show, Armado does not possess a shirt under his doublet. Boyet, in a cruel swipe, discloses that the fantastical Armado wears one of Jaquenetta's dishclouts as a favour. A dishclout it appears is an Elizabethan sanitary towel.[10] The scene now becomes raucous as (in our version) the men find the hidden clout and start throwing it to one another.

So rather than polite banter, it is a scene of unpleasant bullying that we are watching as suddenly the dark figure of Marcade intrudes.

Death enters. The King of France, the father of the princess, has died. 'The scene', as Berowne says, 'begins to cloud'. Navarre tries to comfort his new sweetheart and gets tangled in his own words. As the princess becomes distressed, Berowne soberly interjects, 'Honest plain words best pierce the ear of grief.' But Navarre tries to seek some kind of happy solution:

> Now, at the latest minute of the hour,
> Grant us your loves.

But the princess chides his haste:

> A time, methinks, too short
> To make a world-without-end bargain in.

She tells him instead to remove himself to some remote hermitage, and continues:

> Then, at the expiration of the year,
> Come challenge me, challenge me by these deserts,
> And, by this virgin palm now kissing thine
> I will be thine.

Berowne begs the distracted Rosaline to look at him, saying touchingly:

> Behold the window of my heart, mine eye,
> What humble suit attends thy answer there.

But she in return imposes a tougher sentence than merely to wait out the time. She knew of his reputation as a scathing mocker, a cynical wit, a man for whom a good joke is worth more than a good friend.[11] And as punishment for his flippancy, she insists:

> You shall this twelvemonth term from day to day
> Visit the speechless sick and still converse

---

[10] It is a surprise to read of menstruation in Shakespeare. As it is to hear Gonzalo in *The Tempest* suggest in the storm scene that their sea dog Captain is unlikely to drown though the ship were 'no stronger than a nutshell and as leaky as an unstanched wench'.

[11] Compare Drummond of Hawthornden's opinion of Ben Jonson: 'He will sooner lose his best friend, then his least jest.'

With groaning wretches; and your task shall be,
With all the fierce endeavour of your wit
To enforce the pained impotent to smile.

Berowne's astonished reply suggests there are limits to comedy.

To move wild laughter in the throat of death?
It cannot be; it is impossible:
Mirth cannot move a soul in agony.

Berowne accepts her tough imposition:

A twelvemonth! well; befall what will befall,
I'll jest a twelvemonth in an hospital.

But despite his consent, he reveals his disappointment to the king.

BEROWNE   Our wooing doth not end like an old play;
           Jack hath not Jill: these ladies' courtesy
           Might well have made our sport a comedy.
NAVARRE   Come, sir, it wants a twelvemonth and a day,
           And then 'twill end.
BEROWNE   That's too long for a play.

It's as if the illusion has evaporated: 'Jack hath not Jill'.[12] As if the theatre working lights have suddenly been turned on and the magic disappears. Deflated after the fun.

But Shakespeare has one last treat for us, and for the young lovers, as Armado introduces the debate of the owl and the cuckoo, maintaining Spring and Winter. The song they sing, celebrating spring flowers (with a little warning to cuckold husbands) and winter snow, also reminds us of the cycle of the seasons, and the passing of the year, which may in turn bring about reunion, reconnection and reconciliation.

The picture of winter the song paints recalls Breughel, or those delightful skating scenes of the deaf-mute Dutch painter, Hendrick Avercamp. The details the verses conjure include icicles hanging by the wall, birds shivering in the snow, pails of frozen milk, and greasy Joan, sweating as she keels the pot on the fire, stirring it and making sure it doesn't boil over.

---

[12] Puck says of the ending of *A Midsummer Night's Dream*, as he sorts out the chaos he has caused among the young lovers:

Jack shall have Jill;
Nought shall go ill;
The man shall have his mare again, and all shall be well.

Love's Labour's Won

After one dress run of the show, David Tennant (Berowne) and Nina Sosanya (Rosaline) were deep in conversation. They were saying how disconcerted they both felt about the fact that Shakespeare separates their characters at the end of the play, when the whole process of the narrative, the flirting, the banter, has been leading towards conjunction.

I suggested that we should immediately schedule *Much Ado About Nothing*, where two sparring lovers have the occasion to meet again, both still licking old wounds, and pick up where they left off, and finally with the help of their friends, they are brought together.

The thought began to take hold. The relationship of Berowne and Rosaline did seem to parallel that of Beatrice and Benedick. At their first encounter Beatrice delivers a crushing put-down, 'I wonder you will still be talking, Signior Benedict, nobody marks you', and receives his scathing response 'My dear lady Disdain are you yet living?' The tetchy (and very funny) little exchange ends with Beatrice calling after him, 'you always end with a jade's trick', and adding, with the saddest of inflections, 'I know you of old'.

Could *Much Ado* in fact be an alternative title to *Love's Labour's Won*, one of the plays associated with Shakespeare's name, which is considered lost?

A Lincolnshire minister called Frances Meres had published a commonplace book in 1598 called *Palladis Tamia*, or *Wit's Treasury*. He sets out to compare English poets with their Greek, Latin and Italian forbears. 'As Plautus and Seneca were accounted best among the Latins for Comedy', Meres writes, 'so Shakespeare among the English is most excellent in both kinds'. He then goes on to list a dozen Shakespeare plays: six tragedies and six comedies, to prove his point. Alongside *The Two Gentlemen of Verona*, *The Comedy of Errors*, *A Midsummer Night's Dream* and *The Merchant of Venice*, Meres includes both *Love's Labour's Lost* and *Love's Labour's Won*. The titles suggest that the plays are linked, and if the labours of Love are lost in the first play, as Jack does not get Jill and the couple do not marry, then it implies that at the very least the outcome is different in *Love's Labour's Won*.

Much Ado is not mentioned in Meres's list. The play was published in quarto in 1600, with the phrase 'as is has been sundry times publicly acted' on the cover. So, it may be that it had not been presented by the time Meres wrote his treasury. It was then published in the Folio, though despite Meres's recommendation of the excellence of *Loves Labour's Won*, that play is not published in the Folio. And we have no evidence in the Stationers' Register for an application to publish a play with that title. Does Meres base his recommendations on having read those plays, or merely on the testimony of seeing them?

The Taming of the Shrew is not included in Meres' list, which has led some to suggest that it is a candidate for being *Love's Labour's Won*, but of course Meres may not have included it because he did not think it represented Shakespeare's mastery in the genre. *Shrew* was probably written between 1590 and the closure of the theatres for plague in 1592. Most scholars now believe *Love's Labour's Lost* was written in 1594–5, which would discount the earlier play from being a sequel to the later one.

In the summer of 1603, at Blandford Fair in Dorset, an Exeter Bookseller called Christopher Hunt opened his daybook and drew up a list of plays sold between 9–17

August. It was only discovered in 1954, in the binding of a volume of sermons from 1637. Mr Hunt's list includes both *Love's Labour's Lost* and *Won*, as well as *The Taming of the Shrew*, which is rather singular proof that the two titles are distinct plays.

When I expanded my (by now and to me) definitive theory of the pairing of the two plays, David Tennant shook his head: 'Ah, no, well, but you see,' he said,

> I do actually know what happened to *Love's Labour's Won*. Yes, you see, Dr Who discovered in the seventh episode of the third series, that a hostile alien species called the Carrionites, employed magic based on the power of words which allowed them to manipulate psychic energy, you see, and lines from *Love's Labour's Won*, when spoken out loud could liberate them from their confinement on earth. And to cut a long story short, in the end, all the copies of *Love's Labour's Won* were sucked into a vortex. Sorry.

Nevertheless, I pursued my theory and in 2014, as Artistic Director, I proposed to director Chris Luscombe that we couple the plays, cast-through with the same company. And as we were commemorating the start of the Great War that year, I suggested that we place the plays on either side of that conflict, with *Love's Labour's Lost* set in the long, hot, Edwardian summer of 1914, and *Love's Labour's Won (Much Ado)* set as the soldiers returned from the front in the changed world of 1918.

Never have I known a director so completely embrace an idea and deliver it with such panache. Chris's production, with Ed Bennett as Berowne/Benedict and Michelle Terry as Rosaline/Beatrice, opened to great acclaim and was revived in the West End the following year, when Lisa Dillon took over from Michelle.

Dominic Cavendish of *The Daily Telegraph* called it 'blissfully entertaining and emotionally involving' and remarked that, 'Parallels between the two works – the sparring wit, the sex-war skirmishes, the shift from showy linguistic evasion to heart-felt earnestness – become persuasively apparent.'

21

Twelfth Night

– 2009: Courtyard Theatre, Stratford-upon-Avon;
Duke of York's Theatre, London.

My sister Ruth and I were 'born in an hour'. She now lives in Colorado, so we are separated by geography alone. But the idea of losing my twin haunts me.

I was working with the British Nigerian writer Biyi Bandele, on a production of *Oronooko* at The Other Place. He told me that in Yoruba culture, twins are thought to share the same soul. They carve two little statues called 'Ibeji'. These are made to house the soul of the twins and are reunited in the event of their deaths. I found this symbolism oddly helpful and as my sister and I were about to celebrate turning forty, we decided to echo the practice, exchanging identical clocks on our birthday. Mine sits on the mantelpiece and its comforting chime reminds me of her life seven time-zones away on the other side of the world.

I am often asked what special bond there is between us, how that might manifest itself, what incidents of telepathy have we had. I answer by recalling a bizarre coincidence that happened back at the start of my professional career as an actor.

I was playing Cocky the chicken, in pantomime. We had transferred for Christmas from Nottingham Playhouse to the Towngate Theatre, Basildon, in Essex. During the Dame's song-sheet singalong just before the finale, I would run up to the back of the auditorium, clamber onto the backs of the seats, and walk row by row over the heads of the children, down to the front (no doubt giving some unsuspecting 5-year-olds nightmares for life). Then I would join the Dame back up on stage.

One mid-week matinee, I hauled myself back up on stage only to realize that I had badly pulled my back out. I clucked off to the stage manager in the wings, went back on to finish the show (trooper that I was), and was then rushed to the Basildon Royal Infirmary, still dressed as a chicken, in my green feathers, yellow stockings and red wattles. No one in the waiting room batted an eyelid.

I eventually told the doctor that I needed to hurry as there was the second house coming up. 'You've put both sides of your spine into spasm,' he said, 'you can't possibly carry on with the show. You'll have to be replaced. Here, wear this.' At which point he presented me with a surgical collar.

I put it on, sloped off home, and rang my twin.

I immediately detected in her greeting that something was wrong. 'What is it?' I asked.

'Well, promise you won't tell Mum and Dad 'cos they'll only worry, but I have just been in a car accident.'

'What?' I yelped, 'Are you OK?'

'Oh, it's fine,' she said, 'just whiplash. I have to wear this neck brace.'

For the first time in our lives, on either side of the Atlantic, four and a half thousand miles away from each other, at exactly the same moment, we were both wearing surgical collars around our necks. Now if the absurdity of that story doesn't both prove and disprove the weird symbiosis between twins, I don't know what does.

Later in our lives, in the same year (1987), we had both met men called Tony. And then committed the rest of our lives to those men. Ruth and her Tony were able to get married three years later, in 1990. My Tony and I then had to wait another fifteen years, until civil partnerships between same sex couples were allowed in the UK.

As a result, I have always felt a particular affinity with *Twelfth Night*. There are of course double the sets of twins in *The Comedy of Errors*, but none of them know of the other's existence, so they feel no pain in their separation. Viola and Sebastian ache with it, and their reunion is the more touching because of it.

It has always fascinated me that Shakespeare was father to twins, Judith and Hamnet, and that he should write two plays about twins.

In Elizabethan times Candlemas, the feast day commemorating the presentation of the Christ child in the temple, was also the day when all the green Christmas decorations – the holly, mistletoe, rosemary and bay – had to be taken down, a task which today we associate with the Epiphany, or Twelfth Night. It was on this day, 2 February 1585, in Stratford-upon-Avon, that Shakespeare presented their twin babies at Holy Trinity Church to be baptized. Their mother Anne would not have been allowed to be present, as she would not have been 'churched' yet.

Seventeen years later, on that same day in 1602, a Candlemas Feast, to mark the end of Christmastide, was held at Middle Temple in London. John Manningham, a student, recorded the event in his diary: 'At our feast, we had a play called *Twelfth Night* or *What You Will*.' It struck me that the first recorded performance of *Twelfth Night* came seventeen years to the day since Shakespeare had registered the births of his twins. In the final act of the play, he can reunite the fictional twins separated in a shipwreck; in life he cannot. Judith would have spent her seventeenth birthday, a few days before, alone, without her twin to share it with, for Hamnet had died six years before, aged eleven, on 4 August 1596.

In 2009, Michael Boyd had launched his three-year ensemble company, which was now in full swing. They had completed Year One, in the Courtyard Theatre, and were heading for a new work season at Hampstead before beginning rehearsals for Year Two. I would finally be working with the actors on a production of the *Morte d'Arthur* in an adaptation by Mike Poulton. In the meantime, in a break from the ensemble, I would direct a solus Shakespeare in the Courtyard, and I chose *Twelfth Night*.

With designer Rob Jones, our first job was to explore where to set the play.

Shakespeare locates the action in Illyria. The name evokes a place of lyrical delirium, but perhaps that fantastical reputation stems more from the popularity of the play itself than from the actual location, which for Shakespeare's audience was a very real place. Illyria was a wild corner of the Ottoman Empire, on the eastern shores of the Adriatic

Sea, notable for its pirates and for the frequent shipwrecks along its rugged coastline. It roughly equates with modern day Albania.

Shakespeare draws on the country's unruly, dangerous and exotic reputation. Antonio warns Sebastian that, to a stranger 'unguided and unfriended', the area can be 'rough and unhospitable'. Shakespeare peppers the play with pirates and renegadoes, shipwrecks and sea-battles. There are references to eunuchs and mutes and the court of the Sophy, the Shah of neighbouring Persia.

Despite these Middle-Eastern references though, *Twelfth Night* seems populated by a decidedly English bunch of characters. This led me to the idea of exploring a period two centuries later when the English presence in the Near and Middle East hit the headlines. The wilds of Illyria were made famous when they were visited by the young Lord Byron. Since the late seventeenth century, the Grand Tour around the great capitals of Europe: Paris, Geneva, Venice, Rome, had been a vital part of the education of young British aristocrats. But at the start of the nineteenth century, as the Napoleonic Wars prevented European travel, the English tourist ventured further east into Greece, Turkey, Syria and Lebanon.

What's to do? Shall we go see the relics of this town?

Act Three Scene Three

Sebastian seems the very epitome of a young man on the Grand Tour. 'I pray you, lets us satisfy our eyes / With the memorials and things of fame that do renown this city' he suggests to Antonio.

Byron's exploits, including his assumption of Albanian dress (which he described as 'the most magnificent in the world'), his famous attempt to follow the mythical Leander and swim across the Hellespont, and his dalliance with both alluring countesses and dark-eyed Greek boys, all contributed to the romantic idea of the Aegean Peninsula.

But he was only one of many visitors with a taste for the area. Before he arrived, Lord Elgin had parcelled up two hundred cases of marbles for shipment home, earning him the wrath of Byron who called him 'the greatest patron of larceny Athens ever saw'. Although Byron himself had told a friend 'I have some idea of purchasing the island of Ithaca; I suppose you will add me to the Levant Lunatics.'

One such Levant Lunatic was without doubt Lady Hester Stanhope, a niece of William Pitt and friend of Beau Brummell, who travelled to the near East with her long-suffering physician. They were shipwrecked off Rhodes. Having lost her entire wardrobe, she decided to dress as a Turkish man. Lady Hester spent the rest of her life in the Levant and never put on women's clothes again.

So here we had our setting. Lord Byron, with his romantic passions and obsessions, would mirror Orsino. In Lady Hester, dressing as a man after she was shipwrecked, we had a model for Viola. The ex-patriot English community, bored and frequently drunk, would accommodate the world inhabited by Sir Toby and Sir Andrew, and the Grand Tour would explain the presence of Sebastian and his sister. It all fitted perfectly. In fact, perhaps it fitted rather too perfectly.

*   *   *

I had been pestering the actor/director Richard Wilson to play Malvolio for the best part of a decade. As a close friend of Tony, I had known Richard in his pre-Victor Meldrew days. In fact, I remember him turning down the role in the BBC sitcom *One Foot in the Grave* that would make him famous, and which he would eventually play for over a decade from 1990–2000.

Richard's reluctance to take on the role for which he seemed so ideally suited was, I think, precisely that. Everybody kept saying how right he was for the part that he feared living up to all those high expectations. Richard never made a secret of the fact that he had something of a block with Shakespeare, attributing it to his background, growing up in a working-class area of Greenock with little access to the classics. How he loyally endured all the Shakespeare productions that his best friend Tony Sher had been in all these years, I don't know.

There had been a run of unhappy productions of the play at Stratford in recent years. Michael Boyd's own production in 2005 had been plagued with catastrophes of one sort or another. Lindsay Posner discovered that he had to direct his 2001 production on a grey season stage, which might have worked well for the other plays in the repertoire, but drained the joy from *Twelfth Night*, and Adrian Noble had (for him) a very rare flop with the play in 1998.

Only Ian Judge's 1994 production with Des Barrit as Malvolio, set in Elizabethan Stratford, had enjoyed real success, going on to enjoy a revival and subsequent tour. As Michael Billington pondered, 'Give British directors a really difficult play like *Titus Andronicus* or *Timon of Athens* and they normally triumph. Present them with arguably the greatest comedy ever written, *Twelfth Night*, and they often falter.'

Once I had landed Richard as Malvolio, secured a solus production and a West End transfer, I set out to cast the play to the hilt. I was delighted that Richard (Bill) McCabe agreed to play Belch as this character drives the plot and Bill, apart from being a very fine comic actor, has an unerring instinct about pace and how to motor a play. James Fleet who, like Bill, had been in my first season at Stratford in 1987 and who had found TV fame as dim-witted Hugo in *The Vicar of Dibley*, accepted the role of Andrew Aguecheek.

Nancy Carroll would play Viola and Alexandra Gilbreath would play Olivia, to me the most under-rated comic role in the canon.

Both women had taken part in Michael Wood's *In Search of Shakespeare*, for which I pulled together an acting company to perform a number of Shakespeare extracts in locations where Shakespeare's own company might have performed: a coaching inn in Gloucester, a guildhall in Leicester, the school room at King Edward School in Stratford, and Hampton Court.

As the actors gathered on the first day of rehearsals for the TV series at St George's Church in Bloomsbury, I introduced Nancy to Jo Stone-Fewings who had played the Bastard for me in *King John*. I swear a high voltage spark like an electric charge cracked between them, witnessed by the whole company. As Phoebe says, in *As You Like It*:

Dead shepherd, now I find thy saw of might:
'Who ever loved that loved not at first sight?'

Act Three Scene Five

Nancy and Jo became inseparable throughout the week's filming and nine days later became engaged. I was officially invited to their wedding the following summer in my role as Cupid. Jo played Orsino to Nancy's Viola.

As an exercise at the start of our rehearsals for *Twelfth Night*, I asked the cast and the creative team to supply an answer to the question posed by Feste: 'What is Love?' Some people wrote their own anonymous responses, others found quotations which best summed up an answer. Here are some of my favourite replies:

> — Love is the irresistible desire to be irresistibly desired.
>
> *Mark Twain*

> — Love doesn't make the world go round,
> Love is what makes the ride worthwhile.
>
> *Elizabeth Barrett Browning*

> — Love is like quicksilver in the hand. Leave the fingers open and it stays.
> Clutch it and it darts away.
>
> *Dorothy Parker*

> — We can only learn to love by loving.
>
> *Iris Murdoch*

And the following responses were not attributed:

> — Love is . . . feeling less lonely.
> — Love is friendship set on fire.
> — Love is discovering, to your delight, that you are no longer one of two, but half of one.

Everybody falls in love in Illyria. Viola with Orsino; Antonio with Sebastian; Malvolio with Olivia; and Olivia with Cesario. Maria has a crush on Sir Toby, Feste might be in love with Olivia, and even Sir Andrew 'was adored once too'. And Shakespeare nails the moment, alerting the actor to the very heartbeat in which love arrives.

When Viola (disguised as the boy Cesario) arrives at the Countess Olivia's house to present Count Orsino's embassy of love to her, she is treated with considerable disdain by the vain Countess. And Viola, because she has nothing to lose (she is already in love with her master, so Olivia is her rival), gives as good back again.

VIOLA   Good madam, let me see your face.
OLIVIA   Have you any commission from your lord to negotiate with my face?
     You are now out of your text: but we will draw the curtain and show you the
     picture. Look you, sir, such a one I was this present: is't not well done?
VIOLA   Excellently done, if God did all.

Notice the scene is all in prose up this point. But now it shifts into verse as Love enters the conversation. As Cesario describes the strength of his master's passion he/she becomes ravishingly eloquent, overwhelming the Countess with a cannonade of violent images, which crash against the metre.

> VIOLA   My lord and master loves you: O, such love
>   Could be but recompensed, though you were crown'd
>   The nonpareil of beauty!
> OLIVIA   How does he love me?
> VIOLA   With adorations, fertile tears,
>   With groans that thunder love, with sighs of fire.

[You sense that Olivia feels she has to put a stop to this.]

> OLIVIA   Your lord does know my mind; I cannot love him.

Almost imperceptibly, Olivia has suddenly shifted efficiently towards verse. The audience may not yet notice or realize why her language has become abruptly heightened, but the actor playing her must.

Now Viola can't help revealing the depth of her own obsession. Listen to the pain in her love, the suffering, 'the deadly life' (an arresting oxymoron, all too easily passed over!):

> VIOLA   If I did love you in my master's flame,
>   With such a suffering, such a deadly life,
>   In your denial I would find no sense;
>   I would not understand it.

Olivia, swept up in this whirlwind of feeling expressed with such earnest sincerity, now prepares us, asks us to pause and, after the turbulence, attend to what amounts to a song of unrequited love:

> OLIVIA   Why, what would you?
> VIOLA   Make me a willow cabin at your gate,
>   And call upon my soul within the house;
>   Write loyal cantons of contemned love
>   And sing them loud even in the dead of night;
>   Halloo your name to the reverberate hills
>   And make the babbling gossip of the air
>   Cry out 'Olivia!' O, You should not rest
>   Between the elements of air and earth,
>   But you should pity me!
> OLIVIA   You might do much.
>   What is your parentage?

There are interesting choices in how Olivia responds to Viola's canton of love disdained. Does she pick up her cue and complete the half-line with 'You might do much'? Or does this aria so impress her that it takes a beat for her to think of what to say but can only come out with banalities: 'you have a very promising future. Who are your mum and dad?'

She recovers well enough but manages to insult the young servant by offering him a tip, which he roundly refuses. As soon as Cesario has exited we realize that Olivia is smitten. 'How now', she gasps, 'Even so quickly may one catch the plague?'

Having sent Malvolio in chase after Cesario, with a ring, she seals her new condition immediately and precipitously yielding to the inevitable, with a joyfully rhyming couplet:

Fate, show thy force: ourselves we do not owe;
What is decreed must be, and be this so.

*   *   *

After six weeks of rehearsal, finally we arrive in Stratford ready to go into the tech and previews in the Courtyard Theatre.

To welcome the company to Stratford, I take them to a special place with a particular association to our play.

The knot garden of New Place is a jewel box. It was visited by J.B. Priestley on a little jaunt to Stratford: 'spring in blue and gold'. He wrote about the experience in an essay he published in 1928. He imagines Shakespeare keeping an immortal eye on his birthplace and roaring with laughter at the Midland Bank 'trying to look Elizabethan and romantic'. He pokes fun at how conscientiously thatched and beamed everything is. I wonder why he doesn't mention the theatre, but then realize that having burnt down in 1926, and the Art Deco building by Elizabeth Scott not opening until 1932, there was probably very little to see beyond a building site.

Then he mentions our play and I read it to the company as we stand together in the garden.

And there was one moment, the other afternoon when I really did feel I was treading upon his own ground. It was when we were in the gardens of New Place, very brave in the spring sunlight. You could have played the outdoor scene from *Twelfth Night* in them without disturbing a leaf. There was the very sward for Viola and Sir Andrew. Down that paved path Olivia would come, like a great white peacock. Against that bank of flowers, the figure of Maria would be seen flitting like a starling. The little knot garden alone was worth the journey and nearer to Shakespeare than all the documents and chairs and monuments. It was a patterned blaze of tulips, the Elizabethan gentlefolk among flowers. The white ones, full open and very majestic, were the great ladies in their ruffs; and the multicoloured ones, in all their bravery of crimson and yellow, were the gentlemen in doublet and striped hose. The little crazy-paved paths added a touch of pride and fantasy and cross gartering, as if Malvolio has once passed that way. And then, to crown all, there were tiny rows of sweet-smelling English herbs, thyme and sage and marjoram, and misty odorous borders of lavender. I remember that when we left the garden to see the place where Shakespeare was buried it didn't seem to matter much. Why should it, when we have just seen the place where he was still alive.

J. B. Priestley, *Apes and Angels*, 1928

Opening night. I normally gather the company on stage before the press night. It's important to connect. To do a bit of work, nothing new. And to get people to focus on the play and not on the distractions of the event: have they written first-night cards to everyone? Did they leave the ticket for their agent, or the keys for the family? Did they iron the frock or the shirt they want to stun everyone with at the party afterwards?

Today I conclude with a few thoughts to remind them that a press night is a hall of mirrors, some of the reflections will horribly distort what we think we have achieved; some will flatter; some (but not many) will show back what we believe we have done. If we step into that hall of mirrors together, accept the credit if it comes, deal with the brickbats if they are thrown, then we'll be OK.

I tell them to remember not to carry the baggage if things go wrong, I thank them for all their work, and say how proud I am of every one of them, and then I ask their indulgence for a personal reflection of my own. I say how special this play has always been to me, partly as I have no doubt mentioned many times in rehearsal that I am lucky enough to be a twin myself. And then I say, 'And as it happens, my twin is here with me for tonight's show, and I have asked her to pop on stage.'

To a cheer from the company, my twin Ruth walks up the aisle and joins me on stage.

*   *   *

Now, the melancholy god protect thee; and the tailor make thy doublet of changeable taffeta, for thy mind is a very opal.

Feste bestows his enigmatic benediction upon Orsino, but every director of *Twelfth Night* should pray to be blessed by it too.

The melancholy god predominates over this play. Not the 'sable-coloured' moodiness of the Prince of Denmark. Not the fantastical affectation of Don Armado. Nor the wallowing humour of Jaques who 'can suck melancholy out of a song as a weasel sucks eggs'. *Twelfth Night* has a melancholy all its own.

It should be dressed in 'changeable taffeta', with the warp and weft of joy and pain that produce its peculiar iridescence.

And its tone must be opalescent, with sparkle in its depths, and a rare ability to change and reflect moods from light and warmth to wind and rain.

I think perhaps I didn't achieve that. I should have. I had such a great cast. But I was so pleased to have found what I believed was the perfect setting for the play. I thought it solved every detail, but in truth it was more picturesque than pertinent. Decorative, rather than revelatory. Perhaps its effect was to trap the play's anarchy and tame its craziness. To tidy up its grief and neaten its rapture and abandonment. I needed to shake up all those ingredients, and risk losing control. The production needed to let is hair down.

In the end, I didn't attend to the play's title. The feast of *Twelfth Night* is presided over by the Lord of Misrule. I had been too polite.

I want to do it all over again now.

22

Julius Caesar

– 2012: Royal Shakespeare Theatre, Stratford-upon-Avon;
Novello Theatre, London; Moscow Arts Theatre;
Brooklyn Academy of Music, New York; Southern Theater, Columbus, Ohio.
– Filmed for BBC Four.

30 April 2001. London.

Tony and I were on the balcony of South Africa House, overlooking a packed Trafalgar Square. We had been invited by the High Commissioner, Cheryl Carolus, with whom we had been working on a show to celebrate the new rainbow nation.

The 82-year-old Nelson Mandela was guest of honour at the Freedom Day concert. He received a hero's welcome as he was led out onto the stage by the prime minister, Tony Blair. Blair did not get quite such a warm reception, having just delayed the general election, and having been criticized for his handling of the foot and mouth crisis. We watched as Mandela paid tribute to the part played by British people in the fight against apartheid. He then returned to the balcony to watch the rest of the concert.

The previous weekend an article had appeared in *The Observer* by Anthony Sampson, the author of the first biography of Mandela. He deplored the crass decision by the education department in Gauteng Province, Johannesburg, to drop Shakespeare from the syllabus. *Hamlet* was 'not optimistic or uplifting'. *King Lear* was 'full of violence and despair' with a plot which was 'rather unlikely and ridiculous' and *Julius Caesar* apparently was sexist because 'it elevates men'.

Sampson argued how important Shakespeare had been to the continent, revealing that Mandela had had access to a copy of Shakespeare in prison, and had put his signature alongside a quotation from *Julius Caesar*. I was dying to ask the great man himself about it.

When Mandela appeared, Tony, who had met him once before, introduced me to him. I want to say that we had a profound conversation about the influence that reading Shakespeare on Robben Island had had upon him, why he had chosen that particular quotation, and what he felt about that play, but in reality I was so overawed I can hardly remember what I burbled. What I do remember, however, as he shook my hand, was that he placed his other hand on top of mine, as if to assure me that (for those few seconds at any rate) I had his full attention.

Tony and I finally got to see the 'Robben Island Bible' when we helped bring it to Stratford-upon-Avon five years later (with its owner Sonny Venkatrathnam), for display in the Complete Works exhibition at Nash's House in 2006.

Sonny had been an inmate on Robben Island during the 1970s with Mandela, Walter Sisulu and others. Sonny's wife Theresa explained that as literature was not allowed in the prison, she had smuggled in his Collins Complete Works of Shakespeare but had covered it in old Hindu Diwali greeting cards to disguise it as a religious text and prevent it from being confiscated by the guards. I loved the idea of Shakespeare being protected by Rama and Sita. The book was covertly passed around to other prisoners such as Sisulu, Billy Nair and Govan Mbeki to read and mark up their favourite passages. Sonny placed the precious book in my hands to look through. I turned to the page Madiba himself had signed.

He had chosen Julius Caesar's words on the night before his assassination.

Cowards die many times before their deaths
The valiant never taste of death but once.
Of all the wonders that I yet have heard
It seems to me most strange that men should fear,
Seeing that death, a necessary end
Will come when it will come.

And he had signed his name N.R.D. Mandela (Nelson Rolihlahla Dalibhunga Mandela) alongside the passage and dated it 16/12/77.

The date was not insignificant. 16 December was celebrated as Dingaan's Day in South Africa. It marked the anniversary of the Battle of Blood River in 1838, when 470 voortrekkers were attacked by thousands of Zulu Warriors, and against all odds, defeated them. The victory was taken as a certain sign that their supremacy was ordained by God. The voortreker monument in Pretoria was inaugurated on 16 December 1949 to commemorate Dingaan's Day, and the religious holiday renamed the Day of the Covenant in 1952.

But Mandela may have been recalling another significance of the date, as it also marked the founding of Umkhonto we Sizwe (Spear of the Nation), the military arm of the ANC, on 16 December 1961. That day, leaflets were dropped on the streets warning, 'The time comes in the life of any nation, when there remain only two choices; submit or fight. The time has now come.' A series of sabotages signalled the decision to embark on an armed struggle against the apartheid regime.

Mandela's choice of Caesar's lines has a very different resonance in this context. They seem to articulate the need for determination, for defiant fortitude, to continue the struggle even at the ultimate cost of life.

When he became the first president of the newly democratic South Africa, Mandela renamed the public holiday the Day of Reconciliation, deliberately choosing to represent national unity by combining a day that had significance for both the Afrikaner and liberation struggle traditions.

*   *   *

Sol Plaatje, one of the founders of the African National Congress, once quoted a Bechuana Chief in Mafeking calling Shakespeare William Tsikinya-Chaka or William Shake-the-Sword. Of all Tsikinya-Chaka's plays, *Julius Caesar* seems to have been most frequently translated into African languages. Plaatje himself, in South Africa in the 1920s, translated it into Tswana.

Julius Nyerere, the first president of Tanzania, created *Julius Kaisari*, a Swahili translation, as a gift to the nation to celebrate its first anniversary of independence in 1961. He followed it by translating a version of *The Merchant of Venice: Mabepari wa Venisi*. I bought a second-hand copy online, and when it arrived, I discovered an inscription on the inside cover. It read, 'To Lord and Lady Olivier from Julius Nyerere'.

I asked the great South African actor and activist, John Kani, why the play was so popular on his continent, and he said, 'It's simple, Greg; it's Shakespeare's African play.'

That really struck me. If you look at the history of Africa in the last fifty or sixty years since many of the countries gained independence from imperial rule, you find a history of leaders coming to power on a wave of popularity, beginning to gather all that power to themselves, then being overthrown in a military coup that plunges the country into civil war. That's the plot of *Julius Caesar*.

When I began to think about directing the play, the thought of translating the action to an unspecified African country seemed an obvious choice. The decision seemed all the more exciting, as there are now so many fine Black actors in the UK with real classical chops able potentially to redefine those great roles for an entirely new generation.

My first instinct was to test the idea: to get a group of actor friends together, sit around the play for a couple of days, and invite experts to reflect on the meaning of the figure of Julius Caesar in Ancient Rome, and in the Renaissance. I wanted us all to consider how the history of modern Africa might illuminate the text.

So, in July 2011, that's exactly what we did.

Tom Holland, author of *Rubicon*, an absorbing account of the end of the republic, detailed the significance of the man in Ancient Rome, and the catastrophic forward planning of Brutus and Cassius after his murder. Cicero said the conspirators brought 'the spirits of men, but the foresight of children'.

Professor Richard Wilson[1] discussed how Shakespeare steeps classical history in contemporary political concerns. A Swiss doctor called Thomas Platter saw *Julius Caesar* at the newly built Globe Theatre on 21 September 1599. A week later, the Earl of Essex stormed into London and burst into Queen Elizabeth's bedroom, an incident that would escalate within eighteen months, into his putsch against her crown, the Essex Rebellion.

Journalist and historian Martin Meredith, meanwhile, outlined the Big Man Politics he had witnessed as a correspondent in Africa over the last forty years. Africa has no monopoly on dictators, but Martin gave harrowing accounts of power hungry tyrants like Idi Amin in Uganda; Bokassa in the Central African Empire; Charles Taylor in Liberia, West Africa's most notorious warlord; through to Mugabe in Zimbabwe. He charted the wave of some forty successful coup attempts and countless attempted coups in the two decades since African countries sought to shake off their colonial rule and gain independence. He was also careful to point out the futility and hypocrisy of Western governments in mishandling these international challenges.

---

[1] Not to be confused with the actor, Richard Wilson.

Yasmin Alibhai-Brown, the Ugandan-born, British journalist and author, moderated our discussion.

One of the major difficulties of performing *Julius Caesar* today is to find ways that the audience can both understand the political motives behind the action, and sense how they seem to operate in a mythic universe: where dreams can influence decisions; soothsayers disturb the course of governance; storms seem to quake the foundations of society; and lions can walk the streets.

It's too easy, in a production in Western modern dress, to feel as if the conspirators are simply trying to remove a particularly cantankerous chairman of the board, rather than pull down a tyrant whose fall will shake the earth.

The South African author Can Themba suggested, 'The turbulence of urban African life is like the stage of Shakespeare's Elizabethan world.' He asserted that if Shakespeare were alive now he would recognize Elizabethan England more readily in Africa than in his own country as it is today. He wrote, 'Shakespeare reaches out a fraternal hand to the throbbing heart of Africa.'

We concluded the two-day symposium with a read-through of the play. Paterson Joseph as Brutus even started to see what the language would sound like with a light East-African accent. It was thrilling. We finished the workshop in very high spirits. Yasmin Alibhai-Brown summed up the experience by concluding that the play had yielded a completely fresh resonance. This context could potentially be very exciting, urgent and immediate.

As the summer of 2011 progressed, the events of the drama seemed to be playing out across north Africa, as what was being dubbed the Arab Spring continued to unfold, only enhancing the contemporary echoes in Shakespeare's play. The big questions in Libya were not, 'Are they going to get rid of Colonel Gaddafi? Will they assassinate Gaddafi?' That seemed an inevitability. As in *Julius Caesar*, the big question was 'What happens next?'

In fact, 'What happens next?' is the key to preventing the play becoming broken-backed as it so often seems in production.

Surely the single best-known fact of the entire pagan world has to be that Julius Caesar was assassinated. How, therefore, do you preserve the tension, and the audience's interest, after he dies? Well, surely the focus has to be precisely that question: what happens next? What was clear from our symposium was that Brutus and Cassius, by not thinking beyond the assassination of Caesar, merely opened a power vacuum into which much more ruthless men would rush. And that must be the focus of our rehearsal. Apart from cutting the interval (which inevitably contributes to the sense of anti-climax in the second half) we would have to investigate the play's momentum beyond the forum scene, and urgently ask: what happens next?

*   *   *

By October, the production of *Julius Caesar* had been scheduled for the following spring and would be the RSC's contribution to a 'World Shakespeare Festival' as part of the Cultural Olympiad. Many of the actors from the symposium had eagerly signed up. Paterson Joseph would play Brutus; Adjoa Andoh, Portia; Ray Fearon, Mark Antony;

Joe Mydell came on board as Casca; Jeffery Kissoon would grace the company by returning to play Caesar; and finally we managed to land Cyril Nri as Cassius.

Meanwhile I was deep in rehearsal for a new play by David Edgar, for the Swan. *Written on the Heart* had been commissioned to coincide with the 400th anniversary of the translation of the King James Bible in 1611. It was a complex, powerful play, which took every ounce of my wit to keep up with the mammoth brains of its author.

With a fortnight to go until the press night, Michael Boyd announced his resignation as Artistic Director of the RSC.

Having together accomplished the extraordinary feat of opening the newly transformed Royal Shakespeare Theatre, Michael explained to me that his executive director, Vikki Heywood, had decided it was time to move on. Michael felt that after nearly a decade in the job, he would follow.

So what was I going to do this time round? Could I bear to put my hat in the ring for a second time?

> There is a tide in the affairs of men,
> Which, taken at the flood, leads on to fortune.

Brutus's famous line echoed in my ears. He is urging his co-conspirators to seize the fleeting opportunity to change the regime. But of course, whenever this line is quoted, it is intended to highlight the enticing opportunity that fortune may afford. It is easy to forget that Brutus' action leads to disaster. The very thing the conspirators are trying to achieve, the survival of the Republic, is lost and they are annihilated.

I felt sick. Under Michael I had had the freedom to continue to direct what I chose and to concentrate almost entirely on that.

* * *

Shakespeare has a joke in *Julius Caesar*, at the expense of the great Roman orator Cicero, one of the most eloquent and voluble voices of the ancient world. Shakespeare makes him an incidental character in his play, and the butt of Casca's barbed wit. Cassius asks Casca if Cicero had anything to say about Caesar being offered the crown by Mark Antony at the games, to which Casca responds:

> Ay, he spoke Greek.

When Cassius presses him as to the effect of his oratory he snipes with withering disdain:

> Nay, an I tell you that, I'll ne'er look you i' the face again: but those that understood him smiled at one another and shook their heads; but, for mine own part, it was Greek to me.

When Cicero eventually appears, he is completely unperturbed by the terrible portents that have so shaken the normally cynical Casca: the 'tempest dropping fire', or his reports of a slave holding aloft his burning hand, or even the glaring lion, which walked 'surly by' him, near the Capitol. Shakespeare only allows the legendarily garrulous Cicero a laconic eight and a half lines in the entire play.

Perhaps Shakespeare had suffered too many gruelling Latin lessons at King Edward School, trying to translate Cicero's famous oratory, and was getting his own back. Nevertheless, *Julius Caesar* ably demonstrates Shakespeare's skilful facility with rhetoric. 'The art of winning the soul by discourse', as Plato described it, was formalized by his pupil Aristotle into a system.

Then, centuries later, in a great revival of the art of rhetoric in Ancient Rome, that system was refined by Cicero, who wrote a treatise on it, defining the structure of a great speech from the exordium to the peroration.

In young William's day, rhetoric was one third of his basic education. The three-part grammar school curriculum, the trivium, was based on grammar, logic and rhetoric. Ever since he was a schoolboy, he has understood how to place himself in the mind of another and how to use the oratorical box of tricks to articulate their thoughts most effectively.

What emerges in the forum scene is the way that Shakespeare, with piercing insight, is able to distinguish between the oratory of Brutus and Mark Antony. Brutus' speech is full of conscious sound bites ('not that I loved Caesar less, but that I loved Rome more'), deliberate verbal constructions designed to impress, but his technique is too obviously on show. His speech is all in prose.

Mark Antony on the other hand is hesitant, apologetic for his lack of ability, and yet in a matter of minutes he has turned the entire hostile crowd against the conspirators into a howling destructive mob. His speeches are all in verse.

In March 2012, I was invited to meet the board of the RSC to discuss whether I might take over from Michael Boyd as Artistic Director. So, I decided to prepare myself by applying rhetorical discipline to my argument as to why, this time around, I should be appointed to run the company. I would structure my argument on Ciceronian principles.

I would begin with my 'exordium': setting out my stall and the arguments for choosing me, making sure to present my credentials, my track record, my Ethos ('I know this company, I have been with the RSC for twenty-five years'), then move on to the narration to set out the facts. This must have brevity, clarity and especially plausibility. Then, I would present the counter arguments (Division) in order to deal with them head on: 'I may not be "fresh" or "new" but I represent a dedication to craftsmanship and a devotion to the discipline required to do Shakespeare well.' Thus I would seek to influence the panel by reason (Logos), setting out all the arguments for picking me, smashing the arguments against (Refutation). And then my peroration, and via emotional appeal (bags of Pathos) perhaps a joke to get a good laugh, because laughter is involuntary assent – make 'em laugh, make 'em cry, make 'em agree! Then cranking it up (Auxesis) to an irresistible climax: 'Don't employ me because I've been around the last quarter-century, and represent continuity after a period of change, and rebuilding, and might steady the boat; don't employ me because I have great if veteran support from all the past Artistic Directors, and many of the broadsheets; don't even employ me for what I have done, but for what we can do together. I know how to run this company, and if, as Shakespeare himself says, "the readiness is all", then I am ready now.'

Wednesday 7 March 2012.

The day of the interview.

Tony waved me off from the front door, as if I was off to my first day at school. I took the Victoria line to Green Park and decided to walk from there to the venue for the interview, Great Peter Street in Westminster. But as I crossed the Mall the heavens opened. I pulled on my raincoat, tugged the hood over my head, and trotted across St James's Park.

When I arrived at North House I handed in my sopping wet coat. The receptionist smiled at me sympathetically and said there was a bathroom on the first floor. I went upstairs, walked in to the bathroom, and looked in the mirror. I was wet through. I had cooked inside the mac as I jogged across the park, and was now drenched in sweat. My shirt was soaked, there were dark patches under the arms of my jacket, and there was no way of disguising either. In a mild panic, I took my shirt off, and tried to wring it out as I towelled myself dry. I would have to explain to the board that this was not nervous perspiration, just the result of a spring shower.

Facing the board, all thought of Cicero went out of my head. I did manage to quote the ancient Greek satirist Archilochus, who said, 'The fox knows many things, but the hedgehog knows one big thing.' 'I am a hedgehog,' I admitted, 'I know a bit about Shakespeare, but I do also know a lot of foxes.' I was hoping to imply that to run the Royal Shakespeare Company the most important qualification is surely someone who is passionate about Shakespeare. And I also happened to know a lot of folk who could help me with all the bits of the job I knew little about. The chairman's eyes seemed to glaze over. Perhaps he was imagining the headlines: 'RSC appoints hedgehog'.

When we started work in earnest on *Julius Caesar*, one sunny morning in late March 2012, I had become the company's sixth Artistic Director. Regime change had occurred without conspiracy, assassination or civil war.

* * *

Michael Vale's design created the equivalent of a Roman forum in an African setting. It was a crumbling concrete football stadium with steps surrounding a central vomitorium. Behind it, a grandiose metal statue of Caesar, hand raised aloft in salute, presided over the action. It would topple later.

At the start of the play the stadium was filled with members of our Black community chorus, recruited from Birmingham, Northampton and Coventry. And our band, who wittily dubbed themselves 'the Vibes of March', created a real sense of carnival, for the Lupercal holiday. When Caesar and his party entered, Caesar, preening smugly, and flicking his fly-whisk, even condescended to dance with the crowd.

What we soon realized as we rehearsed the play was how evenly balanced Shakespeare is. Just as you begin to be persuaded that Brutus is right to rid Rome of a tyrant, suddenly we see Caesar after a sleepless night, a little old man in his slippers, anxious and frightened.

As soon as you decide Brutus is a republican hero, the writing makes you think again, perhaps after all, he is just a vain wishy-washy liberal who hasn't thought it through. Ultimately Brutus is both idealist and vain egotist, and Paterson caught that ambivalence, that intellectual vanity and quixotic self-regard perfectly. Brutus in many ways is a self-righteous blunderer, who makes a series of catastrophic tactical errors.

Cassius is the real strategist, with genuine political savvy. He understands the world and would be the greater leader if only he could control his volatile temperament. Cassius threatens to kill himself in every single scene except the one in which he actually kills himself.

The conspiratorial senators arrived for the senate draped in black waxed cloth, resembling the togas of Ancient Rome, while echoing the ceremonial wear of many contemporary African States.

Jeffery Kissoon brought a terrifying self-deluding grandeur to his Caesar, and when the senators circled to kill him, he glared at them, daring them to strike. Like a great buffalo, wheeling as a pack of hyenas try to take him down, Jeffery's Caesar finally succumbed with a roar as Brutus delivered the fatal blow. Paterson had decided to include a detail from one of the contemporary accounts of Caesar's death and stab his mentor in the genitals.

Ray Fearon arrived into the bloody stadium, as if the playboy Antony had only just recovered from his hangover of the night before. The edgy sense that no one really knows what he will do, or what will happen next, was paramount to the success of the scene. Would one of the nervous conspirators stab him? Would he lunge at them? At one point in our production, Cassius himself nearly breaks ranks and stabs Antony. But he is prevented by Brutus.

And now Brutus makes another catastrophic decision, which everyone around him knows to be wrong. To Cassius's despair, the self-righteous Brutus insists that Antony should be left alive.

When left alone to mourn over his dead friend, Antony apologizes to Caesar for his weakness. But as Ray built through to the climax of that speech a primal lion roar of anger and revenge, all the classical skills that Ray has learnt and honed over many years with the company were unleashed to spectacular effect.

The forum scene is one of those astonishing scenes in Shakespeare where the crowd themselves morph into a character. One of the challenges in production is to field enough bodies to make a convincing crowd. For this production our sterling community chorus, reinforced with those few members of the company that were free, kept the edgy reactions of the company both fresh and precise during the whole Stratford run.

The platform above the central 'vom' provided a great speaking platform to address the crowd, and from which to descend onto the thrust stage as Antony asks permission to come down among them. Then we used a scissor lift to raise Mark Antony and the dead body of Caesar on a rostrum above their heads. This put him right in the centre of the theatre space, on a level with the gallery of the auditorium, allowing Ray to address not just the teeming onstage crowd, but the entire crowded auditorium.

The death of Cinna the poet was a little scene left out of production for most of the play's history. In fact, it was not restored until the 1930s. Today it seems to contain a dangerous truth about the way violence spreads and brutalizes society. Cinna the poet is mistaken for Cinna the assassin, and murdered in the street, even though the mob realize they have wrongly identified their man. 'Kill him for his bad verses' they laugh. Art is the first victim of unlicensed brutality.

The tent scene shouldn't work. It's a twenty-minute scene for most of which two men shout at each other. But in truth it's a love scene. Cassius and Brutus, full of recrimination and anger, tear at each other. Brutus accuses Cassius of corruption. Needy Cassius threatens and blusters. Brutus eventually reveals he has received news of his wife's death. 'How 'scaped I killing when I crossed you so?' says his friend. They are reconciled.

Paterson Joseph and Cyril Nri played the scene with lacerating cruelty, concealing genuine love and deep affection. Shakespeare is keenly aware of how to shift the mood of a scene, and after the sheer volume of the row he allows a moment of relief as the boy Lucius, who is always falling asleep, plays to him. In our African context we chose a kora, a sort of lyre built from a calabash gourd covered with cow skin, with a stringed bridge, which produced a dreamily liquid sound. Simon Manyonda as Lucius was able to master the kora sufficiently to produce a very convincing sound.

But of course, it's the calm before the storm, and heralds the arrival of Caesar's ghost, ominously prefiguring the outcome of the battle at Philippi.

In the final scene Brutus collapses for a few moments of respite with his 'poor remains of friends': Clitus, Dardanius, Volumnius and Strato, none of whom we have met before. Brutus asks each of them privately in turn to kill him and each refuses. In the end it is Strato – described by Messala as 'my master's man' – who briefly falls asleep, and then performs the deed.

We wanted to heighten the relationship between Brutus and his servant boy Lucius, by making Lucius a boy soldier accompanying his master into battle. So it seemed appropriate that it should be the exhausted Lucius who has fallen asleep. As he also falls asleep in the orchard, and in the tent, then this seemed an apt conclusion to his narcoleptic character trait. Somehow it was much more intensely moving when Brutus persuades his own boy to help him kill himself. I like to think Shakespeare would have approved.

23 April, Shakespeare's birthday.
A month after starting rehearsal, we began to film the play in a derelict Chinese hypermarket in Colindale, north London. We had been invited to do so by BBC Four, as their contribution to the Cultural Olympiad. But they needed the finished film for broadcast before the Olympics began in July, and we would only just have opened the play by then. There would be no time to film it.

My solution was to look at the play from a public and private perspective. We would film all the private conspiracy scenes – the backstage scenes as it were – on location, mid-rehearsal. Then we would film the public scenes, like the central forum scene, during live performance in front of the audience in Stratford-upon-Avon.

The anonymous architecture of the hypermarket provided a great number of different locations. We created a pan-African market in one area, where Casca meets Cassius in the rainstorm. We lit fires in oil drums in a sort of breeze block stockade to represent Brutus's orchard. We filmed the assassination of Caesar on a defunct escalator, as if he had been making his way up to the senate session in Pompey's Curia. We had the acting company film the murder of Cinna the poet on their mobile phones which gave the scene a dangerous chaotic immediacy. We hired an army jeep and built a bivouac for the tent scene. There were some very dodgy looking meat fridges where we could snatch close-ups of the proscription murders, and a series of trashed greasy kitchens where the battle scenes could take place.

I noticed an odd phenomenon during the filming. At the start of the day, we would get loads done. After lunch, everything always seemed to slow down. 'Ah,' a wise voice said, 'there is a saying in the industry, "Ben Hur in the morning, Benny Hill in the afternoon"!'

The production aired on Sunday 24 June. This was the ninth version of the play the BBC had broadcast, from its first production in 1938 to the most recent in 1979, making it (according to John Wyver, our producer) the most popular of Shakespeare's plays on television.

None, I think, can have been quite like this one. As we edited together the footage of the assassination scene, I felt a sense of awe at how Shakespeare manages to speak to us, centuries ahead of his own era ('not for an age but for all time'). This impression was captured for me nowhere so profoundly as in Cassius's exultant and prophetic cry over Caesar's corpse:

> How many ages hence
> Shall this our lofty scene be acted o'er
> In states unborn and accents yet unknown!

23

Richard II

– 2013: Royal Shakespeare Theatre, Stratford-upon-Avon;
Barbican Theatre, London.
– Filmed, broadcast live and available on DVD, as part of Live from
Stratford-upon-Avon.

On becoming Artistic Director in 2012, the single most important decision I made in planning terms was to embark on a journey through the entire canon in the RST. In the decade from 2000–2010 the RSC had mounted five productions of *Romeo and Juliet*. I felt that frequency undervalued the currency of the plays. I wanted each play to be an event. We would work our way through the canon, without 'hesitation, deviation or repetition' as they say on BBC Radio 4's *Just a Minute*.

I decided to explore Shakespeare's second history tetralogy. Instead of presenting them immediately as a cycle, we would examine them each in their own right, before 'tetralogizing' them, as it were. We would open with a solus of the great lyric verse drama, *Richard II*; and then proceed with the hurly-burly of court and country that were the *Henry IV* plays in the following season, mounting *Henry V* the following year to coincide with the 600th anniversary of the Battle of Agincourt. Then, if appropriate, we would bring the plays together in 2016 in time for the 400th anniversary of Shakespeare's death.

I invited David Tennant to play Richard. To my great delight, he agreed.

*　*　*

Designer Stephen Brimson Lewis and I began by thinking of the play not in terms of period, but of verticality.

Richard II was the first monarch who insisted on being referred to as 'His Royal Highness', and in the play he enjoys his elevated position above the common herd of his subjects. At the lists at Coventry, he deigns to descend from the scaffold to fold his cousin Bolingbroke in his arms. On his return from Ireland, when he learns he has been deserted by his nobles, in abject despair he crumples to sit on the ground and tell sad stories of the death of kings.

The short-lived rally in his spirits climaxes when he makes his appearance high on the battlements of Flint Castle, 'As doth the blushing discontented sun / From out the fiery portal of the East', as Bolingbroke describes him. But he submits, erratically perhaps, and riffs on his fall from grace, with lyrical self-dramatization:

Down, down I come like glistering Phaeton
Wanting the manage of unruly jades.
In the base court? Base Court where kings grow base
To come at traitors calls and do them grace.
In the base court ? Come down? Down, court! down king!
For night owls shriek where mounting larks should sing.

His abasement is then completed when he is locked in the deep dungeon of Pomfret
Castle, an oubliette, a pit of despair, where ultimately, he is murdered. It's a giddy
journey from the top of the wheel of fortune to the very bottom. In his last lines, as he
dies, he aspires once more to ascend:

Mount, mount my soul! Thy seat is up on high,
Whilst my gross flesh sinks downward, here to die.

In the design we tried to exaggerate those extremities: Flint Castle would be played on
a bridge, which could descend from the flies; with the dungeon at Pomfret, a wretched
island in a dark abyss of hollow stage.

The play begins with a tricky piece of back-story to tell. The king is implicated in the
death of his uncle, Thomas of Woodstock, the Duke of Gloucester. Woodstock is one of
the seven sons of Edward III: 'one vial full of this most sacred blood', as his widow, the
Duchess of Gloucester describes him. An audience needs to know that Richard's
original sin is that he has, at the very least, sanctioned the murder of his own uncle.

There was an untitled Elizabethan play about the duke's death usually referred to as
Thomas of Woodstock, which could just as easily be called *Richard II Part One*. We read
it in rehearsal and presented a staged reading at the Barbican during the run there. It
has a number of characters that appear in both plays, including Edward III's sons: 'old
John of Gaunt, time-honoured Lancaster' and Edmund Langley, Duke of York; as well
as Richard himself, and his hangers on, those 'caterpillars of the commonwealth': Bushy,
Bagot and Greene, and for good measure the ghosts of the king's father the Black
Prince, and his grandfather Edward III.

If the audience watching the original production of *Richard II* were also familiar
with the history of Woodstock via the earlier play, it might explain Shakespeare's rather
cautious treatment of the king's implication in the murder of his uncle. The king is
asked to arbitrate a dispute between his cousin Bolingbroke and Thomas Mowbray.
Mowbray is accused of squandering money meant for the soldiery, but more
sensationally of murdering Woodstock. Bolingbroke's father, John of Gaunt, believes
that Richard himself is responsible for killing his uncle.

The first scene of *Richard II* is fraught with tension. Did Mowbray conduct the
assassination on the orders of the king and therefore now expects protection? Will
Richard risk Mowbray spilling the beans, or will he find a way to guarantee his silence?

A visit to Westminster Hall (the setting for the abdication in the play), gave us the
inspiration for how to play the first scene. Richard himself had Westminster Hall
rebuilt with a fine hammer beam roof decorated with angels carrying the royal arms,
and his emblem the white hart. Significantly, the hall has been the location for the

lying-in-state of many notable figures, from Gladstone to Winston Churchill, and most recently then the Queen Mother in 2003.[1]

The duke's murder is the elephant in the room in the first scene of the play. We decided to heighten that tension by staging it at the funeral of Woodstock, with his body lying in state and mourned by his widow as the play begins.

Richard rules that the truth should be determined through trial by combat, in the lists at Coventry upon St Lambert's Day. We are left with the grieving Duchess faced by her brother-in-law, John of Gaunt.

I was lucky enough to land two RSC greats for this challenging but crucial scene, with Michael Pennington as Gaunt, and Jane Lapotaire as Gloucester's widow. Two years after playing Katherine of Aragon, Jane had suffered a massive cerebral haemorrhage while teaching in Paris, in 2000. This was her return to the stage, and to her RSC home.[2]

Jane portrayed the Duchess with a fierce grief, and a burning determination for revenge.

As the tournament begins, we should be aware of what a catch-22 situation this is. If Bolingbroke wins, it means Mowbray did indeed engineer the death of Woodstock, and surely Richard's involvement will be exposed. But if Mowbray wins, might the king find himself too deeply in debt?

There was a thrilling moment in rehearsal when David Tennant gave the banished Mowbray (Antony Byrne) a piercing stare as if daring him to spill the beans about the king's part in Gloucester's murder.

*   *   *

David always navigates Shakespeare's precarious line between comedy and tragedy masterfully. In *Richard II*, Shakespeare's own sympathies seem to swing between his sources.

The first two acts reflect Holinshed's[3] anti-Ricardian prejudices. The king is petulant, preening, monstrous, deliberately provocative. Take the moment, when having baited Gaunt, and provoked his uncle's scathing diatribe, he hears that the great duke has died. David gave the briefest of pious platitudes before smacking his hands together,

---

[1] Our research trip also included a trip to the National Portrait Gallery to see the Wilton Diptych, a fourteenth-century altar-piece, which shows King Richard with his three patron saints on the left panel, and the Virgin Mary surrounded by angels, all draped in gorgeous lapis lazuli, on the right. The Christ child seems to be reaching towards the kneeling Richard, and towards a pennant that one of the angels is presenting. The pennant is the cross of St George, and is surmounted with an orb. Recent cleaning of the picture has revealed a tiny image on this little globe, of a castle, a silver sea and a boat in full furl, 'a sceptred isle', as Gaunt puts it:

> ... this little world,
> This precious stone set in the silver sea.

[2] Jane wrote about her terrible ordeal and her astonishing recovery in an autobiography with the best title you could imagine: *Time Out of Mind*.

[3] Shakespeare used these chronicles of the history of England, Scotland and Ireland as the source inspiration for most of his history plays as well as *Macbeth, King Lear* and *Cymbeline*. A few months after his massive work was licensed, Raphael Holinshed retired back to the village of Bramcote, in Warwickshire, where he had served as a steward.

dismissing any tedious grief, with a 'So much for that,' and gets his minions to start carting off all Gaunt's goods, his 'plate, corn, revenues and moveables'.

The later acts are more indebted to the sympathetic French sources. David charted the slide from ruler to martyr, with painful accuracy, marking each fizz of the collapsing balloon, until he seemed as hollow as his crown.

On the battlements of Flint Castle, Richard is at his most self-absorbed, and yet most honest. 'Now mark how I will undo myself', he says, putting on one final show, somehow both inside and outside his own life.

But the greatest scene is to come, and it is all Shakespeare's own invention. The deposition scene is Richard's most dazzling performance, and his most heart-breaking. The real king never endured such a humiliation. David, in his long auburn hair, made the most of his Christlike image in this scene:

He surveyed the room:

> Yet I well remember
> The favours of these men: were they not mine?
> Did they not sometime cry, 'all hail!' to me?
> So Judas did to Christ: but he, in twelve,
> Found truth in all but one: I, in twelve thousand, none.

Richard is at his most mercurial here, mocking and self-indulgent, his wit flecked with panic, and David was almost unbearable to watch.

Richard runs rings around poor old Bolingbroke, outsmarted in what should be his own moment of triumph. Nigel Lindsay was hooded, brutal and ruthless as the man who would be king.

Bolingbroke seemed a good sort at the start of the play, dumbfounded by the extreme sentence imposed so casually upon him. But, supported by the wolfish Northumberland, it is not long before he has rounded up Richard's cronies, and is brandishing their severed heads in bloody sacks. Shakespeare always reminds us how mucky the approach to power can be.

Casting director Helena Palmer and I had a useful shorthand when auditioning for the play. Richard and his followers were the cricket team. Bolingbroke and his supporters, the rugby team.

*   *   *

I have to admit that in performance, I have frequently been baffled by the presence of the Aumerle subplot in Act Five of *Richard II*. It always seems very late in the day to add such a new twist.

One of the French sources, Jean Creton, says of Aumerle: 'There was no man in the world that Richard loved better.' Up till now, he has spent the first four acts of the play navigating the difficult minefield of political allegiance in this shifting context of power.

When the king exiles Bolingbroke at the start of the play, Aumerle accompanies him on his way, but then has to defend his action to Richard and his caterpillar lickspittles when he comes back.

Aumerle joins Richard on his journey to Ireland and is with him on his return. He is by his side for his moments of deepest self-reflection on the battlements of Flint Castle. Here his tender feelings for Richard are most apparent. And in our production led to a kiss between the two men.

Aumerle (Oliver Rix) then has to face the opposition of the lords at Westminster, before Richard's abdication. It's a scene of comic macho bravado, with a lot of slapping down of gauntlets. His loyalty to Richard feels close to his undoing.

Aumerle's father, the Duke of York, then discovers that his son is involved in an act of treason, a plot to assassinate the new King, Henry IV. His mother (Marty Cruikshank) insists that Aumerle throw himself on the King's mercy, and there follows a comic chase to get to the king, with the father determined that, despite the family connection, justice should be done, and the mother as determined to save her son. The whole tone of the play seems to have shifted to the absurd, as Henry himself declares:

Our scene is alter'd from a serious thing,
And now changed to 'The Beggar and the King'.

In the end King Henry forgives the wayward boy. But his final words seem to contain a warning, and perhaps a deeper implication:

Uncle, farewell: and, cousin too, adieu:
Your mother well hath pray'd, <u>and prove you true.</u>

How should Aumerle ensure that he prove himself true to the new regime? To what lengths might he be prepared to go to demonstrate he's been born again politically?

Then the play moves to its bleak denouement and the murder of Richard by (the hitherto unknown) Sir Piers Exton.

I had deliberately not cast Sir Piers before we started rehearsal, knowing that the role would inevitably be doubled. But as we worked through the play, he felt like a very creaky bit of plotting.

It is as if Shakespeare had been heading in a different direction entirely, and for whatever reason had drawn back from it. To make sense of the Aumerle plot, and rescue it from being a mere comic diversion, it felt as if the shady Sir Piers should actually be Aumerle. That Aumerle should demonstrate the sincerity of his newfound allegiance to his crown, and prove his undying loyalty to the unsettled Henry, by ridding him of the man he loved.

In deciding how to the frame the murder of Richard at Pomfret Castle, Shakespeare seems to be borrowing from another instance of a king despairing of a thorn in his side and requiring his closest associates to demonstrate their loyalty by taking the initiative into their own hands.

In a scene of a mere ten lines the new character of Sir Piers Exton suddenly introduces himself:

EXTON   Didst thou not mark the king, what words he spake,
         'Have I no friend will rid me of this living fear?'

                          Was it not so?
SERVANT   These were his very words.

I could only hear an echo of Henry II's cry 'Will no one rid me of this turbulent priest?' which prompted the four knights to murder Thomas à Becket in 1170. Was Shakespeare borrowing from history to link Bolingbroke to the death of Richard?

And who was Sir Piers Exton? The records seem to suggest that there was no such person, as no tax records exist for him. Maybe he is a cover. If so, Shakespeare, in writing the entire Aumerle plot, was indeed heading towards the poignant conclusion of his vacillating loyalty by killing the man he had most loved to buy his entry into the new king's affection. Why, then, did Shakespeare not go through with it?

The answer may lie in a detail that Shakespeare includes, which can seem an irrelevance, Aumerle's changing name. In Act Five Scene Two, Aumerle's mother, the Duchess of York, greets her transgressing son.

Here comes my son Aumerle ...

But her husband corrects her, promptly completing her half-line:

                                   ... Aumerle that was,
But that is lost for being Richard's friend,
And madam you must call him Rutland now.

Why, we wondered, should Shakespeare bother with a name change so late on in the play? Is it possible that he is making a deliberate connection with someone in the audience?

The title of Rutland died with Aumerle. But the earldom was re-created by Henry VIII. The Fifth Earl of Rutland, Roger Manners, was a royal ward of Queen Elizabeth. Her favourite, the Earl of Essex, threw Rutland a grand ceremony when he received his MA in February 1595, at the age of nineteen. Later that year, the earliest recorded performance of *Richard II* took place privately (on 9 December 1595), in the house of Sir Edward Hoby, in Canon Row. Hoby was the son-in-law of the Lord Chamberlain, the patron of Shakespeare's company. It is certainly possible that Rutland was part of that influential crowd. And if not he could certainly have seen the play at the theatre.

In an intriguing letter by Rowland Whyte,[4] dated 11 October 1599, we hear of Rutland's friendship with Shakespeare's patron, the Earl of Southampton:

My Lords Southampton and Rutland come not to the court, the one doth, but very seldom. They pass away the time in London merrily in going to plays every day.

---

[4] To Robert Sidney, then Governor of Flushing. Whyte was his business manager, whom he relied upon to lobby for him at court.

So, Rutland and Southampton were frequenting the Globe together within a month or so of its opening.

It must have been considered pretty incendiary to mount a play that presented the abdication of an English monarch on the public stage. And Queen Elizabeth clearly understood the connection. The antiquarian William Lambarde famously quotes her majesty as recognizing her person behind the portrayal of Richard II, complaining that the play has been played openly forty times during her reign, and saying bitterly 'I am Richard II! Know ye not that?'

Rutland's relationship with the two noble Earls of Essex and of Southampton would get him into seriously hot water, when they began the dangerous plot to overthrow the queen in 1601. As part of the build-up to the planned rebellion, the Lord Chamberlain's company were approached to mount a special performance of the play, despite it having fallen out of their repertoire.

The Quarto editions of *Richard II* published in 1597 and 1598 do not include the abdication scene.[5] It has widely been assumed that the scene was cut on the order of the master of the Revels. But might it instead have been especially written for that pre-rebellion performance, as has recently been posited? And if so, might Rutland and Southampton have cooked up the idea of getting Shakespeare's company to remount *Richard II* on the eve of Essex's rebellion to overthrow Queen Elizabeth? Might they have been the ones to have encouraged Shakespeare in the construction of the new scene? They have after all been proposed as collaborative candidates for the authorship of Shakespeare's plays. So who knows?

In his very next play, *Henry IV*, Shakespeare gets into trouble for calling the fat reprobate knight Oldcastle, and is forced to change his name to Sir John Falstaff, when a descendant of the Oldcastle family, Lord Cobham objected.

What would Roger Manners, the 5th Earl of Rutland, have made of hearing his title, even if not his direct descendant, implicated in a plot to assassinate the monarch? Particularly on the eve of such an attempt? Or would he in fact have been proud of the implied association, confident of the success of the next day's coup?

In fact, Rutland's role in the failed coup landed him in the Tower of London, and though his life was spared, for some unexplained reason, he was fined £30,000, three times more than any other prisoner. Perhaps as the authorities combed through the script of the offending play and discovered his name there, their suspicions were confirmed. All delicious speculation of course.

Whatever Shakespeare's original intentions may or may not have been, I decided we would not introduce a new character into the final scenes of the play; and so as Richard was stabbed in the back, he pulled the hood off the face of his attacker, to reveal Aumerle. His remorseful howl

For now the devil that told me I did well,
Says that this deed is chronicled in hell.

seemed a more potent betrayal in the mouth of the man who had protested his love.

---

[5] It appears in short form in the Quarto published in 1608, and its full version is only in the 1623 Folio.

I try the whole theory out on Shakespeare scholar James Shapiro, and when he watches a run of the play, and sees the ruthless internal logic of Aumerle appearing at Pomfret to kill the king, he walks across to my desk in the Clapham rehearsal room and writes on my notepad, '... if Shakespeare did not intend this, he should have done!'[6]

17 October 2013, press night.
A moving moment of theatre legacy, tonight. Actor Ian Richardson's widow, Maroussia, gave David Tennant the ring that her husband had worn when he did the play in 1973/4, famously alternating the role of Richard and Bolingbroke with Richard Pasco. It was said of Richardson's Richard that he was 'like Charles I in the first half and Jesus Christ in the second'. Ian died in 2007, and his ashes were buried in the Royal Shakespeare Theatre during its transformation. He is just in front of the stage under Row A. Patrick Stewart is reported to have said, 'Now we'll never get Ian off from downstage centre.'

Live from Stratford-upon-Avon

Perhaps the second most important decision I made becoming Artistic Director was that we would film every production and live-stream them to cinemas not only across the country but around the globe. And the man to help me achieve that would be media producer John Wyver.

I had known John since we worked together on the filming of *Macbeth* in 2000. Since then, we had attempted to get broadcaster interest in filming *All's Well That Ends Well* in 2004 (which after all had Judi Dench as the Countess, who by then had won the Oscar for her eight minutes on screen as Queen Elizabeth in *Shakespeare in Love* and her ninth BAFTA for *Mrs Brown*), but to no avail.

John and I nearly persuaded the BBC to film *Antony and Cleopatra*. We pitched an idea inspired by the 'soap opera' serialization of *Bleak House* on the BBC the previous year. We would release our version over a week in 5 episodes of 25 minutes each. Shakespeare writes in a cliff-hanger at the end of each act: Will Antony go back to Rome? What will Cleopatra do when she realizes he has married Octavia? Who will win the battle of Actium, Antony or Octavius? What will Cleopatra do now that Antony has killed himself? However, none of the broadcasters took up the idea, nor the opportunity of seeing Patrick Stewart return to his classical roots at the RSC after years trekking around the galaxies in *Star Trek*.

In 2008 when we were playing *Hamlet* in Stratford, John had introduced the idea of following the innovative example of the Met in New York, who had been live-streaming operas to cinema since the end of 2006, with the idea of becoming the first theatre production to do so. The idea was rapidly embraced by David, but others were more

---

[6] For a surprising reappearance of Aumerle, see page 260 in Chapter 26 on *Henry V*.

sceptical. The proposal eventually collapsed. Although we did then film the production for BBC Two, the National Theatre ran with the idea of streaming productions, with NT Live starting with *Phèdre* with Helen Mirren the following year (2009).

In my new role as Artistic Director, I started working with John on how to create vivid versions of the plays for a cinema audience. I wanted to capitalize on the fact that these productions would be coming live from Shakespeare's hometown. In 1959, a film had been made of Charles Laughton as Bottom in Peter Hall's production of *A Midsummer Night's Dream*, direct from the Shakespeare Memorial Theatre in Stratford-upon-Avon. It was introduced by Laughton himself, in a montage of shots of Stratford, looking in many ways much as it does today. Laughton mooches about, and rows on the Avon, before heading into his dressing room, and handing over to a very fresh-faced Peter Hall to introduce the production.

We landed on the title for our series of broadcasts: Live from Stratford-upon-Avon. We would partner with Picturehouse Entertainment (later Trafalgar Releasing); and our first broadcast was on 13 November 2013. To be successful our task would be to complete the canon.

Robin Lough (who would be screen director for over half of the Live-froms[7]) really understood the 'verticality' we were trying to achieve in the production, Richard's giddy journey from the top to the bottom of the wheel of fortune, and employed a camera crane to lift the viewer right up to the battlements of Flint Castle, and could express the hurtling descent to the depths of the dungeon in Pomfret.

As I sat in the broadcast van during that first exciting recording of *Richard II*, we received a tweet from a satisfied customer who wrote, 'really enjoying this RSC production of *Richard II* in my UCI Whiteley's Cinema, eating my chicken korma'. Well, I thought, I am glad I am not sitting next to you and your Indian takeaway, but if that's how you want to enjoy your Shakespeare, why not?

Another reaction to the screened production came from one of the grips (the people operating the crane in the filming) who went to see an encore screening and declared the result was 'gobsmackingly phenomenal'.

---

[7] Robin also directed the screen version of *The Winter's Tale* from the Barbican for Heritage Theatre in 1999.

24

Henry IV, Part One

– 2014: Royal Shakespeare Theatre, Stratford-upon-Avon;
Barbican Theatre London; and tour to Beijing, Shanghai, Hong Kong;
Brooklyn Academy of Music (BAM), New York.
– Filmed, broadcast live and available on DVD, as part of Live from
Stratford-upon-Avon.

If *Hamlet* is Shakespeare's statue of David, then the *Henry IV* plays are his Sistine Chapel. Every detail in this vast, spectacular panorama of court and city and country, each character, has been drawn with incisive care. After the great sweeping lyricism of *Richard II*, the *Henry IV* plays are a babble of voices, some raucous, some refined.

I did *Henry IV Part One* for O-Level at the Preston Catholic College. Many people who have studied a particular Shakespeare play in detail at school harbour fond memories of it for the rest of their lives (others distinctly do not), but I fell head-over-heels for it. My mate Richard and I hitchhiked to Stratford to see the two plays in 1975, in Terry Hands's production with Brewster Mason and Alan Howard. But due to some schoolboy oversight we managed to see *Part One* twice.

What I knew from that production, if nothing else, was that you needed a marvellous ensemble to play it.

*   *   *

In the last scene of *Richard II*, Bolingbroke, now crowned Henry IV, laments the death of the man whose throne he has usurped:

I'll make a voyage to the Holy Land,
To wash this blood off from my guilty hand

At the start of *Henry IV Part One*, the King, now that the civil wars are over, still intends to keep that promise, announcing a crusade to Jerusalem:

Therefore, friends,
As far as to the sepulchre of Christ,
Whose soldier now, under whose blessed cross
We are impressed and engaged to fight,
Forthwith a power of English shall we levy.

But he makes no mention of expiation for the regicide in which he is implicated; now the purpose of the voyage is:

> To chase these pagans in those holy fields
> Over whose acres walk'd those blessed feet
> Which fourteen hundred years ago were nail'd
> For our advantage on the bitter cross.

Two hundred years before Henry ascended the throne, crusaders had indeed chased 'these pagans' out of the Holy City, capturing Jerusalem and seizing the *Templum Domini*, the name attributed by the Crusaders to the Dome of the Rock, the site of the Temple of Solomon. The Knights Templar regarded their mission as the protection of that holy site and located their headquarters nearby in the Al-Aqsa Mosque.

I had once had occasion to visit this holiest of sites, on a flying visit to Jerusalem. Tony's father had passed away suddenly while his parents were attending a family funeral in Israel, and we flew out to be with his mother. On the Saturday, the Jewish family were all sitting shiva. As we were not first-degree relatives and were not required or expected to participate in this mourning ceremony, Tony's mother urged us, as we were only going to be in Israel for the weekend (I had to be back in rehearsal on the Monday morning), to go and do some sightseeing.

We decided to take a taxi to Jerusalem and visit some of the holy places. The taxi driver took a look at the two of us and said, 'Christian or Jewish?' 'Both,' we replied. 'So which holy places?'

'All of them,' I said, realizing afterwards that we might be in for quite a long day. So we visited Temple Mount, and the Wailing Wall, and there was a moment in his fairly hectic zip round the ancient city that we found ourselves actually reversing up the Via Dolorosa.

I think my most moving memory was a visit to the Church of the Holy Sepulchre, containing two of the holiest sites in Christendom: *Calvary* (or *Golgotha*, the place of the skull), where Christ was crucified, and *the tomb* where he was buried and from which he rose again. The church was crushed with pilgrims. It was very difficult to see anything among the clouds of incense, but my abiding image was of candles, devotional candles being lit and carried. Their light glinted on the gilded lamps which hung in a circle above our heads, echoing the shape of the church built around the tomb.

The circular construction of this church became the architectural model for the Templar churches all over Europe. The Temple Church in the City of London is one such. The Round Church, as it is known, was constructed by the Knights Templar as their headquarters in England and was built to be London's Jerusalem. And Jerusalem to the mediaeval mind (and according to the guide to the Temple Church) was the centre of the world. To be in the Round Church was to be in Jerusalem.

I took Jasper Britton (who would be playing King Henry) to visit it during our early rehearsals.

The entrance to the Temple Church is hidden away behind the bustle of Fleet Street. The church is quiet as we enter. There may be nothing of the fervent urgency of the pilgrims in its original in Jerusalem, but it is a prayerful place. The curving walls are built of honey-coloured Caen stone and lined with gothic arches. We are drawn to the centre, the ring of dark grey Purbeck marble pillars that lead upward, their shafts supporting a triforium of interlacing semi-circular arches. The light is a cold grey London light, not the hot sunlight of the Holy Land, but nevertheless it seems to lift your thoughts upward like prayer.

There are nine stone effigies of knights in armour on the floor. Though none of them were Templar knights, some have their legs crossed, which may indicate they went on crusade.

In our play, Henry IV is wracked with guilt, and his prayers to journey to Jerusalem are fervent. However, news that rebellion is stirring among his subjects forces him almost immediately to abandon his plans.

Our visit to the Temple Church gives Jasper and me a very real sense of the pull of the Holy Land on the minds of the men of the mediaeval period, and the sense that Henry's ambition combines both pilgrimage and crusade, in what he believes is his divinely sanctioned Christian duty to protect Jerusalem.

Designer Stephen Brimson Lewis wonders if there is a way of echoing the shape of the church for the scenes in which King Henry appears. For the first scene in particular, in which Henry expresses desire for the crusade, and especially for the challenging scene in Act Three where father and son encounter each other for the first time in the play. Henry berates Hal with his behaviour and taunts him with the example presented by Hotspur's bravery. I tell Stephen about my memory of gilded hanging lanterns in the church covering Christ's tomb.

Our next stop takes us to the other end of King Henry's journey. The Very Reverend John Hall, the Dean of Westminster, has agreed to take the *Henry IV* company on a bespoke guided tour around the Abbey, and at the end he accompanies us to a very special place.

It's a chamber in what was the Abbot's house, dating back to the reign of Richard II, and his initial 'R' is painted on the original timbers of the ceiling. The room is lined with linen-fold panelling made of cedar wood brought back from Lebanon, and tapestries that are sixteenth-century French. It was here, in 1413, that Henry was brought, when he became ill while praying at St Edward's shrine in the Abbey. It's thought he had a stroke. He was laid in front of the fire. When he recovered consciousness, he asked where he was and was told the name of the room: Jerusalem.

Shakespeare makes these King Henry's final words:

It hath been prophesied to me many years,
I should not die but in Jerusalem;
Which vainly I supposed the Holy Land:
But bear me to that chamber; there I'll lie;
In that Jerusalem shall Harry die.

As Jasper quietly takes in the chamber, he lifts his head to look at the initial of Richard II on the beams above. 'So if the dying King Henry was lying here in front of the fire,' he says, 'the last thing he would have seen when he looked up would have been the insignia of Richard II, the man who had haunted his entire reign!'

There is a plaster bust of Henry in the Jerusalem chamber, copied from the effigy on his tomb in Canterbury Cathedral. Jasper poses for a photograph beneath it. On the other side of room is a bust of Henry's son, Prince Hal.

*   *   *

After the huge 'Transformation' project of rebuilding the Royal Shakespeare Theatre, Michael Boyd decided he would open the RST with *Macbeth*, and I was charged with the reopening of the Swan. I had been working for some time on Shakespeare's 'lost' play *Cardenio*, and the tantalizing possibility that a remnant of it might be extant in *Double Falsehood*, as presented by Lewis Theobald in 1723.[1] The story is based on an episode in Cervantes' *Don Quixote*. It seemed like the ideal project, as the Swan was originally dedicated to Shakespeare's contemporaries, and related apocrypha. We reopened the Swan with *Cardenio* in April 2011.

The villain of the piece is the aristocratic Andalusian libertine, Fernando. He was played in our production with Machiavellian panache by Alex Hassell. Alex, who is co-founder of the experimental Factory Theatre Company, has a wonderful anarchic energy on stage, balanced with a passionate rigour about Shakespeare's text. Apart from being dashingly handsome, with chiselled good looks and enormous expressive eyes, he has an unquenchable grin, and an infectious laugh that never seems far from his lips. I thought he had exactly the charisma needed to play Prince Hal and asked him to come on the journey with us right through to *Henry V*. I was very pleased that he said 'yes'.

We cast actor Trevor White as Hal's nemesis, Hotspur.

I believe Hotspur is one of Shakespeare's great creations. However, he shares this play with Shakespeare's greatest, Falstaff, so perhaps Hotspur's brilliance has been overshadowed.

The moment Hotspur appears he opens his mouth and out comes a speech of over forty lines. It's made up of only three sentences. The first sentence, describing the popinjay who appeared on the battlefield at Holmedon demanding his prisoners, takes up all but two lines of one whole page in the 1598 quarto. Hotspur hardly draws breath. (It's a very familiar audition speech choice.)

Worcester promises to reveal his secret plan. Its execution will be dangerous, or as he puts it:

> As full of peril and adventurous spirit
> As to o'er-walk a current roaring loud
> On the unsteadfast footing of a spear.

A tightrope over a torrent: one of those utterly arresting images with which Shakespeare surprises us. It thrills Hotspur. It gets his own imagination going. He picks up party games like this very quickly, which tests his father's patience.

---

[1] I wrote about our experience of reimagining Cardenio in *Shakespeare's Lost Play: In Search of Cardenio*, Nick Hern Books (2012).

By heaven, methinks it were an easy leap,
To pluck bright honour from the pale-faced moon,
Or dive into the bottom of the deep,
Where fathom-line could never touch the ground,
And pluck up drowned honour by the locks . . .'

Uncle Worcester bewails his nephew's spiralling imagination, and congenital lack of focus:

He apprehends a world of figures here,
But not the form of what he should attend.

As we work through the scenes, Trevor notes how Hotspur's mind seems like that of a hyperactive impulsive child with an attention deficit disorder. He is also volatile, prone to sudden angry outbursts when he thinks he is being crossed, or deliberately misunderstood, with delusions of his own victimization.

Why, look you, I am whipp'd and scourged with rods,
Nettled and stung with pismires, when I hear
Of this vile politician, Bolingbroke.

And just as suddenly he swings to a mood of the giddy excitement of a child anticipating Christmas as Worcester reveals his rebellion plans and Hotspur cannot wait for the physical thrill of the battlefield:

O, let the hours be short
Till fields and blows and groans applaud our sport!

Shakespeare leaves us with a sense of anxiety that such a dangerous plot, relying on secrecy, should depend on such a wild card as Hotspur.

Trevor and I explored our conviction that Hotspur was frankly unstable, and exciting possibilities began to occur. How much further could we push this?

Our next sight of Hotspur is in the scene with his wife Lady Percy (Kate), back in Northumberland. He is arguing with a letter. One of the allies has refused to join up. And he works himself into a furious prose lather, and decides to set out straight away, only to be interrupted by his wife. Her rational plea to her husband is delivered in calm verse. Though she frequently invites him to respond, with direct questions, he avoids her gaze and does not reply.

Instead, he calls his staff and asks questions of them, a rattling exchange about arrangements and deliveries, and preparations for his immediate departure. Kate asks why he is leaving: 'What is it carries you away?' Hotspur's answer, 'Why, my horse, my love, my horse', is usually played as a clever evasion, where he ducks the issue with a deliberate joke. But following through our growing sense that Hotspur may be on the autistic spectrum, Trevor answered his wife's question literally, with no wink or smile.

Lady Percy tries a number of different tactics to get an answer out of her husband, even threatening to break his little finger. In rehearsal, Jennifer Kirby as Kate tried to tease Hotspur into submission only suddenly and violently to be thrown to the ground, as if the petulant child-man was abruptly halting the game-playing, and instead resorts to bullying, insisting he does not love her.

The scene explores the deep complexity of a loving couple: she, fearfully aware of her husband's impulsiveness, yet enduring his mood swings with patience; he, unable to lie to the only woman he trusts in the world.

The volatility of their relationship is tested even further in the great Welsh scene. And further evidence emerges that in writing Hotspur, Shakespeare may have been aware of the traits of a high-functioning autistic character long before they were clinically described as such.

We are introduced to Owen Glendower, one of those roles that is unforgettable despite only appearing in one scene. Joshua Richards, in a quick change from playing Bardolph, plays the Welsh Wizard. Although based in Yorkshire for most of his life Josh has the rich lilting baritone of his native Wales, and brings to Glendower an immediate sense of high status and self-belief as he says:

> At my nativity
> The front of heaven was full of fiery shapes,
> Of burning cressets; and at my birth
> The frame and huge foundation of the earth
> Shaked like a coward.

Hotspur, disregarding the fact that Glendower is his host, and he is a guest on Welsh soil, makes no concession for his elder's claims that his birth had supernatural repercussions, and disputes it. Not in snide little asides but in open contradiction. Something you feel Glendower has never experienced before, and it prompts him to further extravagant mythology, my favourite example being:

> The goats ran from the mountains, and the herds
> Were strangely clamorous to the frighted fields.

The tone here is quite a subtle one to achieve, because although Hotspur's apparent rudeness is breathtaking, and Glendower's postulations pompous and preposterous, both men are there to make a deal, which adds extra tension to the scene.

Shakespeare is clever to couch what might have been a dry scene about the business of war, in the context of two such contrasting characters: one flamboyant, the other hot-headed and resolutely literal. He brings their contention to a head over the map, and the proposed division of the country. Hotspur says that in order to make his portion fairer, he will have a river moved. Glendower will not allow it, prompting a racist comment from Hotspur.

HOTSPUR   Who shall say me nay?
GLENDOWER   Why, that will I.
HOTSPUR   Let me not understand you, then; speak it in Welsh.

It's a crossroads. Whatever happens next will determine the nature and success of this potential alliance. Will the Welsh Wizard explode? He has kept his dignity admirably until now, in the face of the young man's impoliteness.

Glendower calmly reminds Hotspur that he was brought up in the English court, and cannot only speak the language as well as Hotspur, but while there:

> I framed to the harp
> Many an English ditty lovely well.

A skill he doubts Hotspur has, and which Hotspur quickly agrees with, tellingly revealing his aversion to poetry.

> I had rather hear a brazen candlestick turn'd,
> Or a dry wheel grate on the axle-tree;
> And that would set my teeth nothing on edge,
> Nothing so much as mincing poetry:
> 'Tis like the forced gait of a shuffling nag.

Shakespeare writing a speech about hating poetry – what a delight – and delivering it with such expertly clashing consonants and rhythms, conjuring the clumsy tension in the haltering clip-clop of an old mule being urged to go faster. His philistinism is so unapologetic it makes Glendower laugh and he relents. The situation is saved. Hotspur hilariously defines his aversion to Glendower's 'skimble-skamble stuff' in an image of wild absurdity:

> I had rather live
> With cheese and garlic in a windmill, far,
> Than feed on cates and have him talk to me
> In any summer-house in Christendom.

We next meet Hotspur at Shrewsbury, where the rebel forces are preparing for battle. Hotspur's father Northumberland has sent word he is sick and cannot support him, which Hotspur says, 'in such a rustling time' is 'a very limb lopp'd off'. Vernon warns Hotspur not to engage before they are ready. Some of their reinforcements have only just arrived.[2] Then we hear the king is on his way, followed by Hotspur's chief adversary, the Prince of Wales. Ricocheting from gloom to giddy optimism, Hotspur launches his rallying cry: 'Doomsday is near; die all, die merrily!'

In Act Five, Hotspur and Hal finally meet. Action man meets the reluctant prince. Their differences will be tested in their climactic duel. As the battle swings this way and that, and King Henry has several decoys dressed in his own armour, and Falstaff flits nimbly between the canon shots, Hotspur and Hal finally come face to face. 'Two stars

---

[2]   Vernon has the line, 'Your uncle Worcester's horse came but today.' I point out to Jim Hooper, playing Vernon, that if delivered too quickly, the line risks sounding dangerously like a bit of Shakespearean product placement: 'Uncle Worcester Sauce'.

keep not their motion in one sphere' says Hal, the Shakespearian equivalent of 'This town ain't big enough for both of us.'

In the script you are given very little to work on. It simply says '*They fight*'. And then '*Hotspur is wounded and falls*'.

As Trevor White and Alex Hassell prepared for this pivotal fight, we chatted through the narrative very carefully with Terry King, who produced, I believe, one of his very best duels, in this production.

We decided that it was not necessarily an even fight. Hotspur is, after all, a seasoned fighter. Hal, after the late-night excesses of the Boar's Head Tavern, is probably not even in very good shape. Hotspur relishes the sphere of combat. He is in his element here.

There was a thrilling moment when the company saw the hair-raising fight for the first time, on stage, with Paul Englishby's very precise, gripping underscore. Trevor White had by now dyed his hair a Nordic blonde. With his ice-blue eyes and armed with two swords he seemed a maniacal if not invincible opponent. Alex, as Hal, to begin with seemed overwhelmed by the superior skill of the young rebel, and less confident in his own cause. Hal lost a sword but grew in anger. As the fight progressed and got faster and faster, the tables turned and suddenly Hal dealt the blow that would bring Hotspur down.

The fight had been invented, refined, then drilled rigorously for eight weeks for the very start of rehearsals. The actors delivered it with extraordinary skill, alacrity and speed. It looked really dangerous. That is the technique; the art is covering up that technique.

As Hotspur falls, he proves as pragmatic about 'brittle' life as he is fearless of death, as disdainful of intellect and thought, as he is impulsive for action. His brutal philosophy is dismissive and stoical:

> But thought's the slave of life, and life time's fool;
> And time, that takes survey of all the world,
> Must have a stop,

When Olivier played Hotspur, he famously had a stutter. So that his last prophesy

> ... No Percy thou art dust and
> Food for w-w-w ...

was completed by Hal:

> ... For worms brave Percy.

It is in fact only later in *Part Two* where we learn anything of a potential speech impediment in Hotspur, in the scene where his widow Lady Percy tells his father that he was so admired by his troops that they would imitate his impediment, which she calls 'speaking thick'. It is a fine epitaph to remind us of an extraordinary man made more so in Shakespeare's vivid portrait of his imperfections:

> He was the mark and glass, copy and book,
> That fashion'd others.

*   *   *

One of the great joys of *Henry IV Part One* is the juxtaposition of entirely different worlds, and the juggling of contrasting storylines. It's a soundscape of colours and voices, piecing together a fabulously textured patchwork of England.

The court scenes of Act One have hurled us into a vortex of fermenting cross-border rebellion, and suddenly, at the start of Act Two, we are at a very seedy inn on the Rochester road. Instead of talk of the calamitous national crisis, two carriers are discussing how much the establishment has gone downhill recently.

As I read it, and as we begin to rehearse it, I can't help imagining Shakespeare overhearing exactly this conversation, and committing their speech patterns and phraseology to memory, like Alan Bennett on top of a bus in Leeds, eavesdropping on a pair of old dears gossiping, and jotting it down for future use,

SECOND CARRIER   This house is turned upside down since Robin Ostler died.
FIRST CARRIER   Poor fellow, never joyed since the price of oats rose; it was the death of him.

They are in the stable yard setting out, in the early hours, to carry their wares to market in London, and waiting for the ostler to bring out their horses. They complain about the poor fodder, the fleas ('I think this be the most villainous house in all London road for fleas: I am stung like a tench').

They sound like a pair of sales reps discussing Travelodges on the A2, but having set the scene, the carriers are spooked by the arrival of a lowlife highway robber. He has a deal with the chamberlain of the inn, who gives him information about the travellers using his premises, in return for a cut of his takings. He is called Gadshill.[3]

Matisse once said that a good sketch should be fast enough to capture a man falling out of a window, before he hits the ground. Gadshill is only a thumbnail sketch of a character, a vocal one, but is vivid, nevertheless. He has shreds of menace about him, assumes an air of tatty mystery, and speaks like no one else in the play. He has an extravagance, which is as pretentious as it is beguiling.

Poins calls him their 'setter', which might suggest 'fixer', or possibly the function the gun dog fills in hunting, silently seeking out the game and then freezing in a 'set' when it is spotted. He is delighted to find himself part of the troop that Poins has arranged to entertain Prince Hal, and fool Falstaff. Being elevated into such company, Gadshill pours scorn on his own class of petty thievery that he thinks he may temporarily have risen above:

I am joined with no foot-land rakers, no long-staff sixpenny strikers, none of these mad mustachio purple-hued malt-worms.

Don't worry about diving for editors' notes, or dramaturgical help with rewrites, just listen to the music. He talks as if he might be high. And indeed, that is exactly what he is. As he brags:

---

[3]   Rather confusingly as that is the name of the rendezvous chosen by Poins to meet up with Falstaff and his cronies. We renamed him Rakehell.

We have the receipt of fern-seed, we walk invisible.

A fantasy the no-nonsense chamberlain quickly punctures:

Nay, by my faith, I think you are more beholding to the night than to fern-seed for your walking invisible.

Gadshill has very little else to say in the play, and dutifully fulfils his role in the robbery, and is part of the fall out as the story is relayed and relived back in the tavern. But Shakespeare has carefully created Gadshill, to lay out the territory. Jonny Glynn seized every hint the text gives to develop a completely recognizable shady creature, a druggy weirdo, who in seconds you would cross the street to avoid.

Gadshill may only be a tiny patch in this great quilt of a play, but he provides a colour that sets off the pattern.

*   *   *

Now, you will have noticed that I have said almost nothing of the most famous character in the play, that primal urge, that life force, that assertion of everything it is to be human, that gross embodiment of appetite and desire, the irresistible 'Hill of Flesh', Jack Falstaff.

Well, to begin with, I just couldn't find him.

The search was getting desperate. I had already asked some of our most distinguished actors. Derek Jacobi had politely declined. 'It's just not my part, Greg,' he apologized, 'I saw Richardson do it, and can't get him out of my head.'[4]

In early 2012, I was sitting despondently, gazing down into the quad of Brasenose College in Oxford. I had been invited to be the Humanitas Visiting Professor in Drama. In between lectures, I had scuttled back to my little room to await yet another call. The phone rang. It was Ian McKellen calling to say that he was delighted to be asked and had wondered for a while about playing him being in love with Hal, but had finally decided the part just wasn't his. Then he said to me, 'But Greg, why are you looking for Falstaff when you are living with him?'

Ian had just been to see Tony in Nicky Wright's play *Travelling Light* at the NT. It opened at the Lyttelton in January 2012. The play took place in a remote Eastern European shtetl and was a tribute to those immigrants who left to become major players in Hollywood's golden age.

Tony was giving a magnetic performance as Jacob Bindel, an ebullient timber-merchant. He's a cross between Tevye in *Fiddler on the Roof*, and Zorba the Greek. Jacob, with his wily peasant guile, encourages a young man's passion for cinematography. One of the critics claimed, 'It is one of those performances in which the actor seems to have expanded to twice his usual size.'

Tony finally agreed to play Sir John, having never considered himself in the role, and went on to give one of the performances of his life. He wrote about it definitively in *Year of the Fat Knight*. So, I will say very little here.

---

[4] Ralph Richardson said of Falstaff that he 'proceeds at his own pace, like a gorgeous ceremonial Indian elephant'.

It is perhaps worth noting that Tony was the first actor to play Sir John Falstaff in China. Audiences in the West might well be familiar with this character, who long ago burst beyond the confines of the plays in which he appears. But when we took the *Henry IV* and *Henry V* plays to Beijing in 2016, under the banner title *King and Country*, the Chinese audiences had never seen them before, and knew nothing of the roguish knight.

I remember our first night at the National Centre for the Performing Arts, known as 'The Egg'.

It was a packed house, with a balance of women and men, of all age groups, with lots of young people. They were quiet in the first scenes. I wasn't sure if the surtitles had caught the play's wit. Or if they were keeping time with the dialogue. I needn't have worried.

Hotspur, the hot-headed action man, broke the ice first. Forbidden by the king even to mention the name of the rebel Mortimer, he swears he will teach a starling to say nothing but Mortimer and give it to the king to squawk it at him day and night. Laughter. Recognition of the absurdity, of the imaginative brain of the motormouth Harry Hotspur.

Laughter: at the Gadshill plot, where Falstaff and his henchmen decide to play highwaymen and rob travellers on the London road, only to be hijacked in turn by the dissolute playboy Prince Hal, and his mate Poins.

And then in the tavern scene as Falstaff exaggerates his bravery to the prince, pretending he fought off assailants in ever increasing numbers: great waves of laughter from our Chinese audience.

Despite any perceived language or cultural barriers, they got it ... they got Shakespeare. I became quite emotional.

I hoped that they might respond to the great epic sweep of dynastic rivalry, of deposition, followed by conspiracy and rebellion. And they did: seeing in Prince Hal's tempestuous relationship with the king a common truth about fathers and sons. They recognized Shakespeare's insight that wars are often fought for individual, personal agendas as much as for national ones. And they particularly seemed to enjoy the political out-manoeuvrings, conspiracies and serial back-stabbings. Chinese TV is filled with such historical pageants.

They loved the laconic, malmsey-nosed Bardolph, and the garrulous pint-pot hostess, Mrs Quickly. They even warmed to the maniacal Pistol with his Tourette's outpouring of incomprehensible fustian.

But they adored Falstaff. It was as if that deliciously wicked, disreputable charlatan had always been there in the Chinese psyche, as if he was one of the most ancient of Chinese folk characters.

At the end of the Battle of Shrewsbury, after Prince Hal defeats Hotspur in a duel, Sir John tries to take the credit for killing him to Prince Hal's face. When that venal, mendacious scoundrel declares 'Lord, Lord, how the world is given to lying', the audience got the laugh even before the punchline had landed. Well of course. The world *is* given to lying, wherever you are in it.

But there is a sort of universalizing dogma about Shakespeare: that he is indisputably, unquestionably, the world's greatest writer. And to suggest otherwise is some sort of dangerous heresy. And I admit I have been suspicious of this claim, as a bit of Great British propaganda. But that first night in Beijing was evidence, living proof of his genius unfolding before my very ears and eyes.

In truth it would seem Shakespeare has become fashionable in China. Premier Wen Jiabao had started his visit to the UK in 2011 by visiting Stratford-upon-Avon. The previous autumn, President Xi Jinping had been presented with a copy of Shakespeare's Sonnets by the Queen. Brush up your Shashibiya[5] and it's an index of just how outward-looking and open-minded you are, proof of your cultural awareness, a lifestyle credential. We just did not know if that would translate into actually enjoying watching his plays in performance, and in English.

When Tony and I were doing *Titus Andronicus* in South Africa, Sello Maake Ka-N'cube, playing Aaron the Moor, challenged me about Shakespeare:

'Greg,' he said, 'you told me Shakespeare was English!'
'Yea,' I muttered, 'I think that's indisputable.'
'Uh-ha!' said Sello, 'Shakespeare is Zulu!'

On our first night in Beijing, Falstaff proved that Shakespeare is also Chinese.

---

[5] Shashibiya is the generally accepted transliteration of Shakespeare in Mandarin Chinese since the 1920s.

25

Henry IV, Part Two

– 2014: Royal Shakespeare Theatre, Stratford-upon-Avon;
Barbican Theatre London; and tour to Beijing, Shanghai, Hong Kong;
Brooklyn Academy of Music (BAM), New York.
– Filmed, broadcast live and available of DVD, as part of Live from
Stratford-upon-Avon.

Did Shakespeare set out to write two plays about Henry IV? Or did the first prove such a 'get-penny', so successful at the box office, that a second instalment was demanded? Was the first play originally advertised as *The History of Henry IV*, as the first Quarto suggests, or *Part One of the History of Henry IV*? Somewhere during the plotting of a play about Henry, did Shakespeare decide that he wanted to take the history right the way through to the reign of Henry V, and that he had enough material for two plays on the reign of Henry IV, or did Falstaff just demand to swagger out onto the stage for a second time?

During rehearsals of *Part Two*, I frequently changed my mind on this issue. There is a danger with sequels, that they simply run out of steam and are not as good as the first, though there are honourable exceptions.

In *Part One* you have the northern rebellion of Hotspur and the Percies, interwoven with the glorious Gadshill robbery, and the exposé of Falstaff's lies in the unsurpassable tavern scene. Then the reconciliation of the king with his errant son, prepared for in the improvisation between Hal and Falstaff standing in for the king, with a cushion on his head instead of a crown. And finally, the encounter between the rebels and the king's forces, Hotspur and Hal. Falstaff has even had a death scene, but his life force proves indomitable and resists it.

In *Part Two*, Shakespeare follows a similar template. Its major focus is the journey of Hal towards kingship, with almost entirely separate improvisations on Falstaff, as he ages and tries to avoid consideration of his end. There is a definite cultish cognoscenti who insist on their preference for *Part Two*. To be sure, its mood becomes elegiac, its tone autumnal, Chekhovian almost, and its conclusion heart-breaking. It is certainly, in my experience, a much harder play to do.

The play is introduced by Rumour, a chorus who proclaims a theme: fake news. He recaps the plot so far but declares that his business is to spread disinformation abroad that Harry Monmouth (Hal), not Harry Hotspur, fell at the Battle of Shrewsbury.

Hotspur's father, who failed to support his son in battle, is hiding 'crafty-sick' back at home in Northumberland. Lord Bardolph arrives to tell him that the rebels are victorious. But he is swiftly followed by a messenger with the true facts, confirmed by another. The sight of a father being told his son is alive, when we the audience know it not to be true, is painful, making the news when it comes even more wounding. Northumberland's agony roots the play and plunges us back into the fray.

But now we want to know about Falstaff. And here he is. Shakespeare does not disappoint our expectation from the very first image we see. Sir John's huge bulk seems even greater next to the diminutive page he has inherited from the Prince of Wales. 'I do here walk before thee' says Falstaff, 'like a sow that hath overwhelmed all her litter but one'. We cast the smallest boys we could as the page and gave Tony Cuban heels to his boots.

Falstaff's first words are about his bodily functions, about piss. He has had the page check out his bowel movements with the doctor. This not only reminds us of the fleshly priorities of Falstaff but hints at his vulnerability. And the vital element that he seems to breathe but also to supply: laughter:

I am not only witty in myself, but the cause that wit is in other men.

His first encounter is with the Lord Chief Justice. Apparently, the prince has been arrested for striking the Lord Chief Justice and has even been (briefly) committed to prison. In rehearsals, we found it rather puzzling that such a huge plot point should be dropped in so casually. It sets Falstaff in opposition with the highest judge in the land, the equivalent to the head of the Supreme Court today.

He is a man of principle, who fears the influence Falstaff has on the heir apparent. Later in the play his importance will be fortified when he refuses to flatter his new monarch by speaking well of the fat knight and is rewarded for his honesty and courage in doing so. He not only keeps his place as Lord Chief Justice in the new reign, but is promoted to the position of the king's advisor. Thus, right at the start of the play, though we do not yet appreciate it, we are being introduced to Falstaff's nemesis.

Falstaff tries to change the subject and discuss the poor health of the king; and argues that he is essentially still a young man himself despite all appearance of age and 'only old in judgment and understanding'. In fact, he generally runs rings around his eminent lordship, pretending he is deaf and then, in the most graciously rude way possible, telling the Lord Chief Justice:

It is the disease of not listening, the malady of not marking, that I am troubled withal.

The Lord Chief Justice calls Falstaff Prince Hal's 'ill angel'. If so, he, on the opposite shoulder, will represent the prince's good angel, and as such Shakespeare is careful that Falstaff does not make a total fool of him here.

But this new surprising plot point about the arrest of the Prince of Wales is clearly key to the story of the prince's developing sense of responsibility. Falstaff refers to it again:

For the box of the ear that the prince gave you, he gave it like a rude prince, and you took it like a sensible lord. I have checked him for it, and the young lion repents.

All settled then.

The incident of the slap is dramatized in an anonymous play called *The Famous Victories of Henry V*. It was performed by the Queen's Men, a company of actors formed at the express command of Elizabeth I in 1583. It tells the whole story of Prince Hal, from riotous youth to hero of Agincourt. Early in rehearsal, I asked my assistant director, Owen Horsley, to present us with a reading of the play, by some of the younger members of the company.

It begins with a Gadshill-style robbery, after which the prince and his companions meet up with Jocky Oldcastle (the prototype for Falstaff). Surprisingly enough a substantial and pivotal part of the plot then revolves around the Lord Chief Justice investigating the theft. He puts out a warrant for the prince's arrest, and even justifies his actions before the king who calls for his son to explain himself. When the prince is released, he seeks out the Lord Chief Justice, demands he release one of his companions, and when his lordship refuses to do so, Prince Henry assaults him.

Some academics suggest that this contention between the Lord Chief Justice and Prince Hal would have been so well known to Shakespeare's audience that a mere reference to the incident would immediately be understood. That may be so. But not to the audience we were preparing to play to.

Watching the younger members of our company perform *The Famous Victories* gave us all a clear sense of some of the structural choices that Shakespeare had made if indeed he used the play as a loose basis for his trilogy of plays about Hal/Henry V. In fact, we enjoyed the play's condensation of the action so much, I commissioned Owen Horsley to create a version of the play (following the Queen's Men structure but with Shakespeare's lines) as our First Encounter project with our Education department to tour schools during the run.

But this little rehearsal room exercise inspired another idea. Why not lift the encounter with the Lord Chief Justice from *Famous Victories* and insert it at the end of the tavern scene in *Henry IV Part One*? At the end of the little 'play-within-a-play', Mrs Quickly announces the arrival of the Sheriff 'and a monstrous watch'.

It's a late-night police raid. The sheriff is accompanied by one of the carriers who were robbed at Gadshill, and they intend to search the house for the stolen money. As Falstaff disappears to hide (and snooze) behind the arras, and the sheriff enters, we insert the ominous and unexpected arrival of the Chief Justice as well. As he demands the arrest of Bardolph (and Bardolph tries to resist, assisted by Hal), there is a scuffle, and the Lord Chief Justice is suddenly slapped in the face.

It was neatly sliced in, and I doubt many noticed its inclusion, or suspected its authorship, as we lifted the lines directly from the source play.

'Very John Barton!' someone commented, which I took as a compliment.

*   *   *

But rebellion is brewing once again. Now we are introduced to the Archbishop of York who 'Turns insurrection to religion', to heal 'a bleeding land / Gasping for life under great Bolingbroke'.

The toughest strand of *Part Two* to direct and to play is the second insurgency against the king, led by the Archbishop of York. It can't match the characters who motored the uprising in *Part One*. No Hotspur, no Glendower. And Northumberland is still dilly-dallying about his participation.

But having sketched in the threat from York, Shakespeare brings back another favourite, in the person of Mrs Quickly. She is about to have Falstaff arrested. Having heard Sir John is to join with the King's forces, she worries that she will not be repaid the money he owes her.

It is a bit like a sitcom. You get brownie points just for coming on stage and the audience recognizing you and investing their love in you. This scene is a case in point. It's a joy to see Falstaff and Quickly together again, but as Tony says, the material isn't nearly as good.

I struggle with the scene. Fang and Snare clearly have some physical comedy to deliver, and huge Youssef Kerkour looks great as Snare, alongside wiry young Martin Bassindale as Fang. And movement director Mike Ashcroft (who has come to my rescue many a time and oft) invents some business with twirling Bruce Lee-style Nunchaku batons. But somehow the whole thing feels strenuous.

Tony has a sense that he can use the inferior detail to Falstaff's advantage, as if it demonstrates the air going out of his tyres. But then Shakespeare delivers one of Quickly's most extravagant streams of consciousness, with their endless tangents and diversions. She reminds Sir John of his promise to marry her, by summoning up the experience, the location, the exact date, the circumstances and the sequence of events, all in such minute and precise and irrelevant detail, that you know the memory is indelibly imprinted on her poor soul. And Paola Dionisotti delivers it with such honesty, with such sensitivity, never for a moment playing for a laugh, that suddenly what seemed strenuous now seems effortless.

Falstaff has one of his best laughs as he tries to shock the Lord Chief Justice by saying that Quickly has been telling everyone her eldest son looks like him. He tells Sir John to pay the money he owes Quickly and instead, in a sadly tender exchange, Falstaff manages to persuade her to lend him even more money. Despite the fact she may have to pawn her pewter plate, her tapestries and even her own gown, Mrs Quickly ends the scene happy with the assurance that she has secured her fat suitor's promise to come to supper. Indeed, she is so delighted with what she has convinced herself is a victory, that she suggests she lay on a prostitute, one of his favourites, Doll Tearsheet.

The prince now makes his late entrance into the play in a rather tetchy little scene with Poins. Alex Hassell and Sam Marks noted in playing the scene that the fun they had as mates despite their unequal rank, in *Part One*, was absent from this scene. Our job in rehearsal was to unravel what might lie behind this deceptively inconsequential exchange.

The action of the scene is slight. We chose to set it in court where the men have just finished a tennis match (there is talk of the tennis court keeper, and where to keep a racket). It is important to understand that, though bored, Hal has not returned to his old ways in Eastcheap. The prince, despite himself, is worried about his father's health. He needs cheering up. Bardolph and the little page (nicely described as an 'upright rabbit') bring a letter from Falstaff, which prompts them to go and surprise him at his dinner with Doll Tearsheet.

The friendship between the prince and Poins, like so much in the play, seems to be unravelling. Poins's very existence depends on the prince, and yet if Hal's father dies, it is unlikely that the heir apparent would continue to employ his old drinking buddy.

Hal never asked to be the Prince of Wales. He was not born to it, nor expected to be in such a position. It is only his father's actions in seizing the crown from his cousin Richard II that has propelled Hal into this responsibility. But his growing sadness about his father's illness seems to parallel a development in that sense of duty.

His banter with Poins has a dark undertow. Poins thinks any show of remorse or sorrow on the prince's part would be read as hypocrisy in the prince, because of his association with the disreputable fat knight. When Hal suggests that bad company would include Poins, his friend bridles. His only crime is being a second brother, i.e., having some social standing, but no inheritance to rely on.

But Falstaff's letter casually accuses Poins of other ambitions, of wanting to marry the prince to his sister, Nell. Poins has been caught out. The subject is dropped, but the underlying intention, whether true or not, has been noted.

It is significant that it is not Poins, the usual master of the revels, the brains behind the Gadshill plot, that suggests the return to the Boar's Head Tavern, but the prince himself. Poins says with revealing ambiguity, 'I am your shadow, my Lord, I follow you.' There is now a sour strain between them.

The scene of our return to Eastcheap comes in exactly the same position as in *Part One*, Act Two Scene Four. But the two scenes could not be more different. We decided to place it in Mrs Quickly's Dolphin Chamber with the round table, the sea-coal fire, and the fly-bitten tapestries she has managed to save from the pawnbrokers – a snug little nook for Falstaff to enjoy his encounter with the prostitute she has laid on, the spiky Doll Tearsheet.

But if we are expecting to see Sir John in love in some cosy rendezvous, we are quickly disillusioned. Doll is vomiting, from drinking too much, from venereal disease (Falstaff says of her later 'she is in hell already and burns poor souls'), or possibly because she is pregnant. Falstaff arrives having prepared himself by filling the jordan (he presents the full chamber pot to the drawer on his entrance). He is disappointed to find his date in such a state and they have a scratchy little row. Doll, remembering that Falstaff is meant to be off to war, decides to reconcile with him, and they settle down to their candlelit supper and await their musical entertainment from the house band 'Sneak's Noise'.

Shakespeare now introduces one of his most surreal characters. It is such an outrageous invention you feel it can only have been drawn from life. And it needs an actor brave enough to explore the extremity the role demands. Pistol has very little function in the play, other than perhaps to provide a firework display, a pyrotechnical explosion of some of the most impenetrable but fertile language in the canon. Enter Antony Byrne.

Mrs Quickly is appalled to hear of the arrival of a foul-mouthed swaggerer in her genteel domain, and forbids him entrance, but Falstaff, promising this potentially violent, possibly psychotic new arrival is as gentle as 'a puppy greyhound', persuades the hostess to relent.

As soon as Pistol enters, a fight flares up with Doll Tearsheet, who knows him of old, and threatens to stab him in 'his mouldy chaps'. It is only Falstaff's intervention, 'No more, Pistol; I would not have you go off here', that momentarily calms the row. But now Pistol launches into one of his fantastical tirades.

Footnotes at the ready, we pick through all the theatrical quotations and references Pistol adopts. It is as if he has been a permanent audience member at the Rose Theatre and has imbibed great bombastic swathes of Christopher Marlowe's mighty lines (quoting *Tamburlaine the Great*'s 'Holla, ye pampered jades of Asia') mixed with Italian proverbs, and he can regurgitate them without the necessary connections that sense requires.

We begin to discuss how we would regard a character like Pistol if we were to meet him in our local pub. Someone suggests we would assume he was suffering from an acute neurological disorder; somebody else that the behaviour feels involuntary, like the tics of someone with Tourette's syndrome. Others think his behaviour and his stream of verbiage suggest he is on some powerfully addictive stimulant, cocaine perhaps, or some sort of hallucinogenic drug, as he swings between hyperactivity and paranoia. Or is he, as Bardolph suggests, just drunk? Tony Byrne says he'll go and do some research into that.

Shakespeare has created a noisy racket of a scene. It appears to have almost no function. It's a wild improvisation, but once Pistol is ejected it allows a sense of calm to pervade Mrs Quickly's Dolphin chamber, and for one of the tenderest and most unlikely love scenes to unfold. As Doll climbs onto Falstaff's knee, she asks him when he is going to stop fighting and patch up his old body for heaven. With a shiver, Sir John begs her: 'Peace, good Doll! do not speak like a death's-head; do not bid me remember mine end.'

She changes the subject and asks about the prince and Poins, at which moment of course the two men appear and eavesdrop on the scene, not entirely to their own advantage.

Again, the scene seems deliberately designed to misfire in terms of the humour, as if what the gentlemen overhear fails to provide the laughter they need. Poins hears yet more about what others think of him, as Falstaff declares that his wit (far from being good) is 'as thick as Tewkesbury Mustard', and well suited to his royal companion who has little more to commend him.

Shakespeare's dramaturgy here is breathtaking. As the crestfallen pair attempt to keep up their spirits, satirizing the genuine affection they witness before them, their banter is juxtaposed with Falstaff begging a kiss of Doll. He admits he is flattered by her attention, and she insists she kisses him with a constant heart. The fat knight with simple words, no self-pity, and surprising but brutal honesty, whispers 'I am old, I am old'.

The man boasted to the Lord Chief Justice earlier that very day that he set himself down in the scroll of youth, bragging, 'You that are old consider not the capacities of us that are young.' Now he has come to a moment of self-revelation that is sad to witness.

When the prince and Poins come out of their hiding place and Falstaff realizes he has been overheard, there is almost none of the joyful comeuppance he receives after his lies about his escapades on Gadshill. Instead, the scene is quickly interrupted by a call to war, and everyone scurries away.

Poins is never seen again in the play.

Falstaff's tryst is not to be. As he says: 'Now comes in the sweetest morsel of the night, and we must hence and leave it unpicked.' Everyone – Doll, Falstaff and Quickly – seem to take things very calmly, holding it back. Very English. They all know they may never see each other again.

But after Falstaff has left the scene, Shakespeare writes a curious little coda. Quickly recalls her long acquaintance with Sir John: 'I have known thee these twenty-nine years, come peascod-time' – a thought that hangs in the air. But then, suddenly, Bardolph calls for Doll to come to Falstaff.

'What is going on?' I asked the company.

'Isn't it obvious?' said Nia Gwynne (playing Doll). 'After all that English stiff upper-lip nonsense,' (Nia remember, is Welsh) 'Falstaff has broken and needs a hug.' I think she's right. Quickly cries 'O, run, Doll, run; run, good Doll'. And the Folio adds an unusual stage direction: *She comes blubbered.* It is very rare for a stage direction to indicate an emotional state, but here surely is one.

We staged it with Falstaff, having left our small Dolphin chamber inner stage and gone out in the street alone. Suddenly he breaks down, and like a swelling emotional crescendo, the pox-ridden tatty tart runs into his arms.

*   *   *

Act Three begins with the insomniac king. Jasper imagined him wandering the corridors of the court thinking about all his subjects in their beds asleep. We got to a run of the play in the Union Chapel in Islington, which by this late stage of rehearsal was rather cramped, with all the various stand-in props, furniture hampers and rails of rehearsal clothes, and the large heaters we had to install, as the fan heaters in the hall were too noisy. There was very little room to move our raised stage rostra, so for this stagger of the first half we would just deal with it where it was and stage management would move what they could. Out of necessity, surprisingly, came a moment of inspiration.

Jasper, looking for something to wrap himself in, found the map of the country that had been argued over in the Glendower scene in *Part One*, and which we had reintroduced at the end of the battle, as the king sends his sons in chase across his kingdom to rout the rebels. Now wearing the map like a security blanket, Jasper trudged from the back of the stage over the rostra, where Quickly was lying asleep in her chair in the Dolphin chamber and sat on the front step.

It was as if the king was prowling the streets of his own capital, like a restless ghost. The speech is one of Shakespeare's great camera scripts, tracking the viewer's gaze from long shot to close up. From the 'smoky crib' to the perfumed chambers of the great, from his own sleepless royalty to the ship boy asleep at the top of a mast in a howling gale.

The king is in despair at the state of his country and has subtly shifted the blame away from himself. His contention now is that he had no option but to depose Richard:

> ... necessity so bow'd the state
> That I and greatness were compell'd to kiss.

Henry shudders to recall that Richard had prophesied the civil division that would follow his murder. He rallies on the news of Glendower's death and recommits himself to his longed-for crusade. Somehow the rather feeble rhyming couplet with which he finishes the scene fails to have the requisite ring of confidence about it:

> And were these inward wars once out of hand,
> We would, dear lords, unto the Holy Land.

We opened the second half with the shift to Gloucester. If the portrait of the court and city remind you of the paintings of Hieronymus Bosch, now we are in the world of Pieter Breughel, presided over by Justice Shallow (Oliver Ford Davies) and his cousin Justice Silence (Jim Hooper). Sir John is expected on a recruiting campaign, and the country justices have assembled their required number for him to select from.

Again, this scene echoes the scene in *Part One*, where we see how Falstaff has abused the system for his own financial benefit and press-ganged a skeleton band of recruits. 'Tut, tut; good enough to toss; food for powder, food for powder; they'll fill a pit as well as better.'

The recruiting scene in *Part Two* is less ruthless, giving voice to the motley recruits themselves and their stratagems, which include bribing Bardolph sufficiently to be excused service.

The potential recruits are paraded in front of Falstaff and the country justices. There is Ralph Mouldy, Shadow, Wart, Francis Feeble and Peter Bullcalf o' the green. Their names suggest their intended comic potential from the lubberly Bullcalf to the diminutive Wart, the dusty mildewed Mouldy, and the elusive Shadow. The news that Francis Feeble is a woman's tailor leads to a lot of unsavoury Elizabethan jokes about the dubious reputation of the sexuality of tailors. Nick Gerard Martin playing Feeble pointed out that, despite the prejudice of the panel about his sexuality, Feeble is the only one to offer his services willingly. And as the others pay off Bardolph and are let off, Feeble refuses with a speech of some little nobility:

> By my troth, I care not; a man can die but once: we owe God a death: I'll ne'er bear
> a base mind: an't be my destiny, so; an't be not, so: no man is too good to serve's
> prince; and let it go which way it will, he that dies this year is quit for the next.

Nick even found a tender hint of bravery when Feeble sees little Wart rejected. Feeble stands up for his friend, wishing he had been allowed to go too. 'I would Wart might have gone, sir' he says. Why? We thought it might suggest that their relationship was closer than mere friendship.

But the scene's great joys are the rambling reminiscences of Justice Shallow, recalling the indiscretions of his youth, many no doubt fanciful. In Falstaff's soliloquy at the end of the scene, he shares his gossip about Justice Shallow ('when a' was naked, he was, for all the world, like a forked radish'). The speech afforded Tony Sher the opportunity to hone his stand-up skills. And over the run I watched them develop, as he introduced expectant pauses, and alighted on any particularly raucous laugher in the audience, pointing it out to the rest of the house as if to say, 'he knows what I'm taking about!'

By the time the production played the Brooklyn Academy of Music in New York, the line 'he came ever in the rearward of the fashion' had gained so much in suggestive innuendo it regularly stopped the show.

But now in Act Four, we reach perhaps the most challenging element of Shakespeare's use of the parallel structure with *Part One*, as the Archbishop's rebellion reaches its climax in Gaultree Forest.

Prince John, Hal's younger brother, has proved his mettle at the Battle of Shrewsbury. Now he encounters the rebels. He manages to negotiate peace, offering amnesties and agreeing to their demands. Delighted by this unexpected treaty, the Archbishop and his allies send their troops home. At which point the ruthless Prince John has them all arrested and sent for execution.

The scene takes much considered rehearsal (and some judicious cutting) to keep the argument urgent and bright, to make these characters we know so little of particular and distinct in their perspectives. The thoughtful reasoning of the Archbishop is carefully weighed against the cynicism of Mowbray and the naive optimism of Hastings. And there is some humour to be played here, as for instance when Hastings produces a speech which builds over six lines with a rhetorical crescendo to a flourishing climax of buoyant self-confidence . . . only to be punctured by Prince John's put down:

HASTINGS   And though we here fall down,
                  We have supplies to second our attempt:
                  If they miscarry, theirs shall second them;
                  And so success of mischief shall be born
                  And heir from heir shall hold this quarrel up
                  Whiles England shall have generation.
LANCASTER   You are too shallow, Hastings, much too shallow.

And indeed, the prince is right. When the rebels dismiss their troops (before the prince's forces are dispersed), they have not detected the trap. Hastings comes bounding in with joyful images of his soldiers' fatal departure:

        My lord, our army is dispersed already;
        Like youthful steers unyoked, they take their courses
        East, west, north, south; or, like a school broke up,
        Each hurries toward his home and sporting-place.

His laughter and the exuberance of the soldiers' swift departure like young bullocks, or eager schoolchildren, makes the snapping shut of the trap even more shocking. Prince John's action is calculated and merciless: it will define a new regime.

Falstaff has a short encounter with Prince John and shares his opinion of him with us afterwards. He doesn't drink and you can't make him laugh. So, he is summarily dismissed as of little consequence in Sir John's book.

After the challenge of the Gaultree Forest scene, we are treated to one of the greatest sequences in the play, leading to the death of the King.

As the king hears of his younger son's success with the Archbishop's rebellion, he captures his elation with a blissful image:

> O Westmoreland, thou art a summer bird,
> Which ever in the haunch of winter sings
> The lifting up of day.

It's a synaesthetic observation, combining sensory experiences in surprising conjunctions. But as even more good news arrives the king starts to become ill, complaining:

> And wherefore should these good news make me sick?
> Will fortune never come with both hands full.

At which he falls into an apoplexy and is hauled to his bedroom by his distressed children.

Again, as with the Dolphin chamber scene, Shakespeare enhances the muted tone with music, as the king asks if someone will 'whisper music to my weary spirit'. The crown is laid on his pillow and everyone departs. Enter Hal. It's a marvellous imagining of Shakespeare to have the prince contemplate the crown so intimately while the king is still alive, and even more original to assume in the course of his speech that his father has died, and to depart with the crown.

Jasper would delay the king's reawakening as far as he could. Most of the audience would assume he had indeed died. The elongated pause created a fascinating tension. When he finally spluttered awake, our attention too was jogged back into life. When the prince is found and the king vents his fury at his heir for prematurely taking possession of the crown, he tumbles into a diatribe of invective and bitter prophecy, imagining a debased England enticing every kind of corruption to its shores, and facing cataclysm:

> For the fifth Harry from curb'd licence plucks
> The muzzle of restraint, and the wild dog
> Shall flesh his tooth on every innocent.
> O my poor kingdom, sick with civil blows!
> When that my care could not withhold thy riots,
> What wilt thou do when riot is thy care?
> O, thou wilt be a wilderness again,
> Peopled with wolves, thy old inhabitants!

Prince Henry's remorseful apology to his father is so passionate, so deeply felt and so sincere, it moves forgiveness in his father and settles a deep sense of reconciliation between them. As they sit on his bed, the king confides in his son with a fortified sense of trust. Telling his son, the way to wipe out the memory of the sins of the father (and therefore any further question about his right to inherit the throne) is to distract the population with wars abroad:

> Therefore my Harry,
> Be it thy course to busy giddy minds
> With foreign quarrels; that action, hence borne out,
> May waste the memory of the former days.

As the king's strength fails him, Jasper gasped for air, finding just enough power to howl:

> How I came by the crown, O God forgive;
> And grant it may with thee in true peace live!

Prince John's entrance is marked in the text at this point. But we decided to push it back, so that the young man hears the king's advice about busying giddy minds with foreign quarrels. The idea is prompted by John's final lines spoken to the Lord Chief Justice at the coronation in sinister rhyme.

> I will lay odds that, ere this year expire,
> We bear our civil swords and native fire
> As far as France: I heard a bird so sing,
> Whose music, to my thinking, pleased the king.

With King Henry IV now dead, there is a risk that the play begins to slump as the audience scent that the final curtain cannot be far away. In fact, we have an entire act to go. The pacing of these next scenes is crucial for maintaining attention.

And Shakespeare doesn't exactly help.

He takes us back to Gloucestershire where Shallow is enticing Falstaff and Bardolph to delay their return to London and stay the night. It's a sweetly rural idyll. The servant, Davy, tries to get his master to concentrate on the necessary husbandry of his acres: sowing the headland with red wheat; paying the smith for plough irons and shoes for the horses; and settling a dispute between one William Visor of Woncot and Clement Perkes of the Hill. Meanwhile, Shallow runs through a possible menu for William cook, to prepare for the evening meal: pigeons maybe, 'a couple of short-legged hens, a joint of mutton, and any pretty little, tiny kickshaws'.

All delicious country detail. And Sir John tells us it will give him plenty of material to make the prince laugh when he gets back to Court, which provides us with yet another of those fantastically inventive images from entirely familiar objects, as Falstaff quips:

> O, you shall see him laugh till his face be like a wet cloak ill-laid up!

But to me the scene holds things up, as there is really nothing new for us to learn. I may of course be guilty of missing the point, and that there is irony to be savoured here. We all know the king is dead and Henry is busy considering his new responsibilities, but Falstaff is still blissfully ignorant of the new situation. Maybe that irony creates sufficient tension to justify the scene. Nevertheless, eventually I cut it.

So, our reintroduction to Shallow and co. came in a very mellow scene. 'In an arbour', the tipsy Justice promises, 'we will eat a last year's pippin of my own graffing, with a dish of caraways', and belying his name, Justice Silence is impelled to song. It's a good example of Shakespeare controlling the tone again and lulling us into a slow sweet doze before dropping the bombshell we are all expecting. And who better to deliver this crack shot than ancient Pistol?

He explodes into the scene still speaking with his impossibly convoluted sentence structure and the jumbled syntax worthy of Yoda in *Star Wars*:

> . . . helter-skelter have I rode to thee,
> And tidings do I bring and lucky joys
> And golden times and happy news of price.

Falstaff begs, 'I pray thee now, deliver them like a man of this world.' And when that fails he tries speaking 'Pistol':

> O base Assyrian knight, what is thy news?
> Let King Cophetua know the truth thereof.

They finally get Pistol to impart his news:

> Sir John, thy tender lambkin now is king;
> Harry the Fifth's the man.

In a flurry of excitement, and as drunk as they are, they decide to ride all night to get to London.

We get a quick snapshot of the new order's crackdown on 'crime'. In a swift clean-up operation before the coronation, Mrs Quickly and Doll Tearsheet are being dragged by the beadles before the bench. Doll, in her colourful way, is not helping her case by calling the officer names. 'Tripe-faced villain', certainly conjures up a bad case of acne. She claims that she is pregnant, but the beadle knows that trick, tugging out the cushion she has stuffed up her dress in the scuffle of the arrest. Threats of whipping and prison provide an ugly prelude to the rejoicing and jubilation of the procession that follows.

The new king's rejection of Falstaff is brutal and sudden. It is made more shocking because Falstaff is so ill-prepared for it. Staging this encounter presents some real challenges.

A procession expected. The streets strewn with fresh sweet-scented herbs and rushes. Suddenly 'Trumpet-clangor'. Excited crowds. Roars swelling like the sea. The royal party arrives from the cathedral, and there in his crown and 'new and gorgeous' coronation garments is the young king.

Falstaff, delirious at seeing his boy, steps forward in open-hearted welcome: 'My king! my Jove! I speak to thee, my heart!' But the king's public humiliation of his old friend is chilling, and uncompromising.

I know thee not, old man: fall to thy prayers;
How ill white hairs become a fool and jester!

Falstaff reels. Silent.

I have long dream'd of such a kind of man,
So surfeit-swell'd, so old and so profane;
But, being awaked, I do despise my dream.

He tells Falstaff, 'Presume not that I am the thing I was', and banishes him from his company, with an exclusion order not to come within a ten-mile radius of his person.

Why does he do it? At the climax of the glorious Tavern scene in *Part One*, Falstaff had delivered his jubilant defence of himself, getting the rest of the pub to chorus with him: 'Banish plump Jack and banish all the world.' To which the prince had replied, 'I do, I will.' So, we have been warned.

But we still feel shocked and betrayed. How can Hal reject this old man? Of course, it would not be politically expedient to keep this unreliable old bull-shitter by his side, but we love the life-force that is Falstaff. It's the most painful resolution to any relationship in the entire canon.

The major challenge in staging the scene for the open stage of the RST was whether or not the audience should see Falstaff's face while the king harangues him. It would be impossible for Alex to deliver the whole speech up stage to Tony, and somehow weaker if they simply faced each other across the stage, so we decided to play the scene with the king processing past Falstaff and then turning back for the rejection. Tony in the meantime would face upstage for the whole of the king's speech, wait until he had processed off stage, and slowly turn to face us.

Just holding back, allowing the audience to imagine his face, and how Falstaff reacted to this public humiliation, had huge advantages. The audience seemed collectively not to breathe until he finally turned round, his expression still frozen somewhere between rejoicing and bewilderment as he tried to comprehend the enormity of what had just happened.

Falstaff is still allowing himself to believe this is some kind of tactic on his beloved young friend's part and that he will be called for later, when the Lord Chief Justice arrives ordering him to be carried to the Fleet Prison.

Exit Sir John. One of the greatest inventions of the human spirit.

When we played the production at BAM, the Brooklyn Academy of Music, *The New York Times* critic acclaimed Tony's performance as Falstaff as 'one of the greatest performances I've ever seen'.

26

Henry V

– 2015: Royal Shakespeare Theatre, Stratford-upon-Avon;
Barbican Theatre, London; King & Country Tour.
– Broadcast to cinemas and released on DVD.

On 25 October 1415, the young English king, Henry V, with his ragged band of brothers, and against all odds, defeated the mighty French army and won the battle of Agincourt. Two hundred years later, Shakespeare wrote a play about it.

Seven years after the battle, in 1422, at only thirty-five years of age, King Henry V died. He was buried in Westminster Abbey in London. His tomb stands hard by the shrine of St Edward the Confessor, behind the high altar, at the eastern end of the church. Above it lies his funeral effigy, carved from the heart of English oak. Originally, the head and hands were made of silver, but they were stolen a century later. They were not replaced until 1971, when the hands, if not perhaps the face, were (so rumour had it) modelled on Sir Laurence Olivier, who famously played the warrior king in the 1944 film of Shakespeare's play.[1] Thus, the historical figure and Shakespeare's play are literally fused together on his monument.

Exactly six hundred years after the Battle of Agincourt the Royal Shakespeare Company mounted a production of the play, which I directed.

On Thursday 29 October of that year, six centuries after the news of the English victory reached London, a commemoration of the famous battle was held at Westminster Abbey.

In a spine-tingling moment at the climax of the ceremony, a door opened at the side of the high altar and the ghost of the hero-king seemed to emerge from his tomb. In fact, of course, it was one of the actors in our company, dressed in the crown and armour of Henry V, from our production. He strode across the great Cosmati pavement, and down the nave, delivering the St Crispin's day speech, with which the young king in the play rouses his flagging troops just before the fight. Again, Shakespeare's account of the life of the king is inextricably entwined in the public imagination with the historical figure.

In order to understand more about the historical character, I took the company to Westminster to visit the tomb, and to see the other treasures related to Henry V that the

---

[1] According to Tony Willoughby, the author of *Westminster Abbey and the Theatre*, the hands were modelled on the sculptor, Louisa Bolt's son Peter.

Abbey holds: his funeral achievements (helm, shield, saddle and sword) and even an effigy of the Princess of France, Catherine de Valois, who became his wife.

We also spent time trying to understand what the history of Henry V meant to the audience in Shakespeare's day. In Act Five, the Chorus compares Henry V's triumphant return to London to what might happen when 'the general of our gracious empress' returned from the wars in Ireland, 'Bringing rebellion broached on his sword'. It is virtually the only time in all his plays that Shakespeare mentions a contemporary figure directly. The general was the Earl of Essex, whom Queen Elizabeth I sent to suppress the rebellion of the Irish earls.

In 1599, as Shakespeare's *Chronicle History of Henry V* was opening at the newly built Globe Theatre, Essex was mustering his huge expeditionary force of 16,000 troops on the outskirts of London. The audience would have known that. Many of their fathers, husbands, brothers and sons might have already been involved in the Irish campaign. The war had been dragging on by then for four years (and it would last another five). London streets were full of soldiers wounded in the long war. Indeed, some in the audience would be aware that theatres were sometimes raided during performances to press-gang any likely able young men into the army.

Essex was unsuccessful in his campaign and returned to England, against the queen's explicit command.

So, the play was originally performed to an audience who were alert to the propaganda that presented war as a national imperative and an heroic exercise, yet were only too aware of what war could cost.

In reading the play in rehearsal, we began to realize that it presented a full spectrum of perspectives about war, from the heroical presentation by the Chorus, a frankly unreliable narrator (Oliver Ford Davies in our production) to the brutal realities of the conflict.

Look, for example, at the stirring Chorus at the start of Act Two, 'Now all the youth of England are on fire', which describes the English army preparing to set off from Southampton. But then see what follows it: a petty squabble between the bombastic Pistol and the volatile Nym over the hand of Mrs Quickly.

'Honour's thought / Reigns solely in the breast of every man' cries the Chorus, but it is rather profit that 'reigns solely in the breast' of Corporal Pistol. He is determined to profit by the war, as he confides to Nym '... for I shall sutler be / Unto the camp, and profits will accrue'. A sutler[2] was a civilian merchant who sold provisions to the army.

This constant undermining of apparently noble aims presented itself most powerfully to us in the scenes set on the night before the battle. The Chorus suggests that the young king went around his camp, encouraging and cheering his soldiers, granting them (as he describes it) 'a little touch of Harry in the night'. Shakespeare then proceeds to show us a scene in which Henry, in disguise, finds himself quarrelling with some common soldiers, Williams, Bates and Court, about the justification for the war. This juxtaposition of opposing viewpoints is a common and fascinating feature of the

---

[2] 'Sutler' is one of those words in Shakespeare that is hard to put across in performance. Most of your audience won't know what a sutler is, and you may think you have misheard the word 'subtler' and be confused. We compromised with the word 'victualler' (pronounced 'vit'ller').

play. Opposing patriotic sentiment with cynicism makes it very modern: blood-tingling rhetoric and noble endeavour beside grasping self-interest and ruthless exploitation.

The history of the play's performance elicits varying responses to the text, according to the prevailing attitude to war, particularly within the last century.

For example, at the height of the Second World War, as England was facing the might of the Nazi war machine, Laurence Olivier was filming his version of the play. Prime Minister Winston Churchill urged him to use the film to boost the morale of the nation. Any scenes which represented obstacles on Henry's procession to victory were cut – particularly the traitors' scene.

At the RSC, when Alan Howard played Henry V for Terry Hands in 1975, the Vietnam War was coming to an end. Inevitably the nature of that conflict coloured the attitude to war in that production. Adrian Noble stressed the horrors of war when he directed Kenneth Branagh in the role at Stratford-upon-Avon in 1984. The production played in the wake of the Falklands War; the legitimacy of which conflict was hotly debated within the country. Argentine writer Jorge Luis Borges described the war as 'a fight between two bald men over a comb'. Branagh made his film of the play five years later, in 1989.

Attitudes to war were perhaps even more intensely cynical when Nick Hytner directed the play at the National Theatre in London in 2003, at the height of the Iraq War. He chose to make direct reference to that invasion. The Archbishop of Canterbury in the first act carried a governmental dossier containing the genealogical justification for Henry's inheritance of the French Crown, echoing the infamous 'Dodgy Dossier', produced by Tony Blair to provide justification for the invasion by exaggerating the evidence of weapons of mass destruction stockpiled by Saddam Hussein.

At the International Shakespeare Congress in Stratford in 2016, I was asked to give the keynote speech. The subject was Shakespeare on film, and included a survey of the attempts to record, broadcast and translate stage productions of Shakespeare into film. I titled it 'Think when we talk of horses'.

Henry V, of course, has produced at least two famous films, mentioned above (the Olivier and Branagh via Noble versions). The first Chorus in *Henry V* sets out the challenge of translating the action of history onto the stage, and in so doing outlines the similar challenge of translating a play made up of words, into a medium that concentrates on image.

The Chorus begins by admitting the inadequacy of the resources at the theatre's disposal to create the events leading up to the Battle of Agincourt. He begs our indulgence, and our complicity, if we will allow the actors to work on our 'imaginary forces'. It won't work without that, 'for 'tis your thoughts that now must deck our kings' he says, and then he gets down to specifics:

Think when we talk of horses that you see them,
Printing their proud hoofs i' the receiving earth.

Here lies the challenge that confronts anyone attempting to translate Shakespeare onto the screen. Essentially, on film, we expect to see horses, and are reluctant to accept anything less or to fill in the gaps with our own imagination, and certainly not to 'work, work our thoughts' to create them. For the image, not the word, is the medium of film.

So, if you have horses, you don't need any of the words Shakespeare uses to describe them. But what words! Here is the observant French Lord Grandpre describing the ragged English cavalry drawn up for battle. Listen to how he closes in on the scene, from the horses' eyes to the tackle in their mouths: a final devastating detail:

> The horsemen sit like fixed candlesticks,
> With torch-staves in their hand; and their poor jades
> Lob down their heads, dropping the hides and hips,
> The gum down-roping from their pale-dead eyes
> And in their pale dull mouths the gimmal bit
> Lies foul with chew'd grass, still and motionless.

Indeed, often in rehearsal we talk about how Shakespeare's speeches act like a camera script. Listen to the Chorus calling the shots as the fleet sets sail from Hampton Pier. He focuses on the silken banners, a close-up of the ship boys clambering up the hempen tackle, the shipmaster's whistle, then the wide shot as the sails fill and the huge ships pull out to sea. Cut to the view from the cliff top of the whole fleet like a 'city on the inconstant billows dancing'.[3]

*   *   *

Aumerle (Richard II's 'tender-hearted cousin') makes a surprising reappearance in *Henry V*, although Shakespeare makes no attempt to remind his audience of the connection. He is now Duke of York, having inherited the title from his father. The character has less than two lines. The scene is frequently overlooked, and often cut, but its impact on the action is significant. I include mention of it here because I find it intriguing and unexpectedly moving.

In Act Four Scene Three, York appears and kneels before the king. He asks permission to lead the vanguard, which Henry grants him. That's it. It is York's only appearance in the play.

Two scenes later, the battle is going well for the king, and his soldiers lead in their prisoners. Uncle Exeter suddenly arrives and tells his nephew that the Duke of York sends his majesty his commendations. The king asks if he is still alive as he has seen him three times in the fighting, hacked down, but recovering each time. 'From helm to spur all blood he was.'

Exeter then reports the death of York. His bloody body lies next to the noble Earl of Suffolk, 'Yoke-fellow to his honour-owing wounds' (and a character we have not met). Exeter describes the manner of their deaths:

---

[3]   And Shakespeare uses this technique again in *King Lear*. Edgar, describing the imaginary cliff at Dover, moves from '*the crows and choughs that wing the midway air*' to the samphire gatherer (*dreadful trade*) half-way down, to the fishermen way below on the beach.

Suffolk first died: and York, all haggled over,
Comes to him, where in gore he lay insteep'd,
And takes him by the beard; kisses the gashes
That bloodily did spawn upon his face;
And cries aloud 'Tarry, dear cousin Suffolk!
My soul shall thine keep company to heaven;
Tarry, sweet soul, for mine, then fly abreast,
As in this glorious and well-foughten field
We kept together in our chivalry!'

Exeter tells how he tried to comfort the grieving York, who smiled at him, reached for his hand, and bade him commend his service to his sovereign.

So did he turn and over Suffolk's neck
He threw his wounded arm and kiss'd his lips;
And so espoused to death, with blood he seal'd
A testament of noble-ending love.

The language of espousal signified by a kiss, and of testaments sealed with blood, creates an image of a profound and shameless male love, of a Spartan dedication to a union now made eternal by death. The scene reduces the Duke of Exeter to tears. And Henry admits he too is compelled to weep.

The double death of York and Suffolk, wrapped together, appears nowhere in the sources. It is entirely Shakespeare's invention.[4]

The Arden editor introduces a stage direction that indicates the exeunt of the soldiers and their prisoners before this scene, suggesting that, 'Exeter's dialogue with the king is better without a passive stage audience.' But why? Because the soldiers would be embarrassed, or wouldn't approve of the intimacy between two men, expressed by the duke? On the contrary, Exeter has chosen to speak this eulogy now, in a moment which seems briefly to suspend time, and which directly impels the next shocking beat of the story.

At that moment a new alarum is heard. The French have rallied, and Henry suddenly commands 'that every soldier kill his prisoners'. Scholars argue over the sources, and what precisely prompts the brutal war crime that Henry orders here. In performance (if the York–Suffolk death had not been cut) it is impossible not to relate the two (particularly if the French prisoners are present and hear the speech) and conclude that Henry's actions are prompted by his grief at the tragic loss of two great men, wedded in their courage by death, and his anger at the French turns to outrage.

* * *

[4] Aumerle, the Duke of York, died childless. It was his 4-year-old nephew who inherited the dukedom. He is the York who instigates the Wars of the Roses in Shakespeare's *Henry VI* plays, and would be the father of Richard III.

In preparation for the RSC's first visit to China in 2016 (which would include *Henry V*) I had initiated a collaborative project to translate Shakespeare's plays into Mandarin, and a complementary endeavour to have the many great classic Chinese plays translated into English. I had been introduced to the wealth of this repertoire in 2011 when preparing to direct *The Orphan of Zhao* in the Swan. It is known as the Chinese *Hamlet* and is certainly performed as often there.[5]

The Shakespeare translation project was based on a simple idea: that we open our RSC rehearsal room to Chinese translators; share the process of textual analysis we do at the start of any production; and engage them with the same interpretative choices that the actor and director makes in rehearsal to inform their own translation choices.

In the case of *Henry V*, the translation that emerged from our rehearsal room was to be fully realized and honed in performance, in a production at the Shanghai Centre for the Performing Arts, directed by my now associate director, Owen Horsley. It was scheduled to be presented in September 2016 as part of the celebrations for the 400th anniversary of Shakespeare's death.[6]

There was one rehearsal when the collaborative nature of this process bore particular fruit. It was a moment when one realizes how important it is for a good translation to convey not just the literal meaning of the words, but the sound they make as well.

We were rehearsing the traitors' scene in Act Two, where just before his departure at Southampton, Henry exposes the conspiracy plotted against him, by Grey, Cambridge and Scroop. The coordinator of our Chinese translation project, Shihui Weng, was sitting listening intently to the actors deliver the text. Lord Scroop (Keith Osborn) had got to the obsequious speech where he attempts to demonstrate their loyalty to the King.

So service shall with steeled sinews toil
To do your Grace incessant services.

Shihui said suddenly, 'I don't think I fully understood the line, but you can tell that he is lying.' 'Why?' I asked. And Shihui replied:

'Because he sounds like a snake.'

And she was right. I hadn't at first noticed, attending so closely to the literal meaning of the words, but Scroop's speech hisses with serpentine sibilance. There are at least a dozen suspicious 's' sounds in just those two lines.

That line becomes the cue for the young king to spring his trap on the treacherous lords.

The director of the Shanghai Dramatic Arts Centre, Nick Yu, joined us from the very start of our rehearsals. In the early stages of our discussions, Nick had expressed some not unsurprising concerns about the choice of *Henry V* for this production, and what

---

[5] Our second production of a Chinese classic (which boasted the RSC's first ever entirely British-Asian cast) was *Snow in Midsummer* by Guan Hanqing, adapted by playwright Frances Ya-Chu Cowhig, which played in the Swan Theatre in 2017.

[6] Subsequent productions of *King Lear*, *The Tempest*, *Hamlet* and *Twelfth Night*, in translations initiated in our rehearsal rooms, took place in Beijing, Shanghai, Hong Kong and Guangzhou.

relevance a play about this quintessentially English king would have for a Chinese audience. Was it not surely a play that spoke simply to the British about their own particular history?

As the RSC rehearsals drew to a close in London, I asked Nick what he now thought of the play. Had his attitude changed? Did he still feel it was merely a chronicle of English history? His answer delighted me. He said he had completely reversed his opinion.

Here was a play about going to war. It's a play about what war feels like and what it costs. It's not a piece of propaganda, it's not a manifesto, it's an extraordinary debate, about war. As such it was potentially as relevant and resonant to a Chinese audience as it was to a British one. It justified Shakespeare's claim to universal status, to being a world writer, a writer for everyone. Nick said he was very excited to be doing this great play for the first time in China in Mandarin, at the Shanghai Dramatic Arts Centre.

After our tour to China in 2016, I returned later that year to catch the final performance of *Henry V* by the young ensemble of the Shanghai Dramatic Arts Centre. The production was very different from my own. Owen had in no way produced a carbon copy, but a fresh analysis of the play. It invited the investment of the acting company and their participation, not just in performing the play, but in deciding what it meant, to them, to their audience and what it might say now to the twenty-first century.

I had the opportunity, backstage after the show, to ask some of the actors what the experience of rehearsing and performing *Henry V* had meant to them. One said it had not only changed his view of Shakespeare, but of what it meant to be an actor.

I took that as reason enough (if reason were needed) for the vitality and importance of our Chinese translation project: the opportunity to share insights, and the experience of wrestling with the act of performing these great plays, of continuing to produce not definitive productions – no production can be a definitive account of the play – but what a particular group of actors, of creative teams of designers and directors, and of audiences may make of any play in the context, and the time, in which they attempt it.

'The purpose of playing', as Hamlet says, 'is to hold, as 'twere, the mirror up to nature'. The reflection is not constant, it is kinetic. It changes according to what it sees and how you choose to look at it. That is Shakespeare's genius.

27

King Lear

– 2016 and revived 2018: Royal Shakespeare Theatre, Stratford-upon-Avon;
Brooklyn Academy of Music, New York.
– Broadcast to cinemas and released on DVD.

I couldn't watch *King Lear* for years. Or even read it. The portrait of an old man descending into madness was too close to home.

My dad, a proud Scot, was born in Kilsyth, just after the Great War. In the Second World War, he tried to join up with the RAF, but his irate father marched him back to the recruiting office in Glasgow and demanded his release, on the grounds that he was in a reserved occupation. He was studying chemistry at Glasgow University, and as Hitler was known to be developing chemical warfare, his unit were investigating what measures could be taken against the toxic effects of sarin gas.

After the war, the exciting new British nuclear industry was developing, and by the late fifties, after a stint at ICI in Huddersfield (where I was born), my father landed a job with the United Kingdom Atomic Energy Authority at their plant at Springfields in Preston, and he moved his young family across the Pennines to Lancashire. He was then head-hunted to become General Manager for British Nuclear Fuels at Windscale in Cumbria. In the course of his time there the plant was renamed Sellafield. By the time I went to university, my dad was managing one of the most controversial industrial sites in the UK.

The first time I realized that my father had dementia was in the summer of 2003, long after he had retired. He and my mother stayed overnight with us on the way to a SAGA holiday in the Italian Lakes. I came down in the morning to find my mother in her nightie at the kitchen table. My dad had become unwell over night, but she had not wanted to disturb us. I went downstairs to their room to find him ashen and struggling to breathe. When the ambulance arrived, he was rushed to the Whittington hospital, where they kept him in overnight.

That's when we noticed the first signs.

The hospital phoned to say I needed to come back as my father was confused. When I got to his ward, Dad was in a fury. His mind thought this was a hotel in Lake Garda, after all. The service, he said, was terrible, and he took a pretty dim view of the accommodation. They hadn't even been able to find him a double room, and where was Mum? When he was finally sedated and settled, I returned home. I was called back to the Whittington three times that night.

Dad always wore a tie, every day of his working life, and for much of his retirement. It represented for him a sense of organizational preparedness, focus, presentation, seriousness of purpose and decency. His mind started to unravel, but his tie did not.

The summer of 2004, Michael Boyd had announced a season of Tragedies. Corin Redgrave was cast as King Lear. It was a powerful production with Redgrave puerile then petulant, and finally pathetic. But by then, I had spent too much time watching my own father, an intelligent, devout man, slip quietly but inexorably into the maze of dementia. It was painful enough to observe at close quarters; I somehow had not anticipated seeing it echoed on stage.

We had moved my parents down from the Lake District to be close to where my brother and his family lived on a farm in the Vale of Clwyd. Unfortunately, shortly after the move, my mother died. Without her permanently by his side, Dad was lost.

My father used to go out for an afternoon walk every day. Many times he got lost, and once having managed to get over the cattle grid, and having walked miles out of his way, he was found on the busy main road, and returned by the police. Eventually we moved him into a home. But he would still try to 'escape', claiming he had run out of Bounty bars, and once was discovered in St Asaph Cathedral in his jacket and pyjama bottoms.

It was soon after this that Michael Boyd announced that we would be doing The Complete Works Festival in 2006. I realized that this meant we would be doing *King Lear* again, only two years after the last. I suggested to Michael that he ask Ian McKellen and Trevor Nunn to complete their trilogy of Shakespeare Tragedies (after *Macbeth* and *Othello*) and do *Lear*. After all, McKellen, then in his late sixties, was bound to do it soon, and surely he should do it in Stratford.

It was of course one of the many highlights of that extraordinary endeavour. But by then I found the play almost impossible to watch. By the interval I was shaking. I pondered not going back in for the second half. By the end, I vowed never to see this play again.

My father died in 2010 at the age of ninety. I was in rehearsals for the *Morte d'Arthur* in Stratford when I heard and drove straight up that night. When I was shown into his room, the curtains were drawn. Dad's face was peaceful, his full head of white hair combed and neat on the pillow, and his nose, I remember being surprised to discover, was (as Quickly says of the dead Falstaff) 'as sharp as a pen'. We buried my father with his beloved wife in a quiet churchyard in a secluded corner of the Vale of Clwyd.

*   *   *

I took over as Artistic Director of the RSC in 2012 and began my programme in the autumn of 2013. I knew we would have to pull out all the stops for the 400th anniversary of Shakespeare's death in 2016, and although it was still nearly four years away, I began to plan the programme immediately.

Tony and I had not worked together since *Othello* in 2003, and I suggested we think what we might do together in that special jubilee year. He had done Prospero in a co-production between the RSC and the Baxter Theatre in Cape Town in 2009, beautifully directed by Janice Honeyman. So we began to talk about *Lear*.

I think Tony loved the play as much as I feared it. He had played the Fool twice: once at the start of his career in 1972 at the Liverpool Everyman, and then a decade later, when he joined the RSC in Adrian Noble's production with Michael Gambon, in 1983. So, although he was well aware of the play and the role's reputation as a theatrical Everest, he wanted to climb it. He knew how challenging the play had become for me, but one day he asked me to read it again. 'You see,' he said quietly, 'I know it's a commonly held belief, but I don't actually think Lear has dementia.'

I read the play again.

I began to see a way. I began to think I had just used my anxiety about my father to prevent me from attempting to pit myself against this mighty play. 'If you will hold my hand, and we just go step by step,' I said, 'perhaps we could try, together.'

So after a decade of not collaborating together as actor and director, in 2013 we started planning an exciting new adventure for Shakespeare's big year.

I asked composer Ilona Sekacz to write the music for *King Lear*, and designer Niki Turner to design the production. I had known Ilona since my very first production at Stratford in 1992 when she composed the score for Derek Walcott's *The Odyssey*. Niki and I had first worked together on a production of *Oroonoko*, also at The Other Place, in 1999.

Niki and I discussed the elemental nature of the play. Not just the storm and the bare heath, and the impression of the clifftop near Dover, but the society's belief in the influence of the planets on our lives. It's a faith so scoffed at by Edmund, and so deeply held by his father, Gloucester.

Tony's first experience of seeing Shakespeare at Stratford was a production of *King Lear* in 1968. He remembers the king's arrival. Eric Porter was brought in, carried high on a bier. It is important to establish who is boss right from the top. Niki and I had similar thoughts.

The portrait of Elizabeth I at Sherborne Castle in Dorset shows the queen being borne aloft in procession to Blackfriars surrounded by her Knights of the Garter. She sits in an elaborate canopied litter, elevated and visible to her people. It's an Elizabethan version of the *sedia gestatoria*, the huge ceremonial chair on which popes were carried by twelve footmen in red livery. In 1978, the smiling pope John Paul I refused to use it at his coronation, until he was persuaded that if he didn't, the crowds in St Peter's Square would be unable to see him.

Everybody must see King Lear. Surely we needed something like that for his first entrance?

So, as the Duke of Gloucester announced, 'The king is coming', Ilona's score, a basso-profundo drone and enormous taiko drums would cue the opening of a huge sliding metal door at the back of the stage, and the entrance of twelve of our supernumeraries carrying gnarled golden boughs, heralding the arrival of Lear's two elder daughters and their husbands, the Dukes of Cornwall and Albany, and Cordelia in her white betrothal gown, and then out of the darkness emerged a gilded glass box palanquin carried shoulder-high, in which in remote isolation, Lear sat in his great wolf-skin coat and antique gold crown. Ilona's score rose in a magnificent pagan crescendo, as the palanquin was lowered, and its glass walls descended.

When we first ran the entrance at the technical rehearsal, all the creative teams, the makers and the designers who had worked so hard on this first beat, gathered to watch the spectacle. I said over the microphone, 'Ladies and gentlemen, you have to be married to the Artistic Director to get an entrance like that!'

King Lear starts as grand opera but develops into a work by Samuel Beckett. The play evolves to expose us all as the poor, bare, forked animals we are at root: 'unaccommodated man'. Lear himself begins with all the trappings of kingship, and ends having stripped off his clothes on the heath.

Niki wanted to find a way of charting that descent. The court scenes were played on a gold painted floor cloth, against high dark brick walls. The floor cloth was scooped up in the storm, as Lear and the Fool perched high on a precipitous platform in the centre of the space.

Once the giddy platform descended, Kent (disguised as Caius) finds Lear and tries to help him to shelter in a hovel. The lost king suddenly sees the beggars, the 'poor naked wretches' enduring 'the pelting of this pitiless storm'. In our production, these homeless souls have haunted the stage from the very beginning. It's a moment of epiphany for Lear. It is now (and must have been even more so then, when the play was first performed) a powerful appeal for social justice. A king recognizes the inequalities in his kingdom and says:

> O, I have ta'en
Too little care of this.

We chose to retain the enigmatic mad mock trial. This manic scene of spiralling insanity is present in the first edition of the play, the Pied Bull Quarto,[1] but is not in the revised version printed in the 1623 Folio. Lear, now growing more and more delusional, imagines trying his daughters for their crimes against him. The actors playing the poor itinerant beggars who were taking shelter in this barn, made up the court, presided over by the wildly improvising Edgar, adding to the growing craziness of Lear's world.

Why is the scene there? Why is it then cut from the Folio version? It has very little narrative drive. But it is crucial in the weird path that Edgar is taking us on. But what is he doing? By abetting Lear's 'anatomising' of his daughters, is he prompting Lear to rehearse, and therefore exorcise the cruelty of those daughters? Is it designed as some crazy act of drama therapy in which Lear can achieve catharsis and rest? It certainly provides Edgar with perspective on his own troubles:

> How light and portable my pains seems now,
When that which makes me bend, makes the king bow.

After the mock trial, the Fool disappears from the play. In the production Adrian Noble directed, in which Tony played the Fool, they created a moment that has gone down in theatre history and been much copied since. In the melee, as Lear stabbed at a cushion, he accidentally killed the Fool, and as Gloucester entered to hurry the king away to safety no one realized what had happened.

---

[1] So-called because it was published by Nathaniel Butter at the sign of the Pied Bull in 1608.

I felt differently. To me the Fool's departure from his master is a deeply painful choice. He has been replaced by the gabbling lunatic, Poor Tom, the character adopted by Edgar, who Lear takes to be a profound philosopher. Perhaps the Fool will join the vagrant band, or perhaps with no further purpose, and feeling rejected by his beloved master, he will take a rope from the barn and hang himself.

Of course, one well-established theory is that the actor playing Cordelia and the Fool doubled. At the end of the play when Cordelia has been murdered, this allows Lear's line 'And my poor fool is hanged' to hold a double force. We chose to lift the strangely beautiful and mysterious prophecy the Fool makes and place it here, ending the first half with its bewildering optimism for the Isle of Albion. 'This prophecy Merlin shall make, for I live before his time.'

Graham Turner's genius as the Fool was his ability to deliver his role as entertainer, as well as truth-teller, the 'all-licensed fool'. He was aware of how crappy his vaudeville routine was, and yet was able to thread it with dangerous radical alternative comedy. His utter devotion to Lear made his decision to leave him now, heart-rending.

We began the second half with the blinding of Gloucester. He was forced into a brightly lit glass room (echoing Lear's palanquin), in the centre of the stage. It somehow focused the dreadful torture and would not allow you to look away. As the walls became smeared with blood, the box looked more and more like a painting by Francis Bacon, framing the cruelty and forcing you to watch.

Our hero in rehearsal became the unnamed servant who suddenly can't take it anymore and tries to prevent Gloucester's dismemberment. He draws a knife on Cornwall but is stabbed in the back by Regan. Three cheers for the little guy.

Only then, after Gloucester's blinding did light enter this dark world, as the walls in Niki Turner's set were slowly hauled out to reveal a bright white cyclorama with a single black weather-blown bush, and Edgar in his Poor Tom blanket in existential contemplation. Having reached what he imagines is surely rock bottom, the only way is up. Isn't it?

Realizing this blinded man is his father, Edgar reviews his opinion about reaching the bottom.

> O gods! Who is't can say 'I am at the worst'?
> I am worse than e'er I was.

And he continues discovering truth in the simplest words:

> And worse I may be yet: the worst is not
> So long as we can say 'This is the worst.'

Like Lear before him, Gloucester also has an epiphany, which reiterates a Christ-like prayer for the care of the poor. He prays that those who have more than they need, and who ignore the teaching of God, who cannot empathize because they have no experience of poverty, should feel the potential of that higher power, so that things may change, and no human being should go without. These two epiphanies would inspire Cicely Berry's constant reassertion that Lear is Shakespeare's Marxist play:

Let the superfluous and lust-dieted man,
That slaves your ordinance, that will not see
Because he doth not feel, feel your power quickly;
So distribution should undo excess,
And each man have enough.

The scene that follows, in which two men walk on to a bare stage, one of them falls flat on his face, and then they both stand up and start to walk off again, is surely one of the finest scenes ever written.

We asked ourselves a great deal, in rehearsal, why Edgar doesn't just tell his father who he is. Why would he allow his father to imagine he has reached the summit of a cliff, and knowing his despair, watch him as he believes he is throwing himself to his death?

Edgar does tell us:

Why I do trifle thus with his despair
Is done to cure it.

We found it helpful to feel that, rather than acting out a preconceived plan, Edgar doesn't really know what he is doing and is essentially improvising moment by moment, and indeed might change his plan at any instant. But his actions have taught his father to endure:

Henceforth I'll bear
Affliction till it do cry out itself
'Enough, enough', and die.

This theme of endurance is potent. But the next time we encountered it directly in the play, again in a very short scene between this father-and-son duo, it made us question the direction of the entire play.

*   *   *

Before going into rehearsal of any Shakespeare play, I like to make sure I am as familiar as possible with the source material. In the case of *King Lear* there are a number of inspirations: the historical chronicles, an old play, and some interesting contemporary events.

What surprised me most was that the historical events Shakespeare describes, and the play he may have adapted, both have happy endings. The chronicle on which the events are based tells how the real king overcame his perils and died peacefully in bed. While the earlier play, called *King Leir*, ends not with the carnage that strews the stage in the final scene of Shakespeare's play, but with the marriage of Edgar and Cordelia.

The next time we encounter Edgar and his father things are looking up. However, it is very easy not to notice, to suppose that catastrophe is about to occur. But from these characters' point of view, at this moment, now, there is hope.

One day in rehearsal, as we looked at this tiny scene in more detail, I noticed the opening stage direction that we had ignored or felt was not necessary to stage. It reads:

'*Alarum within. Enter, with drum and colours,* KING LEAR, CORDELIA, *and* SOLDIERS, *over the stage; and exeunt.*'

I thought it was just an indication that battle is being prepared. But it is much more than that. It is raising the stakes and lifting our hearts that all may yet be well.

Goneril and Regan are in disarray, both squabbling over their love for Edmund. Edgar is armed with evidence that Goneril wants Edmund to kill her husband Albany; and, having heard of the approach of Cordelia's army (now joined with both Lear himself and the good Kent), Edgar is heading off towards them.

The strange little scene is beguiling, and on a very basic level represents a pretty radical piece of stage craft. A blind man is left sitting under a tree to watch a battle. The battle then occurs, and its outcome is determined while he listens. Time, we are asked to accept, contracts while we watch him. And bearing in mind that this is Act Five Scene Two, it is quite late in the evening to add any time to the performance.

But what struck me that morning in rehearsal was that Shakespeare seemed to be heading irrevocably and resolutely in the same direction as his source material, towards a happy ending. And that instead of staging it with the foreknowledge that the play does not resolve in that way, I had ignored Shakespeare's instruction to 'make the audience think it's all going to end well'.

So, we staged what I felt Shakespeare's intended beat was – a moment to celebrate the strength of Cordelia's reconciliation with her father and his public appearance before their troops, to suggest unity of purpose and resolve to prevent a slide into anarchy presided over by the voracious Edmund and the fractious sisters.

Niki's set with its white panoramic background could accommodate a letterbox of light with a back-lit silhouette of the King elevated above his cheering troops with Cordelia by his side. Then in seconds, as the blind Gloucester watched the battle with his ears, the same letterbox panorama could reveal a hazy slow-motion battle again in glaucomic silhouette.

As Edgar returns to tell his father that, against the odds, Lear has lost, Gloucester replies:

No farther, sir; a man may rot even here.

And his son's response, even at this most desperate moment, fortifies the need to endure, that despite the misery, our human capacity for resilience, our ability to persist is what gives our lives validity:

What, in ill thoughts again? Men must endure
Their going hence, even as their coming hither;
Ripeness is all: come on.

To which his father replies, with arresting simplicity:

And that's true too.[2]

---

[2]   Which was John Barton's favourite line in Shakespeare.

*   *   *

The production was revived at the invitation of the Brooklyn Academy of Music (BAM) in 2018, but it was not until the following year that I finally understood why Shakespeare had perhaps had a change of heart and brought the play to a tragic conclusion.

When our theatres were closed in March 2020 (see later chapter) I began to realize what impact the pandemic would have on our lives, but also what impact the plague might have had on Shakespeare's writing.

The first fatality due to Covid in the UK was recorded on 2 March. A fortnight later we locked the doors of the RST, and six weeks after that, on 6 May, UK deaths reached 30,000, the highest in Europe. That number struck me, because that was the number of deaths recorded in the outbreak of plague in Shakespeare's London in 1604. But that was the death toll in a city population of 200,000. Fifteen percent of the citizens of the capital perished that year. The stench of mortality must have been intolerable.

I had always assumed that the slippery slide in Shakespeare's writing in the early years of the seventeenth century, from the disillusionment in *Hamlet*, through the cynicism of *Measure for Measure*, the suppurating bile of *Troilus and Cressida*, tipping into the abyss of *Lear*, could be accounted for by the political instability of the new reign, the shattering effect of the Gunpowder Plot, and a sense of a loss of moorings in society, where old certainties no longer applied.

But with the Covid-19 pandemic, another thought occurred. Had Shakespeare originally followed his sources and intended his story to end in reconciliation? But with the soaring death toll of the plague, and loss of faith in any overarching divine plan – which included the belief that in whatever circumstances good should prevail – Shakespeare simply could not carry through his original plan.

I imagined him starting to rehearse the first draft of his last act and suddenly throwing his hands in the air, tearing up the script and telling the actors to go home. Then travelling back across the river, to his lodgings in Silver Street, through streets pestered with coffins, loud with the tolling of church bells in every parish of the city, clamping his handkerchief soaked in vinegar to his mouth, and wafting rosemary under his nose to avoid the rank odour of the piling bodies, and the jostling plague carts. He gets back to his desk, re-reads his last act and finds it dishonest. The world is not like that. There can be no happy endings. So Cordelia must die, and Lear must howl.

We tend to sneer condescendingly at the idea of Nahum Tate's 1681 revision of *King Lear*. When he adapted the play after the Restoration, he gave the play a happy ending. Dr Johnson said we simply could not tolerate it otherwise. Nahum Tate's version of *Lear* held the stage for 130 years. When Edmund Kean restored the original ending in his nineteenth-century production, the audience rejected it and he was forced to revert to Tate's conclusion.[3]

---

[3] Which ends thus: EDGAR 'Our drooping country now erects her head, / Peace spreads her balmy wings, and plenty blooms'. He then turns to his new bride: 'Divine Cordelia, all the gods can witness / How much thy love to empire I prefer!' And building to a rousing final couplet 'Thy bright example shall convince the world / Whatever storms of fortune are decreed / That truth and virtue shall at last succeed.'

As we rehearsed the final act of the play, I came to realize that Tony was right. Though Lear has endured severe periods of delusion, once Cordelia's soldiers find and return her father, he begins to recover.

My brother Mark, a neurologist, pointed out that most dementias are relentlessly progressive. And the delusional states associated with dementia, although frequently accompanied by moments of apparent lucid clarity, are rarely reversible. In other words, people with dementia, like my father, tend not to recover.

But Lear does recover. In what is for me the most moving scene in the play, Lear is brought in asleep, and wakes to see Cordelia. He initially assumes her to be a soul in bliss and wants to know when she died, but as his mind clears, the play reaches a transcendent grace as he says:

> Do not laugh at me
> For as I am a man, I think this lady
> To be my child, Cordelia.

The doctor then confirms:

> The great rage
> You see, is killed in him.

When Edmund Kean decided to restore the original ending to *King Lear*, he was recognizing the unbelievable power of the image of an old man carrying his dead daughter and howling. He told his wife Mary that the London audience 'have no notion of what I can do till they see me over the dead body of Cordelia'. Tony and I had laughed at the advice of Donald Wolfit: 'Get a light Cordelia and keep an eye on the Fool.' But when it came to it we realized that we would need to rethink the famous entrance.

In an onstage fight, on the press night of *Death of a Salesman* at the Noël Coward Theatre in the West End the previous year, Tony had badly wrenched his shoulder. He would later have to undergo an operation to replace the entire shoulder with a titanium implant. There was no way he could carry Cordelia, whatever the weight of the actress we cast.

I decided to use the cart on which Gloucester and Kent, escaping from Cornwall and Regan, had transported the sleeping Lear. Now we would hear Lear's first howl, the great doors at the back of the stage would slide open and there would be the cart, carrying Lear with his daughter is his arms, in a terrible pieta of grief.

Coda: November 2016.
I received a note from a lady who said she felt 'overwhelmed'. She had just seen a screening of our 'Live-From' recording of *King Lear* 'with coach-loads of school children from Red Lodge, in rural Montana, in a converted barn, near a little town called Fishtail, in a bend of the Rosebud river, at the edge the Custer Forest, in the shadow of the Beartooth Mountains'. How much deeper into cowboy country could you get?

28

The Tempest

– 2016: Royal Shakespeare Theatre, Stratford-upon-Avon;
Barbican Theatre, London.
– Broadcast to cinemas and released on DVD.

Imagine the scene. We are in the Banqueting Hall at Whitehall Palace. It's the winter of 1605. We are about to see the *Masque of Blackness*, devised by Ben Jonson and designed by Inigo Jones.

The hall is a large double cube room, not a theatre. Everything has had to be brought in for this one night: grandstand seating, orchestra and scenery. The King sits enthroned on a raised dais at one end of the room. The tiered grandstand-seating around him is packed, with ambassadors, royal guests, lords and ladies, in glorious array. Not only their costly jewels, but the spangles, sewn especially onto sleeves, ruffs and standing collars, shimmer in the light of several thousand candles.

Suddenly there is a great swell of music, a curtain drops, and an ocean tide seems to flood forward. Upon the billows are six blue-haired tritons with fishes' tails, blowing on conch shells. Behind, two great seahorses 'as big as the life' rear and writhe in the waves. On their backs, Neptune-like with tridents and sea-grass garlands, sit Oceanus and Niger ushering in a great concave mother-of-pearl shell, in which Queen Anne herself is placed among her ladies.

To the astonishment of the crowd, the royal masquers have blacked-up. They are dressed in azure and silver cloth with ropes of pearls, but their arms and faces are painted blue-black. Beside them swim six huge sea monsters, each with two torch bearers on their backs lighting the glittering scene.

Imagine a sort of living Trevi Fountain, but in painted cloth and split deal boards instead of travertine and Carrara marble.

In a sumptuous wedding masque called *Hymenaei*, a great globe in blue and silver seemed to hang in the air, which then magically rotated to reveal eight musicians playing within, and Juno accompanied by her attendant peacocks. In *Tethys' Festival*, there was spectacular innovation, as a heavenly circle of stars was seen to move and descend, delivering the masquers in a cloud onto the floor of the hall to dance. In the *Masque of Oberon*, the heir to the throne, young Prince Henry, dressed as the Prince of the Fairies, was brought forward in a chariot, drawn by two live polar bears.

At university, I became obsessed with the elusive and largely forgotten conventions of the court masque. These masques employed the very latest in continental technology to produce spectacular effects. They were extremely elaborate, multi-media affairs, involving lavish scenery, lighting effects and transformation scenes. The RSC would have a hard job to recreate let alone afford these today, even with all our technical know-how.

Just over a year after the *Masque of Oberon* was presented at Court, *The Tempest* was performed in Whitehall as part of the festivities to celebrate the wedding of the king's beloved daughter Elizabeth to Frederick Elector Palatine. No wonder it featured a masque where Miranda and Ferdinand receive a blessing from the gods themselves, watched by the much-admired daughter of the king and her new husband.

Unhappily, Princess Elizabeth's 18-year-old brother Prince Henry died suddenly of typhoid just three months before the wedding.

In *The Tempest*, King Alonso's grief for the loss of his son, whom he believes to have been drowned in the shipwreck, must have struck profound chords throughout the audience in court. Shakespeare might be able to reunite father and son, but King James could experience no such happy ending.

Ships and shipwrecks were much in the minds of Londoners in September 1610. The *Sea Venture*, England's first purpose-designed emigrant ship, was the flagship of a seven-strong fleet, carrying settlers across the Atlantic to Jamestown in the summer of 1609: on board were 150 men and women, and one dog. The flagship hit a hurricane on 24 July and was separated from the rest of the fleet.

The storm blasted the ship for three days before the captain deliberately ran her onto a reef (to prevent her foundering), on the coast of Bermuda. The passengers survived but spent nine months on this uninhabited 'island of Devils', before managing to build two pinnaces from the timbers of the wrecked ship. They eventually made their way to Jamestown, from where one of the men on board wrote an account of their tribulations.

That man was William Strachey, secretary-elect to the Virginia Company. It is thought that Shakespeare must have been aware of the contents of his letter, as some details of it appear in *The Tempest*. For example, during the storm, the terrified passengers witnessed sparks of fire travelling along the masts and bowsprit. The phenomenon, known as St Elmo's Fire, is reimagined by Shakespeare as Ariel divides and flames amazement among the mariners.

The letter contains some terrifying insights into what it must have been like to be on board a tiny vessel in the middle of an Atlantic hurricane. During a workshop on the play, with a number of RSC actors, we read Strachey's letter on board the replica of Sir Francis Drake's ship, The Golden Hind, docked safely on Bankside. To listen to the account of how the caulking between the ship's planks gave way and allowed the water to gush into the hold, while actually crouching below deck, was a sobering experience.

The very same month that Strachey's letter arrived in London, another ship was in the news. But whereas the *Sea Venture* has long been considered an influence on Shakespeare in writing *The Tempest,* this other ship seems to have been overlooked.

It is a gusty Monday morning, just before Michaelmas, on 21 September 1610. In the Royal Dockyard at Woolwich, the shipbuilder Phineas Pett is nervous. At eleven o'clock the King, James I himself, and his family are due to come on board a new ship that Pett has built, at His Majesty's charge, and named for his 16-year-old son, Henry.

The *Prince Royal* is a magnificent vessel, the most significant ship to have been built in James' reign. That morning she is to be 'floated out' or launched onto the River Thames.

Not surprisingly, the spectacular ship attracts large crowds. Pett records in his journal: 'it is not credible what numbers of people continually resort to Woolwich of all sorts, both nobles, gentry, citizens, and from all parts of the country round about'. If Shakespeare himself isn't among the throng who come to see this wonder, many of those who would soon see his play, *The Tempest*, surely are. And Ariel's line 'I boarded the King's ship' would have had extra special resonance.

It is no wonder Pett is anxious. Late the previous evening, an emergency order had been rushed from the court instructing him to search the ship's hold 'for fear some treacherous persons might have bored some holes, to sink her after she should be launched'. An attempt to sink the ship while the royal family were on board would be an unthinkable act of sabotage of Gunpowder Plot proportions.

A wind, blowing hard from the southwest, is unfurling the Royal Standard on the poop deck, but is also affecting the river. It should be building towards full flood at high water but threatens to be little better than a neap tide.

The drums and trumpets are in place on the forecastle, and the Lord Admiral stands ready to welcome the royal barge. The King arrives on time, attended by Prince Henry, and, a little later, Queen Anne arrives from Greenwich with her daughter Elizabeth and younger son Charles. All is ready for the launch. But when the Lord Admiral gives Pett the command to 'heave taut the crabs and screws' (or begin the process of launching) Pett doubts the ship will shift as 'the wind over-blew the tide'. There are so many people on board that the ship resolutely refuses to move.

Eventually, in the late afternoon, the King 'much grieved to be frustrate of his expectation' decided to depart. The humiliating misfortune of being unable to launch the great ship in the presence of the royal party was only compounded when the weather took a turn for the worse. Pett records that shortly after midnight the sky became 'sore overcast'. A violent tempest of rain, thunder and lightning suddenly enveloped the ship 'with great extremity', writes Pett, 'which made me doubt that there was *some indirect working* amongst our enemies to dash our launching'. 'Indirect working'[1] suggests some sort of occult practice.

To imagine that his enemies might be capable, like Prospero, of summoning up a tempest, by 'some indirect working', to damage his project and his reputation, could be paranoia on behalf of the ship builder. But remember, King James himself had charged a group of women in North Berwick of trying to sink his ship when he had brought his young Danish bride back to Scotland in 1590. It's a moment Shakespeare recalls in *Macbeth*, when he has the weird sisters curse a ship 'but in a sieve I'll thither sail and like a rat without a tail, I'll do, I'll do, and I'll do'.

---

[1] When Othello is challenged to refute Brabantio's charge that he used witchcraft to gain his daughter Desdemona's affection, he is asked:

Did you by *indirect* and forced courses
Subdue and poison this young maid's affections?

The squall, however, subsided; Henry arrived back as he had promised, and the *Prince Royal* was successfully launched on the early tide.

It is interesting to note that when they came to secure the ship, Pett writes: 'In heaving down the moorings we found that all the hawsers[2] that had been laid on the shore for land fasts were treacherously cut, to put the ship to hazard of running ashore, if God had not blessed us better.'

So, it was not paranoia, after all. Pett was right to be concerned. There *were* parties conspiring to wreck the king's ship. If these discoveries had circulated among the scavelmen and mariners, and been exaggerated and embroidered in the tavern gossip of Bankside, it is not implausible to think they would lodge in the mind of William Shakespeare and be transformed into the plot of his new play.

*   *   *

Back in Stratford, in April 2014, we successfully marked the 450th anniversary of Shakespeare's birth with an immense firework display igniting a great head based on the outline from the Droeshout engraving. As it flamed amazement in front of the theatre, I was busily thinking of how we would celebrate the 400th anniversary of Shakespeare's death in two years' time.

I had decided to direct *The Tempest*, Shakespeare's last solely authored play, as the climax to the 2016 season, but in order to make it a particularly special event, I set my teams a challenge. I explained how, in writing the play, Shakespeare had been influenced by the masques, which had so astonished the Jacobean court. I wanted to know what the twenty-first-century equivalent might be. How could we astonish our audience today?

Sarah Ellis, our Head of Digital Development, sent me a YouTube clip. It showed a chief exec. in a corporate hotel environment in Nevada delivering a keynote speech. Behind him three large screens projected film of a huge whale, Leviathan, swimming from left to right. 'That's great!' said the chief exec, 'but what if we could do more?' And as he spoke suddenly the whale turned to face us, swam through the screen, and over the heads of the audience. 'That's it!' I said, 'that's what I want for *The Tempest*.'

The event was CES, the Consumer Electronics Show, held annually in Las Vegas. The chief executive was Brian Krzanich. The company was Intel. Sarah reached out. She rang Intel customer services and asked how she could get in touch. Within hours she had set up a meeting. Sarah has chutzpah.

She asked a simple question: would Intel like to work with the Royal Shakespeare Company in developing a new production of *The Tempest* for Shakespeare's 400th anniversary in 2016?

The answer was 'yes'.

So began two years of intense research and development. The result was a production that reimagined the play like never before, performing for the first time with real-time, interactive effects, powered by Intel. It is truly 'a brave new world'.

*   *   *

---

[2] Thick cable used to moor the ship.

Alongside Intel, we began a collaboration with director and producer Andy Serkis and his team from his production company, The Imaginarium. I visited Andy on set for the live-action, motion-capture-enhanced version of *The Jungle Book* that he was directing at the Warner Brothers Studios in Hertfordshire. I was completely captivated watching actors in mo-cap volume suits treading softly through a perfectly realized rainforest jungle. They would eventually transmogrify into the jet-black paws of Bagheera, the panther, as he discovers the baby Mowgli among the tropical vines and creepers of the forests of Madhya Pradesh.

Andy was very welcoming and accommodating to our project as we developed ideas for what the harpy should look like and how it should move, how Ariel might ride on the curled clouds, or appear as a sea-nymph, or be confined in a cloven pine, and how to realize the vicious hunting dogs that Prospero sets on the unwary clowns.

But I knew that no amount of clever effects would solve the play.

At the heart, I needed to secure an actor with the capacity not only to convey intellectual genius and moral gravity, but also to suggest an internal struggle sometimes lacking in the drama.

I met actor Simon Russell Beale for a cup of coffee on Bankside. Simon was living proof of Terry Hands' dictum that the RSC didn't need stars: it made them. Since joining the RSC in the year the Swan opened (1986) Simon had played a whole range of parts: Edward II, Richard III, Thersites, as well as a gaggle of fops. But the last time he had appeared at Stratford was in 1993, twenty-three years before. He had played Ariel in a production by Sam Mendes with Alec McCowen as Prospero.

He immediately put me at my ease, confiding, 'I'm going to do it by the way. I should just say that.' And then we began to discuss what this new technology might mean.

The technical wizardry being developed at The Imaginarium Studios in Ealing was getting very exciting indeed. We had begun by concentrating on Ariel to see how a live actor could create the movement with no latency, no delay in real-time between his gestures and the movement of his technical puppet or avatar.

Mark Quartley, cast as Ariel, was helping to shape the vocabulary.

As we began to involve Simon in these workshops, we realized a few important principles. The first was that Ariel could appear as an avatar, in whatever guise, when he was showing off his clever work to his master, but that as soon as there was business to be discussed Ariel would abandon his avatar disguise, and confront his master face-to-face.

*   *   *

We rehearse the play in the summer of 2016, in the Backstage Trust, one of our new rehearsal rooms in TOP. Normally a new production would rehearse in London and then come up to Stratford just before opening, but because of the amount of new technology we will rehearse the entire production here.

A tumultuous tumble of impressions stays with me from that packed rehearsal period. The cast were finding fascinating stuff. Jenny Rainsford was developing a delightful wit and limpid simplicity, with real anger as Miranda. Joe Dixon was creating a highly original puppy-dog vulnerability in Caliban: both touching and worrying. The comic talents of Simon Trinder and Tony Jayawardena as Trinculo and Stephano were taxed to the limit as they negotiated the very rough magic of the gaberdine scene with Caliban.

The lords were gradually coming more into focus: Jimmy Tucker as King Alonso was growing steadily more panicked by the loss of his son; Joe Mydell was eternally optimistic as Gonzalo, while attempting to keep his temper in the face of the casual racism of Tom Turner's urbane bitter-but-dim Sebastian; and Jonathan Broadbent's Machiavellian Antonio.

And Dan Easton made lovely discoveries about Ferdinand. The king's son is clearly highly educated, though unable to articulate his thoughts without becoming deeply convoluted, and perilously in danger of pretentiousness. Here, for example, he interrupts his would-be father-in-law's stern warnings about any temptation to premarital dalliance and matches him in the scale of his protestation. Try saying the following all on one breath:

> As I hope
> For quiet days, fair issue and long life,
> With such love as 'tis now, the murkiest den,
> The most opportune place, the strong'st suggestion
> Our worser genius can, shall never melt
> Mine honour into lust, to take away
> The edge of that day's celebration
> When I shall think: or Phoebus' steeds are founder'd,
> Or Night kept chain'd below.

To which the frankly baffled Prospero replies laconically:

> Fairly spoke!

*   *   *

We start coming to a much clearer realization as to how the masque is structured. The harpy section with the disappearing feast, haunted by 'strange shapes', is effectively an anti-masque. It is there to prepare you in rough form, for the beauty that is to come.

We also discover that the conjuring of the goddesses is under the control and plan of Prospero himself and is a benediction: his blessing on the union of his daughter and Ferdinand.

But then, the goddesses are seen to whisper, and it transpires, unbeknownst to Prospero, that they have prepared a coda to the masque. The arrival of sweaty, sunburnt sicklemen, ready to relax after hard work in the hot fields, accompanied by nymphs, is not meant to be a bucolic sylvan idyll, but a release of sexual energy.

Prospero watches his daughter and her boyfriend get caught up in the dance as it spirals wildly, getting faster and sexier. He halts the dancing. Not because he has suddenly remembered the conspiracy plot (he has that well covered) but because he cannot bear to watch his daughter discovering her own sexual awakening. No wonder Miranda has never seen him in such a passion. Or so angry.

Prospero's fury turns on Caliban who once tried to rape his master's daughter, leading to his enslavement. Prospero sets terrible hell hounds on Caliban and the clowns at the end of Act Four. He then immediately turns his attention to the lords, as if the savagery he has unleashed on the poor wet drunks has only fuelled his appetite for exacting revenge on his peers.

The scene change – indeed, the change of act – indicated in the Folio text isn't useful here. We remove it, feeling that an exit isn't helpful. Editors have surely only marked it in order for Prospero to have time to get his magic cloak on. It is much more powerful if Prospero can drive on through. He is slavering for the revenge that has been such a long time coming.

When Ariel tells his master how he has imprisoned his enemies 'in the line-grove which weather fends your cell', he conjures an image of old Gonzalo's grief that is so domestic, and so particular it catches the breath.

> The good old lord Gonzalo;
> His tears run down his beard, like winter's drops
> From eaves of reeds.

Ariel suggests that if his master only saw how distracted his enemies were, his feelings towards them 'would become tender'. At which Simon's Prospero snorted derisively 'dost think so spirit?', only to be completely disarmed by his spirit-servant's gentle response 'Mine would were I human'.

Suddenly the breath slows, the heart-rate drops, the anger dissipates, as Prospero realizes that

> ... The rarer action is
> In virtue than in vengeance.

And as Ariel goes to fetch the spell-bound lords, their brains boiled within their skulls, Prospero abjures his rough magic forever:

> Ye elves of hills, brooks, standing lakes and groves ...

In a sentence seventeen-and-a-half lines long, syntactically erratic, full of Ovidian evocation, which meanders through the spectrum of his magical powers, and the weak masters he has employed to summon sea-storms, kindle earthquakes, and it seems wake the dead themselves, Prospero calls upon the island's spirits to attend to his decision.

Once Ariel has delivered the stunned lords, Prospero promises him his freedom. At this point Shakespeare gives Ariel one of his most exquisite songs, 'Where the bee sucks'. Our technology was able to deliver an ecstatic explosion of Ariel and all his quality, dividing deliriously and whizzing around, swooping and diving in exultant anticipation of the liberty he has so longed for.

In narrative terms, the song seems initially to be in an odd position. It serves to fill the time required to dress Prospero in his Ducal robes, but surely from Ariel's point of view this joyous sneak preview of freedom should come once he has been released. In examining this structure, we decided that perhaps Shakespeare wants to strike a different note as master and servant finally part.

Mark Quartley beautifully captured a sense that once granted his freedom, far from lounging luxuriantly in the cowslip's bell, or riding on the bat's back in blissful exhilaration, Ariel suddenly has nowhere to go and nothing to do. His final exit, instead of the usual exuberant flash, was slow and heavy, filled with anxious trepidation at an imagined emptiness ahead.

As we start the technical period on stage, there are breathtaking moments when the technology suddenly all comes into focus. There is genuine amazement after the storm when the body of the king seems to float down, full fathom five, from the tech gallery, as if drowning, his body turning into coral and pearl. The first arrival of Ariel, an azure avatar, scintillating in the ether, is stunning. There is astonishment as Ariel is swallowed inside an enormous cloven pine whose roots and branches suddenly twist and creak, writhing to fill the whole stage. The spectacle of the harpy descending with wings the width of the entire proscenium is harrowing.

I marvel at the liquid grace of the rainbow aurora borealis accompanying the arrival of the goddess Iris, and the drone flight over Hockney-esque horizons, turfy mountains and flat meads, all in primary colours, evoking broom-groves and sea-marges. Then to top it all, the pyroclastic eruption of earth mother, Ceres, from the ground, and a gorgeous peacock's tail fanning out in a shimmering glory, as Juno herself, the queen of the gods, arrives to bless the happy couple.

But of course, it wasn't all plain-sailing.

The twenty-seven projectors required to create the spectacular illusions in the RST's 3D space caused noise issues, a constant background hum of fans, which had judiciously to be negotiated.

Mark Quartley had to have his motion-capture suit (cunningly disguised in his skin-tight Ariel costume) calibrated every performance by our expert in-house team, who had rapidly been learning new skills. But if he then happened to step over a piece of metal concealed in the stage, or a stray wire cable, then the illusion became severely compromised. The avatar's head would suddenly lurch disconcertingly to the side, or his arm would disappear inside his body, and he would have to start the recalibration process all over again.

But in the end, we pulled off the impossible.

The work of all the technical and creative teams – Stephen Brimson Lewis's over-arching design, Finn Ross's astounding kinetic video projections, the avatars and digital characters created by Imaginarium, the understated genius of the lighting designer Simon Spencer – subtly ensuring that the actors themselves did not get lost amid this ravishingly visual feast. And Paul Englishby's music, for the masque in particular (inspired by the marvellous thought that Mozart had been commissioned to write an opera of *The Tempest*) underscores the play with lush splendour.

Our greatest challenge was to ensure that the technology continued to serve the play and that the themes and the story were not drowned among them. It is a tribute to Simon, Mark and the entire acting company that this never happened.

On the day of the first preview of *The Tempest* I felt alarmingly anxious. (Tony could not be on hand to hold my hand. He was in technical rehearsal for *King Lear* at the Barbican.) So many cameras, so many Intel lenses focused on me, and on everything else. Philippa Harland, the then Head of Press, trying to keep all the various film crews in order, and in temper, but tension levels were rising. Had we promised too much?

And to top it all, it took place on the same day as the US elections, which Donald Trump, against all predictions, looked liable to win.

The press night was also scheduled for the same day as the RSC Annual General Meeting, with the press night of *King Lear* at the Barbican the previous Tuesday. How could I have looked at the schedule all those months ago and ever have thought this was feasible, or advisable?

Andy Serkis comes to the opening night with his wife, the actor Lorraine Ashbourne. I meet them beforehand. It's been a hectic few weeks. Lorraine tells me how much she is looking forward to the show and can see how much is riding on its success. She tells me about a documentary she was watching on TV, about the tennis grand-slam champion Serena Williams. Serena was asked how she dealt with all the stress associated with being the highest paid female athlete in the world. She simply replied, 'Pressure is a privilege.' I am going to have that stitched into a sampler and hang it over my desk.

The critics, who were divided on the success or necessity of all the high-tech, universally acknowledge that Simon Russell Beale gave the performance of his career as Prospero.

Reflecting on the production after the furore of the press night and the flurry of reviews, and well into the run, Simon discussed the play and how it felt to perform it now: 'I'm finding it terribly moving,' he said, 'the idea of a man being forced to judge his past life. Shakespeare's last plays are all to do with the nature of forgiveness and acknowledging past mistakes. I think he must have been very exercised by that. *The Tempest* is the play of an older man.'

He said he had always thought of *The Tempest* as a cold play, but had come to realize that he was wrong, and that it has a huge beating heart. I think he's right.

*   *   *

In the winter of 1855, the author of *Les Misérables*, Victor Hugo, and his family exiled themselves from their native France, 'like shipwrecked ones', on the island of Guernsey. His youngest son, François, decided to translate Shakespeare's works in time for the tercentenary of the playwright's birth in 1864. Hugo wrote a book-length introduction to that translation.

Isolated on his island, Victor Hugo reminds me of Prospero.

'There are men, oceans in reality,' he writes. His second chapter is one long tumbling impressionist sentence describing the experience of staring at the ocean: 'These waves, this ebb and flow, this terrible go-and-come, this noise of every gust' ... 'these huge sobs, these monsters glimpsed at, this roaring, disturbing these nights of darkness, these furies, these frenzies, these tempests, these rocks, these shipwrecks' ... 'this vast marvel of monotony, inexhaustibly varied' ... 'this infinite, this unfathomable' ... Hugo conveys the giddily absorbing experience of staring at the sea, which he must have spent long hours doing from the rocky headlands. And that, he says, is like looking into the minds of great men ... like Dante, like Michelangelo, and like Shakespeare.

Coleridge wrote of Shakespeare: 'The body and substance of his work came out of the unfathomable depths of his own oceanic mind.'

29

Troilus and Cressida

– 2018: Royal Shakespeare Theatre, Stratford-upon-Avon.
– Broadcast to cinemas and released on DVD.

King's Cross, Finsbury Park, Potters Bar, Hatfield, Welwyn Garden City . . .

It's the last day of May (2017) and the day is bright, and the railway embankments frothy with elderflower blossom. I am travelling to my first meeting with Evelyn Glennie.

Welwyn North, Knebworth, Stevenage, Hitchen, Arlesey . . .

I want to persuade her to compose the music for my production of *Troilus and Cressida*, next year. And she has invited me to her place of work, in Huntingdon.

Dame Evelyn Glennie, the world-renowned virtuoso percussionist, has been profoundly deaf since she was twelve. If I can persuade her to do this, it will be the first time she has ever composed for the theatre. I want a score that reflects the world of the play and its 'rude sounds' as Troilus calls them.

Biggleswade, Sandy, St Neots . . .

Re-reading *Troilus and Cressida* on the train, I am reminded of just how noisy the play sounds. As the alarums sound for the preparations for battle, Troilus cries:

Peace you ungracious clamours, peace rude sounds!

I love 'rude sounds'. That could be the title of an album. It suggests how out-of-step Troilus is with the warmongering in both Greek and Trojan camps. 'Fools on both sides', he says.

Act Four rings with trumpets challenging each other.

Aeneas (the wily Trojan) has announced Hector's challenge in high and mighty terms declaring:

Trumpet blow loud
Send thy brass voice through all these lazy tents.

While the blare of Ajax's trumpets matches the elephantine lumbering of the man.

Thou, trumpet, there's my purse
Now crack thy lungs and split thy brazen pipe,
Come stretch thy chest and let thy eyes spout blood
Thou blowest for Hector.

After the combat, Hector is welcomed into the Greek camp, and into Agamemnon's tent, with another noisy musical welcome:

Beat loud the tambourines, let the trumpets blow,
That this great soldier may his welcome know.

This clamorous arrival heightens the still silence of the night-time encounter, which Troilus witnesses, between his beloved Cressida and the seducer Diomed. Harmony and music is used to express the discord Troilus feels at seeing Cressida betray him. Troilus cries, 'Yea, so familiar?' And the cynical Ulysses comments 'She will sing any man at first sight', which I take to mean she will pick up a man as quickly as she can pick up a tune, sight-reading straight away.

The climax of the play, announced by drums, is the death of Hector (not of Troilus, whom Shakespeare seems casually to forget at the last moment). The Myrmidons, Achilles' elite fighting force, surround Hector and impale him on their wheel of spears. The Myrmidons were supposed to be ant-men; according to Ovid, when the population of the island of Aegina was wiped out, they replaced the humans and repopulated the island.

We have been looking at footage of how ants communicate through drumming their antennae, and I am interested to see if this ominous sound could accompany the horrible overwhelming of the hero Hector. Achilles then drags him around the walls of Troy tied by the ankles to his horse.

As the train pulls into Huntingdon, I jump into a taxi and make my way to Evelyn's two-storey office in a local business park. I have been a fan of Evelyn's for many years and love the way she talks about the power of music. This is the first time I have met her. She emerges from her office and greets me warmly, her steel grey hair framing a broad beam of a smile. She walks me around some of her marvellous hoard of instruments: Taiko drums, Tibetan prayer bells, a gamelan orchestra of huge exhaust pipes, and piano harps, which she strums or taps as we walk around.

Then we sit down to talk about the project with her assistant, Lee. As I begin to describe how I see the play, set in a dystopian future, a world where endless wars are being fought over scarce resources, sort of 'Ancient Troy meets Mad Max', Lee is getting excited. 'Oh, yeah,' he says, 'that could be great.' I sense I have an ally.

By the time I leave we have riffed all manner of ideas and have agreed she should come up to Stratford to meet the music department and see what resources we have in our magical music store. And she'll meet the designer Niki Turner to discuss how the construction of the set might help amplify the soundscape. I am pretty sure, if she agrees to do it, this will be the first time a composer has been involved in the design of the set at the RSC.

*   *   *

During the Christmas break, in preparation for rehearsals, I curled up in the corner of a sofa and re-read Homer's *Iliad* from start to finish. It's a mighty read, but a thrilling one in Robert Fagles's effortless translation. I am not expecting it to prove revelatory as inspiration for our production of *Troilus and Cressida*, I just want to read it. Shakespeare dispenses at once with all those capricious interfering deities and derides the superhero status of its cast list. Troilus gets only a single mention (in Book 24), but I am surprised by the sudden, very brief appearance of Thersites. Shakespeare is clearly so delighted by the scurrilous misanthrope; he turns him into the play's commentator.

Trying to understand this play's position in the canon, I came upon a mystery surrounding the origins of Shakespeare's play.

A quarto edition (the little single-play paperback version) appeared in 1609 in two different versions. One says on the title page 'The History of Troilus and Cressida . . . as it was acted by the King's majesty's servants at the Globe'. But the second version describes it as a new play, 'never staled with the stage', 'never clapper-claw'd with the palms of the vulgar', and even more graphically, not 'sullied with the smoky breath of the multitude'.

In my facsimile of the 1623 First Folio, *Troilus and Cressida* does not appear in the contents page at all. The text is printed, but without page numbers, unlike the rest of the Folio. Why?

Two decades before the First Folio was assembled and published, *Troilus and Cressida* had been registered for publication. In 1603, one James Roberts had been granted the right 'to print when he hath gotten sufficient authority for it'. Clearly there was some crisis in obtaining the rights for the Folio. They obviously got them eventually, but too late to redo all the pagination.

In my edition, it is squeezed in between *Henry VIII* and *Coriolanus*, between the histories and the tragedies. So is it a history? Should it be classed as a tragedy? Or is it in fact a comedy?

What other research did I need to do?

Tony and I had visited Troy ten years before. Or what, at any rate, is assumed to be the site of the ancient city. Heinrich Schliemann believed he had located Troy in Hisarlik, in modern Turkey, in 1871. Hisarlik means 'fortress' and Schliemann imagined it was the Barbican of the fabled city. Visiting with Tony, it was hard to project the topless towers of Ilium, the mighty walls, or the epic battles fought around them, on to these shifting sand dunes. Alluvial activity has meant that though in its day Troy stood overlooking the Aegean, the sea is now five kilometres away.

I try to convince Tony. But the tacky modern reconstruction of the wooden horse at the entrance to the archaeological excavations has already made him deeply sceptical.

But perhaps these red mud bricks are the crumbling remains of 'strong-besieged Troy'. Is this dry gully the river Simois or Scamander that rose up in torrents against Achilles? Might one of Priam's fabled six great gates have stood here? Dardan and Tymbria, Helias, Chetas, Troien, or Antenorides perhaps, with its 'massy staples' and bolts? Is that the Dardan plain where the Greeks pulled up their black ships and pitched their brave pavilions? If so, where is the island of Tenedos, from where the sea-serpents came frothing over the spume to entangle Laocoon and sons? Might this ramp of polished stones now tufted with grass, and dotted with blood red poppies, be the very ramp that Hector and his returning Trojan warriors climbed after the day's battle?

It was only when we stood on the sandy promontory with our guide and I asked what the headland on the other side of the water was, that myth and history collided for a moment. He told us that the stretch of water before us was the Dardanelles. The spit of land we could see beyond it was the Gallipoli Peninsula. Gallipoli, the very name a blood-spatter, a scar, was the battle ground of one of the greatest disasters of modern warfare. It had all taken place a mere century before, within the view of howling Troy, the pattern for all wars to come, the template of all battles, the fatal warning, fated never to be heeded.

Wars have always been – will never not be. A play set in the place of its mythic original could be set in any era: now, then, or yet to come.

Designer Niki Turner and I chose to set our production of *Troilus and Cressida* in a world that is both elsewhere and elsewhen. We have chosen a dystopian future world of urban and environmental collapse, where war is a blood sport. It allows me to do several things. One of them is to think about the gendering of roles. In such a world, there is no problem having strong women as the leaders of the armies.

So, the cast is exactly gender-balanced, for the first time in the history of the RSC. I cast women as Ulysses, Aeneas, Agamemnon and Thersites. To me, it not only makes perfect sense, but it is a great opportunity to work on Shakespeare with some very talented women for whom the traditionally gendered roles have virtually run out.

Having an actor with the experience of Suzanne Bertish playing Agamemnon, with the authority of a Madeleine Albright,[1] albeit without her indomitable spirit, was a huge asset. Adjoa Andoh aligned Ulysses' Machiavellian guile with a calculating femininity in a male-dominated environment. As the generals lined up to kiss Cressida, Adjoa's Ulysses begged one too, and spat with bitter bile at Cressida's clever put down. We also had Ulysses shoot Patroclus, in order to unlock the stalemate, and prompt Achilles to action over the loss of his lover.

Amanda Harris lent her vibrant wit and dark chocolate tones to Aeneas, pitching his smiling cynicism perfectly; while having Sheila Reid (at 81) as a pepper-pot Thersites, spewing her filthy commentary, was a joy. Thersites' debunking of the male posturing seemed only to be enhanced by having the role played by a woman. And of course, there is nothing new. I discovered that the first time the play was ever performed at Stratford, in a production by William Poel in 1913 (in which Edith Evans played Cressida and Hermione Gingold Cassandra), Thersites was played by a woman called Elspeth Keith, and Aeneas was played by Madge Whiteman.

We also swapped the genders of the soldier Antenor (Gabby Wong) and Cressida's parent, the priest Calchas (Helen Grady). Having Cressida betrayed by her mother instead of her father seemed almost more perfidious.

But all the re-gendering choices were made with vigilant precision. I was careful to ensure that the underlying homoeroticism of the relationship between Achilles and Patroclus was not undermined by any spurious re-gendering, nor did I want to compromise the ludicrous macho posturing of Ajax, faced with the manly valour and integrity of admirable Hector. I was very pleased when the *Evening Standard*, in a

---

[1] The first female Secretary of State in US history, under Bill Clinton.

glowing review, declared, 'This production boasts a 50:50 gender-balanced cast, an RSC first, but I mean it only as a compliment when I say that this is perhaps the least interesting thing about it.'

I also cast a deaf actor as Cassandra. Cassandra was blessed by the Gods with the gift of prophecy but cursed that no one would believe her. Charlotte Arrowsmith came in to audition and as she delivered her speech, she seemed effortlessly to align Cassandra's frustration at not being understood with her own lifetime's frustration at being ignored, patronized, or regarded as lacking intelligence because of her deafness. It was a viscerally powerful and moving performance.

Amber James and Gavin Fowler as the eponymous lovers struggling to negotiate this infected world centred the play's erratic heart, while Oliver Ford Davies (taking over mid-rehearsals from Des Barrit) brought a delicious prurience to Pandarus's suspect interest in the young people in his charge.

At the tech Evelyn Glennie and Niki Turner are admiring their new shipping containers, in which we imagine the Greeks have pitched camp. They have been constructed to work like massive drums, which can be beaten by sticks or dancing feet. Evelyn and Niki have been busy exploring how harmony and discord can work in our production. Shakespeare describes, in a central speech in the play, how when order is upset, what chaos ensues. Ulysses says:

Take but degree away, untune that string
And hark what discord follows.

They have enhanced that image by creating a sort of over-hanging firmament of junk, a galaxy of tat, the sort of space detritus currently orbiting the globe, which itself can jangle and clang to amplify that sense of discord.

How profoundly true is that? Today the world seems particularly challenged by division and discord, and this play articulates just that anxiety.

The Jacobean period was an age of doubt. I would contend that there was just the sense of disjunction and impending apocalypse that many feel present today. While we may approach that with cynicism, with sardonic black humour, and sometimes escape into a positive spirit of optimism, of love, of possible redemption, often we slip back into something like despair at the state of the world, the nature of politics, the fragility of the planet and our place in it.

That is just the place Shakespeare finds himself, writing *Troilus and Cressida*. Frankly I don't think he knows or cares if it is comedy, tragedy or history, because (like life) it is all of those things: inconsistent and contradictory, resistant of the narratives we may attempt to impose upon it.

We are adrift in this unfettered play, while the world decomposes around us. It's heartfelt and merciless. Don't expect it to be what you expect it to be. Let it be what it is. It's a voyage of discovery. Dr Johnson, in his *Preface to Shakespeare*, writes that the plays are 'compositions of a distinct kind ... exhibiting the real state of sublunary nature. ... expressing the course of the world'.

Troilus and Cressida was the favourite play of my friend and mentor, the great, the legendary RSC director and guru John Barton. John's 1980s TV series *Playing*

Shakespeare and the accompanying book are still treasured by drama students and young actors all over the world to this day.

When I told John I was going to direct the play, his eyes twinkled. I spent long hours in his Fitzrovia flat listening to him describe what drew him so especially to this knotty, sinewy, teeming, challenging work. I wish now I had recorded those conversations. John died in January 2018, in his ninetieth year, just as I was preparing my production.

After his funeral, a packet arrived. It contained a few books, some yellowing foolscap sheets and a picture.

The books are four battered editions of the play, the copies John had used in rehearsal for each production. They are filled with his pencil scribbles and edits. There's a note. It's from John Barton's sister, Jennifer: 'I think John would have wanted you to have these.'

Troilus and Cressida became John's signature play.

In the front of the oldest edition, John has scribbled his name J.B.A. Barton (John Bernard Adie Barton). I suspect it is the copy he had at Cambridge when he assisted his Cambridge mentor, George 'Dadie' Rylands, in a Marlowe Society production in 1954. It's one of the pocket-sized New Temple Shakespeares, published by Dent in 1949 with illustrations by Eric Gill. The book has several crusty black spots on the cover. When I wet my finger and dab them, I realize they are dried stage blood. John always choreographed his own fights. He had, perhaps, got too close in one rehearsal and got spattered.

John was credited as the fight arranger on the production he worked on with Peter Hall at Stratford in 1962 as part of a season of comedies. Ian Holm and Dorothy Tutin played the lovers with Max Adrian as Pandarus. The slim blue hardback 1957 Cambridge University Press edition must be the one he used for this production. It is full of stage directions and blocking ideas.

The package includes two very collapsed CUP paperback editions that John used for his next two productions. In 1968 he directed the play with Helen Mirren as Cressida, Michael Williams as Troilus, David Waller as Pandarus and Alan Howard as Achilles.[2]

The picture is an engraving of the heroes of Troy: Agamemnon, Achilles, Nestor, Ulysses, Diomedes, Paris and Menelaus. On the back is a message in blue ink. It reads:

> *Darling John, this must have been meant for you, so it comes in admiration of your Troilus 1968 and brings wishes for its 1969 revival and truly Trojan tour. Love Peg.*

The great actress Peggy Ashcroft had presented John with this nineteenth-century print in celebration of his acclaimed production of the play. In the summer of 1969, the company set off on an extraordinary European tour taking in Zurich, Geneva, Cologne, The Hague, Rotterdam, Amsterdam, and two other dates in the Netherlands, in just two weeks. No wonder Peggy called it 'Trojan'.

---

[2] The final copy of the script is from the 1976 production with Mike Gwilym and Francesca Annis.

But for me the greatest treasure is a sheaf of faded papers, in John's own handwriting, headed 'Directors notes for rehearsal'. They are John's thoughts for the first day of rehearsal of the play.

And as you can imagine, I took them into our first day of rehearsal that September.

John was a self-deprecating man who rarely wrote about Shakespeare, preferring instead to share his vast knowledge and experience in the rehearsal room. So, this scruffy package of notes was gold dust. They date, I think, from the 1968 Stratford production, as there is a reference to the Vietnam War.

John's major premise in approaching *Troilus and Cressida* is not to generalize its mood.

He begins by asking simply: what kind of play is it? Is it comical, tragical, historical, mythical, psychological? What is its tone? Cynical, romantic, obscene, intellectual, absurdist?

Perhaps it's all of these? Perhaps that's Shakespeare's point.

They reveal much of John's approach, guiding actors to mine the text for indications to character embedded within, rather than imposing ideas upon it; and urging them to celebrate contradictions and inconsistencies, rather than flattening them out. To avoid generalization at all costs. Why? Because life, too, is messy and we are inconsistent.

As we rehearsed the play we realized John was right. That if you tried to simplify the character, to play only one perspective, then you missed the contradictions. They are all 'compact of jars'. Like life itself, full of contradictions. Funny one moment, sad the next, noble, then base, chivalric, then self-serving.

I dedicated our 2018 production to John Barton's memory.

But on the morning before the opening night of *Troilus and Cressida,* I heard of the loss of another great RSC character.

I received a phone call to say that the legendary voice coach Cicely Berry had died. Her daughter Sara told me she had died peacefully in her sleep on Monday night. I took half an hour out and walked along the river to Holy Trinity. Acrid, sweet smell of fallen leaves. I knew only one of my grandparents, and he died before I was four. But Cis and John felt as if they had always been for me the company's spiritual grandparents.

I sat in the choir stalls, contemplating Shakespeare's bust, and thinking about a woman who had dedicated much of her life to his work.

I went back and did a director's talk before the show, and then called the company into the wings, to talk about Cis. Though we had dedicated the production to John, tonight we would do it for both these great teachers and human spirits. I popped up to the Ashcroft Room, to do the same for the *Tamburlaine* company who were busy warming up for the show, and then down to TOP where the actors were preparing for a performance of David Edgar's *Maydays*.

Adjoa caught up with me in the corridor backstage. 'Cis would have loved this production,' she said proudly. 'It's political, and it's human, like her. She believed that Shakespeare is for everyone like you do. So, we're OK.'

Back in the office, Cis is sitting on the sofa. It's a tender drawing in red crayon, which Tony did of her. I have been meaning to hang it next to the one he did of John. You can see her listening.

The following spring, we planted a cherry tree for Cis, next to John's behind the Swan. They can stand sentinel together, making sure we honour their extraordinary legacy.

30

Measure for Measure

– 2019: Royal Shakespeare Theatre, Stratford-upon-Avon;
and (interrupted) UK tour; Teatre Municipal de Girona/Teatro Principal de
Vitoria, Spain.
– Broadcast to cinemas and released on DVD.

Five years into running the RSC, I felt we needed to stop for a moment to take stock and check that we were presenting our work in the most efficient way possible. In 2017, I pulled together all the different departments and asked their opinions. The result was a deeply creative and illuminating response.

We began a process of recalibration across the board in a variety of significant ways. Indeed, we began to refer to the 2019 season internally, as the Recalibration Season. It was never going to be a great marketing term, but it described precisely what we would do.

Perhaps the most significant factor was asking two directors to join me to develop the season, instead of asking them individually to direct two specific plays. Kimberly Sykes and Justin Audibert bought in to the idea of creating a company to perform three plays. Only then did I invite them to direct *As You Like It* and *The Taming of the Shrew* respectively. We would have a season designer (our then director of design Stephen Brimson Lewis) who would design the sets for all three productions on a season stage. We would pull the auditorium galleries around in front of the proscenium, placing the band platform on the second gallery. The company would reflect the nation, in terms of gender, diversity, regionality and disability.

I would direct *Measure for Measure*.

We often say Shakespeare is like a magnet that attracts all the iron filings of whatever is going on in the world. *Measure* is the living proof of that contention. Not only does it produce a magnetic field attracting some of the most toxic issues of this moment, but it is positively radioactive, producing some intense reactions. This play seems somehow specifically to be written in response to the #MeToo movement.

Take the plot. There is a draconian moral crackdown in Vienna. A young man, Claudio, is sentenced to death for making his girlfriend pregnant. Claudio's sister, Isabella, at the very point of entering a convent as a nun, pleads for her brother's life. Angelo, the man charged with ultimate authority in the city, agrees to release him on one condition: that she has sex with him. She says, 'I will expose you.' He says, 'Who would believe you?' She turns to the audience and says, 'To whom should I complain?' #MeToo.

On the first preview, when Sandy Grierson as Angelo and Lucy Phelps as Isabella played that scene, there were gasps in the audience at Angelo's exit line 'My false o'er weighs your true'.

In the vox pop that the marketing department conduct at the end of that first preview, as the audience come out at the end, one woman put it succinctly: 'It is the most important play of 2019.'

But yet I run before my horse to market.

In 1908, the vicar of Stratford-upon-Avon stood up in the pulpit of Holy Trinity Church and challenged any of the men in his congregation to say they would dare to take a young lady to see a production of *Measure for Measure* that had just opened at the Shakespeare Memorial Theatre. The Rev Arbuthnot repeated his opinion in the local paper: 'No respectable and modest woman ought to go to it,' he fulminated.

In that very same year, 1908, in Vienna, the city in which Shakespeare sets *Measure for Measure*, similar conservative ideas of what was decent and Christian were being severely challenged. It was a crucible of change. The old guard was about to be swept away. New ideas were provoking established beliefs in the nature of art, of the human psyche itself.

That year, Gustav Klimt exhibited his great 'golden period' masterpiece *The Kiss*, Sigmund Freud revealed the Oedipus complex, and a young painter called Adolf Hitler arrived in the city.

We might have little idea of what Vienna meant to Shakespeare, but the place has very resonant associations for us today, particularly in those first decades of the twentieth century. It was the birthplace of psychology, and the same forensic lens that Freud was turning on the human mind was being applied to the painted canvas in the work of artists like Egon Schiele and Oskar Kokoschka. It was the city of Mahler and Schoenberg, the centre of an explosion in music as well as in architecture, philosophy and political thought.

Vienna was also the capital of the Austro-Hungarian Empire, which, along with many of the Royal Houses of Europe, would shortly collapse in the First World War. Vienna had one of the great cathedrals, the Stephansdom, but was also notorious for having some of the most successful brothels in Europe. The Sacred and the Profane sat closely together in that city.

Those ingredients closely match the elements of the play Shakespeare describes in the London that he knew. His own theatre sat very close by some of the stews of Southwark. I hoped the associations we made (and Stephen Brimson Lewis would evoke in our 1900s Vienna design) might match and illuminate the milieu Shakespeare conjures in *Measure for Measure*.

*   *   *

The cause of the duke's sudden departure from Vienna, at the start of the play, is mysterious. He abandons his office and leaves the city in the care of the neurotic Angelo. Why?

The reason seemed to us to become clear in the prison scene, where the duke, disguised as a friar, counsels the young Claudio on the eve of his execution. Although he knows he has the power to revoke the sentence, the duke prepares Claudio for his end. 'Be absolute for death' he urges, arguing that life is 'a thing / That none but fools would keep'.

The speech seems to convey far more about his own troubled psychological state than Claudio's. He seems to lose himself in his own musing on the futility of life, even suggesting to this very young man that once you grow old, and have some wealth, you have neither the appetite, passion nor looks to enjoy it:

> What's yet in this
> That bears the name of life?

he laments, revealing perhaps his own personal despair, a lonely emptiness, an existential crisis.

James Cooney as Claudio then pleads with his sister Isabella to save his life, with a speech that captures in vivid detail his terror of dying:

> Ay, but to die, and go we know not where;
> To lie in cold obstruction and to rot;
> This sensible warm motion to become
> A kneaded clod; and the delighted spirit
> To bathe in fiery floods, or to reside
> In thrilling region of thick-ribbed ice;
> To be imprison'd in the viewless winds,
> And blown with restless violence round about
> The pendent world; or to be worse than worst
> Of those that lawless and incertain thought
> Imagine howling: 'tis too horrible!

In rehearsal, we experiment with the speech. Is Claudio's focus to persuade his sister of that horror, to make her feel that terrifying void so she will relent and give herself up to Angelo's lust to save him? Or does he lose himself in that extraordinary single sentence, until he is overwhelmed by its imaginative power, crying ''tis too horrible!'

James himself becomes overwhelmed by the rolling cataclysmic force of the language, tears spring to his eyes, his voice cracks, and the speech gets lost in his own emotion. I give him a note that Terry Hands once gave me in my first season at Stratford, when he directed *Julius Caesar*. I played Octavius Caesar in the second half, and in the first half I was assorted citizens and messengers, including the servant who brings Caesar the warning from the augurs, as he is about to set out to the Capitol on the morning of the ides of March.

I ran on in floods of tears, appalled at the horror of the bad omen, and its possible implications for my master.

> They would not have you to stir forth to-day.
> Plucking the entrails of an offering forth,
> They could not find a heart within the beast.

Terry stopped me and said, 'Well Greg, I could see you certainly felt every ounce of that speech.' And as I flushed with pride and burbled my thanks, he continued, 'the trouble is, I didn't feel anything.' I got the point at once. Don't spend all your energy feeling the emotion, wallowing in it, as I had been doing. Instead, make the person you are speaking to feel the impact of your news, and thereby the audience too with any luck.

I told James a favourite piece of advice that Thora Hird had recalled on Desert Island Discs. It had come from her father, who managed the Royalty Theatre in Morecambe: 'Don't show too much emotion: or you won't glean any.'

Claudio ends his account of the soul's journey after death with his own assessment, a direct rebuttal to the Friar's advice.

> The weariest and most loathed worldly life
> That age, ache, penury and imprisonment
> Can lay on nature is a paradise
> To what we fear of death.

*   *   *

> *Some actors have a tendency*
> *Boarding on obsessive*
> *To stress the boring pronouns*
> *And adjectives possessive.*

In an attempt to wean my company off this distracting habit, I presented the above doggerel to the actors during rehearsal. The nouns and verbs have generally much more value and interest, but for some reason if there is a 'me' or a 'my' in the verse line, some actors will automatically stress it, with almost egotistical addiction.

> Friends, Romans, countrymen, lend ME your ears

> A horse, a horse, MY kingdom for a horse.

*   *   *

As we rehearsed the play in the Gatsby rehearsal room at TOP, the company were performing the other two plays in the season, evenings and matinees: *As You Like It* and *The Taming of the Shrew*. The final scene of *As You Like It* and *Measure* have a lot in common. *Measure* seems almost perversely to echo the earlier play, written perhaps three or four years before. And those echoes seemed heightened by the fact that Antony Byrne was playing both dukes.

In the Elizabethan play, Duke Senior brings all the couples together to bless them: Rosalind and Orlando, Celia and Oliver, Phoebe and Silvius, and Audrey and Touchstone. It's an act of affirmation, of celebration, of catharsis.

But in *Measure*, the Jacobean play, none of the unions he has stage-managed so carefully seem destined for great happiness. Will Lucio be a faithful husband to the prostitute Kate Keepdown or a good father to their 15-month-old toddler? Will

Mariana's insistence that Angelo will prove a better husband than he was a fiancé work out? Why is the duke so dismissive of the potential future of Claudio and Juliet with their newborn? And what are we to make of his proposal to Isabella? Is it a hasty burst of ill-timed spontaneity or a skilfully planned manipulation?

The delight of Antony Byrne's performance as the duke was its constant sense of improvisation, as if the duke was working it all out in the moment.

Lucy Phelps was a radiant Isabella, with a firm, implacable faith. She worked through so many choices in the final beat of the play. What does Isabella's silence mean? Other Isabellas had calmly, even gratefully, accepted the duke's proposal and stretched out a demure hand to accept his. Others had turned on their heel and exited, defiantly returning to the convent or to a newly liberated life. We took a different choice. The 'happy couples' all departed, leaving the duke and Isabella alone on stage. He turned to her. She turned to us. Blackout. We are left wondering what happened next, according to our own prejudices or dispositions. Can she get out of this trap that, somehow, she has walked into?

To whom should she complain?

As Harold Bloom declared, *Measure for Measure* is Shakespeare's farewell to Comedy.

* * *

At seven o'clock, as the final preview of *Measure* is about to start in Stratford, I am sitting in a cramped little cubby hole on the corridor outside the Intensive Care Unit of the Wellington Hospital in St John's Wood, waiting for Tony to emerge from open-heart surgery. He's undergoing an operation to repair a mitral heart valve. I'm trying to keep all thoughts of death out of my head. He's been in there for five hours.

That morning Thelma Holt had sent a little pot of pale pink roses with a note that made us chuckle. She has lit a candle to Saint Anthony of Padua, patron saint of lost causes. As Tony and I waited for him to be collected from his room, I recalled a fortune cookie slip I had found in an old diary, a quotation from Walt Whitman. 'I think it went: "There was just the two of us. Nothing else mattered".' 'No,' Tony said. 'It was better than that. "There was just the two of us. No more to be said".' But actually it's much simpler. 'We were together. I forget the rest.'

'We mustn't make a thing about parting,' Tony said.

'No,' I said, and gave his hand a little squeeze. Then there was a flurry and the trolley arrived. 'I was just starting my fish,' the matron laughed, 'and suddenly the surgeon was ready.' They raised the height of the trolley, took a pillow from the bed, and asked Tony to get on.

'Oh, wait a minute,' he said, and lifted his arms to me. We hugged, had a little kiss. And suddenly he was gone.

In the cubbyhole for five hours, my mind wanders all over the place. I hope the *Measure* company are OK. The previews were in very good shape when I left, but nevertheless ...

By the time they allow me in to see him, all plastered, and bandaged and wired up, oesophageal pipes down his throat, drainage tubes from his heart, cathetered, saline drip swinging, blood seeping from various intravenous lines, and his body still smeared with iodine, he is starting to wake up. Machines bleep and LED numbers register his heart rate and blood pressure, and endless other vital statistics.

'Thank God you're here,' he says in a hoarse whisper. 'Thank St Anthony of Padua that you're here,' I reply.

The following day, *Measure for Measure* opened to good reviews in Stratford.

It then went on to the Barbican, and embarked on a six-week national tour, with *Shrew* and *As You*. But then, in the middle of our run in Newcastle, with two weeks in Blackpool still to go, the Covid-19 pandemic brought everything to a halt.

31

The Comedy of Errors: A Lockdown Chapter

– 2020: The two Shakespeare plays in rehearsal when we closed our theatres were The Winter's Tale and The Comedy of Errors.

At the start of the pandemic, we kept everyone on pay for the first six weeks, until the end of April, and then we furloughed 90 per cent of our staff, in order to take advantage of the government's coronavirus job retention scheme. Although they would not be eligible for the scheme, we kept both RST companies on throughout as well, including the actors, assistant directors and stage managers.

In order to keep everyone up to speed with developments, executive director Catherine Mallyon and I recorded regular company briefings which were streamed live. In a silly addition, to keep the acting company's spirits up, I sent out an alphabet of my favourite words in Shakespeare, A–Z, with a new letter every morning.

The fact we had by now recorded three-quarters of the plays in the canon with our 'Live-From' programme became very useful in keeping engaged with our stakeholders. They were shown on BBC Four's Culture in Quarantine slots, and on the online streaming services Britbox and Marquee.

Our projected plans suggested a possible late spring opening, but we then realized that we would not be back until summer and maybe the autumn. This was a deeply depressing moment for everyone. No Shakespeare productions in Stratford for the summer – that hasn't happened since the original Shakespeare Memorial Theatre opened in 1879. Seasons ran annually there even through three of the five years of the Great War.

The old Shakespeare Memorial Theatre burned down one blustery March morning in 1926, but the very next day it was decided that the summer season of plays would continue, without postponement, in the cramped old cinema in Greenhill Street in town, and those seasons happened every year, despite the general strike and the depression, until Elizabeth Scott's new theatre opened in 1932.

Shakespeare's plays were performed here with only a month's interruption, throughout the Second World War. Even though the Luftwaffe used the theatre as a navigational tool on their way up the Avon to bomb Coventry in 1941, still performances continued.

We didn't even stop when we closed the theatre for our reconstruction project in 2007, as we performed in the rusty box of the Courtyard Theatre (now the new TOP) for five years, until our beautifully transformed theatre was ready to open in 2012.

So the plays of Shakespeare have been performed on our stages, on this very site, since 1879 every year, for the last 140 years in a nearly unbroken line. Unbroken that is ... until now.

Over the coming months, the actors contributed to the education department's initiatives like #homeworkhelp, to support parents trying to home-school their children. They engaged with our national partnerships. They recorded *Sonnets in Solitude*, among a whole host of other clever ideas online. And in the summer, they did weekly weekend performances we called *Shakespeare Snapshots* in the Avonbank Gardens, around the stump of the old red oak tree: an actual 'wooden O', as one of them quipped.

From July, I began *Talking Shakespeare*, three series of twenty online interviews with some great Shakespearians. They attracted an online audience from all over the world. I started with Judi Dench, and we included the likes of Patrick Stewart, Helen Mirren and Ian McKellen, David Oyelowo, Simon Russell Beale and Harriet Walter. To celebrate the RSC's 60th Birthday, we ended the series with my predecessors as Artistic Director: Michael Boyd, Adrian Noble and Trevor Nunn. Trevor told me that for all the terrible financial crises and political wrangles he had had to deal with his in his entire time as Artistic Director, nothing had come close to what we were having to deal with in this pandemic. Somehow it was very reassuring to hear that generous response, as there have been so many times when I had felt the scale of the job would simply overwhelm me.

In the autumn, as the government roadmap to reopening got pushed back and back, we began a long consultation process to cut our workforce costs by 30 per cent. I am proud to say that, due to a magnificent effort from the Senior Leadership Team, really imaginative proposals from the staff, and a significant number of people accepting voluntary redundancy, we finally managed to get compulsory redundancy numbers down to single figures. But in the shuffle, I lost my right hand, my beloved PA Jane Tassell. Her encyclopaedic knowledge of the company going back over thirty years, could surely not be replaced I thought. It was like we were burning down a library.

In the winter, we planned a programme of small-scale events for the RST for December, hoping by then that we would be able to perform to in-person audiences. *Tales for Winter* included my own five-hour edit of the story of the Trojan War and its aftermath, as told in the Iliad, Aeneid and Odyssey, in the Augustan iambics of Dryden and Pope. We called it *Troy Story*. The programme also included retellings of Shakespeare's Tales for schools by Michael Morpurgo, a festive concert for Christmas, and an event curated by our Youth Advisory Board, and Next Generation company called *Young Bloods*.

In the new year, as we went back into lockdown, I directed a second concert in the season, called *Swingin' The Dream*.

Swingin' The Dream showcased the music from an extraordinary production which opened on Broadway in 1939, a musical adaptation of *A Midsummer Night's Dream* fusing Shakespeare with jitterbug, jazz and swing. It had Louis Armstrong as Bottom, Maxine Sullivan as Titania and Butterfly MacQueen as Puck. It flopped spectacularly but its story, which the concert told, is intriguing. Though there would be no in-person audience, the concert was streamed live around the world.

This is an extract from my diary, as I took a break during rehearsals to look around the empty theatre.

Tuesday 5 January 2021: Front of House in the RST.

Finally, back on stage rehearsing. The jazz quintet is starting to warm up for a rehearsal in the RST. Wonderful to hear the smoochy sound of the saxophone, the smoky vibe of the double bass, and the too-diddly-oo of the clarinet, all jamming together. I slipped out to look around front of house.

I have rarely heard the ticking of the 1932 clock in the Elizabeth Scott Bar. Normally this Art Deco foyer is humming with chatter and life, people ordering drinks or picking up tickets or meeting friends, and now it's empty and echoey.

The foyer is paved with different tones of English limestone, greeny-blue Hornton stone and a tawny stone from Devon flecked with tiny shelly fossils. But now you can hardly see it, because the lighting department are taking the opportunity of the new lockdown to sort out all their equipment, and it is spread over the whole floor.

Around the stainless-steel Art Deco box office there are piles of carefully wrapped power distribution cables and rows of lanterns: follow-spots and fresnels. By the doors is an army of automated vari-lights, called 'intelligent lights', because they can move and change colour and swivel about. They look like little rows of robots: stumpy matt black Daleks, and compact R2D2s.

On the drinks shelf, where people usually pick up their interval gin and tonics, sits a line of metal top hats with square brims. They are a shutter fixture, which prevent the scatter of light from either side of the lamp. There are ranks of barn-doors and scrollers (which shape the beam of light or can change its colour with gel filters).

Everything is being cleaned and polished and tested, for electrical safety, in preparation for when we can get back on the stage and put on *The Winter's Tale*.

Yesterday, we had the news from prime minister Boris Johnson that we were back in lockdown. The guidance means that the lockdown is as severe as it was back in March last year, when everything closed, but it does allow for theatres to be able to continue with rehearsal, and with filmed performance, so we are able to go ahead with this weekend's concert as part of our *Tales for Winter* Season.

I wander through the shop, by the box office, and down the colonnade towards the Swan. There are racks of bagged-up costumes, from *The Whip* (by Juliet Gilkes Romero), *King John* and *A Museum in Baghdad* (by Hannah Khalil), which were running in the Swan when we closed that theatre. Big packing cases fill the space, black flight-cases on wheels with silver metal trim, from the RSC tour of *Measure for Measure*, *The Taming of the Shrew* and *As You Like It*. We had reached Newcastle and were on our way to Blackpool, when everything closed last year. And in fact, *Shrew* was about to head off to Chicago and Washington and then to Seoul before ending up in Tokyo just before the Olympics, but now all the sets and costumes have limped back here and are being sorted through, before heading for the store.

Tucked behind the scissor lift (a skyjack used to hang the lights) and next to our enormous grizzly bear is one of the programme stalls, and in front of it a rack of brochures from last year's lost season. Here is a brochure for the Swan's Projekt Europa, a Season of European work, curated by director Maria Aberg, a *Peer Gynt* by Barbara

Frey from Zurich, and an adaptation of José Saramago's novels *Blindness and Seeing* directed by Tiago Rodrigues from Portugal. An enormous amount of work. All brought to a cruel halt. I feel a shudder of guilt and disappointment.

There is a dusty feeling of stasis here in the building. I go back in and listen to the rehearsal.

Walking into the foyer space between the old back wall of the 1932 theatre and the drum wall that encloses the current theatre, I glance upwards. Above me hangs a galaxy of circular illuminated panels with production photographs. They're usually lit up, but not at the moment.

We have been working through the entire canon of Shakespeare's plays since 2013, when I started programming as Artistic Director, and these roundels display production shots from each show. So, there's David Tennant with his long braids and gold-painted fingernails as Richard II, in my first production in the job; Tony Sher as Falstaff and Paola Dionisotti as Mrs Quickly; and Alex Hassell as Henry V. As I contemplate the roundels, I find myself surveying our progress through the canon: some exceptional performances, and some of themes that have emerged along the way.

Here are Michelle Terry and Ed Bennett as the sparring lovers in our pairing of *Love's Labour's Lost* and *Love's Labour's Won* (as we called *Much Ado*). Here is Hugh Quarshie as Othello, and Lucian Msamati as Iago, in Iqbal Khan's production. Iqbal also cast Ayesha Dharker as Iago's wife Emilia, which added another complexity to the dynamics of this inter-racial tangle.

Paapa Essiedu played Hamlet in 2016. Here he is in his Basquiat-inspired graffiti suit, with a skull on the back. Simon Godwin's production, described by Billington as 'spiritually refreshing', and Paapa's 'priceless vitality' as the prince, marked another milestone in the way the company has always embraced and championed diversity on its stages.

Josette Simon, another RSC pioneer, who first arrived at the RSC in 1982, is here as Cleopatra (opposite Antony Byrne as Mark Antony) in the 2017 Rome Season. She gave an extraordinary physical performance, full of capricious feline grace. And here is Sope Dirisu as a bloodied Coriolanus. Sope's career as an actor was kick-started at Stratford when, at the age of twenty-one, he took part in Open Stages, our amateur programme, playing the title role in a production of *Pericles* in 2012.

Chris Eccleston appears as Macbeth, in Polly Findlay's 2018 production, with Niamh Cusack as his wife. Chris was seventeen when he hatched the idea of playing Macbeth at Stratford. But he thought a working-class lad from Salford would never be given that opportunity. Over thirty years later, he wrote to me about his ambition, and over lunch, as he started to persuade me that it would work, he discovered he was pushing at an open door. His Macbeth was a rugged soldier, shocked by the scope of his own imagination, poundingly urgent.

Here is Gillian Bevan as Queen Cymbeline in 2016; Kathryn Hunter as Timon of Athens in 2018, and from the same year, the entire company in my own *Troilus and Cressida*, our first gender-balanced production; and Claire Price as Petruchia and the women, in a defiant phalanx of farthingales, power-dressing Elizabethan-style, in Justin Audibert's 2019 gender-flipped *The Taming of the Shrew*.

At the riverside end of the foyer, the last few remaining roundels are empty. We were three-quarters of our way through our journey through the entire canon, and by now at least two more roundels should have been filled, with production shots of *The Winter's Tale* and *The Comedy of Errors*.

That journey was abruptly halted just before they went into technical rehearsal last March. So, the roundels remain sadly blank and unlit for the moment. I begin to brood about whether we will ever manage to finish the canon. Alex beard at the Royal Opera House said that in times of financial crisis, the motto was 'if in doubt put on *Swan Lake*'. For which read *A Midsummer Night's Dream* or *Romeo and Juliet* at Stratford-upon-Avon. But I want us to continue our journey. But will the board contemplate us mounting plays as rarely done as the *Henry VIs*?

Back in the theatre, they are rehearsing the opening number, a swishy swing version of Mendelssohn's Spring Song, with the lyric 'Spring is in the air, flowers everywhere'. Let's hope so.

* * *

Ten days after this diary entry, things moved on apace. The daily death toll had risen to a staggering 1,500, the highest in Europe, and we had to rethink our whole strategy once again. This phase of the disease was the worst that we had experienced, with the new highly transmissible variant, and others emerging in South Africa and Brazil. We could see every day on the news what pressure the NHS and intensive care units were under.

It was clear we could not open before Easter, and that in all probability, it wouldn't be before May half-term, or even June or July. So we had another of our by now very regular company meetings and I had to tell the acting company that with such an indeterminate roadmap, we could no longer afford to retain them. Some very sober, sad faces in the Zoom screen, alas.

With the anniversary of lockdown coming up we created a *Lament for a Year of Lost Theatre*. Two paired sonnets (97 and 98) which speak of the pain of absence, throughout 'the fleeting year', were recorded by Lucy Phelps and James Cooney, to an achingly sad collage of images of the empty theatre, photographed by Sam Allard. Lucy and James had been in Newcastle on tour in *Measure for Measure* (playing Isabella and Claudio) when the theatre doors were locked.

We did manage to persuade the BBC to film Erica Whyman's *The Winter's Tale*, shown on the Lights Up season over Shakespeare's birthday weekend, although it was very sad to think it would never be seen before a live audience. But would *Comedy* ever see the light of day as a production, or should we cut our losses, and release that company?

* * *

On a chilly February morning, at the start of 2021, our Director of Creative Placemaking and Public Programmes, Geraldine Collinge; Stephen Rebbeck, our Technical Director; Head of Technical Design, Alan Bartlett; and Head of Technical Resources, Ben Ranner, gathered outside the theatre, in our wellington boots.

In order to find some sense of certainty in a very uncertain time, we had made the decision (brave or fool-hardy, we would discover) to build an open-air theatre for the summer and stage the other production (alongside *The Winter's Tale*) that we had planned to do last summer: *The Comedy of Errors*.

After an hour or so of deliberation we decided that the best place for our new theatre would be in the Swan Gardens, next to the river. 'I think this is perfect,' said Geraldine (whose inspiration the open-air theatre really was). And as she said so, a flight of swans took off on the river, their wings flapping against the water, sounding exactly like a round of applause. The plans very quickly started to appear.

Meanwhile, director Phillip Breen began a recast and rethink of *The Comedy of Errors* for our new garden theatre. It's the ideal play for our new open-air venture, and it happens to be the shortest of the Shakespeares.

On Monday 12 July 2021, on a balmy sunny evening, I walked out onto the stage for the Lydia and Manfred Gorvy[1] Garden Theatre in front of a live audience. 'We're back,' I said, and the applause expressed not only a sense of relief to be back to the theatre for the first full-scale production in over a year, but the joy of being back as a community to witness together the shared experience of theatre. The laws of inertia state that anything as big as an audience accelerates from a standing start slowly, but when it finally gets moving there is no stopping it. Well, on that particular summer night they defied that law and from the start the laughter exploded like champagne from a shaken bottle.

Mark Lawson's 5-star review for *Comedy* concluded: 'After a period in which *The Comedy of Errors* has been busy as a headline on the government, the RSC gloriously reclaims it for theatre.'

We all felt a huge sense of relief. The wheels were beginning to run again. Now we could turn our attention to reopening the RST itself.

Watching the play, some lines hit home as they had never done before. I don't know why. Perhaps just because they were being spoken out loud, to a live audience, and after such a long break. As Adriana welcomes home her tardy husband (unaware of the fact that it is his twin brother), she redefines a classic expression of the indissolubility of a couple in love.

> How comes it now, my husband, O, how comes it,
> That thou art thus estranged from thyself?
> Thyself I call it, being strange to me,
> That, undividable, incorporate,
> Am better than thy dear self's better part.

For all the hyperbole, her words echo my own experience of the bond of love.

> For know, my love, as easy mayest thou fall
> A drop of water in the breaking gulf,
> And take unmingled that same drop again,
> Without addition or diminishing,
> As take from me thyself and not me too.

---

[1] Lydia and Manfred have been massive supporters of the RSC since an early visit in the 1960s.

*   *   *

Now *here's* a comedy of errors:

At the end of May 2021, it was reported that William Shakespeare had died.

Bill (81), a local Warwickshire man and a former Rolls-Royce worker, had been the first man in the UK to receive the Pfizer vaccine the previous December. In Argentina, Canal 26 reporter, Noelia Novello, announced that she was stunned to tell her viewers that the most important writer in the English language had just died.

32

Henry VI, Part One

– 2021 Open Rehearsal project.
– Filmed and broadcast live, and available on DVD.

On Wednesday 23 June 2021, in a first for the RSC, we live-streamed an open rehearsal run from the Ashcroft Room. The play was *Henry VI Part One*.

During the month-long project, leading up to that broadcast, my life changed.

I had had the idea of conducting a project that would not depend on any government road map – which might threaten our opening plans – but that would keep our work visible, available and accessible. We would allow cameras into the rehearsal room and for three weeks would rehearse a play, under strict Covid-secure protocols. We would let anyone interested watch rehearsal sessions or listen to experts discuss the history and context of the play, or even join us online for warm-ups if they felt like it. We would then, in the fourth week, live-stream the final rehearsal room run. Any of the actors invited to join the project would be fully aware of these unprecedented proposals before they signed up.

Week One.

The Ashcroft Room is indisputably the most beautiful rehearsal room in the world. Like some Viking Mead Hall, or wooden cathedral, its apse of dormer windows overlooks the river Avon, as it flows down to Holy Trinity Church. The room sits above the Swan Theatre, which was built on the site of the original Shakespeare Memorial Theatre. That theatre burned down in 1926. A conference hall was built in its shell, where rehearsals used to be held.

When plans for the Swan were drawn up, Trevor Nunn and his team had to work out where else to find alternative rehearsal accommodation. The architect, Michael Reardon, came up with a clever solution (despite not being in the original brief, and thus not budgeted for). He suggested a scheme to build above the theatre, which would have the advantage not only of creating a great space but would restore something close to the original 1879 Memorial Theatre skyline and make sense of the horseshoe-shaped brick building. Reardon described the form of this new roof, when viewed from the other side of the river, as evoking the idea of a circus tent or a jousting pavilion. The Swan's American benefactor Fred Koch approved of the revised scheme, and supplied the considerable extra sum required to complete it.

It was Adrian Noble who suggested the room should be called the Ashcroft Room, in memory of Dame Peggy Ashcroft, when she died in 1991. Her many awards (including her Oscar for *A Passage to India*) used to be on display in the room, alongside her portrait as Imogen from the 1957 production of *Cymbeline*. Peggy was one of the first leading actors to sign up with Peter Hall for his newly formed RSC. Her superlative performance was certainly as Margaret of Anjou in *The Wars of the Roses*. Maybe her genius will preside over our project now.

Today, this golden round is filled with buttery yellow light which makes the mellow pine wood glow, although the dormer windows are all discreetly covered with grey acetate, a neutral density lighting gel, to diffuse the bright light outside for the cameras.

From the Ashcroft Terrace, we can see down to the Swan Gardens, where gravel is being laid as a bed on which to construct our new garden theatre.

Monday 31 May Bank Holiday.
The company gather for the first day. There are sixteen in the cast, which scholars suggest might have been the number with which the play was originally performed; and we have broadly followed the conjectured doubling pattern that the Arden edition lays out. Only instead of fourteen men and two boys, we have a gender-balanced cast.

We have an induction session, which introduces our Covid marshall, Rachael Barber. I call her our 'plague warden'. She covers all the Covid protocols we have in place, including the one-way system around the theatre backstage. Each actor has their own chair at an appropriate distance from each other around the room, which they take responsibility for wiping down each day.

Our video unit arrive to introduce themselves and get us all used to the presence of cameras, but nothing is broadcast today. Andrew Brooks, the video production assistant, has what looks like a space jet-pack on his back. It's a 'gimbal with a supporting body vest' he tells me, which will allow him to move around the room easily, albeit not entirely unobtrusively.

In the afternoon, I give some background to the play before we settle down to read it.

Henry VI might be the first, the earliest and perhaps the only Shakespeare play for which we know the date of the first night. In Philip Henslowe's diary, on Thursday 3 March 1592, in the first fortnight of the performances he records at the Rose Theatre, a play called '*harey the vj*' is marked as 'ne', which is thought to mean 'new' to the repertoire. Henslowe's notes in this early theatrical account book that his portion of the takings amounts to £3 16s 8d.

Shakespeare uses the past to illuminate the present, both as a warning and a prophecy.

Tuesday 1 June.
We decide for our very first streaming session at noon, to put the play on its feet. We sit in a wide circle, and everyone gets up when their scene comes and reads their lines. The actors are fearless and undaunted. We manage the whole of the first four acts. It's a rough cartoon of the play, and rather suits its knockabout character.

Wednesday 2 June.

The floor of the Ashcroft Room is marked with a diagonal grid, which creates a good sense of what a two-metre distance actually is. This morning our movement director, Polly Bennett, takes the company through some exercises to get used to the space.

After yesterday's trot-through, we now start at the beginning. Polly and my co-director Owen have an offering of a sort of funeral procession to start the play. Bruce O'Neill, our Head of Music, with our house band (Kev Waterman on percussion and Nick Lee playing everything else), improvise a dirge. It is Henry V's funeral. His coffin is represented by an RSC flight case on wheels. 'Hung be the heavens with black'. Mariah (Minnie) Gale as Bedford declares the first lines, and we are off.

The jarring contention between the Duke of Gloucester (Chris Middleton) and the Bishop of Winchester (Mark Hadfield) for control of the young king is both serious and comic. Their dislike for one another breaks out in the first scene over the corpse of Henry V. But the gloves come off two scenes later when Gloucester is shut out of the Tower of London by Winchester, and a brawl ensues between their men: 'blue coats to tawny coats!' Only an intervention by the Mayor of London can break it up. At the start of Act Three, as we meet King Henry for the first time, their slanging match continues, culminating in Winchester's threat 'Rome shall remedy this', to which Gloucester responds cattily 'Roam thither then'.

Finally, the young King Henry insists his warring uncles make up and shake hands. This presents us with a challenge. I consult our Covid marshall, Rachael. The ruling is that they can shake hands if they have sanitized their hands before. And then they should sanitize immediately afterwards.

In fact, this seems like a gift, to me. As their servant squeezes antibacterial gel into their hands, Gloucester proclaims 'This token serveth for a flag of truce'. They shake hands. Then he continues, 'So help me God as I dissemble not.' And as Winchester echoes 'So help me God as I intend it not' they both hand-sanitize again. The ritual only enhances the dislike between the two great Officers of State and amplifies its absurdity.

Thursday 3 June.

Spend some time today on one of the most frequently cut episodes in the play, the Countess of Auvergne's invitation for Talbot to visit her. She is clearly obsessed with his fearsome reputation, claims to have his picture hanging in her gallery, and has probably been fantasizing about his Herculean aspect, and the 'large proportion of his strong knit limbs'.

When Talbot appears, she is underwhelmed by what she sees. 'A child, a silly dwarf', she calls him, declaring:

It cannot be this weak and writhled shrimp
Should strike such terror to his enemies.

The camp comedy of this put-down is amply delivered by Amanda Harris, using her breathiest voice for the invented word 'writhled', which suggests both shrivelled and wrinkled.

Friday 4 June.

Then comes perhaps the most famous scene in the play: The Temple Garden, the setting for the ignition of the Wars of the Roses itself.

An undisclosed debate between Richard Plantagenet (Michael Balogun) and the Duke of Somerset (Mimî M. Khayisa), on some 'nice sharp quillet of the law' as Warwick characterizes it, has got noisy and out of hand in the Inns of Court and propelled the feuding lords into the Temple Garden. Suffolk and Warwick are reluctant to be drawn and remain evasive, preferring to maintain their neutrality rather than commit themselves to either party. But Somerset and Plantagenet won't take no for an answer. As they both insist the truth is on their side, they demand that each choose a rose to determine whose side they favour.

We pull a sword rack from the side of the rehearsal room, with its bristling phalanx of spears and broadswords. I think the huge five-foot swords come from the Peter Hall/ John Barton *Wars of the Roses*. Briony, our inventive ASM, makes up some red and white paper roses and twists them round the briar of blades.

Both parties agree that whichever side ends up with the least roses will yield to the other. But Somerset breaks the deal and insults Plantagenet calling him a 'yeoman' (a man who may own property but is not a gentleman). Warwick might protest that Plantagenet is derived from royal stock, but Somerset counters that his father was beheaded for treason for plotting to overthrow Henry V.

In a hundred lines or so, an undefined squabble has escalated into bitter factionalism that will lead in turn to civil war. As Warwick prophesies:

> This brawl today
> Grown to this faction in the Temple-Garden
> Shall send between the red rose and the white
> A thousand souls to death and deadly night.[1]

Saturday 5 June.

The weather has been beautiful all week, after the soggiest May on record. The garden at our home, O'Cahans, is blushing with foxgloves and pansies. We could play the Temple Garden scene here. On one side of the path is a white rose bush, buds bursting, on the other a red rose bush. The white rose, with deep chalice-shaped blooms and an old English rose fragrance, is called Desdemona. The red rose, a flushed dark crimson, is called Falstaff.

---

[1] The famous 1908 fresco depicting the plucking of the roses in the Temple Garden, by Birmingham artist Henry Payne, hangs in the East corridor of the Palace of Westminster. Richard Plantagenet, on the left in his scarlet houppelande and crimson liripipe, stretches his arm dramatically shaking his white rose at Somerset who, equally elaborately attired in black and gold brocade, reaches for his scabbard. You wonder why this scene, which Shakespeare invented after all, was chosen to decorate the mother of parliaments. Ultimately it dramatizes the moment when differing opinion and nuanced debate calcifies into entrenched positions and polarized party politics.

Week Two.

Monday 7 June.

The noisy Temple Garden scene is followed by a dying fall, a scene of intimate melancholia. Plantagenet visits his uncle, Mortimer (Marty Cruickshank), who has spent much of his life sequestered in the Tower of London.

The scene contains quite an elaborate history lesson, and Marty, Michael Balogun and I spend one of our streamed green room conversations assembling the family tree. We are helped with a series of production photos of actors playing the various roles in the previous tetralogy: Richard II (David Tennant), Henry IV (Jasper Britton), Henry V (Alex Hassell) and even David Rintoul as Edward III, and Jamie Glover as the Black Prince from the 2002 Swan production of *Edward III*.

I pick through the relevant detail, noting that Shakespeare has conflated a few Mortimers along the way for clarity: Mortimer's father was adopted heir by the childless Richard II. King Richard's father was the Black Prince, the first son of King Edward III. Mortimer was descended from his third son, Lionel.

Tuesday 8 June.

There are just too many battles in this play. After a stagger-through, I suggest to Owen that between the significant battles of Orleans and later of Bordeaux, we really do not need another episode at Rouen, where Joan smuggles her men into the city under the guise of being farmers travelling to market and takes the city only to lose it again when Talbot and his forces attack. Talbot's splendidly funny line 'Lost and recovered in a day – again!' rather points to the absurdity of the dramaturgy. Not unsurprisingly, John Barton came to the same conclusion.

Wednesday 9 June.

In the late afternoon, Owen and movement director Polly Bennett are working on the section where Joan la Pucelle (Lily Nichol) appeals to the fiends for their diabolical aid.

> Now help, ye charming spells and periapts,
> And ye choice spirits that admonish me
> And give me signs of future accidents.

I explain what a periapt is. Such a charm is referred to in Philip Henslowe's diary, alongside the accounts of how much the daily takings were at his theatre, The Rose on the Bankside in Southwark. 'Write these words on virgins' parchment with the blood of a bat upon Tuesday morning betwixt 5 or 6 in the morning or at night. Halia JK. turbutzi. And tie it about thy left arm and ask what ye will have.'

What on earth might 'Halia JK. turbutzi' mean? Is it an anagram?

Owen and Polly are doing lovely, inventive work with the fiends. I leave them to it and return home.

Tony is waiting for me at the front door. That morning, Dr Shearman had arranged for him to have an ultrasound of his abdomen. In the afternoon, Shearman had rung unexpectedly to say two shadows, 'patches', had appeared on his liver. They won't really know what the patches are until he has a CT scan next week.

Later that evening, I have an hour-long international call with members of our RSC America board, about possible future plans. Hard to concentrate.

Thursday 10 June.
I have to dip out of rehearsal to meet up with Harriet Walter who has agreed to join me for a press call for our fabulous new costume workshop.

The reception area is very welcoming with the great double height of the old scene dock doors opening onto a glass lobby. As we thread through the building, we keep recalling what was there before. Here was where the costume supervisors' room used to be, and that was where Head of Costume, Alistair McArthur, had his office; over here is where the old dying shed was and that used to be the door to the Nibelung treasure cave that was Alan Smith's armoury.

In the courtyard, the old clay tiles have been carefully removed from the roof, cleaned and replaced. They now look handsome, splendidly preserving this the oldest part of the site. I recognize the old windows that appear in Laura Knight's picture *The Yellow Dress*, which she painted when she was artist-in-residence here after the war in 1948. We have been making costumes on this site for at least that long. But an overhaul was long overdue. We urgently needed to upgrade the facility to accommodate the world-class craftsmanship that goes on here. After all, we now make on average between 1,500 and 2,000 costumes a year in these workshops.

Large windows frame a view of three of them, looking from Alan Smith's new spacious armoury, through to two other brightly-lit workspaces beyond, inhabited by Millinery & Jewellery, and Costume Painting & Dyeing. Around every corner, a new vista opens up. Here are the fitting rooms. This is one of the two spray rooms. There is a stockroom where all the fabric is stored. And then the ladies' wardrobe, a wonderfully bright space, with the cutting tables and sewing machines.

I have saved the pièce de résistance until last: the men's wardrobe. As we walk in, we are greeted by Emma Harrup who runs the team who work here. They are delighted with the amount of light they have to work with now. The sloping roofs have great window lights, and the air seems to sparkle even though outside it's a rather grey day. Eastwards, we can see out over the rooftops of the waterside cottages to the checkerboard pattern on the Swan and the roof-scape of the RST beyond.

Harriet is impressed. The new costume workshop is a magnificent addition to our campus. It brilliantly connects the whole workforce. Whether walking through the building to your desk in the Chapel Lane offices or taking up a new position in these craft spaces, the route reminds us of our shared endeavour: to produce great theatre and share it with the world.

Saturday 12 June.
It's Tony's birthday on Monday, and as I will be working all that day, we determine to celebrate over the weekend. We decide to start by having breakfast in the garden.

We always have soft-boiled eggs on Saturday mornings. It's traditional. Exactly four minutes from when the water boils, as my dad used to insist. Mum used to make us kids a boiled egg for breakfast to set us up for the school day. 'Go to work on an egg!' as the TV slogan for the egg marketing board had it. Tony only really remembers having hard-boiled eggs on family holidays, packed in Tupperware boxes as 'Padkos', picnic food, on the long car journey to Middlepost across the dry Karoo Desert.

I make sure to butter my piece of toast as soon as it pops out of the toaster, slice it horizontally and cut the top half into soldiers. He cuts his diagonally and uses only a sparing amount of Benecol spread.

I hit the top of my egg with the teaspoon, and then lift off the crown. He slices it off with his butter knife. I scoop out the white from the crown. He leaves it uneaten. If there is any runny white, he lifts it out and discards it at the side of his plate. I just eat it.

I shake a little salt into the yolk and dip my first soldier in. He grinds sea-salt onto his plate, scoops out a spoonful, and then taps the back of the spoon in the salt which sticks to the back of it, as he lifts it to his mouth. I think this is rather ingenious, but he can't remember who first suggested this way of doing it. We are so different. I can't think how we've lasted thirty-four years and counting.

As I watch him enjoy his egg, I think I cannot be without him.

In *Hamlet*, Claudius tells Laertes how much Gertrude means to him. He says:

> The Queen his mother
> Lives almost by his looks; and for myself,
> My virtue or my plague, be it either which,
> She's so conjunctive to my life and soul
> That, as the star moves not but in his sphere,
> I could not but by her.

Act Four Scene Seven

Tony is conjunctive to my life and soul.

Week Three.

Monday 14 June (Tony's 72nd birthday).

Our Executive Director Catherine Mallyon and I begin the day with an early trek up the Welcombe Hills together to sort out life. We sit apart on two benches overlooking the Vale of the Red Horse, with Meon Hill way beyond the spire of Holy Trinity.

When I return to O'Cahans to pick up my bag and head into rehearsal, I find Tony stretched out on the bed. He looks drawn and pale and has felt faint again. I tell him I will phone in and let Owen continue rehearsals without me, so I can stay with him. He protests but is relieved not to be left alone.

Later, I get two messages on my phone.

One tells me that I have tested positive for the coronavirus and must immediately self-isolate for ten days. In my hurry to complete my lateral flow test (which the whole company working in the building have to do every seventy-two hours) and in my resolute determination to keep optimistic, I have ticked positive instead of negative.

The second is a furious text from Adrian Noble. He is incandescent on my behalf about a piece in *The Stage*, which someone has alerted him to. It's a snippy little article about Rufus Norris employing his wife Tanya Ronder to write a new musical for the National Theatre. It claims that nepotism is rife in the industry, citing Dominic Cooke commissioning his partner (the writer Alexi Kaye Campbell) when he was Director of the Royal Court, and me casting Tony at the RSC.

I have worked with Tony many times of course. Why wouldn't I? He is universally acknowledged as one of our greatest classical actors, and was so, long before I even joined the RSC. In reality, I have worked with him at Stratford no more times than Sam Mendes has worked with Simon Russell Beale, Nick Hytner with Alex Jennings, Deborah Warner with Fiona Shaw, or Michael Boyd with Jonathan Slinger. What has our relationship got to do with it?

Adrian thinks I should sue. I don't tell Tony.

Tuesday 15 June.

Act Five. Jamie Ballard as the battle-scarred warrior, Old Talbot, is working through the scene where he is joined on the battlefield by his young son John, played by Minnie Gale. He calls him his Icarus, launching into the fray with an undaunted spirit. It is this image to which his father returns when, in the most unexpectedly poignant scene in the play, the son is killed, and his body brought and laid in Talbot's arms.

Covid regulations mean we have to find another way of doing this. Minnie tries carrying in her doublet. She watches her father as he cradles the doublet in his arms, trying to take in the death of his brave boy.

The grieving father, in an image of resolute defiance, pictures himself and his son, another Daedalus and Icarus, escaping the field of Death and flying heavenward:

> Thou antic death, which laugh'st us here to scorn,
> Anon, from thy insulting tyranny,
> Coupled in bonds of perpetuity,
> Two Talbots, winged through the lither sky,
> In thy despite shall 'scape mortality.
>
> Act Four Scene Seven

We consider how 'lither' should be pronounced. It's the only time Shakespeare uses this word. Is it 'lither' as in 'slither', or as in 'blither'? Is it a comparative adjective meaning 'more lithe' and if so, more lithe than what – the thick dense smoke on the battlefield they have just waded through?

Sounding 'lither' and 'sky' together, the assonantal resemblance of the two words would suggest the lighter opportunity. Jamie can float if he chooses on the two continuant vowels amplifying a sense of the yielding air through which their two released souls may escape: 'li-i-i-ther sky-y-y'.

And so the young Talbot soars into perpetuity, into the pantheon of great English heroes, 'the great Alcides of the field'.

In what might stand as Shakespeare's first great review, Thomas Nashe published a pamphlet in 1592, claiming:

> How would it have joyed brave Talbot (the terror of the French) to think that after he had lain two hundred years in his tomb, he should triumph again on the stage and have his bones new embalmed with the tears of ten thousand spectators at

least (at several times), who, in the tragedian that represents his person, imagine they behold him fresh bleeding.

Nashe adds 'there is no immortality can be given a man on earth like unto plays'.

Wednesday 16 June.
Tony opens the front door. He is clutching a piece of paper.
  'Bad news I'm afraid,' he says.
  Dr Shearman has confirmed that the dark patches are indeed cancer. I find myself reeling. I had not expected any diagnosis until the CT scan next week. I am not ready to hear this.
  We sit on the bench in the garden, watching the field. The sheep have gone now. I suppose they have been taken away to be shorn. So, the grass is tall and the clover and the buttercups have grown in dense swathes.
  We start to try and comprehend what Shearman's news means. I fetch bowls of strawberries and a glass of champagne each, perhaps to signify that our approach will be defiant, optimistic and cheerful. As the light fails, the sycamore is suddenly illuminated in a blade of saffron-coloured light.

Thursday 17 June.
Warm-up first thing. We have a stagger this morning, and I want the actors to remember the newness of the words their characters choose. I do this exercise for every Shakespeare. I construct an alphabet of words that appear in the play. They may be the sole use of that word in the entire canon, like King Henry's 'immanity' (perhaps a contraction of inhumanity?), 'lither', 'periapt' or 'writhled'.

Saturday 20 June, morning.
Final run-through. No cameras. Back home for lunch. During a brief siesta afterwards, Tony suddenly shudders violently. He describes the weird sensation of falling backwards through the mattress. I know this is hypertension, but don't know what to do about it.
  Peonies in abundance in the garden.

Week Four.
Monday 21 June.
The film crew arrive. Rhodri Huw, our screen director, has been filming BBC *Cardiff Singer of the World*, until last night. The exciting final was won by Gihoon Kim, a 29-year-old baritone from Korea. One of the judges describes his 'Rolls-Royce voice'. The tenderness with which he sings the aria from Act Three of Wagner's *Tannhäuser*, as Wolfram asks the evening star to guide the way of his beloved's soul, is almost unbearable.
  The team watch a run-through.
  This evening, we work the scene where the handsome Suffolk (Oliver Johnstone) encounters Margaret of Anjou for the first time. Minnie Gale plays the young Margaret. The scene includes lots of asides, as the pair share their thoughts with us, the audience.

It's as if Shakespeare is testing how far this convention of asides can go, and we want to ensure the cameras can catch each of these quick-fire responses, played straight down the lens.

The purpose of an aside is to invite your complicity, to get you on their side. So, we realize that Suffolk is smitten with the beautiful young princess, and that she is puzzled about what his intentions are. While he shares his dilemma with us, Margaret is bewildered by his self-absorption, and confused that he seems to be talking to himself.

He talks at random; sure, the man is mad.

It is sweetly comic. And a fresh note of laughter, late in the play.

Minnie's bump is showing. She is due in November with her second child.

Throughout the rehearsal, I keep feeling I want to turn to the camera, and in my own aside, say: 'What the fuck am I doing here?'

Tuesday 22 June.
The company have the morning free as the cameras set up, which allows me to accompany Tony to Stratford Hospital for an ultrasound scan. We spend an hour in the waiting room beforehand as he has to sip a 'contrast' dye, which will allow the radiologist to see any abnormalities in his liver.

Afterwards, I run ahead to fetch the car. He can't walk very fast these days. In fact, he has found it hard to get around for the last couple of years. A slip on a wet step, during the run of *Kunene and the King* in Cape Town, resulted in him having to have a knee operation, which hadn't worked properly. Now he needs a stick to get about.

It seems a terrible irony that this most physically daring of actors should have his mobility so severely compromised. This was the actor who could scuttle across the stage on crutches as the bottled spider, Richard III; or climb up a rope in *Tamburlaine the Great*, suspended in the middle of the Swan stage, flip upside down and descend arms outstretched while declaiming Marlowe's mighty lines:

Now clear the triple region of the air,
And let the majesty of heaven behold
Their Scourge and Terror tread on Emperors.
Smile Stars that reign'd at my nativity,
And dim the brightness of their neighbour Lamps:
Disdain to borrow light of Cynthia,
For I the chiefest Lamp of all the earth,
First rising in the East with mild aspect,
But fixed now in the Meridian line,
Will send up fire to your turning Spheres,
And cause the Sun to borrow light of you.

Wednesday 23 June.
In the afternoon, we run the play again for a final camera rehearsal before tonight's live streaming.

We get to the scene in which Talbot cradles the dead body of his young son. In one rehearsal, Jamie as Talbot had let out a terrible wail at this point, when the English hero sees the body of his son. It came from somewhere deep in his gut and released a flood of tears.

Although potent and effective in the room, somehow watching it on screen made it feel too big. I had encouraged him to resist it.

This afternoon, Jamie really holds it back. His struggle not to break, not to give in to the howl rising like magma within him was overwhelming, and I began to weep. Of course, it's the tension that has gripped me all day as I have anticipated what Dr Shearman will say, what news he has of the CT scan results, what prognosis he may share of our time left together. I bite my hanky for the rest of the run.

Then I dash away, leaving the team to re-run Act Five for the cameras, not sure if I will make it back for the live stream.

At the Grafton Suite, in Stratford Hospital, Dr Shearman gently takes us through the detail of the CT scan. Tony has hepatocellular liver cancer. It's primary, so has not spread from other organs, and there is no evidence of what he calls metastatic spread – it hasn't infected his surrounding organs. There are two focal lesions, one the size of a satsuma, the other of a walnut, which is now how we refer to them. It sounds like an Aesop fable: 'the Walnut and the Satsuma'.

Shearman is recommending sending Tony to the consultant gastroenterologist at University Hospitals Coventry, so that he can be assessed by a multidisciplinary team. The first step will be an MRI scan. It is probable that they will take a targeted chemo approach to 'zap' the two patches and seal them up to prevent spread (or that is how we understood it in layman's terms). He described this as TACE (transarterial chemoembolization). So many new long words.

Tony feels reassured. Although he has liver cancer, he is living with it, not dying from it.

I ask him if he'd like me to stay with him, but he is adamant that I should go back and watch the live stream. My absence would prompt too many questions.

The run is exceptional. The thought that Owen has put into this; the care with which John Wyver has pulled all the filming together; the work of the actors, of the musicians, the camera crew, the whole team. The open rehearsal project has been a success, giving audiences an unprecedented insight into our rehearsal process. The play itself is not Shakespeare's greatest achievement, but somehow the very transitory nature of this project has suited the roughness of this early work.

On exactly the same date, Midsummer's eve, eight years ago, we had conducted a similarly brave experiment from the same location: a performance of *A Midsummer Night's Dream* played in real time over the weekend. The first act court scene was played on Friday evening. The forest scenes played from 2 o'clock on Sunday night to 4 am. Just as Puck said 'Fairy Lord attend and mark, I do hear the morning lark', the dawn chorus started to sing outside. The final scene, with Pyramus and Thisbe, was played in the dell, by Holy Trinity Church on the Sunday night as a huge orange super moon rose over the Avon. Magical.

Thursday 24 June.
With the live stream done, we have time to do one or two catch-ups, so that when we produce the DVD, as part of our Living Folio, the entire catalogue of the plays in the First Folio, we can give the best account of the production that we can.

Co-director Owen and I meet with screen director Rhodri to work through our notes from last night and discuss what our focus will be for the afternoon's rehearsal. Then we leave him to get on with his note session with the camera team.

I ring Catherine Mallyon and ask if she happens to have any time for me to pop round to her digs in Old Sexton's Cottage. She does. I am very relieved. She has not only been a great Executive Director, in the years since I became Artistic Director, she has been a great friend. And I need to let her know what is happening with Tony.

> Give sorrow words: the grief that does not speak
> Whispers the o'er-fraught heart and bids it break.

Afterwards, I walk back through the gardens, to see the amazing amphitheatre of the new garden theatre which has gone up in record time, during our open rehearsal project. Matt Aston and Tom Watts who head our stage crew have been working on the project flat out and proudly show me their splendid work. We move on.

> Ruin hath taught me thus to ruminate
> That Time will come and take my love away
> This thought is as a death, which cannot choose
> But weep to have that which it fears to lose.

Sonnet 64

33

Henry VI, Part Two (Henry VI: Rebellion)

– 2022: Royal Shakespeare Theatre, Stratford-upon-Avon.
– Broadcast to cinemas and released on DVD.

1 April 2022. The first preview.
This morning the Earl of Warwick tested positive for Covid.

Paola Dionisotti, who plays Cardinal Beaufort, has had it for a week. She's missed the entire technical period and has been sitting in her little cottage in Waterside praying for the faint little second line on her lateral flow test to disappear altogether. This morning it did.

The plan was to get through a dress rehearsal and the first preview with her understudy today and then get Paola properly tech'd and back on tomorrow. But now, not only her understudy Sophia (who has gallantly done the entire tech in Paola's place) will be on, but Warwick's understudy (who has never done it before), will be on too, and a whole series of knock-on understudies beyond those two major roles. So, the dress rehearsal had to be sacrificed, and the company are about to do the whole show for the very first time, in front of a thousand people.

It feels like a very bad April Fool's joke.

The title, on the frontispiece of the Quarto edition of *Henry VI Part Two*, reads like a trailer:

The First Part of the Contention betwixt the two famous houses of Yorke and Lancaster, with the death of the good Duke Humphrey: And the banishment and death of the Duke of Suffolke, and the Tragicall end of the proud cardinal of Winchester, with the whole rebellion of Jack Cade: And the Duke of Yorkes first claime unto the crowne.

I am inclined to accept the theory that this *First Part* was indeed written and presented first, with the play we presented in our open rehearsal last June created as a 'prequel'. We avoid confusion by calling this part *Henry VI: Rebellion*, and using the title *The Wars of the Roses* for *Part Three*. The same company present both plays. Then *Richard III* will follow, later in the summer, and stand alone.

On reading *Henry VI Part Two* initially, the director Owen Horsley and I wondered how to tackle the enormous cast size. With at least sixty+ characters (depending on how you count them, there are as many as sixty-seven roles, eight of which have more than one hundred lines), it has the largest cast in the canon. The multiple doubling would be challenging, the understudying even more so.

Covid had forced us to abandon our original plans to present the cycle in the Swan. Looking at the plays now, with fresh eyes, an opportunity emerged. *Henry VI Part Two* is a series of set pieces, with entirely new characters in each piece. I began to think of them as pageants, like the Mystery Plays presented by different companies and performed on carts at stations around the cities of York and Coventry in mediaeval times.

Each of these pageants is presented by a different group. During the technical rehearsals as everyone comes together, I get the chance to chat to each of the groups.

* * *

The first pageant is undertaken by our Next Generation actors. RSC Next Generation is an initiative which stems from work the company does in disadvantaged areas across the country, working with young people from low-income families who are under-represented across the industry. There are twenty-three young actors divided into three teams in *Henry VI: Rebellion*.

They are playing a group of petitioners who have gathered to present their grievances to the Lord Protector. But their supplications fall into the wrong hands, when Queen Margaret and her lover the Duke of Suffolk receive them. An apprentice called Peter Thump claims that his master, one Thomas Horner, an armourer, has been saying that the Duke of York was rightful heir to the crown, and that King Henry is an usurper. If the claim proves true, it would amount to treason and carry a death sentence. Queen Margaret is thrilled. York is her sworn enemy.

I feel quite inordinately proud of these young people. In a lull in the technical rehearsals as the lighting or sound teams sort out cues with the stage management, I go over to talk to them. I want to ask them about their experience of being in Stratford-upon-Avon and working with the Royal Shakespeare Company.

They initially seem a bit over-awed by the Artistic Director coming over to chat to them, but then Oscar breaks the ice. Oscar is sixteen and from Birmingham. He plays Sixth Apprentice. 'Can I just say,' he says, 'we think your hair is a-mazing.' Oscar himself sports quite an impressive Afro. Jeminah, sitting in the row in front, joins in the conversation. She has long braids. 'Who does your hair?' I tell her that Sandra Smith, our Head of Wigs and Makeup, has cut my hair since I was an actor in the company thirty-five years ago. 'Serious?' she says. Jeminah is nineteen and from Durham. She plays First Apprentice. She tells me she has been with 'Next Gen' for seven years. 'Then you have been associated with the RSC longer than some of the professional actors on the stage with you,' I say. 'I know,' she beams, 'it's sick!' But now Oscar wants to know how I got started and how I got to become Artistic Director.

The Peter Thump in this group is played by another Next Gen vet, Olly from Cornwall. I already know Olly is fearless, having seen him take over the role of Benedick at the last minute in the Next Gen adaptation of *Much Ado about Nothing*, in our garden theatre last summer.

Back on stage, the Lord Protector is about to recommend York to the position of Regent of France, when Suffolk and the queen present Peter Thump and his claim to the court. York is deprived of his promotion until the case can be tried. The poor apprentice Thump and his master Horner will be forced to engage in trial by combat. Whoever wins will be proved right.

Olly will play the first few performances, but the other two Peter Thumps – 17-year-old Scout from Bradford and 14-year-old Shefit from Northampton – will have to wait until May before they get their turn to go on.

* * *

Our Shakespeare Nation actors have the responsibility of presenting the next Pageant: The Tale of Saunder Simpcox.

Shakespeare Nation is our community participation programme run with our partner theatres, and it is aimed at people with little or no experience of Shakespeare, either as theatre-goers or performers. Seventy-four adults are split into six teams – Blackpool, Bradford, Canterbury, Cornwall, Norwich and Nottingham.

Bradford are going first. This group, based at the Alhambra Theatre, did a wonderful project during lockdown: Jaques' Seven Ages of Man speech, filmed around the town with different Bradfordians delivering the lines, some in the many languages spoken in that community: Albanian, Arabic, Kurdish, Pashtu (one of the national languages of Afghanistan), Slovak, Spanish and Wolof (spoken in Senegal, Mauritania and the Gambia).

All of the Shakespeare Nation actors have stories to tell. Saunder Simpcox is played by Ben, an aviation administrator. Kelly (playing the Mayor) teaches animal care and land-based studies. She always wanted to be an actress but being dyslexic and dyspraxic thought she couldn't ever make it. Qaraman was trafficked from Kurdistan in a truck across Europe and pushed out at traffic lights on the outskirts of Bradford. One actor in his fifties in the Nottingham group has never left Nottingham in his life before this. Now they are all on the stage of the Royal Shakespeare Company and doing great work. You get a real sense of a town community on stage.

The tale of Saunder Simpcox is a little morality tale. The king and queen are out hunting when they encounter an excited group of townspeople proclaiming a miracle. A lame, blind beggar from Berwick-on-Tweed has had his sight restored at the shrine of St Alban. He is brought before the king, who praises God for his delivery from darkness.

Good Duke Humphrey is suspicious of Saunder Simpcox, who claims to have been blind since birth, but is able to distinguish the colour of his gown. The fraud is exposed when he calls for the town beadle to whip Saunder unless he leaps over a stool. Saunder protests that he cannot stand but as the beadle produces his whip, he duly leaps over the stool and runs off. The duke's worldly wisdom is thus neatly contrasted with the King's naive faith.

A couple of our Shakespeare Nation actors have some difficulty jumping over the stool, so are allowed to run round it instead.

The duke instructs the beadle that Simpcox and 'his drab' should be whipped through every market town back to Berwick. Saunder's wife spins on her heel and cries 'Alas, my lord, we did it for pure need'. With the escalating cost-of-living crisis the country is enduring at the moment, this line acts like a ferocious exclamation mark punctuating the scene.

*   *   *

As the tech progresses, we reach the start of Act Four. The ship-board murder of the Duke of Suffolk has been devised as the next of our pageants. This one focuses the work of the nine drama graduates, who have joined the company. Young actors training at drama schools over the last two years during the pandemic have had a difficult time, many having to perform their final shows (their big opportunity to impress the profession) on Zoom. So, we decided to audition any of those students who wanted to apply and to cast a group of them in the production.

This pageant has been developed with them by the fabulously named fight choreography duo R.C. Annie (Rachel Brown-Williams and Ruth Cooper-Brown).

The scene opens dramatically, with the ship being boarded by a crew of assassins. They descend on ropes from the flies. John, a scouser who trained at the Royal Welsh College, plays the strangely lyrical captain, cutting one of the prisoner's throats while eulogizing on the setting sun:

The gaudy, blabbing and remorseful day
Is crept into the bosom of the sea.

Al just graduated from my alma mater, the Bristol Old Vic Theatre School; Felixe is from Royal Conservatoire of Scotland; Sophia from LAMDA; Georgia and Emma from Central. Benjamin, who is a RADA grad, doesn't get to be in this scene as he is playing Somerset, and Jack, who trained with the National Youth Theatre and has cerebral palsy, is about to give his Clerk in the next section. Ibraheem, who just graduated from E15, told me that because of training during lockdown tonight is the first time he has been able to play before a live audience. They all seem to be having a ball.

*   *   *

I catch up with Owen Horsley just before the show. I had to withdraw from co-directing the project with him (keeping only a weather eye on rehearsals) and landed him with perhaps the most adventurous and complex production possible. I ask him how he is feeling about not having done a dress rehearsal and congratulate him on his courageous decision not to cancel the first preview. But Owen is remarkably cool. He and his associate Aaron have done a magnificent job.

This is no ordinary RSC show. Tonight, we see the results of everyone's hard work.

For the first time in our history, we have a company of 121 actors: professionals, amateurs and young people from all over the country. It's huge. I am sitting in what is known as 'Death Row', the first row of the gallery, reserved for the creative team, all anxiously scribbling notes, and often biting their nails, during the previews.

The whole collaborative project comes into focus in Act Four, which is in effect one large pageant: the Jack Cade rebellion. When we started rehearsals in January, our TV screens were full of documentaries marking a year since the storming of the Capitol in Washington, DC. And there was Jack Cade, dressed in his Buffalo-horn fur helmet, with his bare tattooed chest, and Stars and Stripes face paint.

The QAnon Shaman with a military service record, motivated by conspiracy theories and manipulated by Trump's shocking stoking tactics, has many similarities to Cade, seduced by York. In our production, Oliver Alvin Wilson as York delivers a vivid description of the lunatic rebel:

> In Ireland have I seen this stubborn Cade
> Oppose himself against a troop of kerns,
> And fought so long, till that his thighs with darts
> Were almost like a sharp-quill'd porpentine.

I don't think we will need the Buffalo headdress or flag on a spear, for the audience to recognize the contemporary resonance.

All the different groups participate in these extraordinary scenes of rebellion, capturing so much of the urgency and heat and passion we have experienced recently in civil protest, at the same time observing the cynical, self-serving agendas of those trying to whip up dissent for their own ends.

The escalation of the violence unleashed by Cade is horrible, and yet sometimes disturbingly funny. Shockingly so, when Lord Saye is sent to negotiate with the rebels. He is beheaded, along with his son-in-law, Cromer. Their heads are stuck on poles and made to kiss. The audience are responding noisily with both gasps and laughter.

Along 'Death Row', I can see Ali Tanqueray, from our props department, making notes on the severed heads. We have already had the head of Suffolk, which Margaret cradles to her breast. Not only do the props department need to make that head look like Ben Hall, who plays Suffolk, they need to prepare one for his understudy if necessary. Luckily the process is now much easier as we 3D-print all our severed heads.

As the play ends, and Cade runs away, our adaptation of the play leaves King Henry on stage alone, fearing that England may curse his wretched reign:

> Was never subject long'd to be a king
> As I do long and wish to be a subject.

Blackout.

The cheers from the audience are well deserved. And as the groups all run on to take their bows: the Next Gen kids, Shakespeare Nation (Bradford), the graduates, and the rest of the professional cast, they are joined by the musicians carrying their instruments. I find myself terribly moved. There are fifty grinning people on stage, in front of a packed auditorium of a thousand people whistling and applauding their efforts. But perhaps we are all applauding ourselves too, thrilled to be back in this space, making theatre.

For my own part, I feel I am standing at a crossroads. Like the crossroads I try to get actors to identify in any text, so they don't run straight across and ignore other options, other routes. But I can't immediately see which way I am supposed to go.

Knowing I have a job to do helps. I will be back in a rehearsal room, starting work on *Richard III* soon. I re-read the play, and come across a line I haven't noticed before, but which speaks to my soul:

> I have not that alacrity of spirit,
> Nor cheer of mind, that I was wont to have.

Richard III, Act Five

34

Henry VI, Part Three (Wars of the Roses)

– 2022: Royal Shakespeare Theatre, Stratford-upon-Avon.
– Broadcast to cinemas and released on DVD.

23 April 2022.

Yesterday, I announced that I was stepping down as Artistic Director of the Royal Shakespeare Company after a decade in the job, and thirty-five years after joining the company as an actor.

This morning, Shakespeare's birthday, I scattered Tony's ashes in the Avon.

I set out just before dawn on my way to the river, the urn safely wrapped in a towel in the canvas book-bag I use to carry my scripts. As I approached the bottom of Bridge Street, men were off-loading the barriers to line the street for the parade and the town celebrations later in the day. The flag poles were already in place. It suddenly occurred to me that, with all the security around, a lone male with a bag slung over his shoulder might be stopped and searched.

There was no one on the footbridge. A man at the boat club on the far side of the river was un-hooking a trailer of canoes. I pulled out the urn and unwrapped it. Tony and I bought this urn in Egypt. There is an odd fault in the alabaster at the bottom which, when lit from inside, looks like a small skull.

I took half of the ashes to Cape Town back in January. Tony's family and I scattered them from Big Rock, a white granite outcrop on Saunders' Beach in Sea Point, the suburb where he grew up. He used to jump from the rock as a child and continued the practice into adulthood. As the particles of dust scintillated in the bright sea air, they ignited a memory: a soggy December morning in 2005, when Tony and I emerged from Islington Town Hall having celebrated our civil partnership (on the very first day you could) and the family pelted us with rice and confetti.

Confetti and ashes, in fistfuls, flung into the air.

Today the ashes fanned out slowly in sandy fingers. The American novelist, Nathaniel Hawthorne, described how the Avon loiters, as if 'considering which way it should flow, ever since Shakespeare left off paddling in it'. A cob swan swam up to investigate. He dipped his long neck under the water to see what had just gone in, then had a nibble of the ash and, uninterested, swam away again.

I gazed about, trying to imprint the moment on my mind's eye. This footbridge was originally built to carry a tramway track for horse-drawn carriages to transport coal from the Stratford Wharf to Moreton-in-the-Marsh. It's just downstream from the old

Clopton Bridge, which Shakespeare would have crossed, and which was built around the same time as Richard III fought the Battle of Bosworth Field.

Looking the other way, from the middle parapet of the bridge you get what the theatre critic and Stratford-lover J.C. Trewin called 'a sovereign view' of the theatre. Elisabeth Scott's building was originally intended to be clad in white concrete, which would have made it look even more like some great ocean liner floating on the Avon. In the end it was thought brick would tone better with the town. When the theatre opened in 1932, it was dubbed the 'Jam Factory', 'as though this kind of factory was peculiarly shocking,' wrote Trewin.

Sometime before he died, Tony and I had decided that this was how we would scatter our ashes, to flow past the theatre where we both spent so much of our lives; past Holy Trinity Church where Shakespeare was baptized and is buried; past Avonside, the theatre flats where we lived for years; over the weir and away to the Severn estuary, the Bristol Channel and beyond. And one day I hope to follow him.

My promise to Tony fulfilled, I decided to walk along the river under the weeping willows and wept with them.

*   *   *

I am so proud that the plays the RSC are presenting for this year's Shakespeare birthday celebrations are two such fine productions. *Henry VI: Rebellion* has now been joined by *Wars of the Roses*. We opened them together to the press on Thursday.

Mark Lawson in *The Guardian* gives the endeavour 5 stars, writing: 'After two years of pandemic disruption and the demoralizing death of one of its greatest actors, Sir Antony Sher, the RSC shows all its strengths in making minor Shakespeare a thrilling major event.'

Arthur Hughes' performance as the young Gloucester is signalled out for praise, and palpable anticipation for the role he is about to undertake. I feel excited. He takes to the huge RST stage as if he has been playing it all his life.

At the cast party afterwards, Erica Whyman makes a speech, thanking everyone for their extraordinary work. Erica has been Deputy Artistic Director since I became AD ten years ago, but she has been Acting Artistic Director since I took compassionate leave to look after Tony. She has been doing a pretty extraordinary job herself. She has been an outstanding support through challenging times.

Taking over the mic, I blithely thank everyone for creating such a great trailer for *Richard III*.

On Monday I start rehearsals. It'll be 25 April. I dip into *Year of the King*, to read about Tony's first day of rehearsals in 1984. Same date: 25 April.

35

Richard III

– 2022: Royal Shakespeare Theatre, Stratford-upon-Avon.
– Recorded live, broadcast to cinemas and released on DVD.

Arthur Hughes is the first disabled actor to play Richard III at the Royal Shakespeare Company.

In February 2022, Arthur travels to Stratford so I can show him around. He comes up to the house for our first proper face-to-face rehearsal. After lunch, I take him in to Tony's studio, the room in which he loved to paint and write. It's full of light.

I show him the cabin trunk that Tony brought with him from Cape Town, as a shy teenager, in 1968. Before he died, we packed it full of all his scripts: a fifty-year career of work, going back to the Liverpool Everyman. I open it. Here are his scripts for *The History Man*, and *Mrs Brown*, for Mike Leigh's *Goose-pimples*, for Pam Gems' play *Stanley*. And all the RSC scripts, *Moliere*, *Tartuffe*, *Red Noses*, *Maydays*, *The Revenger's Tragedy*, *Cyrano de Bergerac*, *The Roman Actor*, *The Malcontent*, *Death of A Salesman*; the scripts he used playing the Fool, Macbeth, Leontes, Iago, Falstaff, King Lear. Tucked in the corner are a stack of the old Penguin editions, which the RSC used to use: *Twelfth Night*, *The Merchant of Venice*, and on top, *Richard III*.

A sharp intake of breath at my side. 'Is that his actual script?' says Arthur. 'Here, have a look,' I say, handing him the tattered copy. 'It's not holy writ.' It has all Richard's speeches underlined in red and on every other page there are little snatched sketches in the margins, of Roger Allam as Clarence, Malcolm Storry as Buckingham, Brian Blessed as Hastings, and Penny Downie as Anne. Tony's bravura performance as Richard III scorched its mark in the annals of Stratford like a thunderbolt.

'Listen,' I say to Arthur, 'there is no such thing as a definitive performance, or a definitive production of any Shakespeare play. You are part of a continuum. That's what's so exciting about doing Shakespeare at Stratford. It's both inspiring and intimidating in roughly equal measure. You're in a line of actors who have played these parts here for a nearly a century and a half. Back to actor-managers like Frank Benson. In 1911, he made the first silent film of *Richard III*, in what is now the Swan Theatre. Tony's performance was highly celebrated. Unbelievably, I never saw it. Perhaps that is a good thing. But we will do what we will do in this moment, alert to the world we live in now, and as long as we bring open minds and full hearts to that endeavour, we can be proud of whatever we achieve. Richard is in your hands now. It's your right. The RSC isn't just its famous history. It's you, now. You are the RSC.'

Propped on one of Tony's easels is a black-wrapped crutch. 'Is that one of the actual ...? Can I see?' Arthur asks. He's almost whispering now. Like every actor tackling Richard for the last forty years, he's been reading *Year of the King*, though he wasn't even born when Tony played the role.

There is an irony seeing Arthur try Tony's famous crutch. Arthur doesn't need to do any of the research into Richard's disability that Tony describes in such detail in his journal. Arthur has insights into the character of Richard that I haven't heard before.

He has radial dysplasia in his right arm. He refers to his 'limb difference', a much better way of describing it than the self-deprecating phrase 'banana-hand', which he used to use at school, to counter the name calling ('four-fingered freak'), which was hurled his way.

As a disabled man, he talks about the way he has often felt overlooked, underestimated. He tells me a story about when he was at drama school in Cardiff and was walking home one night when a group of young men blocked his way. They were spoiling for a fight. But when he pulled his right hand from his jacket pocket, they backed off:

'Oh, see lads, he's got a funny hand. Best leave him.'

Arthur was furious, he wanted to fight them just to show them what he was really capable of. Their threat might have scared him, but their pity enraged him.

This is Arthur's moment. The TV film he did, *Then Barbara Met Alan*, airs on BBC Two just before we start rehearsal for *Richard III*. It tells the story of Barbara Lisicki and Alan Holdsworth (Arthur), the founders of the Disabled People's Direct Action Network (DAN), a disability activism group back in the early nineties. The weight of expectation upon him is huge.

*   *   *

When I started seriously considering directing this play I read *Tyrant*, by the Harvard Shakespeare scholar, Stephen Greenblatt. It began as an article in *The New York Times* in 2016, asking what Shakespeare could tell us about the rise of Donald Trump. The subsequent bestseller analysed precisely the psychopathy of the 45th President without ever mentioning his name.

The parallels he draws between Trump and Richard III are compelling: both display a gift for detecting weakness, a deft use of mockery and insult, palpable misogyny. Both manifest sociopathic indifference to the suffering of others. Both demand absolute loyalty but show no gratitude in return, and are surrounded by enablers who, for a variety of reasons, allow them to flourish.

The book asks why an entire country should knowingly accept being lied to by a leader, manifestly unfit to govern and indifferent to truth. Greenblatt is acutely perceptive about the ways in which a society becomes ripe for a despot.

Luckily, his book has lasted longer than Trump's administration.

Now of course we are rehearsing *Richard III* as another narcissist world leader wields power like his plaything. Putin's 'strategic exercise' in his neighbour's back-yard, known to the rest of the world as the invasion of Ukraine, is in its third month as we go into rehearsal.

Back at the start of the year when we were still defining the design elements of this production the world was gaping at the optics of Putin at his long white table, welcoming diplomats but keeping them thirty feet away. We thought we would introduce the council chamber table as a long white table, to allow a tongue-in-cheek reference. But now that seems too trivial.

At the start of rehearsals, I asked Professor Greenblatt if Shakespeare's metaphors can constantly be reapplied, how his trenchant analysis of Trump might now evoke other parallels and reflect the lethal posturing of Vladimir Putin.

His first response was a plaintive reflection that at least Trump excited occasional if inadvertent laughter. Putin is more deadly and with nothing resembling a comic streak. On the other hand, Professor Greenblatt did then send me a video clip, which inspires a sort of horrid laughter. It shows Putin dressing down Sergei Naryshkin, the chief of the Russian Intelligence Service, at a security meeting about the Russian-controlled territories in Eastern Ukraine, in February this year (2022).

Putin has framed the meeting as a 'frank exchange of views' but in fact he wants to ensure that his council are seen to share the collective responsibility for the decisions he has already made about prosecuting a war in Ukraine. Each of them in turn have been made to declare their unequivocal positions. It is being televised and broadcast nationally.

Mark Galeotti in the *Moscow Times* described the spectacle as a cross between King Lear demanding his daughters' avowals of love and Blofeld in the Bond films, without his white pussycat and the piranha tank. Here is Putin's squirming spymaster being publicly bullied. Despite having been beside Putin for much of his career, Naryshkin is shown no mercy, or respect. He is the designated scapegoat, and his humiliation makes awful but compulsive viewing.

This is equivalent to Richard Gloucester haranguing Hastings, or his brutal refusal to listen to Buckingham's demands for his promised reward, after his momentary hesitation about the murder of the princes in the Tower. This is Richard distrusting Stanley's protestations of loyalty, at the end of the play, demanding he leave behind his son George as a hostage, in case he defects to Richmond. Both Richard and Putin rejoice in sadistic and demeaning demonstrations of their power.

I invite Stephen Greenblatt to share his reflections for our programme. His article arrives promptly. He nails the way Shakespeare achieves proximity and distance: 'It takes only the briefest glance around the world to grasp that in *Richard III* Shakespeare captured something that is still alive, something that surges up to shatter all our norms of decency and order, something that will not disappear and that fascinates even as it threatens and appals us.'

Greenblatt concludes, 'Shakespeare understood the innovative power of the medium he had supremely mastered, and the danger of that power in the hands of the ruthless and the power-hungry. In a world where it was always dangerous to speak out, he used his art to challenge despotism. The warning is as timely today as it was four hundred years ago.'

* * *

14 March.

In the town of Novosibirsk in Siberia, a man is arrested for holding up a blank piece of paper. The absurdity of the situation is a pointed reminder of the dangers of speaking out in a despotic regime. This young man reminds me of a short, fourteen-line scene in *Richard III*. It's a little speech by a little guy. We are given only his job title: a scrivener, a secretary, who has been charged with the job of writing out Lord Hastings' indictment. He is shocked by the speed with which Hastings, the equivalent of prime minister, has been brought down by Richard on trumped-up charges.

> ... within these five hours lived Lord Hastings,
> Untainted, unexamined, free, at liberty.

But he recognizes how evil spreads, by degrees, as individuals who recognize its pervasive power do not stand up to oppose it:
The scrivener says:

> Here's a good world the while! Who is so gross,
> That cannot see this palpable device?
> Yet who so bold, but says he sees it not?

John Peter, the late drama critic of *The Sunday Times*, once told me a story about that speech. He recalled this scene in particular, in a production of the play which opened at the National Theatre in Budapest, in his native Hungary, just months after the death of Stalin. When the actor playing the scrivener spoke those lines, the full house rose to their feet and applauded. The execution of Hastings was an all too familiar terror story: prominent people who had chosen to speak out had been 'disappeared'.

A few weeks later the National Theatre in Budapest had to close *Richard III*. The thunderous applause by the audience every night was too much for the communist government, afraid of insurrection. They were right to be. John told me that that production of *Richard III* was one of the moving and powerful events that led the country within months to the Hungarian Revolution.

*   *   *

As I never do a read-through on the first day, until we have worked through the whole play and paraphrased it all in our own words, it is Friday before we can speak the play through, and Arthur gets to say the lines he has been thinking about for so long.

Richard III is the longest play in the First Folio (not in the canon – that distinction goes to Hamlet).[1] Harold Bloom, the American literary critic, complains of the play's 'exorbitant length', which he describes as 'cumbersome and overwritten'. Certainly, played at its full length, the play would come down around quarter to midnight. In order to achieve a 10:30pm finish I have cut nearly 30 per cent of the text. It reads at 2 hours 7 minutes. I usually anticipate that the running time of the final production will add another 25 per cent to the read-through time. So that should be about right.

---

[1]   The Folio version of *Richard III* is longer than the Quarto and contains some fifty additional passages amounting to more than two hundred lines. However, the Quarto contains some twenty-seven passages amounting to about thirty-seven lines that are absent from the Folio.

Act One.

What strikes us immediately about Richard's first famous soliloquy is that Shakespeare roots his anger, 'in this weak piping time of peace', in his sense of isolation and rejection. He is not 'made for sportive tricks', not 'made to court an amorous looking glass'. He wants 'Love's majesty' to strut before 'a wanton ambling nymph' and is unlikely to find himself capering nimbly in a lady's chamber 'to the lascivious pleasing of a lute'. Richard has not been invited to the party. He feels excluded. Or as he puts it at the end of *Henry VI Part Three*: 'Love forswore me in my mother's womb'. This rejection has clearly fuelled Richard's misogyny.

It is a syndrome that has become horribly familiar in the last few years, and reflects the misogyny that has emerged online among young men who describe themselves as 'incels' (involuntary celibates). Like the 22-year-old student who went on a shooting spree, in Isla Vista, before turning the gun on himself in 2014. He left behind a 141-page document about his deep loathing of women and his own enforced virginity, stating 'I am the true victim in all of this. I am the good guy.' Or the man in Toronto who posted on Facebook 'The Incel Rebellion has already begun' and then drove a van down a crowded street, killing ten people. Or closer to home, in August last year (2021), when a young man in Keyham, Plymouth, shot dead five people including his mother and a 3-year-old girl.

Our research into the mindsets of these 'incels' introduces us to new vocabulary: these young men describe their 'fuckstration'. Perhaps Richard suffers from the same thwarted desire.

*   *   *

18 May.

Today the first prosecution of a war crime took place in Kyiv. A 21-year-old Russian sergeant admitted taking his Kalashnikov and aiming at a 62-year-old Ukrainian civilian who was pushing his bike along the road and shooting him in the head.

The first prosecution for crimes against humanity was at the Nuremberg trials in 1945–46. Robert H. Jackson, US Chief of Counsel at the International Military Tribunal, evoked Shakespeare's *Richard III* in his closing arguments for the conviction of Nazi war criminals. He said (on 26 July 1946):

> ... These defendants now ask this tribunal to say that they are not guilty of planning, executing, or conspiring to commit this long list of crimes and wrongs. They stand before the record of this trial as blood-stained Gloucester stood by the body of his slain king. He begged of the widow as they beg of you: 'Say I slew them not.' And the queen replied: 'Then say they are not slain, but dead they are ....'
>
> If you were to say of these men that they are not guilty, it would be as true to say there has been *no war*, there are *no slain*, there has been *no crime*.

This morning we are rehearsing the Lady Anne scene from which those lines come. What is immediately exciting about Arthur's Richard (apart from his lived experience of disability) is that he is young. Inevitably perhaps, the role is usually played by actors in their late forties and fifties (Olivier, McKellen, Spacey, Fiennes) whereas Arthur is just thirty and (like Ian Holm, Tony Sher and Jonathan Slinger) is closer to the historical Richard's actual age – he was thirty-two when he was killed. His approaches to Lady Anne don't seem so creepily predatory. His chances of success, despite the fact he has killed her husband and her father-in-law, seem achievable.

Arthur's good looks make his Richard a dark angel. He has a compelling boyish quality, at odds with the villainies Richard carries out. It's contradictory, oxymoronic, juxtaposing sweetness and vulnerability with violent psychopathy.

Lady Anne is played with ferocious fragility by Rosie Sheehy.

We discuss the way the scene charts the narrowing distance between Richard and Anne. At first, they are wide apart, separated by Henry's coffin. Richard attempts to close the distance between them, by appealing to Anne to leave 'this keen encounter of our wits, / And fall something into a slower method'. Like a cobra fixating on its prey, he attempts to get closer to her, to insinuate himself into her affections. She repels him with a spit. He admits his crimes against her family, but protests they were committed for love of her, and, drawing his sword, he urges her to plunge it in his chest. As she holds the sword against his naked breast, their physical closeness has increased and, as she drops the sword and he proffers her his ring, that closeness becomes intimate.

It is the first time we have seen Richard touch Anne. Will Anne be repelled? Will she flinch? She accepts his ring, as he slips it off his own finger and onto hers and moves behind her to admire it.

Look how my ring encompasseth thy finger.
Even so thy breast encloseth my poor heart.

He has engineered a proximity to Anne that quickens both their heart rates. You feel they are breathing heavily and in tandem. He asks her for one more favour that he says will confirm his happiness forever.

'What is it?' she asks, in a short half-line.

Their faces are now very close. Is he asking for a kiss? Does she hope for one? The tension of that empty half-line is replete with possibility. It's a dangerous crossroads. He asks if she will be good enough to allow him to take over responsibility for the burial of King Henry's corpse. An apparently chivalrous gesture on Richard's part, but not I think what she was expecting at all. 'Grant me this boon' he begs in another short half-line. She takes a beat to recover perhaps, before pulling herself together to reply, and win back the moral high-ground:

With all my heart and much it joys me too,
To see you are become so penitent.

Rosie and Arthur play the scene with the skill of top musicians feeling the pulse, noting all the rhythms and cross rhythms, the tempo, pacing and dynamics, observing all the nuances the text makes available, as if it was a musical score. As they finish the scene, their fellow actors who have been watching break into spontaneous applause.

Watching the scene, Minnie Gale, playing Queen Margaret, is delighted. Lady Anne is Margaret's daughter-in-law and the wife to her murdered son, Edward. Anne curses Richard almost as vehemently as Margaret does. Minnie feels she has found an ally in the play. Is this why Shakespeare never brings them on stage together? He wants to keep them isolated and lonely, without apparent allies?

*   *   *

We have been working on line endings. What do you do at the end of a verse line? Easy enough if the line is end-stopped and the meaning therefore contained within it. But what do you do if the sentence continues onto the next line and beyond?

Do you just ignore the end of the verse line and continue on, until the thought and the sentence is complete?

Ben Hall, playing Clarence, does just this in the speech in Scene Two, where he describes his dream of drowning:

> O lord, methought, what pain it was to drown!
> What dreadful noise of water in mine ears,
> What sights of ugly death within mine eyes.
> Methoughts I saw a thousand fearful wrecks:
> A thousand men that fishes gnawed upon:
> Wedges of gold, great anchors, heaps of pearl,
> Inestimable stones, unvalued jewels,
> All scattered in the bottom of the sea.

The speed he achieves as Clarence, caught up with the horror of the experience, is impressive. But I am getting only a general impression of his terror. And if he runs over the verse line, why is the speech not just written in prose? What is the effect of the speech being rendered deliberately in verse? I encourage him to observe the line endings, by lifting the last word, suspending it a little, in order to consider – to discover – where the thought goes next. At first, the actor can feel the line endings are just irritating impediments, like speed-bumps on a road you want to accelerate along. But, as Ben tries it again, suddenly the speech seems more spontaneously invented.

By observing the parcel of meaning wrapped up in each line, before developing the thought in the line and the next, Ben takes the audience with him. I begin to feel the pain of Clarence's experience, rather than just witness it.

As he continues, Shakespeare creates the tumble of Clarence's thoughts by allowing these packed sentences to finish mid-line, forcing the actor to pick up his own internal cues and dive into the next memory. Head over heels he goes as he drowns further in the torrent.

*   *   *

Arthur and I have a lunch time interview for a history podcast. The interviewer, Matthew Lewis, comes clean and admits he is the chairman of the Richard III Society. I anticipate a keen encounter of our wits.

When Tony played Richard III in 1984, one of their number wrote to him saying, 'I read in the papers that you are yet another actor to ignore truth and integrity in order to launch yourself on an ego trip by the monstrous lie perpetrated by Shakespeare about a most valiant knight and honourable man and most excellent king.'

But Matthew is charming and readily makes a distinction between Shakespeare's play and historical fact. Good. Shakespeare is writing a play, not a documentary, after all. The search for Richard's body in the Leicester car park in 2012 may have been prompted by a member of the society, but without Shakespeare's play they would never have started looking for it. And surely it proved a bit of an own goal, as the skeleton demonstrated that Richard did indeed suffer from severe idiopathic adolescent onset scoliosis and had a distinctly twisted spine. So, the 'bunch-backed' image was not all invented by Tudor propagandists.

The body count levelled against the real Richard III may not include the murder of his brother Clarence, but Richard was no saint. He did pretty much annihilate Queen Elizabeth's entire family, and organize the trumped-up charges against Hastings, and his illegal execution. The jury may still be out on the murder of the princes in the Tower, but he had declared them illegitimate thus putting them out of the line of succession and placing himself on the throne.

The company have been watching a new BBC documentary, reopening the famous murder case which has tantalized the public imagination for five hundred years. It re-examines the evidence and claims that, after all, Richard probably was responsible for their deaths.

As Warwick says in *Henry VI Part Two*:

Who finds the heifer dead and bleeding fresh
And sees fast by a butcher with an axe,
But will suspect 'twas he that made the slaughter?

Richard had access and motive and the equivalent of a smoking gun beside him.

We rehearse the arrival of the Prince of Wales and the reunion with his little brother, the Duke of York. Prince Edward has been escorted down from Ludlow to London, by the Lord Protector, Richard and the Duke of Buckingham. The young prince enquires where he will be staying until his coronation and is told by his uncle that he will sojourn at the Tower.

Unhappy at the choice of venue (both his uncle Clarence and King Henry VI have been murdered there) Edward engages Buckingham in a debate about the Tower's history, asking him to affirm the story that it was built by Julius Caesar. Buckingham confirms that it was and has been re-edified by succeeding ages. But the prince is not satisfied. He wants to know if there is written evidence to substantiate that claim. When Buckingham declares that there is documentary proof to corroborate the legend, the boy insists that truth should be eternal, and not depend on written accounts.

Methinks the truth should live from age to age,
As 'twere retailed to all posterity,
Even to the general ending day.

It's a curious little digression, capturing the pedantic mind of a 12-year-old. But the discussion also explores what we accept as true, a theme particularly pertinent to the story of the fate of the princes in the Tower.

*   *   *

Our sound designer, Claire Windsor, has been up to the Tower of London to record the ravens. Legend has it that if they ever left the tower, the kingdom would fall. I am expecting the ravens to have evocative names like Corax or Corbaccio, or marvellous Norse names like Huginn and Munnin (Odin's mighty birds), and am a little disappointed to hear that one of them is called Poppy. Nevertheless, her cronking crow lends an ominous shiver to the scene.

Act Three.
We are doing the scene in which Hastings is warned that Richard is laying a trap for him. He is woken up in the middle of the night, so we decide to try rehearsing it in the dark, in the TOP Studio. Caroline Burrell in the lighting department has made up some dark lanterns. These are lamps with a door at the front which can be opened or shut, to shine or cut off the light. Using these torches, the actors can effectively light their own scene. The lanterns are great. They shine a focused beam which can be used to illuminate just the face of the speaker, and not the rest of the stage.

The scene immediately becomes more urgent and dangerous. It works really well for Catesby, the cat. He can steal on, unseen by the audience, to within metres of Hastings, before he speaks and catches Hastings unawares. What is he doing lurking about at 4am?

*   *   *

We work through the scene where Buckingham (Jamie Wilkes) and Richard perform a double act in reverse psychology. Rather than trying to convince the citizens that they should accept Richard as their new king they reveal how reluctant he is to take up that regal position. The citizens end up trying to persuade Richard to abandon his life of prayer and meditation and assume the burdens of kingship. As Richard attempts to avoid their escalating pleas, the scene becomes absurdly funny.

Thomas More tells us of a sycophantic sermon one Dr Shaw preached at St Paul's Cross, the open-air pulpit in the northeast corner of the Cathedral churchyard. He tried to persuade the people that the princes in the Tower were bastards, and that Richard was the rightful heir to the crown. Shakespeare has one of his men run to this Doctor of Divinity, but leaves the attempt to win over the citizenry to Buckingham.

Then Buckingham brings the mayor and aldermen to Baynard's Castle, Richard's home on the Thames.

As the citizens arrive, Buckingham tells Richard to go 'up to the leads', a flat-leaded roof. (More describes how Richard appeared 'in a gallery over them'.) It seems important for the scene to be played with Richard in an elevated position, but in the RST the action is too important to be relegated to one of the side galleries as the sight lines are not good enough for much of the house to see.

Pondering how we might achieve this, I doodle a sort of mobile prie-dieu in my script. It looks like a set of library steps, or a minbar, the raised pulpit in mosques reached by a set of stairs from which the imam delivers the sermon after Friday prayers. I can imagine Richard in his friar's garb and holy beads and the two clergy men (the same two actors who play the murderers) wheeling him about the stage. It's a great thrill when I walk into our rehearsal room one morning to discover the workshops have realized my sketch exactly.

We start referring to this bizarre but strangely feasible contraption as the 'pope-mobile'. The pious charade as Richard (atop the ladder) attempts to escape the urgent pleas of the citizens for him to accept the crown becomes deliciously farcical.

* * *

Wednesday 25 May.
First rehearsal with four of the six boys who will be playing the young Prince Edward and the Duke of York, the princes in the Tower. Jack was in *The Boy in the Dress* – he was 10 then – and Griffin is just 9. While Henry and Isaac are actual brothers, at 9 and 12. They are all as bright as a chuckle, and completely unfazed by suddenly being in a rehearsal room at the Royal Shakespeare Company rehearsing a play with a group of professional actors.

Back home that evening, Channel 4 News runs a piece from Robb Elementary School in Uvalde, South Texas, where a teenager barricaded himself in a 4th grade classroom yesterday morning and turned his automatic rifle on 19 children aged 9–10 and killed them all. Children, little Isaac's age, hunted down. This, just a week after the mass-shooting in a supermarket in Buffalo, in Upstate New York. Dunblane, Columbine, Sandy Hook. Uvalde enters an unspoken league table of atrocities against our children.

The murder of the princes in the Tower produced shockwaves that continue to ripple through history. An attack on innocence. An unbearable indictment of man's inhumanity to man. In the play, the murder marks the moment the audience turn against Richard.

Act Four.
A rehearsal with Tyrell.
When Buckingham hesitates at the newly crowned king's proposal to murder the princes, Richard looks around for someone to help him. He overlooks his trio of supporters: Catesby, Ratcliffe and Lovell.[2] Catesby notices that the king is angry and gnaws his lip. Richard then asks a page who happens to be standing there, if he knows of anyone who might be corrupted by gold, to 'a close exploit of death'. Rather surprisingly, this random page does indeed know such 'a discontented gentleman', his name is Tyrell, and the page is dispatched to find him.

Later, Tyrell reports the death of the princes in the Tower, as it has been reported to him by Dighton and Forrest, the men he has induced to carry out this atrocity. He describes their emotional reaction with chilling detachment, as if perplexed by the lack of self-control of these 'fleshed villains'. Will Edgerton's dark voice, inflected with his strong Wigan accent, lends Tyrell a still, sinister quality, catching his 'humble means' yet 'haughty spirit'. Tyrell is a lone wolf, a sociopath.

---

[2]　'The cat, the rat and Lovell, our dog, / Do rule all England under a hog', a rhyme posted on the door of St Paul's Cathedral, in 1484.

Richard seems disturbingly drawn to Tyrell. He calls him 'gentle Tyrell', 'kind Tyrell' and invites him to 'an after-supper' so he can relish all the salacious details of the children's deaths.

* * *

We are rehearsing Richard's encounter with Elizabeth (Kirsty Bushell) in Act Four. It brings up a fascinating feature of Shakespeare's writing: how he explores conversational 'turn-taking'.

We are familiar with Shakespeare shared lines,[3] and how he indicates when actors need promptly to pick up their cue. And the opportunities presented by pauses suggested by an empty half-line.[4] But even when one character has a long speech, I think Shakespeare indicates opportunities for the character listening to consider interrupting or resolutely not picking up an offered cue.

In everyday conversation we employ a series of techniques to indicate to the people to whom we are speaking that we are about to finish, or that we have more to say. They generally respond by indicating they understand what we are saying, for instance by nodding if they agree, and alerting us that they have something to add, by drawing breath perhaps, raising a finger, or even starting to speak. This is called turn-taking and it obeys certain mutually understood rules.

We rarely overlap each other for more than a fraction of a second, unless in severe disagreement. It regularly happens on Radio 4's *Today* programme, as politicians dodge an interviewer's interrogations. We have tried overlapping some of the lines in the fraught scene between Richard and Buckingham after the coronation as Buckingham demands what he has been offered (the earldom of Hereford) and Richard brushes him off. As the actors overlap each other and each refuses to give way, the emotional mercury rises immediately.

I find it really useful to consider turn-taking opportunities, even when the character speaking has a very long speech.

Essentially, if the sentence finishes in the middle of the verse line, then the character has not finished speaking, and even if their interlocutor wants to interrupt, they are denied their cue to speak. But if the sentence finishes at the end of the verse line, then potentially they may be inviting their interlocutor to respond, whether or not they chose to do so.

I first realized the brilliance of this technique when rehearsing the scene between Laertes and his sister Ophelia in *Hamlet*. Laertes has a very long speech where he lectures his sister in a patronizing fraternal way about what she should expect from Prince Hamlet's affection for her. Ophelia may try to respond to her brother's advice, but he won't allow her to interrupt. Indeed, when he does offer opportunities for her to respond and she then does not do so, and he continues, he may feel increasingly disconcerted by her wilful silence. Either way, what could be a long inert rant can potentially be a charged and active conversation (albeit still largely one-sided).

---

[3] See the chapters on *Twelfth Night* and *King John*.
[4] See the chapter on *Othello*.

Today, in the *Richard III* rehearsal, we explore how this cue-offering might affect the scene between Richard and Elizabeth.

Richard has a challenge on his hands. He wants to persuade Queen Elizabeth to allow him to marry her daughter, despite the fact that he has massacred several close members of her family, including her sons, the princes in the Tower. In some key ways, it is a re-run of the Lady Anne encounter in Act One.

After a tense scene of ferocious rapid-fire deliberation. Richard suddenly makes a long speech. He lightly dismisses his past misdemeanours and proposes to Queen Elizabeth how he might make amends. He lays out this proposal in seven sentences of varying lengths. But note: unusually, all of them conclude at the end of a verse line. (I have separated the sentences for clarity.)

RICHARD   Look what is done cannot be now amended:
    Men shall deal unadvisedly sometimes,
    Which after-hours give leisure to repent.

    If I did take the kingdom from your sons,
    To make amends, I'll give it to your daughter.

    If I have killed the issue of your womb
    To quicken your increase, I will beget
    Mine issue of your blood upon your daughter.

    I cannot make you what amends I would
    Therefore accept such kindness as I can.

    What? We have many goodly days to see.

    Go then my mother, to thy daughter go
    Put in her heart the aspiring flame
    Of golden sovereignty, acquaint the princess
    With the sweet silent hours of marriage joys.

    And when this arm of mine hath chastisèd
    The petty rebel, dull-brained Buckingham
    Bound with triumphant garlands will I come
    And lead thy daughter to a conqueror's bed.

It is immediately evident that Elizabeth, who is never short of a swift response, does not speak. She does not pick up her cues when invited to respond. Her silence is loud. Our work is to make that silence eloquent.

Perhaps at first, she decides not to speak in order to hear what he has to say. But as the scene progresses, other options emerge: that she is rendered speechless by his astonishing effrontery, or by his threat of potential violence; that she is quietly calculating how far he will go; that she is trying to disconcert him by not giving anything away.

And how does Elizabeth's lack of verbal response effect Richard's argument? Is he emboldened by it or disconcerted, delighted that his outrageous proposal is met with attentiveness, and smugly confident that his seductive powers of persuasion are irresistible, that her silence indicates assent, or is he increasingly unnerved by her deliberate refusal to come back at him? Does he manufacture the apparent rallying confidence of the last four lines, or does her inscrutable poker face give his boast a resoundingly hollow ring?

Arthur and Kirsty both start to enjoy the way that what seemed like a swaggering rhetorical brag now becomes a complex conversation between the two of them.

Elizabeth ends the scene telling Richard to write to her, saying ambiguously:

And you shall understand from me her mind.

As Elizabeth leaves, Richard sneers:

Relenting fool, and shallow, changing woman!

But this retort has little of the triumphant relish or the confident misogyny that his soliloquy at the end of the Lady Anne scene rang with:

Was ever woman in this humour wooed
Was ever woman in this humour won?

We are left wondering whether Elizabeth will convey Richard's proposal of marriage to her daughter. In the next scene, we learn that the queen has instead arranged for her daughter to marry Richmond.

Act Five.
We are putting together Act Five. Richmond (Nick Armfield) arrives. We soon realize that Shakespeare is not merely intending us to see Richmond as the knight in shining armour come to rescue the country. The foe he faces is formidable.

Jeopardy is threaded into the final act through the agency of Stanley. We hear that Richmond's side have six or seven thousand men. Richard's battalions treble that number. Stanley's men could either give Richard an overwhelming advantage, or even up the balance of numbers between the two sides. How long will he sit on the fence? Which way will he swing?

Shakespeare even provides a ticking clock through the act, as we swap between the two camps. Our lighting designer Matt Daw makes some detailed notes as we work through the act, noting each of the multiple references to time.

We consult a contemporary almanac. The Battle of Bosworth Field was fought on 22 August 1485. According to the *Trevelyon Miscellany of 1608* in August, 'the sunne setteth' at 7:23, and 'the twy-light' lasts until 9:50. 'Day breaketh' at around 10 minutes past two, and 'the Sun riseth' at 4:37. This helps us pinpoint the time shifts between scenes, and how Shakespeare is compressing time to build a sense of tension and anticipation.

In the first section, it is evening. They are about to pitch tents for the night, at Bosworth Field.

In the next section, Richmond surveys the mighty army of Richard, as the sun sets. Richmond is really going to need Stanley's reinforcement if he has a hope of defeating Richard's army. As the men withdraw into his tent, Richmond notes that 'the dew is raw and cold'.

When Richard begins to settle down for the night it is nine o'clock: 'supper time'. Ratcliffe tells Richard that at 'cockshut time' (when the poultry is returned to the coop), some of his generals have been going from troop to troop, cheering up the soldiers; something Richard makes no time to do so himself. He sends a pursuivant-at-arms to Stanley's regiment instructing him to bring his troops before sunrise.

Later, as Stanley steals to Richmond's tent, it is 'dark night', but already 'flakey darkness breaks within the east'. Stanley tells Richmond that he will support him, but yet can't be seen to do so, because his son is still Richard's hostage.

After the ghosts haunt Richard, Ratcliffe arrives, as agreed, to help Richard arm. He tells him 'the early village cock / Hath twice done salutation to the morn'. It is three o'clock. Richard's 'Friends' are up and buckling on their armour. Richard says ''Tis not yet near day', and (in a typically paranoid beat) he proposes sneaking round the tents to eavesdrop on his men and 'see if any mean to shrink from me'.

And as we switch back to Richmond, we are told it is 'Upon the stroke of four', and the sun is rising. Richmond has slept well, blessed by the souls of those Richard has killed. In a final little twist for the lighting department to play with, in the next section, as Richard emerges for battle, we hear the sun seems not to have risen at all. And 'disdains to shine'.

The ghost scene.

Working on the ghost sequence and the fight that follows it. Queen Margaret has cursed Richard saying, 'the worm of conscience still begnaw thy soul'. The ghosts are manifestations of Richard's conscience. We are echoing the funeral procession of King Henry VI in Scene Two, where Lady Anne accompanies the lonely coffin of the king, murdered by Richard. As Richard settles to sleep, a spectral photo-negative of that funeral arrives. The cowled figures will reveal themselves as the ghosts of those Richard has annihilated.

As we improvise Richard's dream, Arthur rises from his bed to examine the spectral procession. As he approaches the corpse, the king seizes his hand, and in a revision of Henry's stabbing in the tower, the corpse swaps places with Richard who thus finds himself lying on the bier. I have a momentary concern that the hand-grabbing might be a bit like the nightmare at the end of the film *Carrie*, but manage to suppress the thought.

As we work the scene with movement director Siân Williams, the ghosts each approach Richard in turn, bend over his body and whisper their curses in his ear. He writhes, unable to shake off his torpid sleep paralysis and hit out. It's painful to watch. As he wakes, Richard's jagged nerves are reflected in the jumpy staccato of his schizophrenic soliloquy:

Richard loves Richard, that is, I am I.
Is there a murderer here? No; Yes, I am:
Then fly; What from myself? Great reason: why?
Lest I revenge. What? my Self upon my Self?

The ghosts have in turn urged Richard to 'despair and die'. We explore the speech as Richard now contemplates that possibility. We even find a beat where the ghost of the young Duke of York returns the dagger that Richard has given him in Act Two, to furnish him with the means of his own destruction.

*   *   *

We are rehearsing the orations both leaders give to their troops on the morning of the battle. Nick Armfield explores the rhetorical build of Richmond's speech as it cranks up to a rallying climax, but somehow it feels wrong. Richmond is reminding his men that they fight against tyranny and evil, and that therefore God is on their side. I suggest we explore it with the quiet intensity and passionate sincerity with which Volodymyr Zelensky addresses his Ukrainian people in urgent video messages direct to camera. It immediately feels better. We connect with his argument and listen to it.

In contrast, Richard, dazed by his ghostly attack of conscience, seems disorientated. He barks a few feeble sound-bites, before resorting to xenophobic insults. He calls the enemy 'a scum of Bretons' and the man who leads them a 'milksop'. He sounds like a politician who has arrived at a hostile press conference without his briefing notes, or a stand-up comedian dying on his feet before an unresponsive crowd. We try the speech that way, surrounding Richard by the ghosts who haunt his brain.

We decide to carry the role of the ghosts further, making them become not only the horse that carries Richard into battle and then throws him, but the shades that we hear Richard fights with 'seeking for Richmond in the throat of death'. And it is the ghosts, as Nemesis, that then assist Richmond to deliver his fatal death-blow.

*   *   *

Final run in the rehearsal room. We had a 'stagger-through' (a stop-start run) last Saturday morning. The first half came down at nearly one hour fifty five, and the second half had stretched to one hour five, which with the interval will give a playing time of three hours and twenty minutes. That is disappointing.

I don't want to cut any more. So, I rake through the play, urging the actors to think on the line, pick up their cues, and not to wallow. The exercise cuts sixteen minutes off the running time of the final run.

In the tech, we get to the end of the Lady Anne scene. The incel has had an epiphany. Richard has 'crept in favour' with himself.

Upon my life she finds, although I cannot
Myself to be a marvellous proper man.

Richard decides to embrace the way he looks, 'entertain a score or two of tailors' to adorn his body and buy himself a mirror. Perhaps instead of hating his body, he can grow to accept it at last.

As Richard spies his shadow in the sun and descants on his own 'deformity', Arthur delivers Richard's final lines in the scene:

> Shine out fair Sun, till I have bought a glass
> That I may see my shadow as I pass.

We create a beam of light that throws his shadow against the cenotaph. As Arthur stretches out his arms – one short, one long – his huge silhouette is a triumphant image: a version of Leonardo's drawing of the 'ideal' human proportions, the so-called 'Vitruvian Man', reimagined for today.

30 June.

Press night. When I sat down to write my first-night cards this morning, I realized that something was wrong. For over three decades, Tony would come to see a preview of whatever play I was directing, and then draw a silly cartoon of the show to use as his card to me. I would then have the cartoon printed as first-night cards for everyone.

No cartoon today. Just a dull, hollow ache.

I wonder what he would have made of this production. He would have loved the rawness of the Lady Anne scene. I think he would have laughed at the pope-mobile and am certain he would have found the funeral procession of ghosts and the spectral horse powerful.

I pull out one of the portfolios of Tony's artworks. I am looking for a particular sketch among the hundreds of drawings. It's a version of an image that was published in *Year of the King*. It shows the tiny figure of Tony dwarfed against a huge louring face of Olivier as Richard III. Circling the giant. It's a dream Tony had when he was preparing to start rehearsals of *Richard III* in 1984 and wondered how to pit himself against such an iconic performance.

Arthur has seized that baton and run with it with such deft assurance, I know Tony would have been proud of him. I find the drawing. It's still in one of the Daler A2 sketchbooks, with a scribble of Tony as the bottled spider on one of the other pages. I decide not to rip it out but simply to give Arthur the sketchbook.

I call the company in at three o'clock to do a bit of work together, nothing new, just a song-call, a vocal warm-up, and then a little pep talk. I remind everyone this play is a poem, and a pulse, which starts with the word 'Now' and ends with the word 'Amen'.

Then I show them a photo of me as Lady Anne aged thirteen at the Preston Catholic College, fifty years ago. Rosie Sheehy says she will try to live up to that performance but that I have raised the bar rather high.

I thank the company for supporting me through what has sometimes been an emotionally challenging rehearsal period. I tell them that throughout the process, Tony has been on my shoulder, like a bad prosthetic hump, not letting me get away with anything, pushing me to see things freshly, to look harder, explore deeper, fail better.

That, for me, is his legacy. To demand the best. We are the Royal Shakespeare Company after all.

And I tell them, as we step together into the hall of mirrors that is any press night, that whatever the critics may say, I am very proud of what we have all achieved together.

Later, as the performance ends, and with my sister Jo, as always by my side on press night, I choke back a tear as Arthur runs on for his bow, and the audience cheer and, as one, rise to their feet.

36

Cymbeline: An Epilogue

If you look for a good speech now, you undo me: for what I have to say is of mine
own making; and what indeed I should say will, I doubt, prove mine own marring.

Epilogue to *Henry IV Part Two*
(Spoken by a Dancer)

'Bright baffling soul', Thomas Hardy called Shakespeare, and that spirit is nowhere more bright or baffling than in his late play, *Cymbeline*.[1]

I was assistant director on the 1989 production by Bill Alexander. Bill had directed the play at the end of the 1987 season in The Other Place (TOP). It was a revelatory production. Harriet Walter was Imogen and Nicholas Farrell was Posthumous Leonatus. I still remember their long-awaited reunion, as Imogen threw herself into his arms and he said:

Hang there like fruit, my soul,
Till the tree die![2]

George Bernard Shaw famously not only criticized the absurdity of the plot with its endless denouements – he also rewrote it. But the actors in the TOP production made it seem effortless and urgent. As the intricate complexities of the plot worked themselves out, the plot seemed only as absurd as life itself.

But the TOP production made sense for another reason. Somehow you felt intimately connected with the stories of each character. I realized why. In *Cymbeline*, more characters have asides (or soliloquies) than in any other Shakespeare play. Ten of them speak directly to us. Not just the hero and heroine, Imogen and Posthumous, but the villainous Iachimo, the loyal Pisanio, the idiot clot Cloten, the wicked queen, the disguised Belarius and the Roman general Lucius among others.

---

[1]   *Cymbeline* will be the last Shakespeare play in the First Folio I have left to direct. OK, except *The Two Gentlemen of Verona*! That was the first Shakespeare play I produced as Artistic Director, which I was not directing myself. I asked the brilliant Simon Godwin to direct it in 2014. For the sharp-eyed, I have not directed *Pericles*. But to be pedantic, *Pericles* is not actually in the First Folio. It doesn't appear until the second impression of the Third Folio in 1664.

[2]   The exquisite image of that line is somewhat undermined in an online text version of the play which reads: 'Hang there like a fruit, my soul, Till the tree die!'

The effect of the aside is to implore you, the audience, to see the action from that character's point of view. You share their perspective even if, in the case of Iachimo, lecherously leering over the breast of Imogen, with its mole:

Cinque-spotted, like the crimson drops
I' the bottom of a cowslip,

you are reluctant to share his confidence.

These shared intimacies mean that, as the play unwinds, you know what each of the characters are thinking, and are waiting deliciously for their piece of the strange and beautiful jigsaw puzzle to fit.

Bill's TOP production was such a success that the RSC decided to remount it on the main stage. In TOP, the tight budget had meant that everyone had been costumed from stock, and the set was simple and stripped back. But somehow the huge proscenium of the RST, a picture frame demanding a picture, made that elusive elegiac late play much more difficult to grasp.

As I write this, I am just beginning to ponder how best to spin this late play's elusive spell and achieve its hard-won desire for union and its wished-for promise of peace and plenty. The open stage of the RST will, I think, help enormously.

*   *   *

In concluding this final chapter, I am aware I have been applying a narrative structure to my life that has not been so apparent to me before. Perhaps I am getting philosophical as I approach my 'chair-days' as Shakespeare called them.

Soren Kierkegaard, the most famous Danish philosopher after Hamlet, is right: life must be lived forwards, but can only be understood backwards.

The baroque artist Salvator Rosa depicted himself as a personification of Philosophy. Born in the year before Shakespeare died, he applied a Latin inscription to his broody self-portrait: '*Aut tace / aut loquere meliora / silentio*'. It could be translated as 'Be quiet, unless your speech be better than silence' or 'If you have nothing to say . . . shut up'.

As I hand over the reins, and happily assume the title of Artistic Director Emeritus, I have one special hope: that all those who come after me at the RSC will maintain the disciplines and craftsmanship that Shakespeare demands. In the first line of the Prologue to *The Parliament of Fowls*, Chaucer sums up the challenge: 'The life so short, / The craft so long to learn'.

In 1815, Washington Irving (the American author of *Rip Van Winkle* and *The Legend of Sleepy Hollow*), made 'a poetical pilgrimage' to Stratford-upon-Avon and left us an account of his visit.

He thought it only proper to contribute his 'mite of homage to the memory of the illustrious bard' but was puzzled as how best to discharge that duty. He describes the pious custom he had observed on his travels in some Catholic countries, to honour the memory of saints by burning votive lights before their pictures.

'The wealthy devotee,' he writes 'brings his huge luminary of wax; the eager zealot his seven-branched candlestick, and even the mendicant pilgrim . . . his little lamp of smoking oil.' But he continues, 'In the eagerness to enlighten, they are often apt to obscure; and I have occasionally seen an unlucky saint almost smoked out of countenance.'

And so it can be with Shakespeare. 'The commentator, opulent in words, produces vast tomes of dissertations; the common herd of editors send up mists of obscurity from their notes at the bottom of each page; and every casual scribbler brings his farthing rushlight of eulogy or research, to swell the cloud of incense and of smoke.'

This book must serve as my own farthing rushlight.

Appendix A: Continuing the Shakespeare Gym on the Prologue to *Romeo and Juliet*

We explore the use of caesuras: the position that the line is 'cut' in two. The point that the line pivots. Not so much a 'pause' as a 'poise'. That moment of poise can give you opportunities; a moment's tension, a spring-board onto the next word, and into the next half of the line. It not only helps prevent a monotonous flatness of delivery, but it also heightens the excitement.

Caesuras are often marked with a comma, and are usually easy to identify. Particularly in the first quatrain: after 'Two households' in the first; after 'Verona' in the second; probably after grudge in the third. We try that. Good. But what about the fourth line? Someone suggests putting it after 'blood'. Hmmm ... maybe. But then someone says, 'Could you put it after "hands"?' We like that. Why? It's before the last word of the quatrain. It rhymes with 'scene'. And as all the rhymes are deliberate, we are waiting to hear what that rhyme will be.

This is the basis of any limerick. I ask someone to tell me a limerick. Somebody does and that prompts another. It usually takes a while for people to work out if they can tell a rude one, but eventually someone plucks up the courage. Then I ask them to repeat the limerick but leave out the very last word. They do. You can feel everyone anticipating it, and feeling it's absence at the end, nodding the missing beats. We all have an innate response to rhythm, and that is what Shakespeare is relying on at the end of this quatrain.

And suddenly we become aware of just how odd the choice of word is. 'Unclean?' The hands of the citizens of Verona aren't 'unclean'. This feud has been going on for centuries, and its latest outbreak has been violent. 'Unclean' is the understatement of the year. The prologue may not have been assigned to a single character,[1] but that doesn't mean there isn't character to be derived from its language. And 'Unclean', I would argue, could express a detached cynicism, or a bitter spirit, weary of violence. Either way it is not neutral, it is full of character.

In the second quatrain, the caesuras seem to be less obvious. Mostly the group will identify them clearly in the second and fourth lines. Placing one after 'lovers' has the added benefit of highlighting the potential ambiguity we've been alerted to in the phrase 'take their life'; and putting a caesura after 'death', emphasizes the word 'bury' by

---

[1] I have seen the prologue delivered by the Friar, the nurse, the prince, by Benvolio, by Mercutio, by a chorus of young people, and even as a recorded tourist guide to Verona, played over headsets.

allowing the actor to lift 'death', and land on 'bury'. And after all, the poetic choice of transferring the action of burial from their dead children to the parents' rage, is also satisfying.

Something odd happens with the caesuras in the third quatrain. They virtually disappear as one line tumbles faster and faster into the next. If we are right, this giddy, precipitous rush takes you right through to the appalling truth expressed (and discussed above) about the inevitable and fatal consequences of the gang violence on the most vulnerable members of the community.

Someone usually asks whether there could be two caesuras, particularly in the line 'Which, but their children's end, nought could remove'. I try to point out that as the tendency of actors is to over-stress, to 'pong' too many words in the line. One simple choice is invariably better than two: it's the editorial punctuation, rather than the need for two caesuras, which is tempting you.

We then sail into the haven of the final couplet. Each quatrain, gathering in pace as we have seen, builds from exposition through elaboration to conclusion, from exordium to peroration in rhetorical terms. It even ends with another characterful note, as the speaker promises the actors will work really hard on the audience's behalf, 'What here shall miss, our *toil* shall strive to mend'.

It is also worth noting that the chorus appeals to the crowd to attend, 'with patient ears'. We talk about theatre audiences and television viewers. In Shakespeare's day you went to 'hear' a play.

Appendix B: Filmed Productions

The following Shakespeare productions directed by Greg Doran have been filmed and many are available on DVD or online:

1. Titus Andronicus (South African Broadcasting Corporation, 1995)
2. The Winter's Tale (Heritage films, 1999)
3. Macbeth (filmed by Illuminations for Channel 4, 2001)
4. Venus and Adonis (filmed by the V&A, 2004)*
5. Antony and Cleopatra (filmed by the V&A, 2006)
6. Hamlet (filmed by Illuminations for BBC Two, 2009)
7. Julius Caesar (filmed by Illuminations for BBC Four, 2012)

And filmed as part of the RSC's Live from Stratford-upon-Avon series:

8. Richard II
9. Henry IV Part One
10. Henry IV Part Two
11. Henry V
12. King Lear
13. The Tempest
14. Troilus and Cressida
15. Measure for Measure
16. Henry VI Part One (open rehearsal)
17. Henry VI: Rebellion.
18. Wars of the Roses
19. Richard III

* Cardenio (2011) and Oroonoko (1999) were also filmed by the V&A.

Index